*Henry McBride Series in
Modernism and Modernity*

The artistic movement known as modernism, which includes the historical avant-garde, produced the most radical and comprehensive change in Western culture since Romanticism. Its effects reverberated through all the arts, permanently altering their formal repertories and their relations with society at large, and its products still surround us in our workplaces and homes. Although modernism produced a pervasive cultural upheaval, it can never be assessed as an artistic movement alone: its contours took shape against the background of social, political, and intellectual change, and it was always bound up with larger questions of modernity and modernization and with the intellectual challenge of sifting their meanings. Henry McBride (1867–1962) became perhaps the leading American critic to write perceptively and engagingly on modern art. The Henry McBride Series in Modernism and Modernity, which focuses on modernism and the arts in their many contexts, is respectfully dedicated to his memory.

Editorial Committee

Lawrence Rainey, University of York, General Editor
Ronald Bush, Oxford University
Arthur Danto, Columbia University
Charles Harrison, Open University
Jean-Michel Rabaté, University of Pennsylvania
Jeffrey Schnapp, Stanford University
Richard Taruskin, University of California, Berkeley
Robert Wohl, University of California, Los Angeles

Beauty and the Book

FINE EDITIONS AND CULTURAL
DISTINCTION IN AMERICA

Megan L. Benton

Yale University Press
New Haven &
London

This book has been published with assistance from the fund for the Henry McBride Series in Modernism and Modernity established by Maximilian Miltzlaff.

Set in Sabon type by Keystone Typesetting, Inc., Orwigsburg, Pennsylvania.

Printed in the United States of America.

Library of Congress Cataloging-in-Publication Data
Benton, Megan.
   Beauty and the book : fine editions and cultural distinction in
America / Megan Benton.
      p.   cm.
   Includes bibliographical references and index.
   ISBN 0-300-08213-4 (alk. paper)
   1. Fine books — Publishing — Social aspects — United States —
History — 20th century.   2. Limited editions — Publishing — Social
aspects — United States — History — 20th century.   3. Book design —
United States — History — 20th century.   I. Title.
Z479.B475   2000
070.5′73 — dc21   99-38198
                                                                CIP

A catalogue record for this book is available from the British Library.

The paper in this book meets the guidelines for permanence and durability of the Committee on Production Guidelines for Book Longevity of the Council on Library Resources.

10 9 8 7 6 5 4 3 2 1

Contents

Preface

Does the form of a book matter? Is the text all that counts? Is the book merely a package, or is it a cultural creation in its own right, with layers of meaning and value independent from, though intermingled with, those of its text? Questions that might have seemed idle musings a century ago now lurk with growing immediacy as fundamental notions of "the book" are no longer so familiar and ubiquitous as to be culturally invisible. Who has not felt the stab of surprise — and perhaps something more — at first hearing the dramatic claim that ours may be the last generation to read from printed books held in our hands?

It is a familiar theme: few Sunday papers or monthly magazines today fail to remind us that the book is dying, that physical, printed books will soon matter only to sentimental romantics "addicted to the look and feel of tree flakes encased in dead cow."[1] Coined in 1995, that phrase sounds the contemptuous tone that one often encounters in discussions about the imminent demise of the printed book at the hand of its successor in the communication business, the computer. It is a sneer of good riddance, a sense that the printed book is at best an inefficient machine that mainly bungles its purpose, at worst a barbaric relic of corrupt power structures. In some current commentary, the book has been demonized, scorned as enemy to what for so long it seemed soul mate, the text upon its pages. If the book is dying, it is partly because many are condemning it to death.

Disdain for the printed book today invariably begins by divorcing the nature and interests of a book from those of its text, by severing functions of form from needs of content. The printed book is often portrayed as a burden to its text, an intrusive barrier between text and reader that serves the interests of privileged writers and publishers. Even as they complain that print is clumsy and cumbersome, such critics welcome the electronic book, a digital device about the size and weight of a hefty paperback that can load and display thousands of pages, one at a time, deftly replacing those tottering stacks of summer reading, armloads of office manuals, and heavy textbooks bulging from student backpacks. As makers of one version, the SoftBook, sing, "A robust set of patented technologies enable the SoftBook to closely emulate and enhance the traditional reading experience. Opening the cover instantly activates the 9.5 inch display to wherever you were last. . . . The SoftBook's innovative page-turning system displays an entire page at a time — without the need to scroll." Just like a book, only better. Makers of the rival RocketBook boast that switching from print to electronic form can "put a world of books in the palm of your hand." Yet these electronic books are still essentially laptop computers, without keyboards; what you read is a small screen encased in a slim, rigid plastic box. But just around the corner looms a true electronic recreation of the codex book we now know. Researchers are developing electronic paper — thin, flexible sheets of computer screen that can be assembled and attached at the left edge to a narrow circuit board. Stored or online digital texts will then flow into the whole, so that the device becomes in effect a copy of *Newsweek, Jane Eyre,* the Bible, or *Goodnight Moon,* one after the other, instantly, cheaply, quietly, on demand.[2]

For others the glory of electronic technology lies in how far it moves away from print technology, not how close it comes to resembling it. Jay David Bolter was among the first to celebrate the ability to free text from the "frozen" surface of the printed page. He and others argue that print imprisons textual meanings by imposing fixed, controlling structures that privilege producers, while digital forms "liberate" content by enabling fluid, nonhierarchical hypertextual readings that empower users. They insist that the technology of print hinders the intellectual process, impeding rather than fostering development and exchange of ideas and knowledge, and that the sooner content can be freed from its oppressive printed form, the better. As Paul Dugaid puts it, "the [printed] book, no longer its incarnation, has been reduced to the incarceration of the word."[3] It is true that digital texts offer — in fact, require — a radically different kind of engagement with their readers. If print is replaced with electronic technology, the nature of reading, writing, and information will change. Many eagerly hail such change as freedom from the tyrannies of print, a breakthrough to a more powerful era in human knowledge, aptly millennial in scope and significance.

Yet exultant cries of the death of the printed book seem a bit silly when one is in a busy Borders or Barnes and Noble bookstore on a Sunday afternoon, waiting for a cashier or circling the aisles, stepping over readers sprawled on the floor. Talk of death no doubt sells fashionable magazines and newspapers (not to mention, with an irresistible smirk, plenty of books), but it springs more from postmodern theory than from shopping mall reality. The fact is that printed books are no less alive today — when measured by sales, library borrowing rates, and other data — than they have been throughout the century. Publishing industry analyst Albert Greco declared the period between 1985 and 1995 "a veritable golden age," noting unprecedented growth in both unit and dollar sales of consumer books. The nation's spending for books nearly doubled in that decade, more than twice the rate of the consumer price index increase.[4]

That commercial buzz leads, ironically, to the second theme of book-worry. Superstores are selling books in record numbers, worriers concede, but to them that represents only the triumph of conventional bestsellers and ephemeral fiction pumped out by a greedy cartel of multinational corporate publishers. Oceans of such books are hardly consoling evidence that print itself may linger on yet awhile; if anything, they bolster the argument of print's extravagant squandering of natural and economic resources. Many lament that "good books" are drowning in a sea of dubious others; they fear that good or real books are in mortal danger — if not of being replaced by jazzy new electronic forms of information and entertainment, then of suffocating under an avalanche of popular preferences for banality.[5]

The cultural panic that stirs today's book world is sometimes termed a crisis, but it is an eerily familiar one. Eighty years ago, as Americans emerged from a disillusioning war into a seemingly cynical and materialistic jazz age, the book seemed under similar assault. In the 1920s as today, new communications technologies, economic prosperity, and ever-expanding access to and appetites for books led many to fear that the "serious" book was in peril, its dignity threatened by both modern industrialized mass production and the material and commercial cheapness that industrialization enabled. Today, rallying support for the beleaguered book abounds: in a surge of published memoirs and essays; in campaigns to promote literacy and reading habits; in historical and critical scholarship; in myriad book clubs sponsored by librar-ies, bookstores, coffeehouses, and even daytime television moguls.[6] In the twenties, when the future of the traditional book seemed equally uncertain, many similarly declared their commitment to sustaining the qualities that make books essential to a sense of civilized living.

Among the many forms their defense of the book took in the 1920s, one of the most remarkable, in its ideological audacity and its broad social energy, was the unprecedented production and consumption of a special, acutely self-conscious genre of books whose material form was their foremost feature. They were *about* form, exquisite and extravagant testimonies to print as a site that marked something significant and powerful. Such books functioned as vir-tual temples built in reverent homage to a treasured world of ideas, literature, and the human spirit that books seem intrinsically and uniquely to embody.

I first encountered that rarefied world some twenty years ago when, as a young graduate student, I set a stick of type by hand. Stationed before shallow typecases divided into dozens of tiny compartments, four classmates and I slowly assembled the letters that composed Clarence Day's famous dictum "The World of Books." One at a time, each piece of type went in upside down and backward as we laboriously centered each line. "The world of books," our given passage eventually proclaimed, "is the most remarkable creation of man. Nothing else that he builds ever lasts. Monuments fall; nations perish; civiliza-tions grow old and die out; and, after an era of darkness, new races build on others. But in the world of books are volumes that have seen this happen again and again, and yet live on, still young, still as fresh as the day they were written, still telling men's hearts of the hearts of men centuries dead."

This passage, we were told and explained in smaller type at the foot of the page, was written in 1920 to mark the significance Day ascribed to his broth-er's venture as director of the then-fledgling Yale University Press. We added a few decorative ornaments and nervously printed about a dozen copies by hand on an antique press, powered by a foot treadle. What resulted was a page whose sculptural letterforms, modeled on Renaissance Italian types, were borne deep within the thick, slightly ribbed paper, not merely on its surface. We could feel the passage as well as see it. We learned at several levels — tactile, emotional, and intellectual — that this was a special kind of production known as "fine printing." (What made our printing fine, I must add, was not skill but the materials and processes we used and the care we took to create something that each of us has probably saved.)

At the end of that long morning in a dusty library basement, we washed our hands and headed upstairs to the Special Collections room. There, nestled in cradles draped with black felt, were copies of what we were told were the great books of America's fine printing heyday after the First World War. We gazed at a remarkable tableau: Whitman's long lines marching boldly across broad pages, Ishmael falling headlong through a black starry sky at the entrance to *Moby Dick*, Dante's verse shimmering within a pale blue frame as if a medieval scribe had laboriously lined the pages, naked figures cavorting across the pages of *Candide,* and rows of other, equally beguiling books laid out for us to admire. None of us said much as we wandered through the display, but when we did speak it was in a whisper. We brushed the rough, feathery edges of handmade paper as we turned pages, heard the slight creak of seasoned leather as we closed a book to view its binding, and fingered the palpable indent of words and images pressed forever into paper. We did not need to be told that the books' sensuous physicality literally gave them a special dimension of meaning and import as well. They were certainly great books in the canonical sense, but here the term meant more than the status or merit of their texts. The term was new to me but it made sense at once: these, the curator quietly explained, were *fine books.*

Since that day I have been intrigued by the seductive power of beautiful books, and especially by that spectacular profusion of fine editions produced in the 1920s and 1930s. At first I wondered that that bibliophilic ardor could spring simply from a love of books. Gradually I realized that such love is not simple at all, that it conveys a complex mixture of anxieties and desires which surfaced with particular energy during that pivotal period in American history. Why? What about the fine book proved so resonant to its makers and buyers in that age of startling changes and restless modernity? How did contemporaries understand and value it, and what in turn does that tell us about them? This study explores those strong attachments to the printed book by which so many, then as now, defined a vital part of their selves.

I express my gratitude here to those who helped me research and write this book. For astute guidance as it initially took shape, I thank Lawrence Levine, Mary Kay Duggan, and Robert Harlan at the University of California at Berkeley and my colleagues in an NEH seminar on the history of American book culture conducted by Carl Kaestle in summer 1996. In particular, Jane Greer, Michael Keller, Lisa Gitelman, Velma Brown, and James McDonald shared insights and perspectives and offered equally generous good cheer and friendship as I rethought and rewrote. I also acknowledge the support of the Board of Regents of Pacific Lutheran University, which twice granted me funding to pursue this work. Colleagues Philip Nordquist and Audrey Eyler have been especially valued mentors, encouraging my turn to serious historical work. And I thank Paul Porter, for my first conversations about typography and for the smile this book would have brought to his face. To Lawrence Rainey, editor of the Henry McBride Series on Modernism and Modernity, I owe particular gratitude. His energetic and insightful critiques have been invaluable. I also thank Lara Heimert and Nancy Moore Brochin at Yale University Press for their skillful and cheerful handling of this book. Finally, I thank my husband, Paul, whose company helped make this the best possible kind of endeavor, animated by interest, discovery, and a kindred love of books.

Introduction
To Shame the World, to Please the World

Early in 1923 a small group of carefully selected guests gathered at the Carnegie Institute of Technology in Pittsburgh for a historic occasion, the dedication of unprecedented venture in higher education. The room grew quiet as the first speaker, director of the College of Industries, rose to his feet. He paused for a long moment at the podium, glanced at the old-fashioned iron handpress beside him, then solemnly announced, "Civilization depends to a large degree upon the effectiveness of printing. Printing constitutes the life of our marvelous civilization." He continued, "At the back of every enterprise, be it large or small, there is always an individual. We are fortunate in having with us in this college a man who has the genius of a dreamer, who sees things from a righteous viewpoint." He turned to introduce the man of whom he spoke, Porter Garnett.

Though not a large man, Garnett emanated a powerful elegance with his impeccably groomed white hair and stiff high collar. True to his introduction, Garnett gazed at the select band that sat before him. "We are going to make history," he intoned as he lifted a limp, cool sheet of dampened paper, a leaf from a 450-year-old book cut for the occasion by Pennsylvania's Senator David Reed. As Garnett prepared the sheet to be printed, Senator Reed mused that "we who love beautiful things and want to see America have its Renaissance cannot help but be a little moved by the thing we are about to witness."

Garnett carefully positioned the sheet on the open frame of the handpress, folded it over the inked type, and rolled it into position. Dr. Thomas Baker, president of the institute, stepped forward, grasped the bar on the press, and pulled.

The heavy platen descended and groaned faintly as it squeezed paper and type together for a moment, in a motion much like that of Gutenberg's first press five hundred years before. Garnett removed the printed sheet and held it high, triumphantly pronouncing it the "First Impression" of the Institute's new Laboratory Press, over which Garnett was to preside as Master. The sheet bore a six-line text, the poem "Invocation" by English poet John Masefield. Garnett slowly read it aloud, dwelling with particular emphasis on the final two lines: "O beauty through the darkness hurled, / Be it through me you shame the world."

Garnett looked up and asked his enthralled listeners, "Have you ever thought what power and what weakness reside in a printing press? We have here a machine gifted, we might say, with the power of speech. Consider its potentialities. Consider, too, how helpless, how subservient it is. . . . What a splendid thing it would be if we, in whose power it is for good or for ill, should pledge ourselves to this helpless instrument, should pledge ourselves that it shall never be called upon to speak otherwise than for some noble purpose."[1] The First Impression made just such a pledge. Across the bottom of the sheet, below a long description of the text, paper, and participants in the auspicious event, was debuted the motto of the new press, *Nil vulgare, nil pertriti, nil inepti*: nothing commonplace, nothing hackneyed, nothing tasteless.

With these lines Porter Garnett and that small band of visionaries dedicated the Laboratory Press, a special program devoted to teaching the "taste, tradition, and technique" essential to bookmaking practiced as a fine art, strictly for its own sake and unrestrained by economic or commercial considerations. In explicit defiance of contemporary publishing priorities, all work undertaken at the Laboratory Press would aspire only to beauty, dignity, and permanence. Uncompromised devotion to such ideals would not only restore lost integrity to the printed word but reinscribe the value of the Book, upon which civilization itself depended. Garnett vowed that only this rare kind of printing, known as *fine printing,* offered "the powerful cultural force that . . . will supply the leaven needed to make an aggressive and self-seeking industrialism endurable to others than the go-getter and the money-grubber."[2]

Nearly six years later young Bennett Cerf sat thoughtfully in his tiny Manhattan office. On his desk lay the telegram he'd been waiting for, word from San Francisco fine printer Edwin Grabhorn that yes, he would print another book for Cerf's fledgling Random House publishing company. Grabhorn—

whose Grabhorn Press was already legendary in fine printing circles — had at
last agreed to print a fine edition of Walt Whitman's *Leaves of Grass,* and Cerf
sensed that the printer was as keen as he to surpass the beauty and grandeur of
their acclaimed previous collaboration, a fine edition of *The Scarlet Letter.* A
gamble took shape in his mind. Everything Random House had published in
its first two years had glittered like gold; with the Grabhorn bookmaking
magic behind it, how could this new *Leaves of Grass* not be the best, the most
spectacular and important, book yet? Across the country, he reminded himself, thousands clamored for more fine books, each more lavish than the last.
In that heady moment, Cerf scrapped his initial plan for the book.[3] Instead of
an edition of twelve hundred copies to be sold for fifteen dollars each, he
resolved, this would be their first, indeed likely *the* first, American book grand
enough to boast a hundred-dollar price tag.

Proprietor Ed Grabhorn, assisted by his brother Robert, rose to the occasion. After numerous false starts and some eighteen months of intermittent
labor they finally produced in 1930 a book whose physical form and beauty
seemed impressive enough for both Whitman's poetry and the landmark price.
They made what many still regard as the pinnacle of American fine bookmaking: a massive folio, four hundred and thirty pages and measuring fourteen by
nineteen inches, typeset by hand, letterpress-printed on dampened English
handmade paper, with dozens of hand-carved woodcut decorations by Valenti
Angelo, and bound in mahogany boards with a dark leather spine. Long
before the book was finished, nearly two thousand people hurried to reserve
one of the four hundred copies.

These two scenes mark defining moments in what was frequently termed a
"craze" for finely made, physically distinctive books in the fifteen or so years
that followed the First World War, an era in which buyers demonstrated a fre-
netic "willingness to absorb limited editions in limitless numbers." Despite his
and other publishers' best efforts, Donald Friede testified, there were simply
not enough fine editions to supply the demand for them. Early in 1929, fine
book publisher, designer, and unabashed enthusiast George Macy crowed
in *Publishers' Weekly,* the industry's trade journal, that in just the past ten
years, the number of Americans actively interested in finely printed books had
grown some eightfold, from about three thousand serious buyers to more than
twenty-five thousand. While at the beginning of the decade a publisher could
safely count on selling only about five hundred copies of a fine book, Macy
exulted, "today editions of three thousand copies have been oversubscribed
before publication day."[4] There was a seemingly insatiable market for fine
books, whose desirability lay less in their content than in the beauty, extravagance, status, or scarcity of the edition.

Both the reverent dedication rite in Pittsburgh and the extravagant gamble taken in Cerf's Manhattan office illustrate the conviction bordering on audacity that fine printing often inspired. But despite the two men's kindred faith in the value of books made to the highest standards of craftsmanship and "taste," they held often radically conflicting notions of the nature and purpose of such fine books. Garnett vehemently prohibited any taint of marketplace commercialism in the quasi-sacred work undertaken at the Laboratory Press. He insisted that fine bookmaking should never accommodate, never compromise with "popular taste, with outlays and returns, . . . or with machinery."[5] If they resisted the temptation to put profits above quality, Garnett preached, fine printers would restore dignity and stature to the physical book and inspire, or shame, ordinary printers to uphold higher standards when making ordinary "mass" books as well. His ambition was as spectacular as his resolve was righteous: fine printing could redeem the printed Book as the virtually sacred vessel of Western culture.

By contrast, almost from the start Cerf conceived of the Random House edition of *Leaves of Grass* in terms of its selling price; he left it to the Grabhorns to work out later the features that might constitute a hundred-dollar book. He understood the sensuous appeal of fine books and especially the social pleasure they gave, their satisfying heft, color, and artistry, and the pride of owning a uniquely numbered copy of a finely printed classic work of literature. Throughout the postwar years Garnett remained a steadfast idealist, a kind of high priest at the altar of the printed word, while Cerf recognized the lucrative markets eager to pay for a share of the icons. One was the Conscience of fine printing, the other its premier Capitalist; between them lies the little-explored territory of the ideal book in modern America.

The craze for materially beautiful, fine books in the 1920s may at first seem quirky, one more oddball fad in an era famous for its "exuberant nonsense" — Ouija boards, flagpole sitting, and Harold Lloyd. That craze is difficult to take seriously today, when books that cost a week's salary or more would prompt only incredulous laughs, not eager scrambles to secure a copy. Perhaps at times ownership of these books did slip into sheer extravagance for its own sake, a frivolous gesture as excessive as smoking hundred-dollar bills. But the passion for fine books was far more than a game or a flippant pastime among the restless rich. It speaks of deeper social and cultural anxieties that eerily resemble — indeed, prefigure — fears accompanying the modern role of books in our lives. This study explores those anxieties by examining the unparalleled postwar enthusiasm for books created and valued above all for their physical, material "bookness."

"Bookness" invites serious study in its own right. A book, after all, is much more than its text; it encompasses a host of tangible components (paper, binding cloth, glues, inks), visual features (typefaces, margins, colors, illustrations), and what French critic Gerard Genette calls paratextual, often commercial, elements (a publisher's name and logo, a price, promotional blurbs, lists of other books written by the author or sold by the publisher, and so forth). These material aspects, which differ with each particular edition of a text—lurid cover art, cramped lines of type, cheap paper, stiff bindings, a ribbon bookmark, gilded edges, glossy illustrations, and so on—powerfully influence how we approach and understand the text itself. We intuitively tend to read a book with a sturdy binding, large type, and plentiful illustration as a children's book, for example, and perceive its meaning within that context. We cannot read a text without also, simultaneously and inevitably, reading its form.[6]

Because the material and commercial aspects of books are so telling in themselves, I focused particular attention on three hundred fine editions produced in the United States for sale in the 1920s and early 1930s. I gathered a wide range of detailed information about them: editorial and marketing features such as the gender and nationality of authors, the era when the text was written, its price, advertising, discounts, and so on, as well as a host of typographic and production aspects, including style and size of type, dimensions, materials used, and ink colors. This sample of editions, listed in the appendix, is broad and representative. Although I included most work of the era's prominent fine publishers and printers, I did not try to compile a complete bibliography of the genre. These editions offer a wealth of evidence about how and why they were made, and my arguments rely significantly upon that information. Most of my findings are summarized in a series of tables throughout the book.

That part of the investigation, which was relatively easy, also invited challenges. Unlike the vast range of print production—which includes not only trade books but dime novels, school textbooks, Sunday school tracts, local newspapers, and so on—fine books have been carefully preserved behind glass doors in affluent homes and prestigious libraries. In part because they are so sequestered, so removed from their more mundane cousins, historians and others have tended to dismiss fine books as irrelevant to "real world" questions and issues.[7] They are typically deemed beautiful but benign relics of a golden age of bookcraft, touching if self-indulgent gestures of book love. They seem idealistic and disinterested, produced—and preserved—far from the din of commercial publishing and everyday society.

These notions prevail today because they are exactly how postwar fine printers and publishers usually portrayed their work to the public, and hence to posterity. Today's fine presses (more numerous than one might suspect) typically paint the same picture: most operate "privately," which means the venture is supported with income from other sources or is not aimed at earning a profit. In fact, today a fine press seems almost by definition a private press; any committed emphasis on typographic or material beauty seems necessarily to preclude or overshadow marketplace considerations.[8] Little wonder that we assume all those postwar fine editions were produced under similar circumstances: simply for love of beauty, of good literature, of soul-satisfying handcraft.

Yet surviving private correspondence, business documents, and other archival papers tell a very different story. They depict an enterprise that was acutely sensitive to real world needs, demands, and opportunities, and that was no less shaped by and addressed to the complex concerns of postwar society than the many more workaday forms of print. Although Porter Garnett's Laboratory Press students produced idealized small books and broadsides that were hailed as beautiful "orchids," miraculous for having emerged from Pittsburgh's industrial shadows, most postwar fine printing and publishing was a far hardier species.[9] It was a fully professional venture, in which books were intended from the start for sale to a public market. This deliberate foray into the real world is the essence of what was remarkable about postwar fine bookmaking; it sought to exert a force in larger society, not merely among book collectors, type enthusiasts, hobby printers, and bibliophiles. Ideally, fine printing was meant ultimately to make a difference to all books and all readers. That effort — what it comprised, what motivated and sustained it, how it fared — is the subject of this book.

It is useful to clarify at the outset a few key terms, because any discussion of book culture is complicated by slippery meanings of such terms as *printer, publisher, designer,* and even *book* and *edition.* The *printer* is best understood as the agent who produces the physical book. Traditionally a printer also designed the book, making all the aesthetic typographic decisions concerning its appearance and tangible form, but by the twenties the separate profession of book *designer* or *typographer* had crystallized. By the end of the decade a book's visual features commonly were attributed to its designer, while only its manufacture was credited to the printer (although many printers maintained responsibility for both aspects, and the term *printer* often applied to both functions). A *publisher* is fundamentally the party who assumes the editorial prerogatives and the financial risks and responsibilities, paying royalties and the cost of the book's manufacture and distribution. Often a separate *distributor* would be involved as well, undertaking sales and some advertising responsibilities for a publisher. Some of the chief players in the postwar fine book business performed more than one of these functions, and books often passed through several hands along their way to an eventual owner. The books published under the Crosby Gaige imprint, for example, were typically designed by Frederic Warde or Bruce Rogers, produced by the William E. Rudge printing plant, and distributed by Random House to local book dealers. Finally, many fine productions were regarded as *books* even though their texts were slight; their status as books was determined by their physical format (one or more gatherings of folded leaves bound between rigid boards or, very occasionally, soft covers) rather than their textual substance or length. An *edition* refers to a discrete editorial and typographic version of a text.

As do most of the contemporary accounts on which I have relied, I use the general terms *books* and *publishers* without modifiers when they refer to *trade* books and publishing. Very simply, trade books in the 1920s were usually original publications (as opposed to reprints) that were sold through retail booksellers. The full range of printed texts circulating in American society was much larger, of course, encompassing vast numbers of textbooks, so-called pulp fiction, inexpensive mail-order reprints, church and government publications, periodicals, newspapers, and so on.

In describing fine books I use the adjectives *fine* and *bibliophilic* as approximate synonyms, although in fact they have slightly different meanings. *Fine printing* is a well-established bibliographical term, whereas *bibliophilia* refers to book love, which readily extends to books that are not finely printed. However, the fine books discussed here aspired to be bibliophilic in that they were intended for an audience of patrons who typically regarded the book as a particularly meaningful kind of rare and beautiful object. Contemporaries often used the term *deluxe* when referring to these books, although sometimes they did so ironically, expressing disdain for books that merely mimicked features (such as colophons, numbered copies, or deckle-edged papers) characterizing fine books. The context of such usage makes clear its meaning. Finally, I follow contemporary practice in sometimes using the term *limited editions* to refer to fine books, even though the terms are not synonymous. Virtually all fine books were produced in relatively small editions, but as the market for them grew, so did the practice of issuing otherwise ordinary books in arbitrarily limited editions. This practice infuriated many proponents of fine bookmaking, who distinguished between the kinds of limited editions as either "real" or "fake." Here, too, the context makes clear when *limited edition* refers to something other than finely made books.

This study excludes the work of the handful of truly private and noncommercial presses of the day — such as Arthur Rushmore's Golden Hind Press,

Melbert Cary's Press of the Woolly Whale, and Harry and Caresse Crosby's expatriate Black Sun Press—because their books, while often exquisite in form, were made simply to suit the tastes and purposes of their proprietors. I have also excluded fine publications commissioned by individuals or corporate patrons, as well as the publications of private book clubs, notably the Grolier Club in New York and the Book Club of California, because they were distributed primarily to club members, friends, and associates. Similarly, although its commercial posture is germane here, the publications of the Limited Editions Club (LEC), founded in 1929 by George Macy, generally fall outside the realm of this study because members simply paid an annual sum to receive the year's twelve fine editions and exercised no further discretion in their purchasing. Although privately produced and exclusively distributed books are important to the story of American fine printing, they generally lie outside the range of issues and questions I seek to explore here.

Attention here centers on the broader social and cultural phenomenon of fine publishing. The study therefore encompasses the great majority of postwar fine books, the several hundred titles produced by the era's leading commercial (that is, for-profit, for-hire) fine printing establishments. Among the best known and most active were the Grabhorn Press of San Francisco; the Pynson Printers in New York; Boston's Merrymount Press; and the firms of William Edwin Rudge and John Henry Nash, located in Mt. Vernon, New York, and San Francisco, respectively. These printers also occasionally published books, but most fine editions were produced via more conventional practices, whereby a publisher hires a printer to produce the books. A 1929 census of fine presses tallied approximately forty-five American publishers active in for-profit fine book production.[10] The nature and extent of their activity varied considerably. A few, notably Random House, Crosby Gaige, Fountain Press, and Covici-Friede, issued fine editions almost exclusively. Some smaller imprints, such as Philadelphia's Centaur Press and Dunster House in Cambridge, Massachusetts, published as a side venture from a primary livelihood in bookselling. Others, including the Windsor and Spiral presses, were relatively tiny operations in which one or more printer-craftsmen both produced and published fine books exclusively. Finally, several mainstream publishers—such as Alfred Knopf, Harper Brothers, Liveright, Scribner's, and Doubleday Doran—issued significant fine editions in addition to their trade lists.

At its heart, as Porter Garnett so vehemently insisted, the fine book signified virtually everything that modern mass book culture was not: handcraft instead of industrial production, few rather than many, slow and expensive rather than speedy and economical, *Beowulf* and *Moby Dick* rather than Zane Grey and Emily Post. But for a time, for those dozen or so years after the First World War, fine printing sought distinction from the ordinary not so much to avoid it as to compete with it, to model an alternative aesthetic and culture of the Book itself. Although their alternative was fraught with paradoxes and dilemmas, as the following chapters depict, fine printers and publishers worked to construct a cultural and social framework in which good, important, enduring books mattered more than others, and in which that importance was both affirmed and ensured by their superior artistic and material quality. In other words, fine publishers undertook a deeply cultural project: they aspired to make a fundamental difference to American society by redefining what books, as books, should be and mean.

The story of that project unfolds here through the words and labors of those who, like Porter Garnett, struggled to define and produce the modern book beautiful. They are a colorful and provocative cast of characters: moody and mysterious Frederic Warde, sanctimonious but savvy John Henry Nash, New England blueblood scholar-printer Daniel Berkeley Updike, stylish but stuffy Elmer Adler, the droll and often despondent Carl Purington Rollins, prickly iconoclast Ed Grabhorn, and others. The story also involves the lives of those who, like Bennett Cerf, worked to promote and sell fine books in the American marketplace: shrewd and principled publisher Alfred Knopf, wealthy dilettante Crosby Gaige, decadent cynic Donald Friede, hyperbolic showman George Macy, eloquent publicist Beatrice Warde, and others. Yet it is misleading to leave these players divided into such neat categories, because the two functions — principles and practice, production and sales — cannot be separated. Each player contributed in both ways to the complex and compelling enterprise of exalting the book in modern America.

That duality lies at the very heart of this study. While ostensibly rescuing the Book from the popular market forces that threatened to "cheapen" and "vulgarize" it, fine publishers enjoyed a brisk and profitable business. These publishers sought to influence the world even as they claimed disinterestedness; they stood not merely apart from the mainstream but, they hoped, at its forefront. Fine publishers envisioned a role of natural cultural leadership, but worked shrewdly to attract and maintain their sizable following. They sought to shame the world, but also to please it.

The story begins with an eerily familiar lament. Shortly after the turn of the century, American publisher Henry Holt mourned the imminent death of the book as he knew it. With cheap, ever-changing, and colorful magazines available at every city street corner, he sighed, who would prefer the relatively cumbersome, serious, and expensive book? He noted the impending "massification" of print culture — ushered in by near-complete mechanization of production processes, unprecedented literacy levels, and a crowd of entrepreneurial publishers happy to oblige the commonest of literary tastes. Holt feared that the book, in a vital cultural as well as physical sense, could not survive.

By the 1920s many thought the situation seemed even more ominous. Ironically, even as publishing thrived in a new world bursting not only with magazines and newspapers but also with radio broadcasts and even movies, concerns for the cultural integrity of the book intensified. One of the most telling expressions of those anxieties was the unprecedented production and consumption of fine books. Because fine editions were both produced and bought as much to be *owned* as to be *read,* the story of how they were constructed — literally and figuratively — and circulated has much to tell us about cultural ambitions and ambiguities as Americans made their places in the modern world.

Too Many Books
The Glut of the Good Life

As the 1930 Christmas season approached, editor Henry Seidel Canby counseled readers of the *Saturday Review of Literature* not so much to buy books as to discard them. "There are not, as so many complain, too many good books," Canby announced. Rather, he fumed, there are "too many books published only to be bought" (and, he might have added, bought only to be owned), "too many books used as a 'color note,' books as paper weights, books for the baby to sit on, books kept as feeble proof that someone has been educated, books that are everything but good books."

What prompted Canby's front-page tirade? He had taken an inventory of the bookshelves of the typical American living room. From San Diego to St. Paul, Mobile to Manhattan, he suggested, one was likely to encounter living rooms furnished with "stale and unprofitable volumes, unread and unreadable." He made his case graphically. "Observe a stretch of miscellaneous novels," he wrote, "not too happily chosen in the first instance, and now with six out of seven titles dead and forgotten; a set of Battles of the Spanish-American War in cracked leather backs; a Golden Collection of the World's Literature, villainously bound in the early 1900s, and never used then, or later; an edition of Thackeray, probably a wedding present; three volumes of sermons bound in wormy leather, once belonging to great-uncle John; . . . fragments of a Temple Shakespeare; an illustrated Tennyson "sumptuously" bound; a dozen obvious text-books left over from college; a big Bible and a little Bible; three travel books; and Oratory of All the Nations; and forty or fifty dog-eared magazines put in to fill space." He declared this hodgepodge a "depressing spectacle." Not even a few books that seemed to have been thoughtfully selected for the value of their contents could redeem the collection from his scorn or, he urged, from the incinerator: "a *civilized* family should be ashamed to live in such company!"[1]

Canby found the typical home's books offensive in two ways. First, he loathed the specious purposes most of them served, dismissing them as little more than "sacred arcs of culture." He even preferred the "barbarism" of the "newly housebroken who have moved into living rooms in the recent eras of prosperity" who used their bookshelves for "phonograph records, all-story magazines, and the cat's saucer of milk." Theirs, he sniffed, "is at least the honester way."[2] Canby also disdained the books' content and form. That they were largely "unprofitable" and "unreadable" seemed inseparable from their "villainous" material form: cracked backs, wormy leather, dog-eared pages. Both inauthentic functions and corrupt forms pointed to the chief problem: books had become too plentiful, too commonplace. The precious qualities of "good" books had been diluted — if not drowned — in the flood of "too many" others.

Canby's book-detecting journey into the "typical American living room" may strike us today as a curious and possibly arrogant expedition, but contemporary readers recognized this and dozens of similar essays as a familiar subgenre of the 1920s. Throughout the decade — amid much anxious scrutiny of the nation's collective character — sociologists, critics, and others studied book ownership as a "definite and illuminating index of the general state of culture." Sociologists Helen and Robert Lynd, for example, spent much of the decade analyzing life in typically American "Middletown," including book reading and buying habits, while others focused exclusively on American habits of reading and book ownership.[3] Everyone wanted to know — who has books? which books? and what did that mean? The goal, it seemed, was no less than to take the pulse of civilization itself.

Books and Prosperity

The questions were prompted in part by the unprecedented production and sale of books in the decade or so following the First World War. Steady growth in American population and literacy rates throughout the nineteenth century had translated into equally expanding markets for books. This spurred a series of dramatic technological advancements in the book manufacturing industries, which enabled publishers to offer increasingly affordable and accessible books. In 1880 when the population stood at just over 50 million, some two thousand book titles (including pamphlets) were published, but by 1920 when the population had doubled to 106 million, book title output had more than tripled. Industrial production was not the only factor accounting for the growth, of course, but it was a huge one; in a single industry, papermaking, the difference was perhaps most astounding. At the start of the century all paper was made by hand from rag fibers, but after the 1827 introduction of the Fourdrinier papermaking machine in the United States and the switch to cheaper wood pulp at midcentury, by 1900 paper output had increased a hundredfold while its price had dropped tenfold.[4] Books were plentiful in part because it was easy to produce large numbers of them relatively cheaply and quickly.

Yet production usually goes hand in hand with demand. If industrialization in the nineteenth century had revolutionized book production, it was the commercialization of American society in the late nineteenth and early twentieth centuries that revolutionized book consumption. Especially as confidence and the economy began to soar following the war, Americans, as an aggregate, showed an unprecedented interest in owning books. At the simplest level this was completely predictable: Why shouldn't books flourish, just like so many other consumer goods, during the era's fabled prosperity and plenty? It was only natural that people should buy more books than ever before, because they bought more of just about everything else that signaled leisure and luxury. By the end of the decade it would no longer be anything special to own a radio, for example, and millions thrived on a new diet of magazines and daily newspapers, which for the first time in history reached more than 90 percent of American households.[5] A truly mass media blanketed the country, humming with countless messages that the "good life," as gloriously portrayed in ubiquitous advertising, was now within the grasp of more Americans than ever before. Small luxuries like silk stockings and lingerie, fur-trimmed coats, and even canned food skyrocketed in sales — thanks to the softly drawn images of happy consumers that crowded the pages of the magazines and newspapers stacked in seemingly every home. The average American's ability and constantly encouraged inclination to "better his position and acquire . . . the good things of life by his own industry and cleverness" were widely praised as moral virtues.[6] Owning things and getting ahead was not only fun and exciting but also good for you and good for the country.

Books were definitely part of the fun. In 1920 just over six thousand books were published, but by 1929 the annual total had risen to more than ten thousand titles, adding up to more than two hundred million printed copies.

Book sales expanded briskly by some 10 percent each year, and a flock of new and energetic young publishers entered the field, changing the landscape not only of what was published but of how books were sold. After an initial reluctance, publishers learned quickly to market their wares aggressively and creatively.[7] They premiered weekly bestseller lists in order to alert buyers to what their neighbors purportedly were reading, and they tried such flamboyant sales tactics as skywriting, promotional contests and puzzles, and "sandwich men" wearing mini-billboards. Meanwhile, improvements in distribution methods, including vigorous and efficient mail-order techniques and innovations pioneered by the Book-of-the-Month Club in 1926, helped books reach more homes than ever before.[8]

Despite the sense of profusion and plenty in the living rooms across the country, however, for most rural and poorer Americans book-life had changed little. Much of that population had a bit more money, and they too spent it on the kind of treats that the magazines crowed about and the nearest general store might now stock. Even so, they still had parlors — if they were fortunate — not the breezy new "living rooms" found in suburban bungalows.[9] And in those parlors typically lay the same few books that had probably been there a generation earlier.

Moving picture theaters were beginning to appear on main streets throughout rural America, but virtually no bookstores, and for good reasons. Most people in remote and rural parts of the country had little inclination to lay down precious spending money for a book. One in three American homes had no books at all, and most families that did own books already had what they needed. A Bible usually topped (and sometimes completed) the list, and a few well-worn devotionals and a good almanac were almost as common. Mother might have been given a book of recipes and household advice as a wedding present, and the children would have spellers — perhaps the same ones their parents had used — and a favorite storybook, names scrawled across their torn or soiled covers, stashed in a bureau drawer or in the toolshed. Some homes might boast a large book about the Holy Land, the American presidents, or the march of progress, or stories by Mark Twain or Walter Scott. But to most poorer families books were like furniture: in most cases one had hand-me-downs or the rare gift for a special occasion, and there was little need to buy another until the old wore out.

The truth was — as it had been for centuries before and remains today — that among most working-class and poor rural families, books were not a luxury many coveted. The only reading matter the Lynds could detect in Middletown's poorest working-class homes was "yesterday's newspaper," while in those of slightly more means "some magazines may be lying about, but rarely any books." The extravagance of buying books simply exceeded their appeal. When in 1921 the *Ladies Home Journal* published for readers with modest incomes a chart dividing expenses into three suggested levels — *fixed, possible to estimate,* and *necessary to limit* — rent, groceries, and magazine and newspaper subscriptions were included in the first two categories, while books joined out-of-season foods and long-distance telephone calls in the third. That year only some 4 percent of Americans visited a bookstore more than once, and virtually all of them lived in a major city.[10]

In fact, although publishing certainly flourished in the twenties, it saw none of the fabulous expansion and profits registered by many other consumer industries. By the end of the decade, when Americans were merrily spending nearly 5 percent of their annual income on recreational expenses, less than one-half of 1 percent of that income was spent on books. In 1927 alone Americans spent more than three billion dollars on personal "luxuries" — a catchall term for everything from chewing gum to fireworks to jewelry — twenty times the amount spent on books. The cultural implications of this struck many as ominous indeed. What is so good, one writer wondered glumly, about life in a society that buys ten pounds of candy for every book it purchases?[11] While 200 million books bought each year might suggest a nation with enthusiastic reading habits, it amounted to fewer than two books per capita in a population of 120 million. By comparison, *weekly* movie attendance grew from 40 million in 1922 to 95 million in 1929, and continued to rise to 115 million the following year. Price was no doubt a factor; a magazine or admission to a movie cost only a few coins, while a novel usually cost between two and three dollars, and nonfiction between two and five dollars. (Most consumer books were clothbound; the modern paperback did not emerge until the late 1930s.) Yet price alone was not the answer. "We can afford to buy books," one critic put it bluntly, "but we do not."[12]

Books and Better Homes

How do these accounts of only lukewarm interest in buying books square with reports of unprecedented sales, or with Canby's portrait of burgeoning, if haphazard, collections found on "typical" American bookshelves? Oddly, it did make a kind of sense. The fact that even in their relative abundance books scarcely touched working-class America tacitly confirmed one of the dominant truisms of the decade. As Vice President Coolidge put it, "better" homes always have books. In 1924 Coolidge sternly challenged readers of *The Delineator:* "Do you want a mind that is keen, straight-thinking, well balanced? . . . Do you want to be efficient, up-to-date, successful in your work? . . .

Do you want to develop the spiritual side of you—sympathy, imagination, love?" To each query's presumably chastened reply the resounding response was the same: "Then you must read books." There was more to it, however: "you must do more than read them. You must own them, make them part of you. And you must choose the *right* books." At the bottom of the page Coolidge recommended specific titles of history, biography, fiction, poetry, and devotion that would nicely form, he promised, the nucleus of "books for better homes."[13] In this familiar formula, books enable "civilized" living because they lift the mundane, ordinary existence into higher realms. The equation affirms a value system in which quality and merit derive from inner wealth— character, taste, respect for art and culture—not sheer income or amassing of material goods. *Culture* was the flourishing commodity that spurred much of the decade's book sales; you needed it if you cared to distinguish yourself from the static lives of the poor and working classes, and especially from the "barbarians" who neglected books altogether in their postwar lives.

Significantly, it was soon discovered that the inner wealth derived from books often yielded tangible rewards. This was the modern twist: books could expand one's mind and soul nicely, of course, but they also were instrumental to the good life in its material dimensions. Paradoxically hailed as tangible expressions of those important cultural intangibles, books were soon seized upon as a kind of miracle product that could help one "get ahead." Thus, although it did not compare to the mass audiences that formed for radio broadcasts, movies, newspapers, and magazines, the market for books thrived in the 1920s as never before.

These new and avaricious book buyers puzzled and fascinated critics. Just who were they, and what were they after? "There is a new book-buying public," one journalist allowed cautiously, but it "is not yet a public of established tastes, of literary traditions." Another dubbed them the "book Babbitts," invoking Sinclair Lewis's classic everyman of the twenties, George F. Babbitt. They were, or aspired to be, members of what the Lynds labeled the "business classes," typified by their economic prosperity, usually derived from business, their suburban lifestyles, and their largely expedient and somewhat irreverent determination to improve their lives.[14] They proudly pegged themselves average Americans, at once disillusioned and sentimental, cynical yet ambitious.

Across the country, as a New York columnist put it, there seemed to be stirring "a definite hunger . . . for some indefinite thing which [men and women] perhaps call culture." Frederick Lewis Allen suspected that such hunger was more utilitarian than spiritual. He diagnosed what he termed an "epidemic" of outlines of knowledge and books of etiquette as the peculiarly American self-help solution "for those who had got rich quick and wanted to get cultured quick." Indeed, Wells's *Outline of History* topped the nonfiction bestseller lists in 1921 and 1922, to be replaced by Emily Post's *Etiquette* in 1923. Will Durant, whose *Story of Philosophy* was one of the decade's most steady bestsellers, explained that he had written the book to bring knowledge within the grasp of the "million voices" that called out for a book to teach them what "dull, arrogant professors" could or would not. He insisted that its popularity signaled a new democracy of culture, and he noted with pride that sales of classic philosophy texts more than tripled after publication of his *Story*.[15]

Others were not so sanguine about the prospect of a spontaneous cultural democracy. "It seems odd," Howard Mumford Jones remarked, "if 'a million voices' called for the outlines, that hundreds of thousands of dollars had to be spent in high-pressure advertising to get the books sold." While many Americans no doubt discovered genuine new pleasure in reading and learning, they may have been nudged into it by anxieties triggered by the decade's incessant advertisements. One, for example, pictured a tall man in evening clothes chatting amiably as three beautiful women listened raptly, their dresses pooled languidly around their long, slim bodies. Three men stood tensely nearby, the caption explained, watching "the man whose conversation so dazzled the company that the envious dinner-coated bystanders could only breathe in amazement, 'I think he's quoting from Shelley.' "[16] Among the most heavily advertised, especially in magazines aimed at families with relatively modest incomes, were the Harvard Classics, better known as Dr. Eliot's Five-Foot Shelf of Books. Retired Harvard president Charles W. Eliot had selected for the series the "few great books really worth knowing," which the publisher claimed were readily installed in "thousands of cultured American homes." Lured by the prospect of a "liberal education in fifteen minutes a day," buyers hoped that by acquiring the essential "few great books" they could make their homes as cultured as the next. Ads for the series, sold through subscription by P. F. Collier and Sons, were compelling and insistent. Who dared *not* to buy books that promised "the difference between the plodding clerk and the clear-thinking executive. The difference between the deadly bore and the interesting talker. The difference between success and failure — in business and social life"?[17]

Domestic Bookaflage

Many who embraced books for the first time or with new energy did so for the improving and instructive qualities of their content, as Durant claimed. But there was a superficial purpose as well; a good part of books' popularity derived from the benefits they bestowed beyond those gained from actually

reading them. In 1923 Thomas Masson offered tips on "domestic bookaflage."
How easily, he remarked, one might "group a few high brow books at a
strategic point, so that as the guest enters his eye will fall upon them at once."

> Take Gilbert Murray's Greek plays, Galsworthy's "Saga," Milton's "Paradise
> Lost," Plato's "Republic," and Browning, and there you are! Anyone entering
> and seeing these flowers of literature carelessly disposed on a near-mahogany
> table just inside of the living-room bounds, would say to himself at once:
> "Here we have culture! Here we have literary delicacy!"
>
> You do nothing more yourself. You are quite safe. If you talk about the
> latest movie or the approaching golf tournament, your guest again whispers
> to himself: "He's concealing it. Under the specious show of frivolity and the
> mere commonplace, he is hiding the expansive soul of a genuine scholar."
>
> Thus, with the judicious expenditure of a few hundred dollars, you can
> erect an intellectual entanglement that will keep you quite safe in your domes-
> tic trenches.[18]

Masson's essay lampoons a notion that was both proffered and received in all
seriousness in the twenties. Books played a prominent, often featured role in
the widespread preoccupation with fashioning one's home. "These friends, so
dear and full of charm, . . . add warmth and graciousness to any room,"
proclaimed one family and decorating magazine after another.[19]

That books were integral to the good life was readily apparent throughout
the pages of popular magazines. "One of the most forlorn things in the world
is a house without books," one writer warned bluntly. Books appeared in
nearly 30 percent of the decade's ads; everything from Cream of Wheat to
Jergens soap promised to deliver the same wholesome, life-enriching qualities
that books convey. Just like the pleasant book in her lap, one dreamy young
woman's Milk of Magnesia made her "life sweeter," one advertisement assured. Similarly, dozens of articles extolled books' virtues. An essay entitled
"Mental Good Housekeeping" advocated books for maintaining minds as
tastefully and conscientiously as the home and garden. "We Americans are
lavish with books," another writer crowed in *Good Housekeeping;* for her,
books were essential home furnishings. Books in one's home, she declared,
were no less than a shorthand statement of pride in American civilization.[20]

Throughout the decade books were praised for emanating domestic beauty,
virtue, and comfort. Along with firelight and flowers, they conjured a virtually
irresistible picture of the ideal home: elegant yet inviting, beautiful yet personable. Homeowners were repeatedly advised to pair books with the fireplace,
their partner in peaceful dignity and relaxing intimacy: "there is a relationship
between a fire and a book as close and pleasant as between a brook and a
speckled trout." Books also blended perfectly with that other keynote of gra-

ciousness and pleasure, flowers. "Who would not better enjoy the splendid measures of Milton . . . in the perfumed air from a great bowl of roses on a table nearby?" one writer sighed, adding that for best results "Walt Whitman should be read when lilacs bloom."[21]

Owning books, however, was not sufficient; much depended on what one did with them. Several writers cautioned readers of the distinction between books cloistered in a home library and those "invited into" the living room. People who entombed their books in libraries or in cold, inhospitable surroundings — behind glass doors, for example, a treatment likened to "shutting out your best friends" — gained neither the social nor the decorative benefits of book ownership. Books thus treated tended only to intimidate or chastise others intellectually, an act of antidemocratic snobbery that profoundly violated the social ethic of postwar home decor. Books were to be bridges that linked their owners with new and often better territories of gracious civility, not walls that preserved or erected cultural boundaries. The decade's most heeded expert in creating a beautiful home life, Emily Post, bluntly pronounced that "to fill your rooms with books you know you will never open, rather than with those you like, . . . is to produce the same impression of misfit as if you wore a mask and wig." To misrepresent your tastes was fraudulent and, worse still, bad manners. There was a certain justice to the resulting hazard that one would create an oppressive burden of "beautifully bound classics, which you feel you should have read."[22]

Despite her objections to displaying books merely for social ostentation, Post had to admit that the rich colors and connotations of books were too tempting for style-conscious homemakers to overlook. Even if one hadn't read them, she conceded, books were incomparably handy for projecting homey tranquillity and reverence for literature and ideas. Ignoring the logical step from book decor to bookaflage, Post and others rhapsodized about the power of books' bindings alone to achieve domestic warmth and dignity. She even instructed readers how to cover ugly, insignificant books with materials that matched the room's color scheme in order to gain attractive books in a pinch, although only as "temporary fill-shelves" until one could buy more authentic volumes.[23]

Others felt no such qualms. Margery Doud's 1925 "Books for the Home: A Selection for Both Merit and Color" pointed out that "a few red books will . . . brighten up a dark corner on a dreary day," suggesting that because "our great and beloved Mark Twain comes in the red class" it would be an excellent candidate for such a spot. "For those hot summer days . . . there are some thin little, cool little, unpretentious green books with which one may dream away a lazy afternoon," she continued, recommending Barrie's *The Little Minister*.

Constance Lindsay Skinner reported hearing a luncheon-hour radio broadcast in which the program hostess chided the "cultured women listening in" for being content to buy books "merely to pass away an hour or two of leisure." After offending a visitor with the discordant color of a new purchase thoughtlessly laid on the center table of her living room, the hostess declared that thereafter she "never entered a bookshop without a 'small sample' of the velour, chintz, or damask, which gave the 'prevailing tone' to her room." Cultured ladies were advised to do likewise, to purchase books not for "trivial amusement" but as "aesthetic aids in home decoration." Such counsel hit home; one bookseller reported that a customer entered the shop "with a tape measure and asked for three and a half feet of red books. She explained that her walls and chairs were painted gray, her draperies were red, and that there was a four-foot shelf just over the gray *chaise longue* where a big splash of red was needed. She did not want books enough to fill the shelf, did not want them to stand closely and evenly. One book must lean, catty-cornered fashion, from left to right at one end of the shelf, and another must catty-corner from right to left in the middle of the shelf, so as to have that artistic sort of careless look becoming to a sun parlor furnished in enamelled wicker and hooked rugs."[24]

Skinner was appalled at the notion of books as part of one's domestic furnishings — and even one's toilette. "Smart gift shops," she reported, had "combed Europe for rare old books in rich inlaid bindings" to be glued shut, slit open, and hollowed out to make little boxes for earrings, manicure tools, and other necessities of the dressing table. "Here was, indeed, a new synthesis of life for the thoughtful woman," Skinner drolly exclaimed. "And how enlarged was the Author's field! I had cherished the common dream of authors: that my bright fancy might reflect in the hearts of Gentle Readers, but I had never thought of its putting lustre on their fingernails."[25] Books were hailed as affordable, plentiful, colorful dabs of civilization to be lavished throughout the gracious modern American home, and many heeded attentively.

Printing and Civilization

What Skinner mocked, others found less amusing. More serious resistance was evident early in the twenties, particularly among writers, editors, printers, and publishers who felt their professional values slighted in the frivolous popularity of books. To them, the physical and aesthetic degradation of books was inseparable from, even emblematic of, broader cultural decline. Throughout the decade, for many the material qualities of books — the dignity, beauty, and stature of their physical form — measured the cultural authenticity of those who produced and purchased them, and even of America's much-pondered civilization.

Among the small band of those determined to bring new integrity to American bookmaking was a young designer named Frederic Warde. Early in the decade he found himself a rising star in the book world, the newly appointed director of printing at Princeton University Press. With his new wife, Beatrice, who had graduated a few years before from Barnard College, he had practiced calligraphy and taken keen interest in the beautiful limited editions being made in England and the United States, especially those made by the two great American printer-celebrities, Daniel Berkeley Updike and Bruce Rogers. Their books were everything the young Wardes thought fine books should be: handsome, substantial, exquisitely tasteful in demeanor and beauty.

After a brief stint learning the publishing basics at Macmillan — a start in the book world arranged as a favor to Beatrice's mother, a respected New York book critic and journalist — Warde presented himself at the book manufacturing firm of William Edwin Rudge on Manhattan's lower east side. He could not disguise his ambition to work in the same company — indeed, in the same room if possible — with the great Bruce Rogers, who had recently agreed to design books for Rudge's more important clients. Rudge welcomed the young man's eagerness; anyone who appreciated the work of Bruce Rogers was exactly the kind of employee Rudge valued. Once hired, Warde immediately set about to learn book design from Rogers, even if much of the time Rogers was unaware of the silent loner who watched and listened so intently as the great man worked. After a few years with Rudge, Warde's tacit apprenticeship ended in 1922 when he accepted the position at Princeton.

Almost immediately Warde realized how daunting his work would be. Although he was proud to preside as the press's typographic authority, as its arbiter of taste and excellence in bookmaking, the sheer labor of the task often wearied and discouraged him. Even the books that had been made under his exacting directions gave him only small pleasure; their luster was spoiled by the many other manuscripts he'd been given that he found so unworthy, so "plain rotten," that he could only refuse to have anything to do with them.[26] If even a university press could be careless about the quality — textual and material — of what it published, he sometimes thought morosely, little wonder that most publishers seemed satisfied with the drivel that crowded bookshop windows and magazine ads.

That colorful jumbles of new volumes massed insistently on magazine pages and in bookstore displays bothered him; he despised the messy printing inside noisy covers, the slapdash jingle of ornate or just odd typefaces on the title page to give the book "atmosphere," and the skimpy margins stretched around the page like a reluctant belt around a bulgy waist.[27] This was what American readers were gobbling up, relishing badly printed books because they did not have much chance to see, much less appreciate, well-printed ones. At times Warde wondered privately if the few books he had worked so hard to produce to higher standards at Rudge and Princeton would ever make a difference.

Despite the discouragement, Warde felt acutely that his work held cultural import, and he often struggled to grasp its significance. Early in 1924 he confronted the task when he wrote a catalogue to accompany an exhibit of historic fine books in the Princeton University Library. Although he disliked writing and often welcomed his talented wife's offers to help or even do the job for him, he knew that this was one task worth the labor of setting down his own thoughts.[28] He began boldly. Each book selected for the show — magnificent volumes by legendary great printers of past centuries: Aldus, Jenson, Estienne, Baskerville, Bodoni — clearly "reflected the spirit of the age in which it was produced." Shifts in typographic taste were "a matter of national culture," he decided, "for it is the reader, after all, who unconsciously sets the style for typography; he buys what attracts him. In an age of good taste, he will be irked by shoddy types and narrow margins, and he will buy beautiful printing . . . because the printed book actually enters the mind of the reader together with its contents; and the civilized mind demands harmony and beauty."

Warde knew that he must also consider the books in the shop windows. "We can safely take the commercial printed book of any age as an index of the culture of that period," he asserted, then added, perhaps thinking of Bruce Rogers's books, "just as we can take the *edition de luxe* . . . as typical of the ideals of grandeur of its time." In that case, surely "any exhibition of fine printed books will put the visitor in a chastened frame of mind to look at the books that are being published today. He will realize that he has, by tacit consent, been writing down his tastes for future ages in a more careless tradition of sloppy printing than has ever before been allowed. He will also discover that as usual, fine typography has flourished among the few here and abroad, and that already readers are asking why this country can produce a typographic genius like Bruce Rogers and at the same time tolerate shiny paper, fuzzy presswork, and starved margins, not in dime novels but in important editions of books that will last." Why, indeed? Where was that thought headed? Warde must have struggled to regain the sanguine composure that the curators expected from him. He concluded with an optimism that he could only rarely muster: "Public complacency has vanished, and in a few years the reader will take beautiful printing for granted, and not place it in a neat frame labelled 'Art,' or 'Limited Edition, Do Not Touch.' "[29]

In darker moments, Warde doubted the public cared two figs about excellence. Any popular magazine could remind him that many new book buyers simply helped themselves to books, and all that they meant, on the installment plan, as easily as a new Frigidaire and Motorola. Just as linking *mass* and *culture* seemed oxymoronic at times, so did *popular* and *book*. What could be more loathsome, Warde must have wondered, than the modern effusion of pseudo-books, the tableaus of "tone" and color that mocked everything he cared about and worked for?

The Plight of the Genteel

Frederic Warde's concerns were neither idle nor unusual. If a good measure of the postwar attachment to books sprang from "book Babbittry," an equal measure was galvanized to resist it. Canby's editorial catalogued not only the "too many books" found on typical American bookshelves but also the resentments that many book lovers and intellectuals, like Warde, shared as society increasingly condoned, even promoted, such frivolous and expedient attitudes toward books. To them the book was both agent and emblem of the cultivated intellect, soul, and life. As such, books stood at the heart of who they were, or who they aspired to be. They were the remnants of American gentility, typically distinguished by their serious educations, professional vocations, and sense of cultural leadership. Often sympathetic to a philosophical movement in the twenties known as New Humanism, they looked with concern and sometimes despair at what they termed the spiritual indolence of mass society. They felt bewildered, even betrayed, by a society that no longer admired, much less emulated, their disciplined attention to the "hundred small refinements and formalities that together make for decency and civilization." They feared the triumph of a "standardized mediocrity" that promoted quantity over quality and self-indulgent consumption over disciplined productivity.[30] The postwar nonchalance toward books smacked to them of profligacy, a wantonness blamed on the "too many" books that gushed obligingly from publishers' lists. They feared that it might undermine the framework of values upon which American society — indeed, civilization — was built. Much was at risk, they worried, if the cultural integrity of books were overwhelmed by the glut of the good life.

For those to whom books mattered deeply, few issues sparked their energies more than the need to ensure that books regain their place at the heart of what made life worth living. This vague but acute struggle over cultural stewardship of the book took two forms: a spate of testimony and gestures of their own reverence for books, and disdain for anything less. These book lovers strove to make their purchasing "count" in cultural rather than material benefits. Katherine Fullerton Gerould argued plaintively in her 1926 essay "The Plight of the Genteel" that "we who care about things of the mind and the spirit . . . must refuse to let the standards of the majority be ours; must, with a certain bravado, if necessary, spend our tiny surplus for things despised of both Labor and Capital." Books were meant to be among the *higher* things of life, she insisted; she and others did notice and applaud the qualities of books produced at Updike's Merrymount Press or designed by Bruce Rogers, and they were proud to buy such fine books whenever they could afford them. Economist Jessica Peixotto noted that faculty at the University of California at Berkeley "will eat the plainest food and spend resignedly a total sum upon clothing that underpaid clerks would rebel against" in order to maintain a cultured home distinguished by the excellence of its books and music. Those families placed little value on cars or new appliances, and neither radios nor movies were even mentioned in their budgets.[31]

Labor and Capital were both, for different reasons, culprits in this genteel dilemma. In a decade when only slightly more than half the population was both Caucasian and American-born, "labor" hinted pejoratively, at least in part, to the masses of immigrants arriving annually. The threatened "middle class," a spokeswoman attested, was exhausting itself struggling to pay rent in a "reasonably respectable neighborhood" to ensure "association with people of our own race." This was "racial self-preservation, not snobbishness," she explained. Aversion to majority rule in matters of culture, echoing misgivings about democratic rule in general, was similarly touched with xenophobic strains. Good taste was tricky to define, Emily Post confessed, but she knew what it was not. Good taste was not simply majority opinion. "Consider the uncouth millions pouring into . . . our United States," she wrote. "Consider what the charm of living would be, should majority be the criterion of culture."[32]

It was easy to malign the "majority." Some critics merely reiterated the hackneyed maxim that a book appealing to a popular audience could not, by definition, have much merit. In *The Marks of an Educated Man* (1925), Albert Wiggam confessed: "I always suspect a bestseller. I fear it can not be very profound or very accurate because these are the two things that repel instead of attract the great majority of people." Skilled polemicist H. L. Mencken had a field day lampooning the decade's numerous new readers and the writers who fed their appetites. He blamed "the absurd effort to cram every moron with book-learning" for a national cultural chaos fueled by "too much reading, and too much writing." For that majority of "average Americans," he felt that reading and writing were not so much harmful as pretentious and

pointless. Poetry, he remarked, had become "a recreation . . . for the intellectually unemployed . . . who, a few generations ago, would have taken it out in
china-painting."[33]

"The world has gone book-mad," Richardson Wright sniffed in his 1919
essay invoking the popular quip "Let's Buy Her a Book," to which "she already has one" was the familiar retort. Overwhelmed by a brazen new population of "pen waggers," Americans have "bowed to the idol of the printed
page," Wright lamented. Familiar scapegoats for the sins of vanity and vacuity,
women often personified the new book enthusiast. Stuart Sherman described
her as a *jeune fille* who "has no soul, . . . but [who] trusts that the tailor, the
milliner, the bootmaker, the manicurist, the hairdresser, and the masseuse can
give her an equivalent." So, too, she buys books to furnish her fashionable
aura; she visits Brentano's as readily as her tennis club.[34] Wright, Sherman,
and others argued that fewer, better books — circulating among the more refined readers whose educated tastes better enabled them to evaluate and appreciate them — were preferable to a larger but less discerning market. The
new readers made a mockery, it was felt, of authentic book ownership: they
wanted the effects of culture without the substance, just as they styled the
surfaces of their selves and homes.

Many were particularly appalled at the notion of a do-it-yourself liberal arts
education. They felt that correspondence courses, outlines of history and culture, and agendas of reading prescribed by librarians, journalists, ministers,
and even vice presidents only parodied genuine learning. It is not that knowledge "will give wings to our imagination and give a larger, clearer, and sweeter
horizon to our lives," Irwin Edman wrote indignantly. It is that some think
"that knowledge, or a smattering of it, will make us successful or respected,
that a veneer of garbled French will reveal our breeding, or a parade of the
names of philosophers testify to our intellectual curiosity. There is possibly no
clearer index to the remoteness of a native American culture than the eager
indiscriminate voracity with which Americans gobble up tabloid versions of
fields of expert knowledge."[35]

Postwar novelists often used fictional accounts of book ownership to explore these cultural desires and anxieties. Images of narcissistic young women
pursuing book culture along with mah-jongg expertise and titled European
bachelors, for example, recur throughout the twenties. In the bestselling 1925
novel *Gentlemen Prefer Blondes* Lorelei Lee repeatedly declares a great devotion to books because, she says, "I am always reading to improve my mind."
Her energy flags easily, though. As she explains after abandoning a biography
of Cellini: "I mean it was really quite amuseing in spots because it was really
quite riskay but the spots were not so close together and I never seem to like to

always be hunting clear through a book for the spots I am looking for, especially when there are really not so many spots that seem to be so amuseing after all." She instructs her maid to read *Lord Jim* and tell her about it so her mind won't go unimproved that day.[36]

Other literary portraits mocked such naive ambitions by depicting homes in which books were conspicuously owned but obviously unread. A drunken guest at Jay Gatsby's mansion seemed astonished that the books in Gatsby's Gothic library were "absolutely real — have pages and everything." Seizing a volume, he marveled that "it's a bona-fide piece of printed matter. It fooled me. This fella's a regular Belasco. It's a triumph. What thoroughness! What realism! Knew when to stop too — didn't cut the pages." Although the library appeared to have been imported intact from a European estate, the books were literally unreadable because their pages had not been cut apart, making them no better than the fake "fill-shelves" Emily Post had suggested. This roomful of esoteric, impeccably real books (and ironically valuable, in that they remained in the pristine state most prized by collectors) is the extravagant culmination of Gatsby's youthful resolve to "read one improving book or magazine a week," but with it, Fitzgerald tells us, he achieves only an illusion.[37]

On a different scale but no less deliberately, the home of George F. Babbitt similarly deployed books in strategic ways. Following guidelines "right out of Cheerful Modern Homes for Medium Incomes," a "standard bedside book with colored illustrations" rested between the Babbitts' twin beds. "What particular book it was cannot be ascertained," Lewis writes, "since no one had ever opened it." Presumably equally undisturbed, books on the Babbitt living room coffee table were "unspotted and laid in rigid parallels."[38] Only a semblance of book culture could be purchased, these satiric portraits insinuated with a smirk, no matter how expensive, highbrow, or pedigreed the books themselves.

Yet the new book owners — however cynical, pragmatic, or gullible — were not entirely at fault. The glut of books was also blamed on publishers' pandering to the masses for the sake of profit. "Real" books were as threatened by the proliferating outlines of culture, booming book clubs, and crossword puzzle bestsellers (all the rage in 1925) as by hit radio shows, automobiles, and movies. Perhaps more so. To those for whom the traditional values represented by books bolstered resistance to the prodigal society around them, even the publishing industry had seemed to forsake higher things by pumping out thousands of copies of one Zane Grey novel after another, packaged in garish covers and emblazoned with vulgar buy-me blurbs. Even the new book clubs, which catered to relatively well-educated readers, were seen as a profit-hungry threat. With smug and authoritative promises to select "the best books" and deliver them monthly to members' doors, the clubs attempted to "stereotype the American mind," warned publishing executive John Macrae and others.[39] To Macrae, book clubs ominously resembled mass-circulation magazines, movies, and radio programming, all of which offered vastly more people a dramatically narrower range of information and enlightenment than "real" books offered.

Cries of intellectual standardization were a frightening epithet in the twenties, suggesting a cultural equivalent of industrial mass production. Although Aldous Huxley admitted that machinery had given more people more ease and pleasure in their lives, he countered that mass production of "things of the spirit are not so good." When applied to the production of ideas and art, he argued, standardization threatened to "exalt the ordinary" so that "imbecility may flourish and vulgarity cover the whole earth." In his 1929 polemic decrying *This Ugly Civilization,* Ralph Borsodi despaired over the conventional "herd-mindedness" of the American masses: "Is there any doubt that those who look to the education and improvement of the masses of herd-minded individuals as the hope for building a more beautiful civilization, suffer from a foolish delusion?" The automobile, the decade's greatest achievement of mass production, gripped the American imagination as "a symbol for speed in spiritual matters," for fleeting, transitory thoughts and interests. Did not books produced to appeal to homogeneous, standardized tastes and expectations simply offer readers the same speed and efficiency that Henry Ford had offered travelers? "A book is the book of a month or at most a season, and the rapid-transit reader comes to forswear books for the reviews of them, and forswears reviews for excerpts of them in synthetic magazines."[40] Were "real" books and reading headed for obsolescence, like the horse and buggy?

Few things registered the descent of modern books' cultural status more than their physical appearance. It didn't take a professional eye to see that most sported only a careless or blatantly commercial design. Even editions of the classics were typically issued as one-dollar reprints with imitation leather bindings that smelled like castor oil on hot days. The "cheap and gaudy book designs" used to attract buyers only injured the dignity of the serious book and offended its readers, one writer protested. "Can anything be more exasperating than trying to read Emerson under the glare and gesticulation of a red binding embraced by sundry swirls of purple and pink, which reaches out from its shelf and cannot be quieted?"[41]

The freighted epithet of *too many books* and the attendant visions of cheap, ugly, ephemeral "fill-shelves" were a vital spur toward the unprecedented interest in fine bookmaking in the 1920s. Not all who worried about the increasingly commercial nature of publishing sought solace in fine books, of course, nor did all who scrambled to acquire so-called deluxe books necessarily protest the declining quality of ordinary trade books. Many simply joined Canby in urging publishers to resist the temptation to publish whatever would sell, and in exhorting consumers to trim their own excesses. But a significant number of those who sought to save books from the indignities wrought by their changing social and cultural status did so by embracing the fine book.

Revolution, Stark and Brutal

As the decade began, long before Canby's *Saturday Review* tirade, warm New England summer weekends were likely to prompt a casual gathering of friends at Bill and Mabel Dwiggins's old house in Hingham, near Boston. Carl and Margaret Rollins often traveled up from New Haven, Connecticut, to relax with their old friends, and D. B. Updike occasionally joined them as well. On matters of religion and politics the three men often disagreed, but they shared a stronger bond, a serious commitment to revitalizing the quality of American bookmaking.

In 1920 sixty-year-old Daniel Berkeley Updike was the unrivaled dean of American printing. The only child of a proud but impoverished blueblood family in Providence, Rhode Island, Updike's somber, aristocratic sense of his own excellence distinguished his work throughout his life. After learning the printing business at the Houghton Mifflin Company in Boston, in 1896 Updike established nearby his own business, the Merrymount Press. It quickly became the paragon of printing houses in the country. A devout Anglican, Updike always went to church on Sunday mornings, even on his visits to Hingham, but he would take a bathing suit along, hide it under a bush, then walk down to Nantasket for a swim after the service. When he returned to the Dwiggins's house on Sunday afternoon, however, he was invariably again dressed in tie and waistcoat, in keeping with the patrician tone of his voice and measured, cultivated conversation.[42]

The two younger men, both just forty, were rapidly gaining esteem themselves. William Addison Dwiggins was increasingly sought as a freelance book illustrator and designer. He had grown up in rural Ohio, attended the Frank Holme School of Art in Chicago, then followed one of the instructors, the great type designer Frederic Goudy, east to Boston. Like most artists of the day, Dwiggins paid the bills with routine advertising work, but when diagnosed with diabetes he vowed to Rollins that he would henceforth forgo such "hack-carpentering." Determined to leave his distinctive mark on serious and intelligent things that were meant to last — books — Dwiggins resolved to take on only projects that "call for no compromise with the universal twelve-year-old mind of our purchasing public." This meant, he declared, "Revolution, stark and brutal."[43]

That summer of 1920, Carl Purington Rollins was settling into his position as typographic director at Yale University Press. Born in West Newbury, Massachusetts, he had attended Harvard University but did not graduate. Smitten by arts and crafts socialism, he dropped out to serve as printer to a rural utopian community in 1903. The commune soon folded, and he apprenticed himself to the large Boston printing firm owned by Carl Heintzemann. He spent much of the following decade happily ensconced in a small crafts cooperative in Montague, Massachusetts, where his trademark beard, thick round glasses, black five-gallon hat, and unconventional ways led at least one observer to confess, "I *don't think* he is a Socialist, but he is *very* radical."[44] In 1918 he moved to the new job in New Haven, where, despite spells of intense unhappiness, he was managing to feed his young family and keep his ideals alive as well.

On these summer weekend gatherings, the small group typically lazed in big wooden chairs on the back lawn, laughing over lemonade and the dainty cups and saucers that disguised their Prohibition-style "tea" as Dwiggins regaled his friends with his famous droll dialogues. They particularly relished his recent "Investigation into the Physical Properties of Books." This satire, published in 1919 under a facetious pseudonym, highlighted the problem that each man increasingly sensed. Conducted by the fictitious Society of Calligraphers (William A. Dwiggins, secretary), the investigation boldly began with its conclusion: "All Books of the Present Day are Badly Made." An accompanying chart illustrated the point most graphically (see figure 1). Indeed, when considering "Are books necessary to the present social state?" the committee decided "unanimously and conclusively, no." According to the committee, "During the past twenty years many influences have been at work to wean mankind from the use of books. Automobiles, the motion-picture drama, professional athletics, the *Saturday Evening Post* — these operated even before the Great War to discourage the habit of reading. Since the war the progress of society — culminating, in America, in the dictatorship of the proletariat — has effectively completed the process. Books as an element vital to the welfare of the new race have been eliminated."[45]

The society even declared that "wherever there is contact between books and the public, the effect upon the books is deleterious." If "the public, under compulsion, may turn again to books and reading," something would have to be done. Admitting that it was hardly practical to stave off popular demand,

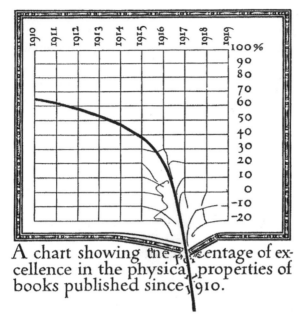

A chart showing the percentage of excellence in the physical properties of books published since 1910.

Figure 1. W. A. Dwiggins, illustration to *An Investigation into the Physical Properties of Books,* 1919.

the committee surmised that the best strategy for saving the book was to force upon the public "such knowledge of the more elementary points of good taste as shall make impossible the further prostitution of standards."[46]

Even if they had not already been honorary members of Dwiggins's phantom Society of Calligraphers (there were no members of any other kind), Rollins and Updike were familiar with the society's laments. They agreed that books had become so shoddily made that they were not "fit to wad a gun with," as the *Investigation* had scoffed: "Most printing looks like it had been done with apple-butter on a hay-press."[47] Yet each knew that Dwiggins's officious satire poked fun at his own real-life endeavor. While among themselves they often bemoaned public taste and the modern fate of books, each was already wholeheartedly in the business of championing alternative book designs grounded in the hallmarks of "good taste." Despite the jesting, few things mattered to them more than the taste and quality of books in modern America.

In the decade that followed, the nearly private lament shared on the Hingham lawn would gain nationwide, even international, currency as concerns for books' material and typographic form — seen as portal to and emblem of their content — grew to unprecedented levels. Dwiggins, Rollins, Updike,

Frederic Warde, and others would find themselves celebrities in posh and well-educated circles across the country, hailed for the beauty and distinction of the books they created. The decade ahead would both embrace their visions of a reinvigorated cultural venue and tangle those ideals in complicated, even dis-illusioning ways. But at the outset, the peculiarly modern ideology of fine printing empowered them as disciples in what soon seemed a veritable cultural crusade.

On Sacred Ground
The Theory of the Ideal Book

The young men who labored so intently under the hawklike eye of Master Porter Garnett at Carnegie Tech's Laboratory Press in Pittsburgh were never able to forget that an even fiercer, unblinking eye watched them as well. While they painstakingly composed type by hand, sometimes mitering and shaving the tiny metal pieces and sometimes slipping tissue paper between them to achieve more harmonious spacing, a large old-fashioned painted eye, the kind that once hung above oculists' doors, gazed down at them from a corner of the ceiling. At some carefully chosen moment each year, Garnett would assemble his charges beneath the baleful eye. As each youth presented his work for inspection, Garnett would say nothing as he peered at each proof. Moving from one to another of the half dozen or so anxious students, he would begin to moan and shake his head. Finally, he would take a deep breath, gesture to the eerie eye overhead, and solemnly explain, "This, gentlemen, is God's Great Aesthetic Eye."[1]

While his right or moral eye had its own agenda, God's left eye was no less busy, one of those students later explained, watching out for "all the shoddy, shabby violations of His aesthetics — violations that we now could see everywhere about us, not only in newspapers, 'slicks' and pulps, but also in many supposedly finely printed books." That Great Aesthetic Eye bore down upon every activity in the Laboratory Press, reminding each young disciple that God himself "saw through our every shortcut, our every shoddy expediency, our every 'lesser evil.'" Garnett was no less vigilant. Once, when conversation in the press grew a bit too casual, too workaday, he dramatically interrupted and insisted that all activities cease. The students quickly put down their tools, washed up, and stood in a row. Then, like a drill sergeant, Garnett inspected their hands, palms down as well as palms up, and sent those with any remaining inky shadows to wash again, repeatedly, until their cleanliness met his standards. "Now I'm going to let you *touch* something," he finally announced. But first they must close their eyes. In solemn silence he produced from his adjacent office a page of the Bible printed in 1903 by England's Doves Press — one of the previous era's most esteemed private presses. Eyes pressed shut, each student slowly ran his fingers, perhaps trembling a bit, over the precious page. After each had partaken in this spontaneous biblio-sacrament, Garnett asked the young men to sit and write down their chastened thoughts. Some filled several pages.[2] The Laboratory Press was indeed a serious place, a kind of typographic sanctuary (see figure 2).

By the early 1930s thousands of print shops across the country and even around the world brandished similar reminders that God was on the side of good printing. "Friend you stand on sacred ground!" rang the most prominent line in the famous "Inscription for a Printing Office" written in 1932 by Beatrice Warde, then publicist for the British Monotype Corporation. In that celebrated declaration she expressed a notion that had crystallized in the years following the First World War, the sense that the printed word represented both the "crossroads of civilization" and its best defense against "the ravages of time." The more one valued those intellectual and cultural traditions preserved by the printed book, the more imperative it was to invest care and quality in its production. Just as opera houses and art museums were being built to resemble temples in reverence to the arts they housed, many felt that the material features of a book should cue more respectful appreciation of its content.[3] The Inscription itself was a good example: composed in all capital letters, each line centered and prominent words in red, its form as well as its content pronounced it a monumental truth (figure 3). More than mere factory workers or machine operators, it proclaimed, printers occupied ground made sacred by their exalted cultural function.

Enshrined at the forefront of this new ethic, fine printing emerged as a kind of culturally ordained priesthood, ready to inspire and guide the flocks of ordinary printers. By adhering only to the highest standards of design and production, it would restore luster to the cultural entity of the book as well as ennoble readers' experiences of particular texts. The decade rang with one manifesto after another as fine printers announced their resolve, as brothers

Figure 2. Porter Garnett and students at the Laboratory Press, Carnegie Institute of Technology, Pittsburgh, ca. 1927. Photo courtesy of the Carnegie Mellon University Archives.

James and Cecil Johnson proclaimed in launching their San Francisco Windsor Press in 1926, "to print the beautiful book, to create the symphony in type, to handle the tools of [their] calling with that divine grace reserved only for the lover of his craft."[4] For many, fine printing was a divinely inspired, if not divinely blessed, cultural mission.

To invoke such sanctions for one's work is no light matter. This remarkable sacralization reflects the righteous ardor with which fine printing was pledged to rescue the book from the postwar vortex of industrialism and commercialism, the two powerful forces that seemed to hold almost everything in their synergistic grip. Driven to sell goods to ever-increasing numbers of consumers, modern industry required relatively low-cost, high-volume production, made possible by machines that could produce huge quantities of identical items. To sell to the large markets, those goods had to be relatively cheap and "popular" by nature, appealing to the most commonly shared tastes, sentiments, and val-

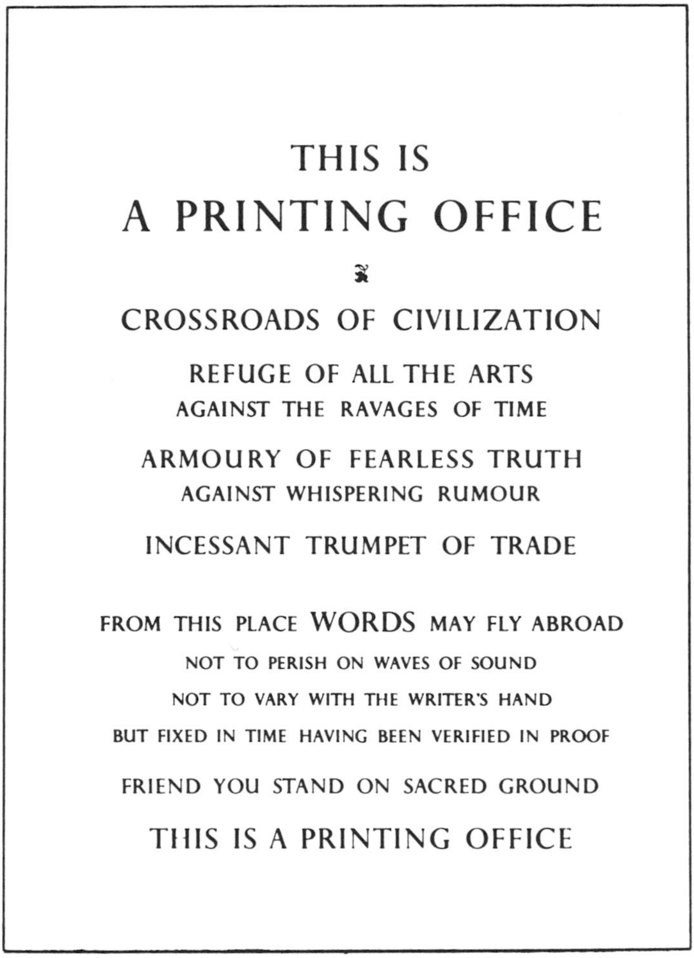

THIS IS
A PRINTING OFFICE

☙

CROSSROADS OF CIVILIZATION

REFUGE OF ALL THE ARTS
AGAINST THE RAVAGES OF TIME

ARMOURY OF FEARLESS TRUTH
AGAINST WHISPERING RUMOUR

INCESSANT TRUMPET OF TRADE

FROM THIS PLACE WORDS MAY FLY ABROAD

NOT TO PERISH ON WAVES OF SOUND

NOT TO VARY WITH THE WRITER'S HAND

BUT FIXED IN TIME HAVING BEEN VERIFIED IN PROOF

FRIEND YOU STAND ON SACRED GROUND

THIS IS A PRINTING OFFICE

Figure 3. Beatrice Warde, "Inscription for a Printing Office," promotional broadside for the Monotype Corporation, 1932.

ues. That formula was perhaps fine for producing breakfast cereal, aspirin tablets, motor cars, or even magazines, many felt, but not for producing books, at least not all books.

Fine printing sought to extricate bookmaking from that industrial/commercial juggernaut. By defying the relentless pursuit of quantity at the expense of "quality," it reclaimed a more serious and dignified aesthetic, technical, and even moral space for that emblem of one of the most serious reaches of human culture, its books. Freed from the economizing and popularizing strategies upon which mass production and sales depended, fine printing focused on intrinsic qualities: sound, enduring construction and materials; attractive and enduring content.

Precedents and Inspirations

Postwar American fine printers were not the first to seek alternatives to modern industrial bookmaking, of course. Three distinct European prewar precedents offered possible guidance or models. Most recent, but also most ideologically alien, was the experimental typographic futurism active primarily in France and Italy after the turn of the century. Futurists protested not the mechanization of commercial printing but the artistic and political dissonance between that industrial production for mass consumption and the bourgeois messages and forms it multiplied. Futurists saw machine production as the foundation for a radical new aesthetic that reflected modern iconoclasm. As theorists, they boldly exploited typographic form to manipulate visual and literary meaning. They were not concerned with pragmatic issues of everyday printing or book production, however; their interests lay in the more abstract power of typography as an interpretive art form.[5]

The two other precedents came from England during the 1890s. One was the activity of The Bodley Head, an imprint founded by John Lane and Elkin Matthews and made famous by its association with fin de siècle so-called decadent writers and artists such as Aubrey Beardsley and Oscar Wilde. The Bodley Head explicitly catered to a small, vaguely avant-garde fringe of British book buyers, cultivating that market by producing books redolent with handcrafted, not machine-made, design features. Those features — handmade papers, generous margins, distinctive decorations and typography, and limited editions — enticed buyers seeking culturally elite, somewhat exotic, luxury goods.[6] In many respects the Bodley Head model prefigured much of the course of American fine publishing, but its precedence was rarely acknowledged. Those who theorized American fine printing tacitly ignored the Bodley Head model because it carried no ideological charge, no claim of ambitions to aesthetic and cultural leadership and reform. At least in principle, the impetus for American fine printing in the twenties held loftier goals; ideally, fine printing was to spur fundamental new notions about books themselves.

Throughout the decade each new fine publisher entering the field defined itself in terms of a pair of assertions: a determination to resist "machine culture," and a resolve to resist "commercialism" — the market considerations that were felt to tyrannize, and skew toward mediocrity, decisions governing content, design, production, distribution, and price. Ostensibly refusing to accept either as necessary or inevitable, fine printers constructed an alternative that was at once deeply conservative and boldly visionary. Although the course of fine printing throughout the decade would soon muddle or neglect its idealistic ambitions, in theory its rejection of industrialized commercial production was but the means to the more forward-looking end of better books for modern readers.

Fine printers posed an alternative approach to bookmaking that revived forms and production techniques from the preindustrial past, hoping to revive as well the traditional cultural values those earlier forms invoked. This fundamental historicism stemmed from the third and most influential precedent of postwar typographic reform, the arts and crafts movement and the private press "revival" it fueled in England in the 1890s and in the United States by the turn of the century. Inspired by John Ruskin and scholar-typographer Emery Walker, a small but influential group of private presses was established to resurrect the largely lost crafts of hand bookmaking. Best known was William Morris's Kelmscott Press, which produced dozens of books printed on handmade papers or vellum by men using an iron handpress that was a recognizable descendant of Gutenberg's press. Kelmscott books were stunning in their contrast to contemporary books. Most striking was their neomedievalism: types and woodcut illustrations and borders modeled on fifteenth-century books, broad margins surrounding dense black blocks of text, and often large dimensions better suited for lecterns than for palms or pockets. Morris's books might have slipped naturally among the treasured books in a fifteenth-century nobleman's library.

The Kelmscott Press also inspired and modeled the second and ultimately foremost tenet of fine printing ideology, its ostensible rejection of commercial, profit-driven bookmaking. Morris's ideas were part of his larger neogothic socialist vision: selling the small Kelmscott editions (typically two hundred to four hundred copies) was almost an afterthought to him, the by-product of his larger mission to protest both the aesthetic and sociological nature of modern mechanized bookmaking. To Morris, fine printing defied the industrialized capitalist structure of modern English society by recreating instead a medieval unity of labor and craft, of production and purpose, not profit. For Morris's postwar American admirers, this model of subordinating sales to ideals achieved two crucial distinctions, at least in theory: the fine printer received (and presumably sought) the pleasure of achievement more than pay for labor, and the books' prices were not inflated by pecuniary motives and hence were "reasonable." In the 1920s, when many agreed with New Humanism's leading light Irving Babbitt that "commercialism is laying its great greasy paw on everything," this model of disinterested vocation in defiance of crass capitalism appealed to producers and patrons of fine books alike.[7] It provided attractive high ground for those disenchanted with modern consumer culture, offering a historic alternative to contemporary commerce. Although most stopped short of Morris's broader socialism, fine printers generally shared some measure of his convictions that the material and design quality of a society's printed books held cultural as well as aesthetic resonance.

The most pervasive theme Morris inspired was the centrality of historical foundations. History provided fine printers with the long view, a framework that diminished the immediate past of the nineteenth century. Just as Ruskin, Walker, Morris, and others had reacted against Victorian industrialism, so their postwar progeny grounded their work in the five-hundred-year tradition of printing and millennia of Western literary traditions. This not only distanced them from the contemporary book industry and its discredited Victorian ancestry but historicized their own activity. By linking themselves to a past they exalted, postwar fine printers gave contextual significance to their own place within that larger continuum.

History offered authoritative models both of physical form — using paper made by hand from rag fibers, for example, rather than the acidic, short-lived papers made mechanically from wood pulp after 1850 or so — and of aesthetic style and literary content. "High standards of quality . . . are the by-products of good taste," W. Arthur Cole noted. "And good taste is the result of long study of source material featuring the work of the old masters." D. B. Updike echoed, "A right taste is cultivated in printing by knowing what has been done in the past and what has been so esteemed that it has lived."[8] It became a virtual canon of American fine printing that merit and skill were largely revealed in the printer's knowledge of historical precedents — if not as outright models, then as inspirations in rightness, in elegance, in *taste*.

The Modernist Challenge

By regarding books of the past as an antidote to modern mass culture, fine printers betrayed an increasingly problematic diffidence toward the spirit of their own age. This ambivalence was most evident in their almost diametric opposition to the great design ideology emanating from Europe in the 1920s, a design school known as modernism. Although American fine printers also focused on present and future needs, and often described their efforts as modern or modernist, most recognized, especially as the decade progressed, that the term *modernism* was most commonly and accurately associated with the new European aesthetic in typography, just as the term had acquired similar (but not parallel) particularity in the visual arts and literature.

The cultural conditions that prompted American fine printers to distrust industrialism and commercialism spurred European modernist typographers in opposite directions. Modernists aimed to topple the traditional typographic framework, reclaimed by Morris and others, that fine printers were busily bolstering. "Instead of recognizing and designing for the laws of machine production, the previous generation contented itself with anxiously trying to follow a tradition that was in any case only imaginary," exclaimed a young Jan Tschichold. With his 1928 manifesto *Die Neue Typographie,* the twenty-six-year-old Tschichold — deeply influenced by the famous Bauhaus community of artists and designers, of which he was briefly a part — became the chief spokesman for the exuberant, strident principles of the New Typography. The triumph of machinery had helped Tschichold and others to break from traditional forms and the social and cultural assumptions about class and order they encoded. Tschichold spelled out a new aesthetic grounded in pure function rather than decoration, suited for and inspired by mass production rather than traditional, craft-based book forms. Its radical implications were clear. "We can only acquire a true general culture (for a culture of the few, as has existed up till now, is no culture but a kind of barbarism) if we remember . . . the indissoluble oneness of all men and all peoples, and all fields of human creativity. . . . [Only] the giving up of personal vanity (up till now falsely called "personality") in favour of pure design assures the emergence of a general, collective culture which will encompass all expressions of life — including typography."[9] While American fine printers sought to preserve human individuality through historicized handcraft, modernists embraced industrial standardization as the long-awaited means of achieving widespread equality of cultural goods.

Modernists praised speed, change, and one efficient aesthetic for all members of society. Traditional typography was suitable for readers "who had plenty of time to read line by line in a leisurely manner," Tschichold allowed, but he insisted that modern printing "must adapt itself to the conditions of modern life. As a rule we no longer read quietly line by line, but glance quickly over the whole, and only if our interest is awakened do we study it in detail." He attacked "fossilized" historical styles as "nothing but proof of creative incompetence." Although he would later modify these bold assertions, Tschichold's youthful manifesto rang with a challenge: "Today the old and decadent, the young and vital, confront one another. The living man, if he does not side with the old and musty, can support only the new!"[10]

Most American typographic leaders took a dim and somewhat condescending view of the modernist challenge, which seemed to them remote and only mildly distasteful throughout most of the twenties. Bruce Rogers brushed modernism away, objecting to its "visual ugliness." William Cole simply appropriated its punch, benignly predicting in 1929 that it "really means the opening up of new channels through which more tradition may be expected to flow." Writing as a wise elder statesman (which to most contemporaries he was), D. B. Updike patiently explained that typography should counter the stressful, disruptive tendencies of modern life, not mirror them. "The trouble with the modernist is that he seems afraid not to throw everything overboard and mistakes eccentricity for emancipation. Thus some books of to-day seem to be the arrangement of a perverse and self-conscious eccentricity. Such printing is often the work of eager, ambitious, and inexperienced young men, and because they are young and God is good, one can afford to be patient; sure that they will, in the long run, outgrow the teething, mumps, and measles of typography."[11]

Despite their patronizing dismissal of the spirit as well as the letter of the modernist ideology, a few American printers did recognize modernism's affinity to postwar life. Douglas McMurtrie remarked that "this is not a contemplative age. We no longer walk through life — we are borne along on vehicles, both spiritual and material, such as our grandparents . . . could not conceive." He felt it was essential that typography strive to understand and interpret the postwar spirit if it was to serve the readers of its own time. McMurtrie pointed shrewdly to the irony that the modernist embrace of machine culture should come from Europe, "that vaunted stronghold of spiritual and intellectual values," while the United States, "the native land of the machine and of machine standardization, so bitterly accused of enforcing upon the world a machine-made life, is also the land of a naive and perplexing sentimentality and of strange adventures with things spiritual."[12] This oblique reference to the hunger for spiritual belonging evident in the resurgence of fundamentalism and charismatic spiritual figures such as Aimee Semple McPherson and Emile Coué astutely suggests that fine printing's traditionalism reflected the sense of loss and alienation that many Americans felt as "progress" carried them further and further from all that they recognized and understood in their lives.

Postwar American bibliophiles labored to preserve, not dismantle, the centuries-old tenets of Western cultural taste and judgment. Those who could afford it often actively vied for the material remnants of the European past following the Great War, adopting a "lost" or rejected (by modernists) Old Europe for themselves by literally buying its cultural artifacts and installing them in the United States. The great art and rare book and manuscript collections of Henry Huntington and Henry Clay Folger, now cornerstones of the prestigious libraries bearing their names, were largely gathered in the teens and twenties. From 1920 until his death in 1927, for example, Huntington spent more than four million dollars on rare books and manuscripts, many of them bought from European owners. Stefan Zweig described this migration of Europe's treasures during its ruinous postwar inflation in a short story that began with a Dresden bookseller lamenting: "The newly rich have discovered their interest in Gothic Madonnas and incunabula . . . considering a wonderful Venetian fifteenth-century book as the equivalent of so and so many dollars."[13] For those with slimmer wallets, modern fine books recreated all the defining features of those coveted books. American fine printers above all strove to evoke a discriminating, tasteful, golden cultural past, making books in studied kinship to their European ancestors. In both its principles and its practices American bibliophilia of the 1920s consciously nurtured much that was antithetical to the modernism emanating from central Europe.

The "Saving Remnant"

One day when Bruce Rogers was visiting the Laboratory Press his host paused while showing the distinguished guest around the room. Garnett glanced up and read aloud the short text of a printed broadside on the wall. It was an excerpt from the T'ang dynasty poet Tu Fu: "Who understands distinctions, who really cares for art?" Without hesitation, Rogers wittily murmured in reply, "Too few, Mr. Garnett, too few!"[14]

A pervasive elitism was seen as an inevitable, if not openly appropriate, feature of any culturally defining effort. It accorded with genteel notions of a natural aristocracy of taste and knowledge, which entailed serious responsibilities as well as obvious status. "Taste is the child of privilege and slow time," declared Dwight Sedgwick: those who enjoyed the latter were charged with cultivating not only their own taste but also, through moral leadership, that of society at large. Irving Babbitt put it more famously: "the hope of civilization lies not in the divine average, but in the saving remnant."[15] Fine printers saw themselves as the saving remnant of the book world, those few whose historically informed sensibilities constituted the "taste" that both distinguished the fine and shamed the ordinary.

The preoccupation with taste in the 1920s was not merely an assertion of personal preferences. Rather, it was a way of attributing those preferences to larger, shared social and cultural values. "Taste is the basis of all that one has," writes Pierre Bourdieu in his landmark analysis *Distinction*, "and all that one is for others, whereby one classifies oneself and is classified by others." Tastes, he continues, "are asserted purely negatively, by the refusal of other tastes. . . .

Tastes are perhaps first and foremost distastes." This notion of taste was central to the era's emerging hierarchy of "brows," whereby personal artistic and especially consumer selections were categorized and judged. This need to achieve distinction through what one rejects as much as through what one prefers is evident throughout postwar American fine printing. Let others "compromise" with "popular taste, with outlays and returns, . . . or with machinery," sniffed Porter Garnett; the truly fine printer would not.[16] In repeated and various ways, fine printing took meaningful shape in terms of what it resisted, opposed, and excluded.

This elitism was first evident in the matter of determining who constituted the favored few, the redeeming remnant. A typographic aristocracy was not readily apparent through family lineage or affiliation with distinguishing institutions. Who were they, then? It was an important question. In 1928 New York fine printer Elmer Adler suggested to Bill Dwiggins that they form an informal club of those making "some definite contribution to the making of better books." There are "few enough," Adler conceded, but that only made the idea more urgent; especially "the youngsters" among them might benefit from the camaraderie. Nearly a year later, on 4 February 1929, the newly dubbed "Crows" met for the first time at the Yale Club in Manhattan. Twenty-eight men gathered around the horseshoe dinner table, considerably more than the ten names Adler had initially proposed, but they did indeed represent most of the designers, publishers, and artists whose work and words have come to define beauty in modern American books.[17]

The evening's host was Elmer Adler. Born into a prosperous clothing merchant family in Rochester, New York, Adler attended Andover Academy but dropped out because he was bored. He went to work in the family business, first in sales and then in marketing, designing some of the company's ads. He became an avid collector of books and prints, gaining from them the typographic education he would employ in his career shift into printing. In his mid-thirties, he "abandoned the apparel industry to those who loved it better," according to biographer Frederick Adams, "and went to the big city to lose his fortune." In March 1922 Adler established the Pynson Printers in Manhattan, a small but sophisticated shop devoted exclusively to "printing in which quality is the first consideration."[18] He became a central player in professional fine printing, mediating among artists, designers, and publishers and promoting higher typographic standards in elite corporate and civic circles, especially in New York and on the East Coast. A talented and knowledgeable designer, Adler was most valuable as an advocate and watchdog; he made sure that fine printing was perceived as an elegant, honorable privilege for its discerning clientele.

Dwiggins traveled down from Hingham, perhaps catching the train from Boston with Updike. Although his professional leadership was more tacit than active, Updike's presence gave a palpable distinction to the dinner. Yet he did not "preside" at the affair and in fact sat silently throughout much of the evening, forgoing the clandestine cocktails beforehand at one guest's nearby home. Carl Rollins, on the other hand, traveled down from New Haven for the occasion only after he'd been assured that the evening's fare would not be "dedicated to the XVIIIth Amendment [or] to a monastic dietary regimen."[19]

Along with Updike, the other celebrity at the dinner was Bruce Rogers. By the late twenties he caused a stir in book circles wherever he appeared, socially and professionally. Oddly, of those who most prominently championed fine printing and its cultural agenda, Rogers was the only one who had completed college. Born the son of a baker near Lafayette, Indiana, he had graduated from Purdue University in 1891. His long and productive career earned him not only celebrity status during his lifetime but the reputation he holds today as the premier American book designer of the twentieth century. Between extended sojourns in England, he spent much of the 1920s designing fine limited editions for William Edwin Rudge, who had relocated to Mt. Vernon, New York.

Frederic Warde had replied that he would come, but he did not attend the dinner. A week later he apologized, claiming gastric illness. He was living near Mt. Vernon and again working for Rudge. Frustrated with his work at Princeton, Warde and his wife had sailed to England early in 1925. Soon after their arrival, Beatrice chose to keep company with eminent English typographer Stanley Morison; consequently, Warde worked and traveled alone in Europe until 1927. Poor and embittered, in 1928 he rejoined Rudge's staff, where he worked with little pleasure for the next four years. He and Beatrice separated in the mid-twenties (she lived in England for the rest of her life), but she retained his surname, eventually eclipsing him as the more famous Warde in the book world.

Many of the decade's leading fine publishers also attended the dinner in Manhattan. Most were young, in their twenties and early thirties. The oldest, at thirty-seven, was Adler's close friend and associate Alfred Knopf. Bennett Cerf and Donald Klopfer, who with Adler had founded Random House two years earlier, seldom missed such social occasions among book friends and generously poured bootleg drinks. They mingled amiably with the printers, artists, and other publishers with whom, in working hours, they sustained spirited — and often witty, good-natured — disagreements. Nearby, for instance, sat the wealthy and urbane impresario Crosby Gaige, whose eponymous fine book imprint gave the partners of Random House (its distributor) endless headaches, and James Wells, who had recently bought Gaige's imprint and renamed it the Fountain Press, but whose business practices would exasperate Cerf no less.

Dwiggins was not the only artist included. A few of his equally celebrated illustrator friends joined the festivities, including the adventurous bohemian Rockwell Kent and fastidious but prolific T. M. Cleland. The other dinner guests that night played a variety of roles in the era's bookmaking renaissance. William Edwin Rudge was invited, of course. Owner of one of the largest and most influential high-quality printing houses in America, he provided unofficial apprenticeships for several of the "youngsters" Adler had invited, men such as Roland Woods and John Fass, whose recently established Harbor Press in Manhattan was already garnering praise. A young Joseph Blumenthal was there as well. After dropping out of Cornell in 1917, he dabbled in business then wandered for a year in Europe, where he encountered contemporary fine printing. He returned to New York, learned the craft at Rudge's, and in 1926 debuted his own imprint, the Spiral Press. A few leading bibliophiles rounded out the select crowd, most notably New York advertising executive Burton Emmett and Henry Watson Kent of the Metropolitan Museum of Art. It was a list of eminent guests, and each man knew that such exclusive distinction was the whole point of the dinner.

The Yale Club gathering of Crows that night came close to encompassing the elite of postwar fine printing, but in fact it only congregated the major players at one of its poles. To be truly comprehensive, the Crows needed a western, or more accurately a San Francisco, chapter. That city boasted a formidable pair of fine presses. One bore the name of the era's most spectacular fine printer, John Henry Nash. Born in Ontario, Canada, Nash was apprenticed at age sixteen to a foundry to learn mechanical engineering. He preferred to become a printer, however, and persuaded his father to apprentice him to a Toronto printing firm instead in 1888. After a series of jobs drifting westward, Nash arrived in San Francisco in 1895, where he would spend his career. In 1916, having earned a reputation for fine printing skills, he established his own shop devoted exclusively to the craft. Throughout the twenties Nash was hailed as a master of dazzling technical virtuosity, and he garnered a stable of wealthy patrons who hired him to produce opulent editions of their favorite books. Nash also produced several books for direct sale under his own imprint, and he occasionally produced books for other commercial publishers.

Nash shared San Francisco fine printing honors, uneasily, with two other immigrants to the city. Edwin Grabhorn was the son of a factory worker in Indianapolis. He completed only an eighth or ninth grade education before entering an uncle's printing business. Yearning to produce fine work in the style of William Morris, Edwin headed West to pursue opportunities for better sorts of work. In 1920 he and his younger brother Robert, just twenty, arrived in San Francisco. Together they constituted the Grabhorn Press, with Edwin as owner, primary designer, and pressman and Robert (who had completed high school and a few months of college before joining the military) as premier employee and compositor.

A minor galaxy of others was significantly involved in postwar fine printing as well, although they rarely joined dinner parties on either coast. Notable among them were William Kittredge, who from 1925 on supervised the Lakeside Press, the fine printing division of Chicago's mammoth R.R. Donnelley & Sons printing firm, and Richard W. Ellis. Educated as a chemist, Ellis fell in love with fine printing after finding a Bruce Rogers book in a secondhand bookstore. He studied the craft and its history and in 1925 established in rural Connecticut his Georgian Press — named to express his fondness for the eighteenth century. Across the country a growing community of librarians, collectors, rare book dealers, artists, printers, and publishers swelled the ranks of those devoted to achieving, and crowing about, a new level of beauty in the printed book.

Audience and Mission

Fine printing was to be undertaken by a seemingly natural elite, a small group identified by the arts and crafts–based ideals evident in their work. The first question they faced was, for whom were their efforts to be expended? Until the 1920s, "simply for oneself" and a small circle of friends and sympathizers had been the easiest and most obvious answer; a special interest in typography and printing or literature was most often indulged avocationally through a private press. This meant producing small editions of books entirely to please oneself in terms of content and form.

The private press was a natural avenue for those with highly particular or avant-garde artistic preferences. In the late 1920s Harry and Caresse Crosby's expatriate Black Sun Press, for example, produced editions of their own poetry precisely as they wished to see it printed. By circumventing the conventional publishing process they were free to print daring or innovative work that the general public was not yet ready to support. Such noncommercial private publishers typically showcased beautiful and enduring material forms, but they differed from fine publishers in their general ambivalence toward any broader purposes of that form.[20] They stepped outside trade publishing simply to ignore its commercial constraints, while fine publishing sought distance from the ordinary to repudiate and ultimately to reform it.

Private presses differed in another, more immediate and fundamental way.

Such complete control required an independent and ample livelihood. Most private presses — including Kelmscott, Black Sun, and many others — were neither intended nor permitted to wholly engage their owners professionally. These presses therefore tended to be the luxurious privilege of those with independent, comfortable incomes who did not need to sell copies or please patrons. By the 1920s, however, the American economy supported relatively few people in such luxury. Those who wished to practice fine bookmaking generally had to do so for a living. They had to produce books that a sufficient number of people would want to buy.

This meant that even as American fine printing adapted the British Kelmscott model for its ideological purposes, it added an important coda. Kelmscott was a private enterprise, a workshop devoted to one person's vision of ideal bookmaking practices and purposes. By contrast, Americans understood that their work was destined for the marketplace, albeit as an oppositional alternative to the mainstream. Even the supremely theoretical Laboratory Press was housed squarely, if warily, amid the nation's largest training school for the printing trades. Fine printing was intended not to bypass the "real world" but to add an unstintingly superior pole to the qualitative spectrum of bookmaking, and thereby to inspire, or shame, all printers to strive for better quality.

This necessary engagement with the marketplace in turn required delicate theoretical (and practical) maneuvering to avoid an awkward clash with fine printers' often-proclaimed anticommercial resolve. To maintain an appealing aura of independence from sales considerations, answers to "Who are these books for?" were carefully couched in terms of *audience* rather than *market*. Notions of an audience preserved a sense that fine printing served more important purposes than merely feeding the printer's family or paying the rent. Serving an audience implied an exchange of knowledge and appreciation, not simply of goods. Fine printing was to be understood as part of a larger cultural project, and an audience was considered a crucial partner in the effort. Notions of a market, on the other hand, connoted unsavory self-serving motives for both producing and buying fine books. In principle at least, fine printing scrupulously addressed itself to an audience, not a market.

The core of that audience was the small and familiar community of those able, financially and otherwise, to appreciate and patronize finely made books as such. This sense of audience invoked traditional notions of a gentility charged with providing not only moral and cultural leadership but also primary patronage of the arts. In theory, both makers and buyers of fine books were committed to keeping alive things of quality and merit in the midst of popular ambivalence. Hailing this audience for its encouragement and support, fine printers underscored their own role of ensuring that books of beauty and taste were available for those few who still valued them. Bruce Rogers confessed that he put his "best efforts into books that will probably go to the discriminating few; and if these few are necessarily people with means enough to gratify their tastes I cannot see why they should not be encouraged to spend their money on costly books as well on costly appurtenances of other kinds. . . . As to depriving the public at large of the privilege of possession, I'm afraid I have no great confidence in the taste of the public."[21]

The depiction of the audience as an elite community of superior tastes and cultural values reinforced the idea that just as there were two kinds of book buyers — "mass" and "class," as Bennett Cerf bluntly put it — so bookmakers naturally adhered to two standards: ordinary and fine. R. L. Duffus defined the two kinds of book patron in America as "a group willing to pay for artistic printing and binding and a larger group of individuals who will accept anything that is legible and will hold together, provided it contains something they want to read." He concluded with a verbal shrug: "The millions demand cheaper books, perhaps. The thousands do not seem to." The formula was seductively simple: the majority of Americans cared more about cost than about quality, but a definite minority valued quality more than cheapness, at least in some of their books. As one patron of Adler's Pynson Printers explained, fine printing was inappropriate for most "routine" work, but he savored the rare chance to splurge on Adler's services "for some special purpose where unerring taste in typography is the supreme end."[22]

For books "expected to last," as critic Paul Johnston described the difference between fine and ordinary, only the highest quality of materials and procedures were to be used. He insisted on papers made from rags and on "real" bindings — in which the body of the book is attached integrally to its covers, not merely glued into a preconstructed case.[23] To hold all bookmaking to such standards, however, was clearly impractical. By contending that most people neither noticed nor cared about quality production, and by devoting themselves to an elite community of patrons, fine printers revitalized a growing sense of hierarchy — of status and expense, as well as material quality and purpose — in the postwar world of books.

Carl Rollins, who more than any of his peers understood and embraced Morris's socialism, proposed a more radical scheme that stratified books less by the taste of their owners than by their intrinsic worth. "The trouble with our values today is that we haven't any," he began. "We confuse quantity and quality. We wanted mass production, and we have it — monotonous, deadly dull, cheap." The only way out, he argued, was "a clearer demarcation between the merely useful, necessary book, and the other sort." He blamed "the modern American ideal of 'business.' . . . Production for sale, the ideal and goal of all the busy manufacturers, is fundamentally unsound and immoral. It results in cheap product, ephemeral literature, five-and-ten trash." Rollins's solution would have delighted Morris. He urged "a situation where the necessary books could be printed in the most economical format possible, and distributed at cost, with profit to no one. . . . Then the worth while books, the books which have a purpose, could be given more careful, leisurely treatment, be finely printed." This two-tiered scheme would eliminate all the dubiously cheap and pointless books produced merely to earn someone a profit, leaving only the purely pragmatic "necessary" books and those with higher, more enduring purposes. Although this production hierarchy was not ideal, it would at least radically reduce the numbers of books printed and published, an important first step toward ensuring that the remaining important books, the "worth while" ones, were produced in "thoroughly good ways."[24]

Rollins realized, as had Morris, that until publishing could be freed from its capitalist moorings fine printing could enhance only a rarefied minority of books.[25] Those few books, it was understood, would be produced in relatively small numbers, accessible to only a tiny fraction of fortunate readers. Most advocates of fine printing accepted as a given that the materials and processes imposed natural limits: handmade papers and printing from type (as opposed to stereotyped plates, or moulds of the composed type cast in harder metals that could withstand many more impressions than the softer lead type) dictated that only a certain number of copies could be printed before the quality of impression would deteriorate. Although this is technically true, the maximum number of good copies is virtually impossible to predict because many variables are involved. Nonetheless, this presumption permeated most discussions about edition sizes.

Those with a more aggressive viewpoint argued that limited edition sizes were more than a necessary by-product of high-quality production. Some invoked the notions of Richard Le Gallienne, who a generation earlier had urged publishers to limit the number of copies produced in order to curtail the "careless procreation" of contemporary publishing practices. What better solution to the problem of "too many books" that some perceived? If books were "more arduously come by," Le Gallienne reasoned, they would be deemed more precious by those who owned them. It did not bother him that fewer copies usually meant higher prices; it was better that books remain expensive treasures accessible only to those who appreciated them "than that any sacrilegious hand should fumble them for threepence." He exclaimed, "Let us not vulgarize our books. . . . Let us, if need be, make our editions smaller and smaller, our prices increasingly 'prohibitive,' rather than that we should forget the wonder and beauty of printed dream and thought, and treat our books as somewhat less valuable than wayside weeds."[26] Expensive scarcity was perhaps an inevitable feature of fine bookmaking, Le Gallienne and others allowed, but it did not require an apology. Rather, they felt that preciousness underscored the inherent value of books, a central objective of the fine printing agenda.

The assumption that the audience for fine printing was strictly limited, however, both raised ideological inconsistencies and invited accusations that it pandered to snobs. The latter criticism dogged the movement throughout the decade. "The words 'fine' and 'printing' are dangerous bedfellows, for they are apt to beget monstrosities," warned Holbrook Jackson. He found the concept arrogant, an anachronistic "survival from a period when one small class was content to surround itself with beautiful things as a means of escape from a distasteful environment." Aldous Huxley, although sympathetic, warned that preoccupation with handcraft and "ancient decorative forms" draws attention away from the larger reform task; it may yield beautiful books for a privileged few, but it "condemns ordinary readers to a perpetuity of ugly printing."[27]

Although the audience (as well as the market) for fine printing was undeniably elite, most fine printers squirmed at the notion that they were abandoning the less fortunate masses to the ugly sterility of commonplace bookmaking. They were caught in the familiar tension between impulses to preserve and to disseminate things of cultural import. They readily embraced, therefore, the notion that fine printing's "otherness" offered less a disdainful retreat from the ordinary than a better, more authentic alternative. To the extent that their mission was conceived in terms of quasi-genteel responsibility for cultural leadership, they were ultimately pledged to serve, not evade, the public interests. Thus, theoretically, the sense of audience expanded to include all readers, even if the benefits of improved typographic standards reached most of them indirectly.

The theory that fine printing ultimately served an all-encompassing audience eased consciences considerably. It provided a kind of trickle-down rationale that justified the more elite realities. The general public would benefit, the argument ran, as fine printing inspired producers of ordinary books to exercise greater care and taste in their work and eventually taught readers to recognize and appreciate better books. Even if the means of fine printing were elite, expensive, and often contemptuous of everything "ordinary," its ends were ostensibly democratic, neatly deflecting at least some of the accusations of snobbery. In theory, then, fine printing was to raise production standards for all books by educating printers and publishers and the general public in the lost principles of excellent bookmaking.

This mission to educate took several forms. Among the most popular was the public exhibition. Throughout the twenties and thirties libraries and other institutions across the United States gathered and displayed collections of finely printed books, typically spanning the five centuries since Gutenberg. In part, these exhibitions helped viewers recognize the historical veracity of the modern fine book whose designs they inspired, cementing a prized sense of continuity with a noble tradition.[28] A related effort was the publication, usually heavily illustrated, of introductory overviews of Western printing history, typically culminating with Rogers's or Updike's prewar work. These surveys similarly lent historical credence to claims of a contemporary renaissance in typography, and they presented historic figures as heroes in the great cultural enterprise. Such studies spoke of Gutenberg, Aldus, Jenson, Estienne, Baskerville, Bodoni, and others in reverent terms, quickly canonizing their names and works.[29] Courses devoted to printing history were developed at a few prestigious universities. Librarian George Parker Winship taught such a course at Harvard University, hailing it as "the most fundamentally cultural course in the college." Similar courses debuted at Yale, including one taught by Carl Rollins. Elmer Adler was approached about teaching at Columbia, but he preferred to offer noncredit evening courses in his own offices.[30]

The most visible educational activity was the work of the American Institute of Graphic Arts (AIGA), founded in 1914. In 1923 it initiated its annual "Fifty Books" competition, in which fifty books produced the preceding year were selected to demonstrate the high standards to which others presumably would aspire. The brainchild of Burton Emmett, New York advertising executive and avid book collector, the competition included a traveling exhibit of the honored books. As expected, fine books dominated the show during its first decade; eager to lead the way in matters of taste and execution, fine printers sought and proudly garnered most of the awards. It is no surprise that members of the printing trade sometimes resented this, noting for instance that only twenty of the 1926 selections were trade books available to general audiences, and nine of those were small-run books published by university presses. Consequently, the average price of the books exhibited was over twenty dollars, seven times the price of an average trade book.[31] Most, however, accepted this dominance as well as the higher prices and limited edition sizes as natural and necessary costs gladly incurred in the larger cause of providing yardsticks by which ordinary books would be measured.

Porter Garnett knew that the mission of the Laboratory Press, devoted to educating the first generation of professional, formally credentialed fine printers, had to articulate precisely the relationship between fine printing and the larger publishing industry. He phrased it with exceeding care: "By dealing with the traditional, scholarly, and philosophical aspects of the craft, in its relation to the civilization of the future as well as of the past, it was hoped to create in the minds of the students an attitude of sympathy towards the refinements of printing, which might bring about, in time, a general raising of standards."[32] Garnett's cautious language couched perfectly the diffused sense of fine printing's centrality to "civilization" and of its eventual, though not immediate, concern with "a general raising of standards" for ordinary books. It was germane to the larger contemporary book world, but not exactly in service to it. Paradoxically, its very timelessness — its adherence to standards of quality and beauty that transcended particular eras, agendas, and fashions — was seen to be fine printing's most valuable contribution to its own age. Civilization itself would benefit, even if only a relatively small number of individuals actually encountered fine printing first hand.

The Professionalization of Printing

On a mild Oakland evening in 1923, a group of Bay Area printers gathered to celebrate Mills College's decision to bestow upon John Henry Nash an honorary master's degree for bringing glory to San Francisco and California through his service to literature, art, and culture. Seated at the head of the banquet table, Nash swelled with pride. Dressed in a suit nearly as expensive as those worn by his millionaire clients, he indeed looked the part of a distinguished honoree. Many found it remarkable that, in the person of Nash, a printer could now mingle among the weekend houseguests at Hearst Castle in San Simeon or at Senator William Clark's Los Angeles mansion. Nash had accepted the satin and velvet hood with great pleasure, just as he now basked in his peers' accolades, beaming at the momentous recognition of this new status accorded a printer.

Seated well back at the table, squirming in their Sunday collars and clean white shirts, sat Ed and Bob Grabhorn and several of Nash's less reverent colleagues in printing. As the speeches grew longer and the room grew warmer, their restlessness became increasingly obvious, as did the rounds of beer they'd downed beforehand. Finally, as an advertising executive droned on at excruciating length about the significance of a printer's name being adorned with those precious initials "M.A.," one drunken voice from the unruly far end of the table hollered in exasperation that it meant "My Ass!"[33]

The lofty notions of fine printing's cultural responsibilities and privileges gave printers a new — and sometimes ill-fitting — mantle of significance and authority. Despite the back-row scoffing of the Grabhorns and a few others, one of the most telling aspects of the typographic renaissance in the twenties was the growing professionalization of the fine printer. As machines were demoted in importance, their masters took on new status, acquiring renown as experts with rare gifts of knowledge and taste. Twentieth-century fine printing was transformed from an avocational craft into a cultural profession approaching, some argued, the ranks of doctors and lawyers.[34]

First, however, fine printers had to establish the sources and evidence of that authority. Education was key. Even though their own formal educational backgrounds varied inauspiciously, most fine printers regarded a liberal arts education as foundational for the fledgling profession. Garnett believed that a student of fine printing must be thoroughly grounded in liberal arts learning, including fluency in the major western European languages and Latin. He lamented that the challenge was especially great in America, "a country without artistic traditions" where "public taste is dominated by the false standards of semi-intelligence, of fake culture," and he urged his students at Carnegie Tech to travel widely in Europe.[35] In months of lectures, he immersed them in European cultural history before allowing them to print anything.

Bourdieu contends that a great deal can be learned about an aesthetic field by examining the credential-granting institutions that recruit or limit recruitment into its ranks. Such an approach is fruitful here. Both Garnett and later Adler emphatically resisted efforts at Carnegie Tech—the country's leading school for the printing trade—to incorporate fine printing into its general curriculum. They insisted that fine printing was properly the concern of only the very few with the necessary talent and aptitude. In fact, Garnett's educational work at the school's Laboratory Press is nearly matched in significance by his efforts to limit access to that education. He strenuously objected when school administrators proposed that all printing students take a semester of fine printing, countering that no more than twelve students should be admitted. Even those students had to earn their way into the course. Each spring, senior and second-year students with "good above-average grades in English and hand [type] composition [were] invited to write papers on fine printing and its place in civilization," one proud graduate reported. Only writers of the best papers, usually between six and ten each year, were invited to take the year long course. Even after Garnett had resigned in 1935, Elmer Adler (among others) refused when asked to deliver a lecture on fine printing to Carnegie Tech students. Such a lecture would be "pointless," he explained, because it would take many months to do the job properly, not a mere forty minutes.[36] Most agreed that fine printing was a rarefied realm that many aspired to but few inhabited.

The new profession was also authenticated in other ways that appropriated the style and effects of social gentility. Most fine printers created workplaces

Figure 4. Willa Cather reviewing materials in the library of the Pynson Printers, New York, ca. 1926. Photo courtesy of Princeton University Library.

that conveyed wealth and aristocratic taste, complete with fireplaces, chandeliers, leather library furniture, oriental rugs, fresh flowers, and the like. Those who entered the offices of Adler's Pynson Printers — housed in the New York Times building on Forty-third Street in Manhattan, purportedly so that its aura would dignify the newspaper operations as well — found a spacious and impeccably decorated suite of rooms. One young visitor gushed to Adler his admiration of the "richness, quiet dignity, and good taste" of the workplace, calling it an "inspiration." Adler cultivated such awe; he hosted a weekly tea in his offices, inviting a steady parade of prominent artists, authors, printers, publishers, collectors, and patrons, and authors settled there in comfort to sign the elegant books he produced (figure 4). Richard Ellis similarly established a salonlike atmosphere by hosting literary teas at his Georgian Press in Westport, Connecticut, housed in a restored eighteenth-century barn that one admirer called "one of the shrines of graphic arts in America."[37]

One striking feature of these highly styled workplaces was the presence of a library. For obvious reasons this room presented a social and professional

Figure 5. R.R. Donnelley & Sons Memorial Library, Chicago ca. 1930.
Photo courtesy of R.R. Donnelley & Sons Company Archive.

focal point intended to impress, if not dazzle, customers, guests, and employees. Edward O'Day described Nash's San Francisco shop library as a "room of inspiration." "Garamond, Bodoni, Morris and others of the Nash tradition look down from the walls," he wrote. "Gutenberg carved in wood stands above the fireplace, and a bronze bust of Franklin in heroic proportions dominates the room." And any doubts about the postwar sacralization of the fine book would be quickly dispelled upon entering the R.R. Donnelley library, located on the top floor of the huge Chicago printing plant (figure 5). To University of Chicago English professor James Weber Linn, the Donnelley library conveyed the spiritual splendor of the printing craft; he declared it a monument of "devotion to an ideal, . . . which is symbolized by one beautiful room, a room so beautiful that it turns work into worship and a factory into a shrine."[38]

The printer's library was far more a gallery and showplace than a place for reading; most books were there as specimens of noteworthy printing rather than texts to be read. Such libraries created an elegant aura of scholarship and intimate kinship with the great figures of printing history, whose portraits and busts as well as books graced the premises. In the Rudge company library, for instance, its rich wood paneling, oriental rugs, and glass-fronted bookcases prompted one visitor to recall reverently "the days of parchment and illuminated manuscripts." A client received at the Merrymount Press felt reassured that its fifteenth-century books and other historically rich surroundings created the "appropriate atmosphere for carrying on in the old tradition, applying eternal principles to commercial work."[39]

Even printers who did not display or enshrine them proudly collected famous books produced by past masters. Ed Grabhorn boasted that within a few years of arriving in San Francisco he and his brother had acquired "the Kelmscott Chaucer, the Doves Bible, and the Ashendene Mort d'Arthur," masterpieces of the three great private presses of the English revival.[40] Such trophies of typographic history were like rare baseball cards; they were emblems of "insider" acquaintance with the field, badges of self-gained scholarship and authority. They acquired a kind of brand name iconic status. Shorthand references to owning "three Baskervilles, two Aldines, and a Bodoni," for example, helped to forge an elite camaraderie among those who understood the argot. Printers' libraries were an important visible testament to the cultural capital of historical knowledge upon which their professionalized status was built.

When at last Porter Garnett deemed that his students were ready to try their hands at fine printing, he always gave them the same initial task. They were to typeset a sentence from *The Journals of Henry Marston:* "The young men of my generation who wish to live the creative life on any level must learn to resist the menace of exploitation." As they labored for days to compose it in flawless typography, they were asked to ponder its message with equally focused care. The sentence expressed Garnett's resolve that fine printing was a precious and vulnerable cultural treasure, at constant risk of corruption or betrayal at the hands of those who understood it only superficially or pragmatically. Garnett argued that the fine book was but a symbol of the greater effort it embodied, renewed reverence for the printed word as the repository of human thought and spirit. What made a book truly fine, then, was not merely its material features but the larger context in which it was made. Ideally, fine printing was to be as much about process and purpose as about product.

In reality, however, that mission was seldom so clear. The "menace of exploitation" was not at all easy to distinguish from the eager reception that greeted fine books throughout the postwar decade. The ideological high ground that Garnett so imperiously guarded left little room for actual operations. Those exacting principles essentially crippled the central imperative of modern fine printing — to present superior models of bookmaking taste. To the extent that virtually every means by which fine books were produced for and disseminated to the "real world" involved some pragmatic accommodation of that contemporary reality, Garnett's unbending credo would hamper efforts to introduce the ideal book to modern America.

3

Man and Machine

Frederic Warde could hardly contain his dismay when he arrived at Princeton in August 1922 to begin his new post as director of printing at the university press. "The whole show was a roaring collection of presses and printing machinery able to turn out a million Lux packages or cartons a day," he exclaimed to his friend William Kittredge. "The Kelly presses were trying to exceed the speed of the Miehle-Vertical—while the Miller Pony beat them all," and the ink was "the God awfulest stuff" he had ever seen. He could find no safe haven from the thunderous machinery; his office was tucked into a corner of the shipping and mailing room, where half a dozen typists "were hammering away all day on the worst old wrecks which one might suspect as having been typewriters perhaps in the days of Mark Twain." No matter where he turned, Warde complained, he could not escape a "din that sounded like a clod-hopper's ball on a tin roof."[1]

All that machine clatter and bustle should have prepared him for the inferior printing that resulted, but his disgust deepened when he described the first trial page he requested. "Whatahell," he snorted, "it was a beauty! I swear it was set in Lithuanian." He was immediately overwhelmed with contemptible work to try to salvage, "heaps of it, and nearly all of it set in the most damnable sans-serif block letter type—condensed, expanded, dried up, worn-out, battered down, wrong font rubbish you ever saw."[2] Though appalled at the conditions in which he was expected to work, Warde knew exactly how to proceed. For the next two years he ruthlessly imposed stringent new standards for workers and equipment alike. He insisted that nothing could be printed without his final approval of the composition and "make-ready" — the minute adjustments that ensure the page prints with uniform inking and pressure. Exhaustive labor and mechanical obstacles mattered little to him: one letterhead was reset eleven times before earning Warde's approval. Pressmen labored for hours, sweat and apprehension blended on their faces when Warde examined their preparations. One recalled finally getting the go-ahead to print and running the job with extreme care, only to have Warde pass by, take one look at the top sheet of the printed pile, and run a pencil down the side of the whole stack. It still wasn't good enough.[3]

Meanwhile, not far to the north, Carl Rollins faced an almost identical struggle at Yale University Press, where he found his work so abysmal and "distressing" that he saw it as little more than "a chance to barely support the family." "There are so few people in New Haven interested in what I am concerned with," he mourned, that he felt lonely and discouraged. One of his worst moments, sadly representative of his dilemma, came when he discovered a dusty, scuffed copy of William Morris's handcrafted masterpiece, the majestic Kelmscott edition of Chaucer, plopped on the floor outside the Yale Art School library, its great bulk reduced to holding the door open. He promptly rescued it from this menial role and, after much effort, persuaded the school's rare book librarians to adopt it into their dignified collection.[4]

Forced to earn livelihoods as best they could, Rollins and Warde struggled to wrest acceptable results from the printing machinery in their charge. Both men learned to live and work with machines, uneasily, but Rollins could never conquer his distrust and dislike for them. In 1924 he described the Linotype typesetting machine as "a wild beast — obedient under the trainer's whip, but a wild jungle beast at heart."[5] One could subdue and control it, Rollins allowed, but the machine by nature threatened to devour what was most human about the society it was meant to serve. To him and to most fine printers, this belief seemed most alarming in the production of the printed word.

The machine loomed throughout the 1920s as a powerful metaphor of both good and evil. Defenders of "machine civilization," as it was commonly called, boasted that machines offered "the greatest opportunity for extending the good life to the masses that the world has ever known." To them machines meant freedom for workers, liberation from drudgery: "Hard labor is for machines, not men," Henry Ford announced, prompting one disciple to proclaim that "the masses have more to hope for from captains of industry than social reformers' panaceas." Another writer linked machinery with the sacred natural order of things: "It isn't the material machine . . . but the spirit behind [it] which scientists and engineers worship. . . . The machine is visible evidence of the close union between man and the spirit of the eternal truth which guides the hand of nature."[6]

To fine printers and many others, however, the machine was more tyrant than benefactor, robbing expressiveness and individuality from maker and product alike. If proponents of machine civilization spoke with hyperbole, it was in part because significant skepticism greeted them. By the 1920s fears that industrialism diminished the human worker seemed frighteningly plausible as mechanization and assembly lines transformed one industry after another. Once the pride of a factory, workers became incorporated into the mechanized process, often in a subordinate, degrading role. One writer described an automobile plant at which workers' sole tasks were to insert steel sheets into a machine that promptly cut and punched them. If workers became fatigued or distracted or if monotony dulled their alertness, the machine would cut off their hands. To remedy this, managers handcuffed the workers' hands to a lever that pulled them away as the machine's blades descended. The workers, who could not control the movement of the machines, were able only "to stand before the press, their hands jerking back and forth. There they work, chained to their machines, as the galley slaves were chained to their oars."[7]

The vision of the factory bred a host of cultural fears prompted by alarming changes in American life and society. These fears were tinged with tones of xenophobia, because nearly all the immigrants who had arrived after 1890 took factory jobs. In a world increasingly dominated by machines and immigrants, who seemed to some "less than human" in their often docile compliance with low wages and shop discipline codes, the factory seemed an ominous threat to core notions of America as a nation of strong individuals. One essayist described "the grim reality" of mass production, predicting that thirty years hence (in 1956) workers would form a line "uniformed from head to toe and marching lock-step to the factory." After a day of standardized labor and a "tabloid dinner, standardized on the authority of Johns Hopkins University Medical Department," the writer warned, "from seven to nine, a standardized radio plays standardized jazz and furnishes to what is left of the cubicle-dweller's mind an assortment of standardized misinformation. After which machinery removes his standardized clothing and casts him into his standardized bed."[8]

American trade book production was no different from any other mechanized industry. Manufacturers scrambled to produce unprecedented numbers of books as inexpensively and rapidly as possible. The physical character of the resulting books was shaped largely by those standardized, streamlined methods of mechanical papermaking, typesetting, and printing. According to a spokesperson for Simon and Schuster in the 1930s, ideal manufacturing considerations dictated that a book's dimensions would not exceed 8 by 5 3/8 inches, because that was the largest page size that could be printed in 64-page forms; it would be printed in only one color, because each additional ink color required a separate trip through the presses; it would include no illustrations other than relief line cuts that could be printed with the text; it would be bound in a standard color and grade of cloth readily available in the plant's stock; and it would "be completely devoid of any extra features" like folding maps, headbands, stained edges, and so forth, which would add cost and time to the manufacturing process.[9]

In stark contrast to European modernists, who celebrated the economy and efficiency of machine production, American fine printers sought to restore a primary human presence in bookmaking. They blamed the nineteenth-century mechanization of the bookmaking trades for severing the spiritual link between a book's creators (author and printer) and its readers.[10] This conviction was inspired by John Ruskin's belief, championed by William Morris, that workers in Gothic society had achieved some expressive scope in their craft. Ruskin contended that by wielding tools rather than operating machines, medieval workers had been able to express the "roughness and majesty of their souls," escaping what he saw as the brutalizing effects of Victorian factory labor. Like Ruskin, Morris argued that modern machines divorced workers from the fruits of their labor, yielding a meaningless, sterile product. The Kelmscott Press, then, like Morris's many other artistic endeavors, was as much about the morality of labor as about the beauty of the printed book. He sought to reunite art and labor, concept and execution in all their dimensions.[11] What resulted were books that seemed almost animate, their beauty infused with their maker's personality and convictions about life, art, and work.

In a long and impassioned letter to Edmund G. Gress, editor of the *American Printer,* Carl Rollins clung to hopes of a modern society in which machines would be used only to produce "absolutely necessary commodities of a very simple sort," and only when "all the shop workers will be cooperative owners of the shop or at least the owner will be a workman working every day in the workroom." Rollins was one of the few American printers who understood Morris's socialism, even though he knew full well that his beliefs cut across the grain of American politics. "What we *need* is visions," he protested, "not visions of more dollars and more machines, but of service, of production for *use* not profit. . . . To pretend that more machinery, either in the workroom or in the business office, is the way of salvation is to blaspheme the eternal verities. And no art in the past has ever been — or in the future will ever be — produced except by the effort of man's hands. . . . and the more we rely on these inhuman machines the less scope we offer to man's soul."[12]

In America, a whole generation of young book lovers was seduced by the romantic Kelmscott vision. Carl Rollins was perhaps most intoxicated by the Kelmscott "superb craftsmanship," but most other fine printers paid some sort of homage as well. John Henry Nash, whose work aspired more than anyone's to emulate the revival grandeur, commissioned a portrait of Morris to hang in his elegant San Francisco business quarters. A few blocks away at the Grabhorn Press, Edwin Grabhorn displayed the framed title page of the Kelmscott edition of *Reynard the Foxe,* and he was so indignant when the visiting head of the printer's union pointed out the apparent typo in the title that he vowed never to join such a hopelessly ignorant and tasteless association.[13] Mere awareness of the revival, epitomized by Morris's Kelmscott achievement, bred a deep sense of fraternity. Even though most quickly outgrew an inclination to imitate Morris's neomedieval style, fine printers rarely wavered in their admiration for the ideals of the private press revival. Chief among those ideals was a wariness of machine culture.

In defying machine production, fine printing attracted many acolytes eager to awaken the "roughness" and "majesty" of their souls. By the 1920s the Merrymount Press had become something of a mecca for the seriously smitten, and Updike entertained a number of idealistic job seekers hoping to try their hand at the noble craft. One day a young applicant interrupted her interview with a question: When you've just completed a beautiful piece of work, have you ever experienced craftsman's ecstasy? Taken aback, the elder statesman of the craft assured her that he had never suffered such an attack, and that he was not entirely sure he would recognize its symptoms if one did occur. The earnest young woman patiently explained that when one had created an especially beautiful bit of typography, it was not uncommon to fall into an awed trance when gazing at one's achievement. Although Updike imagined that one might perhaps swoon with surprise at such a moment, he confessed that he derived no such rapture from his work. Disappointed, the young woman soon left Updike's office, no doubt in search of a workplace with more ecstatic possibilities.[14]

The search for such a workplace would not be difficult, for several practitioners testified that the craft did indeed offer an almost transcendent experience. Joseph Blumenthal attested that "there is a rare spiritual lift to articulate hand labor in the pursuit of craft in association with a meaningful text. One of the great rewards is the profound satisfaction of seeing crisp, sparkling type pages coming off the press on exquisite dampened handmade paper. Such printing . . . is a profound humanistic experience." The Brothers Johnson (as James and Cecil called themselves) confessed that to them "the beautiful book should be approached as a poem which enthralls with its finish and delights with its verve. To the craftsman his book is a sacred thing." Their craft was their "great religion"; they worshiped "that sacredness attaching to any production which has been a labor of love, and doubly so in this machine age when handwrought art is the exception rather than the rule. . . . Its sheer divinity must be apparent to the connoisseur and novice alike, conjoining them to participate in the song of the craftsman's heart."[15]

Printing at Its Best

In his weekly fine book review column in the *Saturday Review of Literature,* begun in 1927, Carl Rollins worked out his definitive ideas about "printing at its best." For him, truly fine printing could derive only from hand processes of type casting and setting, papermaking, and printing. The small but unique variations intrinsic to craftwork produce a "charm" and "virility" unmatched by the monotonous sameness of machine-made products, Rollins contended, making handmade books "more interesting, more attractive." He urged "a modest revival of simpler ways of printing" and a "revolt of the workers in handicrafts against the spiritual dominations of the machine." Rollins considered mass-produced, machine-made books grotesque, "all too redolent of the iron monsters which gave them birth."[16] In a similar manifesto, Porter Garnett defined the ideal book exclusively through handwork: it was to be printed from hand-composed types—and if images were included, from hand-engraved relief cuts—on handmade paper with a handpress powered entirely by human labor.

Emulating Morris, who in turn was inspired by production techniques of the fifteenth century, Garnett and Rollins insisted that the best printing was achieved with a handpress—a nineteenth-century iron version of the wooden press used by Gutenberg. This style of press and procedures of operating it have changed little from the 1450s; one inks the type prior to each impression by hand, manually places each sheet of paper into position, and presses the two together with a hard pull on a leverlike bar. Printing with a handpress offered maximum opportunity to control the results, which enabled Garnett to pronounce exacting models of ideal bookmaking. As one student recalled, Garnett's "concept of perfect inking [applied by hand with a roller] was a theoretical film of fine ink only one molecule in thickness."[17] To attain the perfect impression, or slight indentation created by the contact between the paper and the inked type, Garnett declared, the paper must first be dampened—a manual process, appropriate only for handmade papers, of moistening the sheets before printing to make them soft, limp, and especially receptive to the contact with type. This labor-intensive procedure yields what Garnett called "a certain almost-indefinable something that can perhaps best be described as a living quality. This ultimate grace . . . is sculptural. No printing that is lifeless . . . can be called fine printing." In the actual moment of printing, Garnett felt, "any impression in the sheet much deeper than 1/500th of an inch was too much."[18]

This value system with handcraft at its apex was readily apparent in professional fine printing as well. In 1927 John Henry Nash, who unlike Garnett earned a lucrative income from the craft, defended handcraft as foundational to the highest possible standards of production quality: "Good books, well made, set by hand, and printed on hand made paper, are just as much in demand today among the discriminating as they have ever been. . . . To print wet or by hand is, and always will be, legitimate if it results in the perfection to be desired in a given book. . . . I print by hand from hand set type on hand made deckle edge paper and have been doing this for forty years and hope to continue for many years more." Handwork was often a point of professional pride, a measure of commitment to high standards in bookmaking. David Magee's 1940 bibliography of the Grabhorn Press noted with admiration that less than a third of the press's work relied on machine composition, for example. In 1927 Elmer Adler took offense when a publishing outfit called the Marlowe Society claimed to produce the only American volumes set entirely by hand. Adler bristled with indignation, informing the "ignorant or deceitful" directors of the society that "practically every book that goes through this shop [the Pynson Printers] is handset." He suggested they retract the hapless claim, reminding them that many of the "Fifty Books" selected by the AIGA each year were handset as well.[19] Hand production was a distinction not to be invoked casually.

When a particularly ambitious or important project was envisioned, that specialness was often indicated by the handwork included in its plans. Frederic Warde boasted when he established the Watch Hill Press with Crosby Gaige in 1929 that "there will not be any wheels or electric motors or anything but the human hand for producing the results we want in the work." When George Macy launched the Limited Editions Club in spring 1929, he promised prospective members handset types and imported handmade papers, enticing them with claims that the books' texts would be "printed from type only" and that illustrations would be printed from "original woodblocks, engravings, or lithographic stones." Throughout the twenties, Updike continued to use only foundry types for handsetting because machine composition did not yet measure up to his standards. Even R.R. Donnelley's Lakeside Press, the company's high-quality division devoted to diminishing the gap between fine printing and machine printing, recognized that the gap was often a large one. Press manager William Kittredge conceded in private to Bill Dwiggins that to achieve "a surpassingly fine" edition of Poe's *Tales,* management "is willing to set the entire book by hand." British writer George Moore, who relished seeing his work in fine editions, captured the prevailing sentiment when he rhapsodized that hand-composed books offered the "delight that only the humanizing touch of a printer's fingers can give to a page, the faint irregularities which are the ultimate perfection."[20]

The Reality

Predictably, such perfection was elusive. In truth, the antimachine rhetoric far outpaced the reality. While the use of machinery meant different things to different printers, none adhered fastidiously to the hand-only production ideals. In fact, none of the fine editions offered for sale in the 1920s was produced in absolute compliance with the ideal criteria described by Rollins and Garnett.[21] A few such books were made in the decade, to be sure, but their fidelity to the highest ideals of handcraft rendered them unsuitable for the bibliophilic marketplace (like the Kelmscott books, they were produced "privately," or avocationally). Despite the exhortations, bookmaking by hand was not economically — that is, professionally — viable. Instead, postwar fine printing invariably involved machinery to some degree; consequently, it emphasized the spirit rather than the letter of the term *handcraft.*

The hand production standard that most commercial fine printers exalted was only loosely and partially descriptive of actual practices (see table 1). In this sense, handcraft represented the humanist value system of fine printing (which, most people soon realized, was more easily conveyed through design than production), and so fine printers tolerated the inevitable use of some machinery. As if to compensate, most showcased whatever handcraft was involved in their books, ranging from labor-intensive features like hand-rendered illustrations or embellishments to little more than a number handwritten in each copy. These gestures of handcraft were highlighted in the colophon, or statement describing the book's making, typically on the final page. Colophons — construed as a service to the growing number of bibliophiles who were knowledgeable or at least curious about the particulars of bookmaking — thus more shrewdly enabled publishers to point out the craft-based aspects of production that distinguished fine bookmaking from ordinary.

The tacit accommodation of modern machinery in fine bookmaking was most apparent in the printing process itself. Although many fine printers proudly owned a handpress (and it is remarkable how often they were photo-

Table 1. Fine Book Production Processes

	1920–26	1927–28	1929	1930	1931–32	All
Total books	61	67	65	66	41	300
Composition						
Hand	38	30	30	30	18	146 (55.9% of known)
Machine	17	27	25	28	18	115 (44.1% of known)
Not known	6	10	10	8	5	39 (13% of total)
Paper						
Handmade, all copies	33	31	25	17	7	113 (39.1% of known)
Handmade, some copies	2	4	3	1	1	11 (3.9% of known)
Machine- or mouldmade	24	32	36	43	30	165 (57.1% of known)
Not known	2	0	1	5	3	11 (3.9% of total)
Image-printing technique						
Relief (wood- or linecut)	23	22	20	26	13	104 (78.6% of illus.)
Offset (photography)	5	7	11	9	6	38 (26.2% of illus.)
Other	0	0	1	1	1	3 (2.1% of illus.)
"Printed from type" in colophon	2	5	4	2	4	17 (5.7% of total)
Hand embellishment						
In all copies	2	3	4	1	1	11 (3.7% of total)
In some copies	0	1	2	1	0	4 (1.3% of total)
Numbered copies						
All	33	36	43	48	31	191 (63.7% of total)
Some	3	0	1	0	1	5 (1.7% of total)

graphed with it), none produced books for sale with one. Because its very simplicity required extreme skill and care to achieve the best results, the handpress was used only for small projects, occasional proofs, or by the most extreme purists, who were not attempting to earn a living from the work. Even Porter Garnett, one of those extreme purists, could not manage to assemble and operate a handpress successfully until more than two years after he launched the Laboratory Press. Because the handpress was so vital to his ideas about fine printing, he persuaded officials at Carnegie Tech to buy one, but when it arrived it lacked an essential part for edition printing, a frisket — the thin metal frame over which paper or parchment is stretched to protect the page from stray ink. A frisket was ordered, but even with it Garnett could not get the press to work properly. In fact, the ceremonial "First Impression" taken with such fanfare in April 1923 was the only printing done on this handpress. The school agreed to buy another press, but (after more discoveries of missing parts) it took another year before Garnett and his students could master its operation well enough to produce satisfactory results. In the meantime, the first twenty highly touted student *projets* (as Garnett called them) were discreetly printed on the modern presses in the school's trade printing department—machines that Garnett publicly loathed but on which, in a pinch, he depended.[22]

Professional fine printers, including the Grabhorns, Nash, Adler, Ellis, and others, used those more efficient modern presses from the start, without any apparent qualms. One press style—called a jobber press because of its common use for small-sized commercial jobs like tickets, handbills, and letterhead—features a clamshell action in which type is locked up in an open iron frame and inserted vertically into the press. Inked rollers pass over the type as the operator slips a sheet of paper into position on the platen, which then carries the paper into contact with the type. The Pynson Printers and the Grabhorn Press relied on presses of this design. In both shops, much of the "hand" production work was done on Colts Armory presses with fourteen- by twenty-two-inch platens that defined the largest sizes of paper sheets or type forms that could be printed at one time.[23]

The second commonly used style of press was a cylinder press, in which type is positioned on a flat horizontal bed (as with a handpress), across which pass inking rollers and a cylinder carrying the paper. Updike relied on three cylinder presses and two jobbers throughout the 1920s. Richard Ellis, although he acquired a handpress in 1923, did not actually print books until five years later when he had added a Babcock Optimus cylinder press to his shop.[24] Both platen and cylinder presses were commonly powered by electricity but set to run slowly enough so that paper could be fed by hand and the operator could inspect each impression and monitor the inking. This lent some accuracy to the term *hand printing,* which simply indicated a distinction from the work of very large, automated rotary and cylinder presses used for rapid, high-quantity commercial printing.

When the printer exercised constant control over the press it could be regarded as a tool rather than as a machine. Fine printers who used modern platen or cylinder presses in this modified way could thus be seen as authentic artisans, their work expressing the all-important ascendancy of man over machine. It is significant that librarian and printing scholar James Hart used anthropomorphic language when he admired the Grabhorns' presswork for its strength and "virility." Pressman Ed Grabhorn "did not merely let the type kiss the [dampened handmade] paper lightly and discreetly but instead embedded it in a forceful embrace that could be felt by fingers as well as seen by eyes." Grabhorn, Hart, and most bibliophiles preferred a deep impression to the more controlled, slight one advocated by Garnett; it was ready evidence of the human eye and hand (if not biceps) at work in the process, and a clear contrast to the brief, light contact between type and paper that typifies mechanized printing on dry paper. The heavy impression throughout the massive edition of *Leaves of Grass* that the Grabhorns printed for Random House thrilled many owners. Press biographer Roby Wentz recounted that "the massive [Colts Armory] press shuddered at each meeting of platen and the two heavy folio pages [of type]." He added the often-told tale that because the presswork on the book was so strenuous, involving 87,000 total impressions for the 430-page book, Ed Grabhorn quipped at its completion that the colophon should state "400 copies printed and the press destroyed."[25]

To print images, fine printers similarly preferred traditional relief processes to the planographic options made possible by offset lithography. Although offset is now used for virtually all text and image printing, it did not seriously rival letterpress until the 1960s for book production.[26] It was an increasingly feasible option for printing images in the twenties, however, because it could better reproduce toned or shaded images, like photographs, than could the starker black or white relief techniques. Even so, fine printers generally resisted offset-printed photographic images in their books for several reasons (see table 1). First, offset printing would have to be done separately and usually at another plant, involving problems of cost and coordination. Second, photographs are best printed on a smooth and even slightly coated or glossy paper that not only contrasts with the text paper but also must be inserted into the bound book, usually as a separate gathering or section of pages, invariably isolating text from illustration. Third, the overtly mechanical process of photographic image-making, coupled with the machine-made and chemically treated papers upon which photographs were printed, violated fine printing's central emphasis on handcraft. Instead, fine printing spurred a modest renaissance in traditional relief images, notably woodcuts and wood engravings, as well as line drawings that could be readily (if mechanically) transformed into line cuts. These methods of making and printing images preserved — and revived the prestige of — book illustration as an art form, which in turn added value to the fine book.[27]

Significantly, however, fine books were seldom bound using traditional handcraft. Apart from a small number of books, usually produced by the San Francisco printers, the great majority of postwar fine books were bound at commercial binderies. Most of these binderies demonstrated especially high standards of workmanship, such as the H. Wolff or E. C. Lewis companies in New York, which bound most of the books printed by the Pynson Printers. Bindings were important to fine editions, certainly, but in this regard distinction from trade books was achieved almost wholly through design rather than production.

Fine printers' relative ambivalence to handcraft in binding is intriguing. Perhaps it simply reflects the centuries-old discontinuity between printing and binding; until the nineteenth century books were sold either unbound or in temporary bindings, because owners were expected to have their books bound professionally to custom specifications. Yet fine printers did not follow their historical mentors in this; they conformed to the modern publishing practice of selling books in finished, bound form. Given the widespread anxiety about modern books' cultural as well as material cheapness, it is odd that fine printers failed to distance themselves from this one obvious dimension of industrial book production. One possible explanation is the traditional dichotomy of labor in bookmaking along lines of gender: while papermakers, compositors, and printers were typically men, binding had become women's work. From the earliest days of the Industrial Revolution, bookbinding relied on female labor, perhaps because folding and sewing were primary tasks. (This also suggests one reason mechanization in binding had lagged somewhat behind that of other book trades: labor costs were considerably cheaper, as women earned roughly half the wages paid to men.[28]) Perhaps fine printers felt less artistic integrity was at stake in bookbinding, that mechanical reproduction of women's labor was less troubling than that of men's work. At least as pertinent, however, must have been economic considerations; hand binding would add considerable production time and cost to the already expensive fine bookmaking enterprise. Finally, too, fine books were meant to be sold to modern buyers, who expected their books to be bound. As long as their bindings conveyed dignity and stature, fine books offered sufficient nuances of handcraft in the other aspects of their making.

Hand labor in the composition of type, however, remained a hallmark of postwar fine bookmaking long after the Monotype and Linotype mechanized typecasting and composing systems debuted in the late 1880s. Because selection and arrangement of type was foremost to a book's typographic integrity, resistance to machine composition continued well into the twenties. At first machine composition allowed only crude adjustments (notably in the distribution of space between words so that a line aligns at both ends, or justifies) and offered only the typefaces commonly used in newspaper and other high-volume printing, the "weak" nineteenth-century typefaces reviled by Morris and his followers. Hand typesetting offered two significant advantages: a more desirable range of typefaces available in foundry fonts, and greater control over spacing and arranging. The meticulous standards enforced at the Laboratory Press, for example, could be achieved only with fastidious hand labor.

When Garnett composed the type for *That Endeth Never,* a fairy tale written for him by a friend, he set the entire slim book in an italic typeface of sixteenth-century origin. Inordinately careful hand labor enabled him to use capital letters of a slightly smaller size than the lowercase to make them less obtrusive, and he used swash characters (those with extended flourishes) judiciously throughout to better justify each line and to enhance the overall decorative quality of the book (see figure 6). Citing both better typeface selection and more control of details, most fine printers snubbed the new technology for failing to satisfy their standards of quality.[29]

In composition as in presswork, however, limited use of machinery gradually gained acceptance in the 1920s, even though the conversion came reluctantly and erratically. After the war, machine composition steadily improved in the variety and quality of available typefaces and in the sophistication of spacing systems, size ranges, and so on. In particular, the Monotype Corporation commissioned "faithful reproductions" of the historical faces fine printers had vigorously argued were superior. The company's publicist, Beatrice Warde, explained that its policy was to put design first, "persuading the machine to produce [good design] perfectly, rather than subordinating the proportions of the face to any supposed limitations of the machine."[30] Those American fine printers most closely associated with commercial production quickly concurred with Warde's assertion that machine composition could rival handsetting. Even as he offered Dwiggins hand composition if necessary for the Lakeside edition of Poe's *Tales,* Kittredge admitted that he preferred Linotype as "the way modern things should be done."[31] Fine printers used machine composition primarily for unpublicized reasons of expediency — economy and speed or, occasionally, because Monotype or Linotype offered better typeface options than did foundry sources.

As the technology and available type designs improved, most arguments insisting on handsetting petered out. Particularly for longer texts, machine composition increasingly offered an alternative whose advantages were hard to resist. In fact, a flurry of new type designs based on historical models and developed for machine composition went hand in hand, somewhat paradoxically, with the boom in fine book production in the 1920s and early 1930s. Fine printers soon worked out rationales and procedures that allowed them to enjoy the convenience of machine composition without sacrificing the care of handcraft. As Richard Ellis explained, "I love to have a book set by hand, and many of our books are, [but] I use the monotype, in our large undertakings, and then carefully go over every page and correct any slight imperfection in spacing, etc." Elmer Adler spoke of a similar strategy when he urged Wharton Esherick, illustrator for the Centaur Press's 1927 edition of *The Song of*

shone under his forehead with Wisdom and Fair Reason, flashing like the swift travel of a falcon.

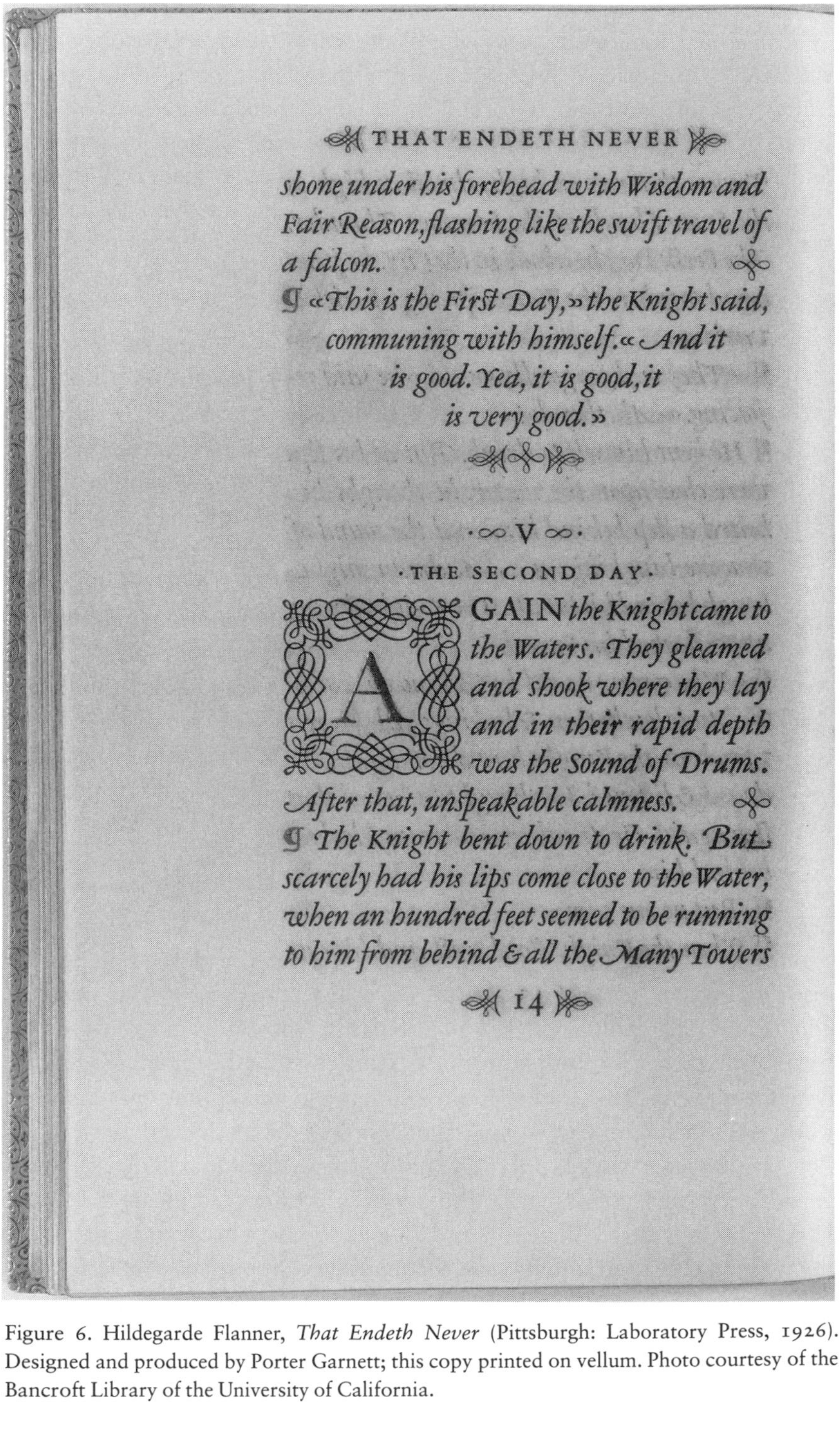

¶ «This is the First Day,» the Knight said, communing with himself.« And it is good. Yea, it is good, it is very good.»

·∞ V ∞·

·THE SECOND DAY·

A GAIN the Knight came to the Waters. They gleamed and shook where they lay and in their rapid depth was the Sound of Drums. After that, unspeakable calmness.

¶ The Knight bent down to drink. But scarcely had his lips come close to the Water, when an hundred feet seemed to be running to him from behind & all the Many Towers

⚜ 14 ⚜

Figure 6. Hildegarde Flanner, *That Endeth Never* (Pittsburgh: Laboratory Press, 1926). Designed and produced by Porter Garnett; this copy printed on vellum. Photo courtesy of the Bancroft Library of the University of California.

of the City seemed leaning over him about to
fall. Again he heard a Voice, as of a Madman weeping into his hands. The Knight
sprang up & drew his Sword.

¶ «Who comes? Who comes?»...But no one
came....There was not even any Echo of a
Madman weeping.

¶ The Knight bent low again to drink. The
air grew heavy with the nearness of an Un-
seen Thing. But the Knight bent low and
drank, looking and listening. When he rose
there was Nothing to be seen, only Himself
reflected there in the Water, the very Image of
his Green Plumes waving, his Sword aloft
in Strength, his Armour gleaming bright,
the whole Knight there rehearsed upon the
Waters, Straight & Sure.

¶ «This is the Second Day,» said the Knight
aloud. «And it is good, yea very good.» But
communing with himself he said, «What
will the Third Day be?» He was tempted

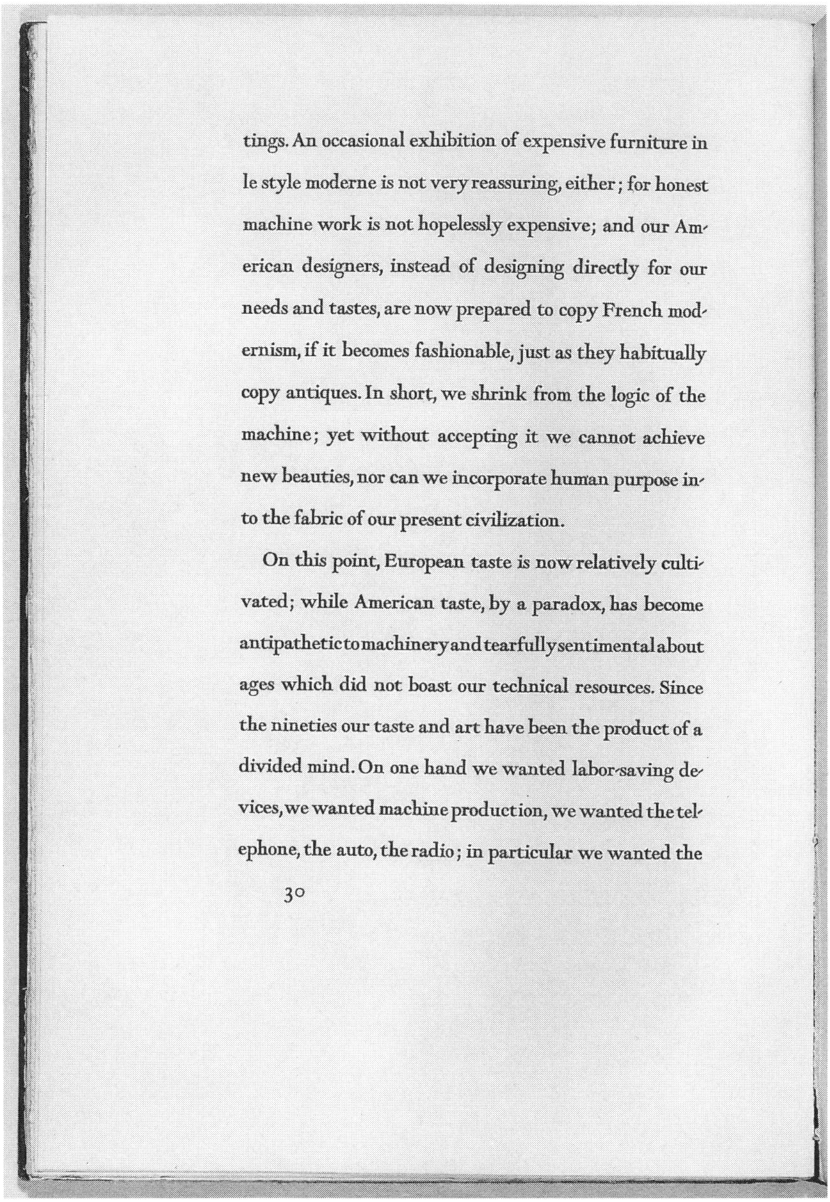

tings. An occasional exhibition of expensive furniture in le style moderne is not very reassuring, either; for honest machine work is not hopelessly expensive; and our American designers, instead of designing directly for our needs and tastes, are now prepared to copy French modernism, if it becomes fashionable, just as they habitually copy antiques. In short, we shrink from the logic of the machine; yet without accepting it we cannot achieve new beauties, nor can we incorporate human purpose into the fabric of our present civilization.

On this point, European taste is now relatively cultivated; while American taste, by a paradox, has become antipathetic to machinery and tearfully sentimental about ages which did not boast our technical resources. Since the nineties our taste and art have been the product of a divided mind. On one hand we wanted labor-saving devices, we wanted machine production, we wanted the telephone, the auto, the radio; in particular we wanted the

30

Figure 7. Lewis Mumford, *American Taste* (San Francisco: Westgate Press, 1929). Designed and produced by Robert Grabhorn and Oscar Lewis. Photo courtesy of Special Collections Division, University of Washington Libraries.

Solomon, to "individualize" the machine-cast typographic ornaments by altering them slightly with his gravers. Adler feared that "too much regularity and machine appearance" would detract from the book's appeal.[32]

Given this largely successful effort to render machine composition acceptable by handwork standards, it is significant that hand composition continued to dominate fine bookmaking in the 1920s, even for books produced in the final few years of the boom market, 1929 to 1932 (see table 1). By that time both Monotype and Linotype offered an excellent selection of well-designed versions of the historical typefaces that fine printers revered. Why, then, were these books composed by hand? Ed Grabhorn candidly admitted that they continued to compose most of their books, even long ones, by hand simply because it was cheaper: they often hired women to do the work, who accepted lower wages.[33] Others offered the argument that hand composition ensured better spacing, but that of course depended on the care that printers took to achieve it; hand composition perhaps enabled ideal spacing, but it certainly did not guarantee it. The Westgate Press 1929 edition of Lewis Mumford's *American Taste,* for example, handset and printed by the Grabhorn Press, includes several exceedingly tight lines (see figure 7).

The best explanation for the persistence of hand composition is that "handcraft" in fine bookmaking came to signal features more ideologically than aesthetically meaningful. It became a sign more of value than of quality per se. Hand production, with its emphases on costly materials and small edition sizes, therefore became one of fine books' primary products for sale. Hand production in fact accomplished two ends that were as important commercially as aesthetically: in theory it set natural limits to the quantity that could be produced, and it yielded a product that sold human presence or skill rather than mechanical efficiency.

Accordingly, several other features of fine bookmaking conveyed similar gestures of handcraft. Most expensive and uncommon was hand artwork. Despite the high costs, a small number of fine editions featured hand embellishments, most with calligraphed opening initials, reminiscent of scribal practices, or hand-colored illustrations (see table 1). Sometimes such handwork yielded deluxe copies available for a higher price, as when ninety-five copies of the 1928 Random House edition of *Candide,* illustrated to great acclaim by Rockwell Kent, were offered with illustrations hand-colored by workers following color templates prepared by Kent.[34] A portion of the edition of John Gay's eighteenth-century essay *Rural Sports,* published by Rudge, was similarly offered with hand-watercolored versions of the illustrations by Gordon Ross, and Rimington and Hooper's 1929 edition of Voltaire's *Zadig* was available with hand-colored Valenti Angelo illustrations. Sometimes the entire

THE PALETTE KNIFE

BY

CHRISTOPHER MORLEY

illustrated by RENÉ GOCKINGA, published

by THE CHOCORUA PRESS, at Chelsea,

NEW YORK and made by the Pynson Printers

in the year nineteen hundred and twenty-nine

YOU WON'T MIND if this smells a bit of kerosene

and turpentine and linseed oil; because I have just, very

Figure 8. Christopher Morley, *The Palette Knife* (New York, Chocorua Press, 1929). Illustrated in original watercolors by René Gockinga; designed and produced by Elmer Adler, Pynson Printers. Photo courtesy of Princeton University Library.

edition of a fine book featured original (not printed) art. In the most extravagant instance, each copy of *The Palette Knife,* a short story by Christopher Morley produced by the Pynson Printers for the Chocorua Press in 1929, featured a series of six original watercolor paintings by René Gockinga, as well as a title page that depicted an artist's palette knife dripping blotches of real red paint down the page, between the opening lines of text (see figure 8).

Hand embellishments were a trademark of the Grabhorn Press in the mid- and late 1920s while Valenti Angelo served as resident artist. For twenty-five dollars a week he provided whatever artistic services were needed; most commonly this meant drawings or woodcuts to illustrate the press's books. Sharing Ed Grabhorn's fondness for things medieval, he expanded his role into "illumination" — manually adding ornamented initials, rubrication, marginal decorations, and color to printed woodcuts. Owners of the medieval fictional account of the *Voiage and Travaile of Sir John Maundevile* (published by Random House in 1928), for example, were treated to pages that Angelo had lovingly adorned with red, blue, and metallic gold inks, just as late medieval scribes had completed many of the earliest printed books (see figure 9).

Original art or hand embellishment was the rarest and most extravagant form of inscribing the human endeavor upon which fine printing was premised. Most books delivered that aura of handcraft in less literal and labor-intensive ways; the best single source was handmade paper. Its use said little about the skills of the printer, of course, except perhaps in dampening the paper, but it implied a knowledge of and commitment to the highest standards of bookmaking. Indeed, handmade paper was an index of a fine book's fineness. William Morris contended that "hand-made paper, with its infelicities of rough edges, hard face, and uneven size and thickness, is more trustworthy than that made by machine." He preferred it in part because it virtually compelled the hand bookmaking that he prized: for best results, "you must wet the paper and print upon a hand-press by the old methods."[35]

Porter Garnett concurred. He warned that machine-made paper not only betrayed the critical spirit of handcraft but also confounded efforts to achieve fine results (in mechanical papermaking, fibers align along one direction of the sheet only, yielding a strong grain that makes the paper curl badly and cockle when dampened and resist folding in the opposite direction). Probably more than any other feature, handmade paper emphatically declared material difference in a book (see table 1). Even so, because the use of handmade paper requires financial resources more than actual skills, this paper is a relatively unexacting token of the handmade aura so coveted among bibliophiles.

Handmade paper's expense was often daunting, however, and here as in other matters a machine-aided compromise was available. So-called mould-made paper offered the look and something of the qualities of handmade at a cost closer to that of machine-made paper. Mouldmade paper is created by a machine that approximates the hand papermaking process, yielding features of handmade paper such as watermarks and deckle edges, and it is commonly made from higher-grade rag pulp instead of the wood pulp of industrially made paper. Predictably, though, Garnett scorned it. "Style and character at their utmost are peculiar (for reasons that have to do with the methods of manufacture) to hand-made paper only." Mouldmade was simply "imitation paper," he pronounced. "Ideally, then, the fine book, in the fullest and strictest sense of the term, can be printed on no other than paper that is hand-made and of the best quality."[36] Yet most fine printers trying to earn a living necessarily saw the situation in less absolute terms; virtually all the fine printers and outen begynnyge and withouten endynge; that is, with outen qualitee, good, and with outen quantytee, gret; that in alle places is present, and alle thinges conteynynge; the whiche that no goodnesse may amende, ne non evelle empeyre; that in perfeyte Trynytee lyvethe and regnethe God, be alle Worldes and be alle tymes. AMEN, AMEN, AMEN.

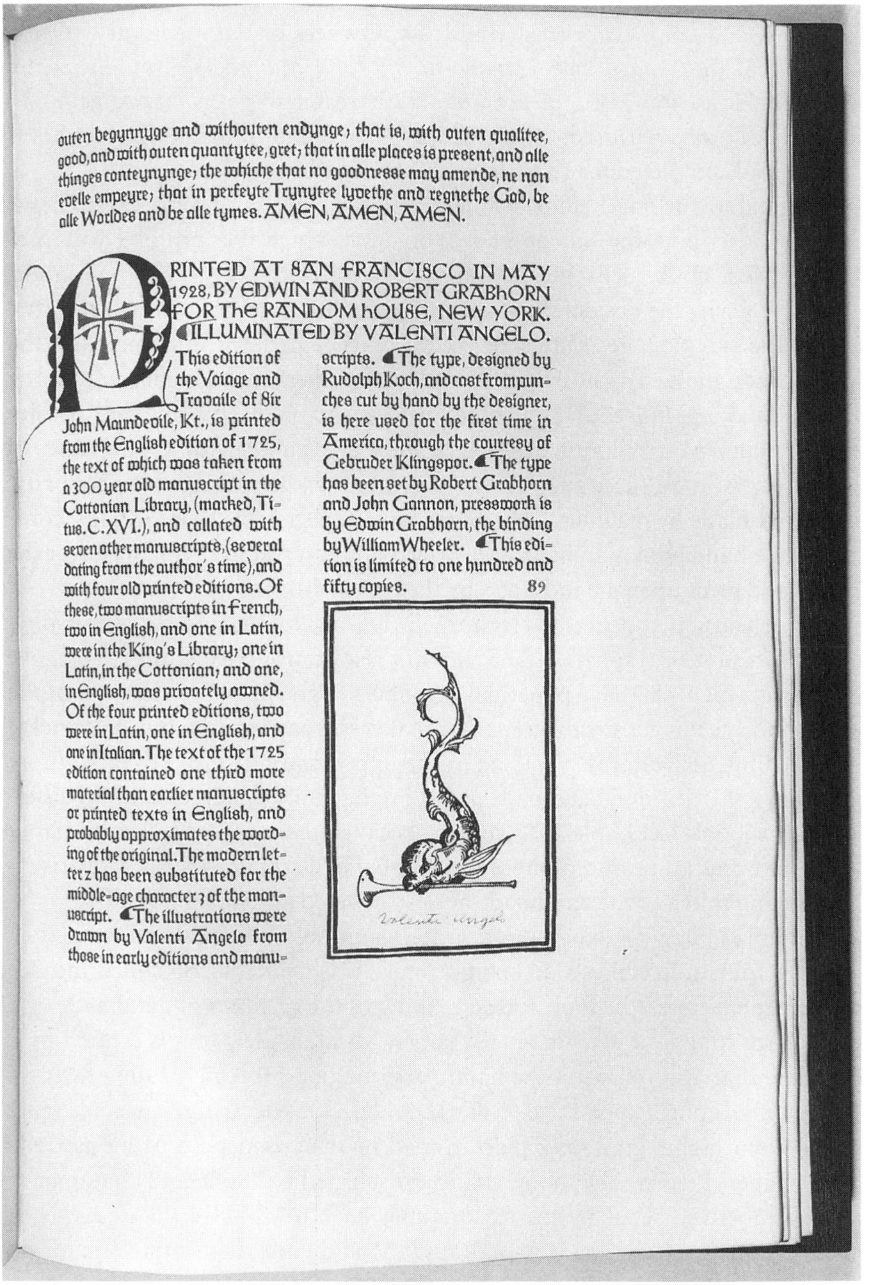

RINTED AT SAN FRANCISCO IN MAY 1928, BY EDWIN AND ROBERT GRABhORN FOR ThE RANDOM hOUSE, NEW YORK. ILLUMINATED BY VALENTI ANGELO.

This edition of the Voiage and Travaile of Sir John Maundevile, Kt., is printed from the English edition of 1725, the text of which was taken from a 300 year old manuscript in the Cottonian Library, (marked, Titus. C. XVI.), and collated with seven other manuscripts, (several dating from the author's time), and with four old printed editions. Of these, two manuscripts in French, two in English, and one in Latin, were in the King's Library; one in Latin, in the Cottonian; and one, in English, was privately owned. Of the four printed editions, two were in Latin, one in English, and one in Italian. The text of the 1725 edition contained one third more material than earlier manuscripts or printed texts in English, and probably approximates the wording of the original. The modern letter z has been substituted for the middle-age character ȝ of the manuscript. The illustrations were drawn by Valenti Angelo from those in early editions and manuscripts. The type, designed by Rudolph Koch, and cast from punches cut by hand by the designer, is here used for the first time in America, through the courtesy of Gebruder Klingspor. The type has been set by Robert Grabhorn and John Gannon, presswork is by Edwin Grabhorn, the binding by William Wheeler. This edition is limited to one hundred and fifty copies.

89

Figure 9. *The Voiage and Travaile of Sir John Maundevile, Kt. . . .* (New York: Random House, 1928). Illustrated by Valenti Angelo; designed and produced by Edwin and Robert Grabhorn. Photo courtesy of Special Collections Division, University of Washington Libraries.

publishers of the day produced at least a few books printed on mouldmade papers.

A more subtle feature of distinguishing craft was the assurance, via the colophon, that a book had been "printed from type." This phrase informs the reader that the printer did not follow the common trade practice of making hard-metal electrotypes of assembled pages of type. Electrotypes enabled more copies to be printed without deterioration of quality, and they could be stored and used again if additional copies were ever needed, avoiding the expense of recomposing the type. It seems counterintuitive, however, that a fine book, whose edition size was invariably limited, would *not* be printed from type. The statement thus suggests that some fine printers were using electrotypes, perhaps to preserve their foundry type from wear. But most of the books bearing this phrase were composed by machine. Perhaps printing from the type itself was seen to mitigate the compromise of using machine composition, or perhaps the phrase conveyed a commitment to give a book's owners "the real thing," pages printed from the type composed for it. Ellis declared that at the Georgian Press "we always print from type, even in our hand set books — I have an aversion to electrotypes and will not use them." The phrase became another way to register devotion to historically authentic sources of quality in bookmaking.[37]

In at least one other way fine printers conveyed difference in the material production of their books. Bookmakers commonly wrote a number in each copy of their books, a practice that established a distinct, if minimal, link between a book's maker and its owner. Typically, the number was inscribed on the colophon or "limit statement" page. Assigning each copy a unique number underscored the limited size of the edition, ostensibly clarifying its rarity and consequent value to collectors. But the practice also delivered a modicum of hand production. This single feature was admittedly a small gesture toward "fineness," but it reinforced bibliophilic aspirations, especially when composition and printing were likely to be machine-derived (see table 1).

Ideal Imperfections

Attention to handwork focused on achieving both the ideal book as Morris and Garnett defined it and a humanistic alternative to the sterile "perfection" of mechanized production. Paradoxically, human-made perfection was most admired for the tiny *im*perfections that distinguish it from the unvarying sameness — however technically masterful — of machine work. Bruce Rogers warned that "if the mark of the tool has been superseded by the marklessness of the machine, it merely means that another humane element has disappeared out of the world." David Greenhood, a Laboratory Press graduate, similarly lauded fine printing's "kindly faults" and "genial humanity," "relaxing it from the rigidities of perfection." Bibliophiles often found something cold and even insolent in the precision of mechanical typesetting; like medieval tapestry weavers, they cherished the tiny flaws that revealed human labor. One enthusiast jubilantly noted that he had spotted a "character turned wrong" in a Pynson Printers book, speculating that it may have been Adler's deliberate way of keeping the book from being "perfect."[38]

One consequence of this paradox was an occasional ambivalence about the quality of hand production work. Most fine printers naturally understood that only excellent bookmaking would keep them in business. Above all this meant well-composed type (without unsightly gaps between words, typos, scratched or broken letters, and so on) and well-printed pages (consistent inking and impression throughout). At times, however, the human energy that ensured such care flagged. Copies of the Fountain Press edition of James Joyce's *Haveth Childers Everywhere* and the Windsor Press edition of the *Ballads of Villon* are both poorly printed, for example, marred by uneven inking. The Windsor Press's edition of Rudyard Kipling's *Legs of Sister Ursula* reveals a different problem; the linoleum cut illustration on its title page has been damaged, leaving a noticeable gap in the middle of a flower's stem. Most notorious for erratic production quality, however, were the Grabhorn brothers. Their books could encompass dazzling care and skill, or they could be flawed by elementary oversights. Bibliographer David Magee claimed that most of their books had at least one typo, and some were plagued by peeling ink and especially by stiff or cracked bindings. Roby Wentz noted that the Grabhorns could be "careless, even sloppy, in their presswork. On an off-day Ed would growl, 'Hell, that's good enough'" and whatever resulted would have to suffice. Even Bob Grabhorn conceded that their presswork was of uneven quality: "We were never what you could call finicky."[39]

The Grabhorns understood that patrons eagerly sought their books in spite of these small vagaries, and even to some degree because of them. This attitude toward imperfections prompted one of the harshest criticisms of fine printing: it indulged a sentimental "worship" of flaws that achieved character at the expense of function. These critics, notably Holbrook Jackson and to a lesser extent Paul Johnston, drew upon ideas most memorably expressed by Thorstein Veblen in his landmark polemic, *The Theory of the Leisure Class*. Published in 1899, Veblen's indictment of adulated handcraft described with uncanny perceptiveness several aspects of fine printing's appeal more than twenty years later. "The point of material difference between machine-made goods and the hand-wrought goods which serve the same purposes is, ordinarily, that the former serve their primary purpose more adequately. . . . Commonly, if not invariably, the honorific marks of hand labor are certain imperfections and irregularities in the lines of the hand-wrought article, showing where the workman has fallen short in the execution of the design. The ground of the superiority of hand-wrought goods, therefore, is a certain margin of crudeness. This margin must never be so wide as to show bungling workmanship, since that would be evidence of low cost, nor so narrow as to suggest the ideal precision attained only by the machine, for that would be evidence of low cost." Veblen protested the "exaltation of the defective" in the perception that handmade goods were more beautiful and valuable than their machine-made counterparts. He particularly chastised Ruskin and Morris for an eager "propaganda of crudity and wasted effort" in the revival of hand bookcraft. To Veblen, Kelmscott books illustrated the "predatory" canon of taste that holds that "the product, if it is beautiful, must also at the same time be costly and ill adapted to its ostensible use."[40]

Three decades later the *Saturday Review of Literature* remarked with less acidity but similar astuteness on the relative values assigned to the machine-made and the handmade. An editorial pointed to the boom in fine bookmaking, with its featured dedication to handcraft, as part of a larger postwar social and literary phenomenon. "No sooner had machine made goods triumphed than people of taste began to collect the hand made in rugs and furniture, and soon the wealthy followed, until now . . . there is a better market than ever before, and handiwork, in a machine age, is actually increasing. Something of the same kind is happening in literature. The little theatres, poetical renaissances, limited editions, cult writers, coteries — these are all signs of a revival in the 'hand made' in literature, made possible by the greater wealth and greater leisure resulting from the use of machines."[41]

The last remark pointed to an irony that troubles virtually every aspect of postwar fine printing. The fine book cult was able to exalt handcraft only by exploiting aspects of the machine culture that it purported to resist. For patrons this paradox typically rested in the source of their wealth, and for producers it derived from their tacit, pragmatic accommodation of machinery. As the *Saturday Review* editorial continued, its words were eerily applicable to the fine printing craze: "this fostered state of literature . . . has a museum smell to it. It is a little like that Tudor Gothic of American universities which, made possible by profits from machines, and practicable because it is a casing upon a framework of machined steel, has no more relation to the life that uses it than any other imitation of the past. Which is obviously not to question its possible value as architecture, but to challenge its vitality as an expression of anything current in life."[42]

Masters of the Machine

The growing use of machinery in their work did indeed bother many fine printers, but not for the reasons expounded by Veblen and his followers. They worried that acceptance, however wary, of machinery threatened to subordinate the human role in production—anathema to most bibliophiles. A modified philosophy emerged, voiced most clearly, if plaintively, by Rollins. Anguished by what he saw as the dehumanizing forces of industrialism, he persistently viewed the machine as an inhuman adversary that threatened to usurp the worker's role and identity. Ironically, he was employed to supervise machine-based production at Yale University Press. Facing the situation as constructively as possible, however, he developed a more accommodating philosophy that recognized the place of machines in the printshop—a place ever subordinate to the printer's. The modern printer must accept the machine, he reluctantly conceded, but only as a tool to be controlled utterly by its *master's* human will and judgment. "Much as I dislike slavery," he wrote, "I much prefer that the machine should be my slave than my master." The key for Rollins was not to disavow the machine but to exert absolute mastery over it. "When I am surrounded by type cases & printing-machinery which is so simple that I am fully aware of exactly what each part of it is doing throughout its whole cycle, so simple that I can . . . dissect & reassemble it, or have it repaired by local mechanics; when I am free . . . from the necessity of hiring a high-priced hand to operate that machine at requisite efficiency; then I am the master of the machine, and it accomplishes what I want to have it do."[43]

This notion of fine printers as masters of the machine, although formulated to include machine management in their repertoire of skills, ironically facilitated a subtle but far greater shift. As fine printers surrendered basic components of actual production processes to machinery they gained in professional stature. Once viewed as artisans with the skills to make a book, they were soon regarded as figures with the knowledge and power to make others (machines and their operators) produce books at their direction. This more abstract managerial sense of fine printing dovetailed nicely with the other ways in which the new typographic profession took shape in the twenties. With each ascending credential of knowledge, cultural refinement, and taste, fine printers moved further from the "hands on" skills associated with actual printing. Several printers "cast handicraft twaddle aside," as critic Paul Johnston approvingly put it, and became experts increasingly distinguished by what they knew, not by what they could do. Fine printers became *designers* or *typographers* rather than *printers* per se. Even though it remained ideologically paramount, the Ruskinian notion of handcraft soon seemed too romantically quaint, too narrow in vision and scope, to convey what postwar fine printing ultimately aimed to accomplish. A young protégé of Garnett's wrote that the ideal book could only "emanate from the efforts of a single person . . . a scholar-artist-printer." Upon devising a plan for a book, this person would "work only as a supervisor" in guiding "competent craftsmen" to carry out instructions. "Now that the word 'craft' has been appropriated by designers of lamp-shades," declared Frederic Warde, "we are coming to speak of the typographer's profession as we do of the architect's: for in each case we ask an expert to solve certain structural problems by using his acquired knowledge and inherent good taste."[44]

This model increasingly prevailed. In fact, several of the era's best-known fine "printers" could not or would not operate a printing press in anything more than a rudimentary way. Garnett, Adler, and Nash — those who most ardently exalted the cultural importance of printing — lead this group. Adler proudly noted that his role was to plan, orchestrate, and supervise subordinates' work: "I have never put two pieces of type together . . . it has not been necessary for me to actually work at production." Garnett did not compose his first stick of type until three years after he launched the Laboratory Press. He explained that his "relation to bookmaking in the past had always been more or less indirect; that is to say, the mechanical part has always been done by other hands." Even Bruce Rogers, who virtually defined the new profession of typographer or book designer, could neither set type nor print with any special skill; his time and talents were devoted to conceptual artistry that others were to execute. Rogers's services were so exalted that one publisher paid six hundred dollars for his meticulous design of a single title page — a sum equivalent to three months' salary of the skilled workers who actually composed the page.[45]

Even fine printers who were skilled craftsmen usually delegated production responsibilities to others. Joseph FauntLeRoy, John Henry Nash's talented and scrupulous shop superintendent, admitted that the myth that Nash composed the type for his books was just that, a "legend that it was profitable to perpetuate." In truth, as Nash's biographer Robert Harlan has pointed out, "after having decided on the format of a book and after having set its title page, dedication, colophon, and a sample subtitle and running head, Nash turned over all further responsibility for composition and presswork to FauntLeRoy." Actual printing of Nash's books was farmed out to several Bay Area printing firms. For many modern fine printers, as for Morris, Ruskin's ideal of unified art and labor was largely illusion.[46] Despite the stirring rhetoric, it was the "roughness" and "majesty" of the master's soul that was to be expressed, not that of those who actually composed and printed the books.

This division between art (or design) and labor was not a modern hypocrisy, however, but a concept openly modeled by typographic masters of previous centuries. Modern printers emulated their historical counterparts, pointing to a noble tradition of great scholar-craftsmen such as Aldus Manutius in fifteenth-century Venice, Johannes Froben in sixteenth-century Basel, and others who had presided over salonlike ateliers where great authors, artists, editors, and printers mingled and collaborated. Garnett, Adler, Rudge, and to some extent Updike clearly embraced this model, but Nash exploited it most deftly; one admirer fawningly dubbed him the "Aldus of San Francisco." The vigorous historicism pervasive throughout modern fine printing and this authoritative human "master" thus helped to counterpose the dominant machine culture of the day. This alternative model, in turn, ironically helped rationalize the use of machinery by dismissing it as merely an expedient option — neither intrinsically desirable nor necessarily definitive — available to the professional fine printer, upon whose authoritative discretion its use presumably depended.

Fine printing thus distanced itself both from mechanization in principle and from actual craft in practice. Not everyone welcomed this development. Most persistently iconoclastic were the Grabhorn brothers. Their shop was no shrine but a cluttered, often chaotic jumble of projects in various stages from composing stick to press to folding table. In 1928 the press personnel published a good-natured protest in *Publishers' Weekly* against the elevation of printing from a craft into an art, which brought with it new rules and canons arbitrated by critics. Until recently, they wrote wryly, customers "were actually selecting books according to their own tastes and enthusiasms." They called for a return to less pretentious times, when printers were printers rather than typographers, and when they had only to please themselves and their patrons, not the new critics.[47]

Despite such occasional debunking of the aggrandizement of their work, for most fine printers the enterprise became intellectualized, a product of serious study, art, and inspiration. For craftsman and designer alike, the heart of the work remained its assertion of human judgment and skill over machine-defined production. "A machine cannot create," declared Ed Grabhorn, "it can only assist, directed by the mind and imagination. The more that is left to the machine, the worse the work."[48] Fine printing exalted human creative will over mechanistic determinism and sameness, but it did so more through pronouncement and gestures of handcraft than through actual abstinence from machine-based production processes.

4

Gilded Goblets
Strategies of Fine Design

The evening's speaker had captured the London audience's attention long before she spoke a word. There was a tinge of illicit glamor to Beatrice Warde, the young expatriate American who had left her husband to work with the great Stanley Morison, himself still married to an absent, ill wife somewhere in the country. Usually the only professional woman at the august gatherings of the British Typographers Guild, Warde relished the attention she drew, not for her scandalous personal life (of which nothing was openly said) but for her aggressive American "charm" (of which much was said) and her stunning eloquence. When chosen in 1928 to respond to the toast at the first Ladies' Night at Stationers' Hall, home of the venerable 400-year-old Worshipful Company of Stationers, she had gleefully confessed that she planned a very brief reply: "just enough to show that I have on a perfectly ravishing new evening frock — black chiffon, all over black crystal beads, which makes me look like Greta Garbo, especially with orchids on the shoulder." She saw little point to a longer speech, "for all they'll hear of it while they're feasting their eyes."[1]

Warde was older and a bit wiser when, four years later, she stood to address the guild. Her words, not her daring outfit or animated gestures, immortalized the evening. "Imagine that you have before you a flagon of wine," she directed her rapt listeners. "You may choose your own favorite vintage for this imaginary demonstration, so that it be a deep shimmering crimson in color. You have two goblets before you. One is of solid gold, wrought in the most exquisite patterns. The other is of crystal-clear glass," she declared, raising high her thumb and forefinger as if pinching the delicate stem of a glass, "thin as a bubble, and as transparent. Pour and drink; and according to your choice of goblet I shall know whether or not you are a connoisseur of wine. For if you have no feelings about wine one way or the other, you will want the sensation of drinking the stuff out of a vessel that may have cost ten thousand dollars; but if you are a member of that vanishing tribe, the amateurs of fine vintages, you will choose the crystal, because everything about it is calculated to *reveal* rather than to hide the beautiful thing which it was meant to *contain*."[2]

Beatrice Warde's famous crystal goblet metaphor captured her generation's most potent and enduring typographic ethic.[3] By the end of the 1920s it had become a truism that typography should be the transparent medium through which an author's words would reach readers clearly and directly. New traditionalism (as critic Robin Kinross terms it) insisted on functional simplicity achieved through utter adherence to familiar, historically sanctioned designs. Book typography "requires an obedience to convention which is almost absolute," pronounced Stanley Morison, its leading spokesman. Anything in a book's appearance that reminds the reader of its design is impudent, wrote Paul Johnston; another critic chastised the "impertinence of self-expression."[4]

Of course, typography is never invisible; it is necessarily a filter through which a reader perceives a text. "Typography is to literature as musical performance is to composition," writes poet-typographer Robert Bringhurst. Just as we hear music only by listening to a particular performance of it, we read a text only by viewing a typographic presentation of it. Typography, then, is "an essential act of interpretation, full of endless opportunities for insight or obtuseness." It becomes invisible not through some neutral objectivity (which is impossible) but by its compelling rightness: when typography subtly steers the reader toward appropriate, accurate, or empathetic perceptions of textual meaning and purpose, when it successfully effaces (but does not neglect) its own interpretive enterprise, it is invisible.[5] What makes typography visible, then, is dissonance between the visual and the textual messages.

The mandate of invisibility repudiated nineteenth-century book design as ugly, thoughtless, and intrusive; modern books were to be uncluttered, cleansed of their Victorian commotion of mixed type styles and ornamental frippery and recast in sober, quiet, purposeful design. The new design principles denounced the forms of nineteenth-century books for their subservience to the machines that produced them and to the tastes of the "masses" who bought them. It is true that the thin, fine strokes of Victorian typefaces were well suited for industrial production: their delicate forms required (or allowed) only a slight moment of contact with the paper in the printing process, and their minimal surface area was well served by the thinned inks that enabled the high-speed machine presses to run most efficiently. But by the 1880s many thought book pages looked anemic, their texts a furtive, diluted gray that seemed to float on the page.[6] It is also true that Victorian typography was unusually generous with "white space" between lines, after punctuation, and even between letters, and commonly positioned each text block in the center of its page, creating a wide unprinted column down the center of an opened book (see figure 10). This practice was partly economic in that publishers sometimes bulked out texts to justify higher prices, but the extra space was also a significant concession to the throngs of less skilled readers who joined the ranks of book buyers as machine production made books more plentiful and less costly.

Protesting these Victorian practices, the English private press revival of the 1890s presented alternatives. Revivalists called for new attention to materials, renewed attention to craftsmanship, and especially new typographic standards. They rejected much of Victorian book design as no design at all, merely a capitulation to mechanical and commercial demands. In keeping with the preindustrial, craft-based production methods they advocated, revivalists' design principles were modeled on medieval and renaissance typography. William Morris's mentor, Emery Walker, distilled these principles into a few tenets that had become widely accepted among typographic enthusiasts by the 1920s. He preached unity, balance, and symmetry. This meant, for example, that two facing pages should be treated as a single element, that density of color created by type, images, or ornaments must be balanced across both pages. He advocated heavier, darker letterforms set closely together in the line, reduced space between the lines, and a smaller gutter or center margin to give the pages a more solid, robust, and integrated appearance.

Morris's interpretation of Walker's design prescriptions hit the book world as something of a bombshell. Morris's taste for all things medieval led him to pre-1500 books as models. The types he designed for his books were based on some of the earliest gothic, or "blackletter" types and on the roman type used by Nicolas Jenson in Venice in the 1470s — which was one of the first versions of the new Renaissance style of letter. The lavish woodcut borders on many of Morris's page spreads similarly echoed gothic incunabula, as did his densely fitted rectangles of type, dazzling black inks, and sculptural impressions into handmade papers (see figure 11). Other revival presses turned to equally revered but less archaic-looking Renaissance models for inspiration.

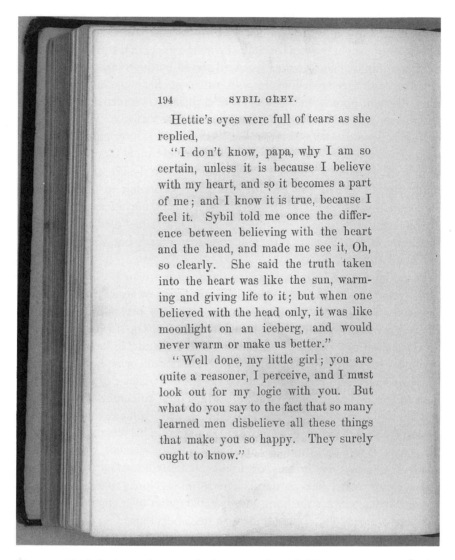

194   SYBIL GREY.

Hettie's eyes were full of tears as she replied,

"I do n't know, papa, why I am so certain, unless it is because I believe with my heart, and so it becomes a part of me; and I know it is true, because I feel it. Sybil told me once the difference between believing with the heart and the head, and made me see it, Oh, so clearly. She said the truth taken into the heart was like the sun, warming and giving life to it; but when one believed with the head only, it was like moonlight on an iceberg, and would never warm or make us better."

"Well done, my little girl; you are quite a reasoner, I perceive, and I must look out for my logic with you. But what do you say to the fact that so many learned men disbelieve all these things that make you so happy. They surely ought to know."

Figure 10. Typical nineteenth-century book typography (*Sybil Grey; or, a Year in the City* [New York: American Tract Society, n.d.]).

By the 1920s, however, a huge and obvious gap yawned between typographic invisibility and the models provided by revival reformers. To contemporary eyes such pages were acutely visible. But to reformers, nineteenth-century tastes and practices, though familiar, were the anomaly; revivalist principles simply returned to the path from which Victorians had strayed.

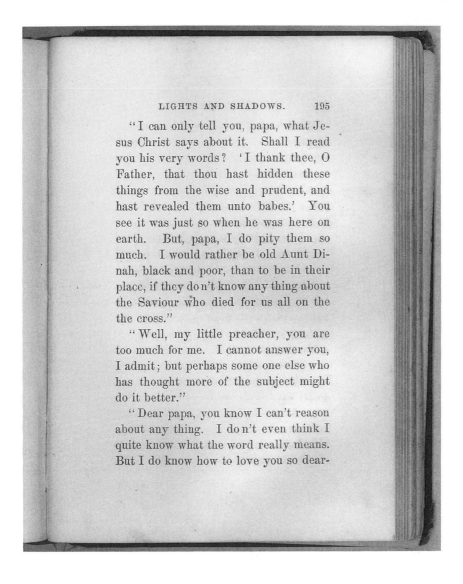

LIGHTS AND SHADOWS.   195

"I can only tell you, papa, what Jesus Christ says about it. Shall I read you his very words? 'I thank thee, O Father, that thou hast hidden these things from the wise and prudent, and hast revealed them unto babes.' You see it was just so when he was here on earth. But, papa, I do pity them so much. I would rather be old Aunt Dinah, black and poor, than to be in their place, if they don't know any thing about the Saviour who died for us all on the the cross."

"Well, my little preacher, you are too much for me. I cannot answer you, I admit; but perhaps some one else who has thought more of the subject might do it better."

"Dear papa, you know I can't reason about any thing. I don't even think I quite know what the word really means. But I do know how to love you so dear-

Reformers believed that their alternatives, sanctioned by hundreds of years of historical practice, were so self-evidently superior that they would indeed become transparent in their natural rightness once readers' eyes adjusted to the differences. It was merely a matter of time. Ideally, the pioneering work of fine books was to resurrect and model the better, more authentic typography.

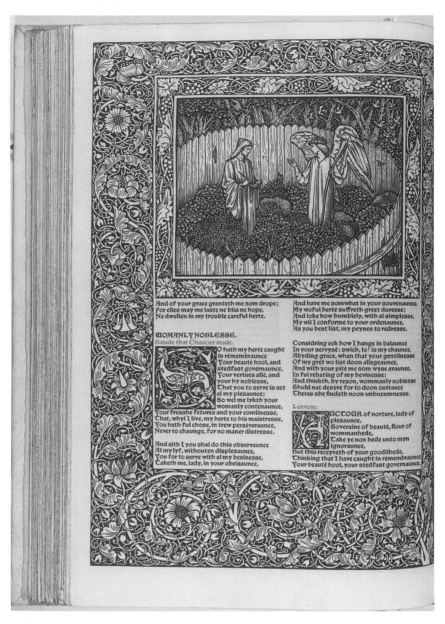

Figure 11. *The Works of Chaucer* (Kelmscott Press, 1896). Illustrated by Edward Burne-Jones; designed and produced by William Morris. Photo courtesy of the Bancroft Library of the University of California.

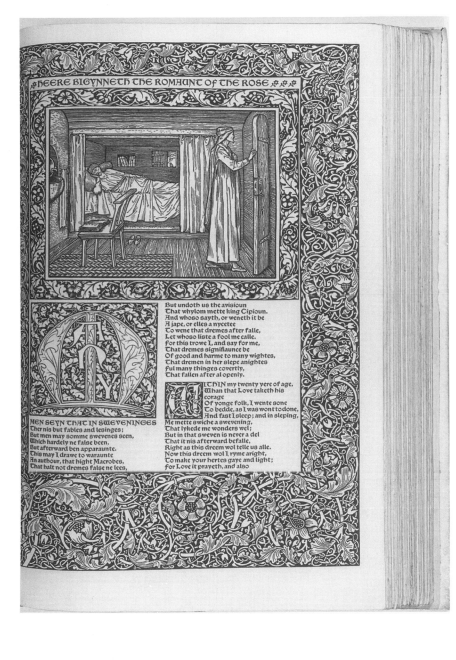

HEERE BIGYNNETH THE ROMAUNT OF THE ROSE

But undoth us the avisioun
That whylom mette king Cipioun.
And whoso sayth, or weneth it be
A jape, or elles a nycetee
To wene that dremes after falle,
Let whoso liste a fool me calle.
For this trowe I, and say for me,
That dremes signifiaunce be
Of good and harme to many wightes,
That dremen in her slepe anightes
Ful many thinges covertly,
That fallen after al openly.

MEN SEYN THAT IN SWEVENINGES
Ther nis but fables and lesinges;
But men may somme swevenes seen,
Which hardely ne false been,
But afterward ben apparaunte.
This may I drawe to waraunte
An authour, that hight Macrobes,
That halt not dremes false ne lees,

WITHIN my twenty yere of age,
Whan that Love taketh his
corage
Of yonge folk, I wente sone
To bedde, as I was wont to done,
And fast I sleep; and in sleping,
Me mette swiche a swevening,
That lykede me wonders wel;
But in that sweven is never a del
That it nis afterward befalle,
Right as this dreem wol telle us alle.
Now this dreem wol I ryme aright,
To make your hertes gaye and light;
For Love it prayeth, and also

Table 2. *General Design Features*

	1920–26	1927–28	1929	1930	1931–32	All	% of Known
Total books	61	67	65	66	41	300	
Historical origin, inspiration of type							
16th century or before	31	27	20	14	12	104	39.1
17th and 18th centuries	12	18	22	28	17	97	36.5
19th century	10	12	14	6	6	48	18
20th century	1	7	3	5	1	17	6.4
Not known (11.3%)	7	3	6	13	5	34	
Printed ink color(s)							
Black plus 3 or more	0	8	2	2	3	15	6.7
Black plus 2	10	3	4	6	1	24	10.7
Black plus 1	21	24	21	20	17	103	45.8
Black only	16	16	19	22	10	83	36.9
Not known (25%)	14	16	19	16	10	75	
Leather/vellum in binding							
Full leather, all copies	3	4	3	2	3	15	5.5
Full leather, some copies	1	0	0	2	0	3	1.1
Part leather, all copies	3	7	5	6	6	27	9.8
Part leather, some copies	3	0	0	3	1	7	2.7
Leather label only	0	1	1	1	2	4	1.5
No leather	43	52	50	45	29	219	79.6
Not known (8.3%)	8	3	6	7	1	25	

Fine design, paradoxically, featured the typographic strategies and judgments deemed most effective in achieving that discreet but powerful transparency.

This reform project was stymied, however, by a problem with type—the defining element of any printed work. Revivalists had solved the problem by commissioning proprietary types designed and cast exclusively for their private use. After the war, most reform-inspired printers had neither the resources nor the desire to operate so privately; they wanted to broadcast their work and ideals to the typographic culture of the day. But before they could initiate their bibliophilic renaissance, they needed to acquire the styles of type considered intrinsic to the reform impulse. They needed supplies of the types used in preindustrial bookmaking.

To meet this demand and help advance the reform effort, throughout the 1920s a gallery of new types based on historical models emerged. It is no small irony that they came primarily from Monotype and Linotype companies, although traditional foundries such as the American Type Founders (ATF) similarly issued new faces based on types from the fifteenth through the eighteenth centuries. The names of these types bespoke their historical genesis, immortalizing the original designer, the printer who first or most often used it, or the title or author of the book that provided the model. Most of these now-digitized typefaces remain stalwarts of book composition today, so that just as in the 1920s even the most casual user of type is familiar with the names of the major figures in Western typography, however unwittingly. Among the most enduring have been *Bembo* and *Centaur* (and its companion italic *Arrighi*), based on the earliest fifteenth-century Venetian roman letterforms; several versions of types cut by the sixteenth-century Frenchman Claude *Garamond;* eighteenth-century English types of William *Caslon* and John *Baskerville;* and the neoclassical types of Frenchman Pierre-Simon *Fournier* and Italian printer Giambattista *Bodoni.*[7] It is difficult to imagine the course of twentieth-century typography without these resurrected types; postwar fine designers depended heavily on these new, historically derived typefaces (table 2).

In theory, then, fine books were to lead the way toward a more beautiful, dignified, and authentic typography, to introduce new norms that would soon become invisible through their intrinsic superiority. Yet almost from the start, most recognized that fine design clearly, even emphatically, exceeded the dictates of transparency, and soon it was tacitly exempted from the dogma it purportedly advanced. While clear, simple, conventional typography was prescribed for books for the masses, something more "artful," more embellished, was not only acceptable but welcome in books for the few. Fine books could retain the "extras" because in a skilled designer's hands they would be meaningful, part of the artistic package. The distinction rested in a presumed though seldom-spoken divergence of function: for connoisseurs of books, as distinct from readers, typography was in fact what one looked *for* and looked *at,* not merely *through.* Virtually everyone involved in the world of fine books in the 1920s and 1930s accepted this double standard, if only implicitly. The crucial — if cynical — point was that postwar fine books were both produced and purchased to be *owned* more than to be *read.* More than mere books per se, they were exquisitely self-conscious objects of "bookness"; the vessel was the whole point, and the more radiant, striking, or distinctive it was, the more memorably that point was made.

So what did fine books look and feel like? How were revivalist design principles applied, adapted, or perverted? The answers naturally defy any blithe generalizations. The books' content ranged from ancient biblical stories to bibliographies of modern authors, from Virgil to James Joyce, from political treatises to whimsical erotica, and their material and visual forms ranged in similarly dizzying scope. Despite these differences, however, virtually all were exalted material objects meant above all to signal the traditional cultural values at the core of typographic reform. This purpose was expressed in three major approaches to fine book design. First were the efforts to recreate and publicize features of preindustrial typography — whose history offered a new aesthetic vocabulary and new models of how books should look and function. Second, designers used that historicized visual vocabulary to articulate a fresh, even personal, interpretive presentation, defining the new in terms of its affinity with and appreciative mastery of the old. The third approach sought primarily to construct iconic, monumental forms of the book per se — often at the expense of textual considerations. These three broad strategies of design, each orchestrated by a highly visible (usually named) printer/scholar/artist in charge, were often intertwined, and they governed virtually every aspect of fine bookmaking.

Setting the Stage: Allusive Design

An advertisement for the 1931 Cheshire House edition of *Shakespeare's Sonnets,* produced by Richard Ellis at the Georgian Press, lavishly describes Ellis's design approach: "Consonant with the richness of the Shakespearean sonnet is this small volume. The use of an old type face [Garamond] and an antiqued paper lends an atmosphere of mellow age and austere style, while the luxurious binding [full red leather] is a tribute to the spirit of splendor that pervaded the era of the Virgin Queen."[8] The historicism of postwar American bibliophilia was most apparent in a particular strategy known as allusive design. This term of art referred to the casting of a book's typography in the style of the place and period in which its text was originally written. At a minimum this was accomplished with type, rules, ornaments, layout conventions, and illustration styles dating from, popular during, or otherwise alluding to, that time or place. Allusive typography also sought fidelity to the text's genesis through design decisions involving paper, ink color, format, binding, and even production methods.

Because paper has its own history, it played an important role in allusive bookmaking. All papers were handmade until the early nineteenth century; a telltale feature was the deckle edge, the slightly rough, often feathery edge made when pulp fibers seep under the edges of the deckle, or enclosing frame, in the papermaking process. Until the mid–eighteenth century handmade paper also bore a faint grid pattern left by the tiny wires and thin wooden ribs supporting the screen surface of the mould; such paper is called *laid*. By contrast, in the mid–eighteenth century John Baskerville pioneered a new style of paper mould, yielding what is called *wove* paper because the screen wires are woven together, like window screening, rather than laid across ribs. The most authentic allusive design, then, ensured that the paper coincided with the historical era evoked in the typography. Indeed, while allusive typography could be reduced to gratuitous typographic cliché, in most cases it achieved a thoughtful evocation of the manner, style, and spirit of the era in which the text originated or was cast.

The most celebrated practitioner of allusive typography was Bruce Rogers, who described the technique as "in a small way something like planning the stage setting for a play. An up-to-date style for an ancient text would compare with staging *Hamlet* in modern dress. However novel and effective in its own way, you feel it to be strange, and this sense of strangeness is an annoying distraction; you are forced to think of the setting and the designer rather than of the text." Here Rogers invokes the dogma of invisibility, criticizing any design "strangeness" that calls attention to itself, but he turns the notion on its head; allusive design was anything but invisible to modern readers. An old text presented in modern typography would look strange only to those acquainted with its contemporary form, not to the many more readers unfamiliar with, in this case, early seventeenth-century English bookmaking. Rogers remarked elsewhere that he designed books so that their authors would feel comfortable and pleased with the presentation of their texts; when an author lived in an earlier time or in an exotic place, the design visually alluded to that otherness, nudging the reader into its aura.[9] Allusive typography sought to be invisible to readers of the author's day, not to contemporary audiences.

Because "typography" properly refers to a text's presentation in *print*, the earliest era to which allusive typography turned was that of incunabula, or books printed between the 1450s and 1501. Just as most incunabula were printed editions of texts that had existed previously in manuscript form, so neo-fifteenth-century typography was commonly applied to texts that pre-dated it. Allusive typography recreated the two broad styles of the fifteenth century — the still-medieval style of the first books printed in Germany, France, Spain, and northern Europe, and the more humanist style that emerged in Italy, reflecting the new art and linguistic interests of the Renaissance. Although there were many typographic differences between the two styles, the most apparent was in the typefaces used; gothic (or blackletter) letterforms were common in the former, while roman and, by 1500 or so, italic letterforms distinguished the latter.

Neomedieval typography had been done in breathtaking fashion by the Kelmscott Press, leaving few postwar fine printers brash enough to move fully into the master's typographic arena. Even so, those who admired William Morris's work and who shared his love for medieval art and life sometimes expressed that kinship by immersing books in a neomedieval setting. Ed Grabhorn, for example, had a penchant for gothic types. Shortly after arriving in California the Grabhorns bought proprietary rights to a neomedieval typeface designed by Frederic Goudy that they named Franciscan in honor of their adopted city, and they soon imported another neomedieval type from Germany. Designed by the eminent typographer Rudolph Koch, its name, Koch Bibel, suggested how it had been most commonly used. But the Grabhorns used it for three books whose archaic titles further cement their neomedieval cast: *The Voiage and Travaile of Sir John Maundevile* (see figure 9), and two books published by Bob Grabhorn and Oscar Lewis under their Westgate Press imprint in 1930 and 1931, respectively, *Fables of Esope* and *Robyn Hode*. The Grabhorns' books also reflected the preference of resident artist Valenti Angelo for illustration and handwork in the medieval tradition. *The Voiage of Maundevile,* which describes Angelo as its "illuminator," delighted buyers with hand-drawn initials and marginal embellishments in red, blue, and gold. Here allusive bookmaking went beyond design to production, incorporating hand-rendered art as well as hand composition.[10]

The most popular typographic era for postwar fine printers to revisit was the eighteenth century. In part this reflects the avid indulgence in neo-eighteenth-century design by a single printer, Richard Ellis. Ellis's Georgian Press books typically featured lesser-known canonical works, including two books by Oliver Goldsmith, hand composed in Oxford and Caslon types, and Alexander Pope's *Pastorals and Discourse* (1928), handset in Baskerville.[11] The eighteenth century was a favorite for allusive design because it was the age in which English bookmaking at last broke into the forefront of European typography, thanks to the contributions of William Caslon and John Baskerville. It was the century in which colonial American literature took root as well, so nationalist typographic impulses often proudly evoked the era of Ben Franklin to herald the beginnings of an American literary and printing tradition. The Rimington and Hooper 1928 edition of Franklin's *Poor Richard's Almanac,* for example, was composed predictably in Caslon (virtually the only type available to colonial printers). This vogue for eighteenth-century typography echoed a craze in the twenties for early American antiques — rag rugs, copper kettles, Cape Cod architecture, and the like — representing a more homespun, colonial version of the attempt to reconstruct Europe's grand past in more serious architecture and institutional interiors of the day.

Bruce Rogers, whose allusive skills nimbly spanned all five centuries of typographic history, found a particular niche in the eighteenth century. Two of the many noteworthy projects throughout his long career showcased this affinity. *The Journal of Madam Knight,* a diary account of Sarah Knight's 1704 journey from Boston to New Haven, recreates the orthographic quirks of its time, including free abbreviations with superscript letters: y^e for *the,* w^ch, and so on (see figure 12). Rogers gave the book an unmistakably eighteenth-century character when he debuted the new ATF version of Garamond, a type created in the sixteenth century but still prevalent in English typography until the 1730s. Rogers's most significant contribution to neo-eighteenth-century typography was the eighteen-volume edition of a recently discovered cache of personal papers of James Boswell that had been hidden in his Scottish estate. The *Private Papers of James Boswell from Malahide Castle* was regarded as a typographic tour de force adeptly evoking the era of Boswell's life and work. Rogers had the book typeset in Baskerville, and with myriad typographic embellishments — catchwords, archaic ligatures (ſt, ct, ſy), and swash characters — his allusive touch was sure and effective. The project also illustrates the infinite pains that Rogers took with details of letterspacing, leading, character alignment, and so on, through which so much effective allusion is achieved.

Given the animosity toward nineteenth-century bookmaking, it is hardly surprising that few fine editions of nineteenth-century texts (which in fact were plentiful; see table 6) recreate that typographic era. Only a handful did so, all successfully. When Bennett Cerf asked Updike to produce for Random House a fine edition of Walt Whitman's youthful 1842 temperance novel *Franklin Evans; or, The Inebriate,* Updike admitted that he found the book "a pretty dreary affair," but "as I do not have to read what I print," he continued, he agreed to undertake the task. He found some calligraphic ornaments commonly used in the 1830s, paired them with the era's popular Scotch type, and created a book that Whitman's original audience would have read

ticularly with regard to the number of the inhabitants, and the facilities and accommodations prepared for travellers. Over that tract of country where she travelled about a fortnight, on horseback, under the direction of a hired guide, with frequent risks of life and limb, and sometimes without food or shelter for many miles, we proceed at our ease, without exposure and almost without fatigue, in a day and a half, through a well peopled land, supplied with good stage-coaches and public houses, or the still greater luxuries of the elegant steam boats which daily traverse our waters.

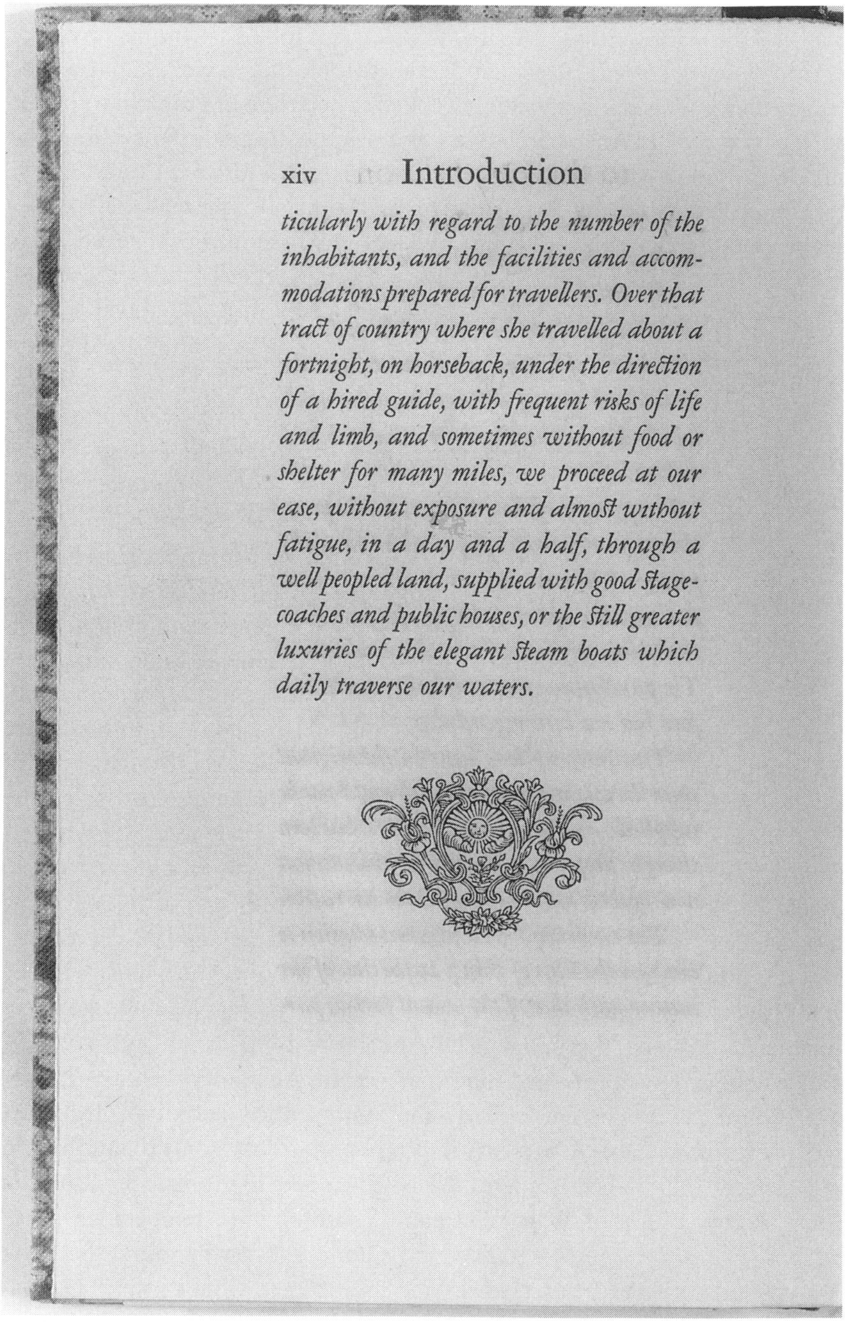

Figure 12. *The Journal of Madam Knight* (Boston: Small, Maynard, and Co., 1920). Designed by Bruce Rogers. Photo courtesy of the Bancroft Library at the University of California.

THE
JOURNAL
OF
Madam *KNIGHT*.

❖❖❖❖❖❖❖❖❖❖❖❖❖❖❖❖❖❖❖

Monday, Octb'r. y^e second,
1704.

ABOUT three o'clock afternoon, I
begun my Journey from Boſton
to New-Haven; being about two Hundred Mile. My Kinſman, Capt. Robert
Luiſt, waited on me as farr as Dedham,
where I was to meet y^e Weſtern poſt.

I

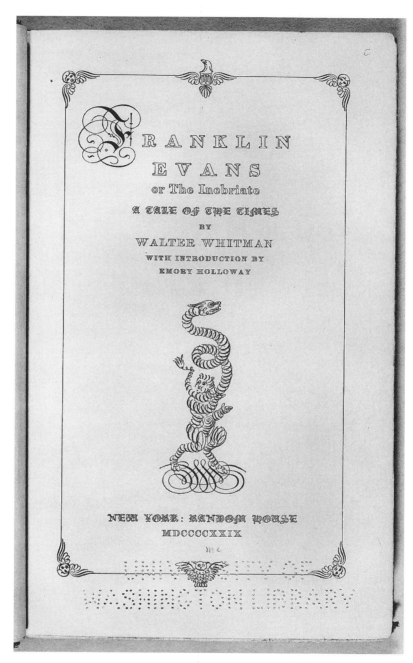

Figure 13. Walter Whitman, *Franklin Evans* (New York: Random House, 1929). Designed and produced by D. B. Updike. Photo courtesy of Special Collections Division, University of Washington Libraries.

comfortably. As with most good allusive typography, Updike's effort was not a slavish copy of past style but a lively design that transcended its historical idiom. He incorporated into the title page an ornamental nineteenth-century penmanship exercise design that reminded him, he told Cerf, of "a man enmeshed by a serpent — The Serpent of Drink!"[12] (See figure 13.)

Allusive typography showcased detailed historical knowledge of European printing traditions, both establishing the printer's scholarly expertise and imparting that knowledge to patrons. Frederic Warde described allusive typography as a "graceful game" that offered the growing number of printing enthusiasts a "subtle challenge" to their learning and taste.[13] It was clearly pedantic to some degree, tacitly teaching patrons to recognize eminent traditional typographic styles, not least so that they might better appreciate designers' skills in using them. As the postwar fine printing community became better informed about historical features of the craft, allusive typography lent a kind of in crowd status to those who recognized it. This community therefore succumbed at times to a kind of visual name-dropping made possible by the growing fashion for bibliophilic scholarship. Historically informed typography set itself apart from ordinary book design in part by establishing a camaraderie of elite knowledge among bibliophiles.

Allusive design was not immune to criticism, however. Its deference to past styles prompted some of the harshest complaints about fine bookmaking in the decade. Critics regarded it as design by default, a failure to develop a twentieth-century typographic style. In an essay titled "The Modern Style — If Any," Walter Dorwin Teague complained that modern American printers only reproduced work from the past. Carl Rollins similarly chided his colleagues for a "timidity" that rendered them unable to "make printing consonant with our times." America has exceedingly clever "archeological" printers, he conceded, but no truly creative artistic talents. Another critic labeled allusive typography "epidemics of theft," producing only " 'period' printing as tedious as 'period' furniture and as worthless." Updike, who more than anyone led the way toward traditionalism in modern design, nonetheless recognized a crucial difference between an authoritative command of typographic tradition and attempts simply to dress a text in historical costume. He dismissed a 1924 book designed by Frederic Goudy in a "pseudo-antique" manner reminiscent of Morris and Kelmscott with the remark: "Isn't it funny that Mr. Goudy has never gotten over this sort of thing! It reminds me of the story of the little boy who was taken to see the Masonic procession and asked his Papa what it was all about. 'That, my son,' said his father, 'is a procession composed of men who never had a good time when they were little boys!' "[14]

The relationship between modern American fine printers and the traditions of their craft was typically conflicted. These printers struggled between efforts to master that tradition, to achieve a kind of dominance over their forbears by assimilating the older styles, and a rhetoric of self-effacing deference to the supreme "rightness" of what had been achieved in the past. Just as Americans vacillated between celebrating their nation's preeminence in the postwar world and lamenting the impoverishing decline of European cultural traditions, fine printers labored to understand their role as bridge between past and future. While most considered it arrogant folly to jettison that past as irrelevant, they also recognized the danger of trivializing it.

This conflict occasionally led to frustration with a present that both consumed the past and lionized it. Nowhere is this better expressed than in the extraordinary correspondence of Frederic Warde, who wrote from Europe to William Kittredge several long polemics on the subject. Warde, whose work was almost aggressively traditional in a fastidious, intellectualized way, had nothing but contempt for "these filthy modern copies and imitations of old books." He railed, "What I want to see is a modern book in which tradition gets a good slap in the teeth. The finest, the best, the most beautiful book is yet to be printed, and believe me when it is printed it will be a book which has been produced in a modern way by the most modern methods. . . . I cannot imagine what I may have written to you that would give you the idea that I had any interest in any of this "diploma printing" or otherwise, the painted ladies of the craft. . . . You could never find me when it comes to entertaining gold teeth and spats in typography. . . I quite agree with you that it is high time all these genteelizms in typography and printing be burnt out of all consideration. They are the assassinating bacteria in the life of any work." Warde understood typographic history as abstract principles rather than literal particulars. He considered William Morris "dead before he was born" because he tried to express living thought to living readers in forms borrowed from a dead age.[15] Many agreed, though in less vitriolic terms, that modern American fine printing ought to pay more attention to the spirit of its own time and place.

Although this sounds like a simple enough task, the problem of defining "modern" postwar typography was an awkward one for American designers. By the late 1920s, the word invoked the radically opposite, combative design ideology emanating from central Europe. "Just as it is absurd today to build villas like Rococo palaces or Gothic castles," a young Jan Tschichold proclaimed in 1928, "so people tomorrow will smile at those who continue to practice the old typography." He declared that modern civilization reflected the machine's spiritual triumph over the backward-looking "romanticist," and that the printed book should do no less: "new needs and new contents create new forms which look utterly unlike the old. And it is just as impossible to argue away these new needs as it is to deny the need for a truly contemporary style of typography."[16] American fine printers could agree passionately that new needs abounded in the postwar world, but they disagreed utterly about what was needed. The polar contrast between modernist and traditional values was most evident in design and typography, in the myriad decisions that determine how a book looks, feels, and performs.

European modernism sought to bring characteristics of mechanized production — speed, standardization, precision, economy — to book design. In his manifesto on the "New Typography" associated with the Bauhaus in the 1920s, Tschichold declared that typography must be brief, simple, and clear. He scorned the traditional practice of centering lines of type, for example, likening a central axis to "an artificial, invisible backbone: its raison d'être is today as pretentious as the tall white collars of Victorian gentlemen." Asymmetric arrangement better reflects the logic, energy, and rhythm of a text's message, he argued. He also preached that illustration must rely on exact images — photography — instead of artistic versions of them, that dimensions and formats should correspond to new international standards in the papermaking industries, and that organization and clarity should rely on strong contrast rather than close integration of elements. Tschichold dismissed ornamentation as inessential and fanciful, the remnants of a "childish naivety" — a "fear of pure appearance" that reveals only an effort to "cover up bad design!"[17] (See figure 14.)

Most notably, Tschichold argued that only sans serif types are "in spiritual accordance with our time," that their geometric plainness and universality better achieved the clarity and anationalist neutrality needed for modern typography. He even espoused the radical orthographic economy of discarding capital letterforms. Because lowercase letters are easier to read in continuous text, the change (particularly in German, which capitalizes all nouns) would "result in great savings of spiritual and intellectual energy." As Kinross explains: "our script loses nothing through writing in small letters only — but becomes, rather, more legible, easier to learn, essentially more economical. for one sound, for example "a," why two signs: A and a? one sound, one sign. why two alfabets for one word, why double the quantity of signs, when a half achieves the same?"[18] Capital letterforms were in fact abolished for a time at the Bauhaus in 1925.

Because their fundamental notions of the purpose of books differed so radically from those of European modernists, most American fine printers paid little heed to these bold new design ideas. They tended to view modernist typography, and particularly sans serif types, with condescension, regarding it as perhaps useful for the eclecticism of advertising (which has no tradition,

JAN TSCHICHOLD

DIE NEUE TYPOGRAPHIE

EIN HANDBUCH FÜR ZEITGEMÄSS SCHAFFENDE

BERLIN **1928**

VERLAG DES BILDUNGSVERBANDES DER DEUTSCHEN BUCHDRUCKER

Figure 14. Jan Tschichold, *Die Neue Typographie* (Berlin: Bildungsverband der Deutschen Buchdrucker, 1928).

Paul Johnston remarked) or as a "passing fancy" soon to become one more historically resonant style to be added to the traditionalist palette. Bruce Rogers considered lowercase sans serif letterforms "unfit for reading anywhere," though he allowed that they might be suitable for printing the work of modern writers like Gertrude Stein or James Joyce.[19] Most ignored or sidestepped modernists' broader assertions about the nature of print culture. Their own ideological framework invoked a radically different sense of audience, purpose, and — consequently — design criteria. American fine printers labored to reinvigorate cultural connections to the preindustrial past from which modernism sought to shake itself free; they exalted traditional forms of type design, book design, and bookmaking.

Design Personality: Interpretive Typography

If an allusive designer functioned as a stage designer, in interpretive typography the designer was the center stage performer, star of the show. When Bill Dwiggins designed and illustrated an edition of Robert Louis Stevenson's *The Strange Case of Dr. Jekyll and Mr. Hyde* for Random House, for example, his shifting visions charted a typical interpretive course. From the start, he intended to create contrasts in the book's form that would echo the text's theme of linked opposites. In August 1927 he explained to Elmer Adler, who supervised the book's production, that he envisioned a plain black cloth binding and a slipcase printed in vivid colors—a "very sober book in a very gay box." Over the next several months his design ideas developed and drifted: in January 1928 he thought of presenting the book as a "glorified romantic legal document" with tinges of a "police tale" to it, but by late June he was after a "semi-sensational police detective" with a "newspaper scare-head" look to it. He thought of the title page as placardlike, with a "£5000 Reward" feeling. He assured Adler that a potboiler look could still be "within the bounds of artistic bookmaking," but Adler balked at producing a fine book designed to look like the cheap thrillers that crowded newsstands of the late nineteenth century—perhaps anticipating the dismay of buyers asked to pay ten dollars for the book—and Dwiggins soon deferred to his friend's uneasiness. In the end, the chief visual contrast was in alternating styles of illustration throughout the book: one "rich and juicy" and the other "sharp and acid," as Dwiggins described them.[20]

Interpretive design invited printers to express their artistic personalities. In 1926 Otto Ege published a "decalog" of axioms to govern fine book design. The tenth axiom proclaimed that the "personality of the craftsman and his friendship for and sympathy with his text should be evident. His style, his method of interpretation, that which is his power and his only, should be clearly displayed. . . . The best materials, energy, and skill are valueless without the magic of a dominant personality." *Personality* became the special, highly visible ingredient that elevated a book's design from ordinary to fine, a quality even more crucial than expensive materials or meticulous craftsmanship. Even Stanley Morison admitted that fine printing required something extra. "The fine printer begins where the careful printer has left off. For 'fine' printing something is required in addition to care—certain vital gifts of mind and understanding. . . . A fine book is something more than 'something to read.' The amateur looks for character in printing. The book therefore which assays to rank above the commonplace, will, while not failing in its essential purpose, carry the personality of its maker no less than that of its author and its subject."[21] A designer's personality and artistic vision pervaded a book; typography blended into illustration. This partially explains the keen market for fine editions of texts readily available in other formats; many fine books of the 1920s were published solely to offer, say, Rockwell Kent's or Bruce Rogers's interpretation of some literary classic.

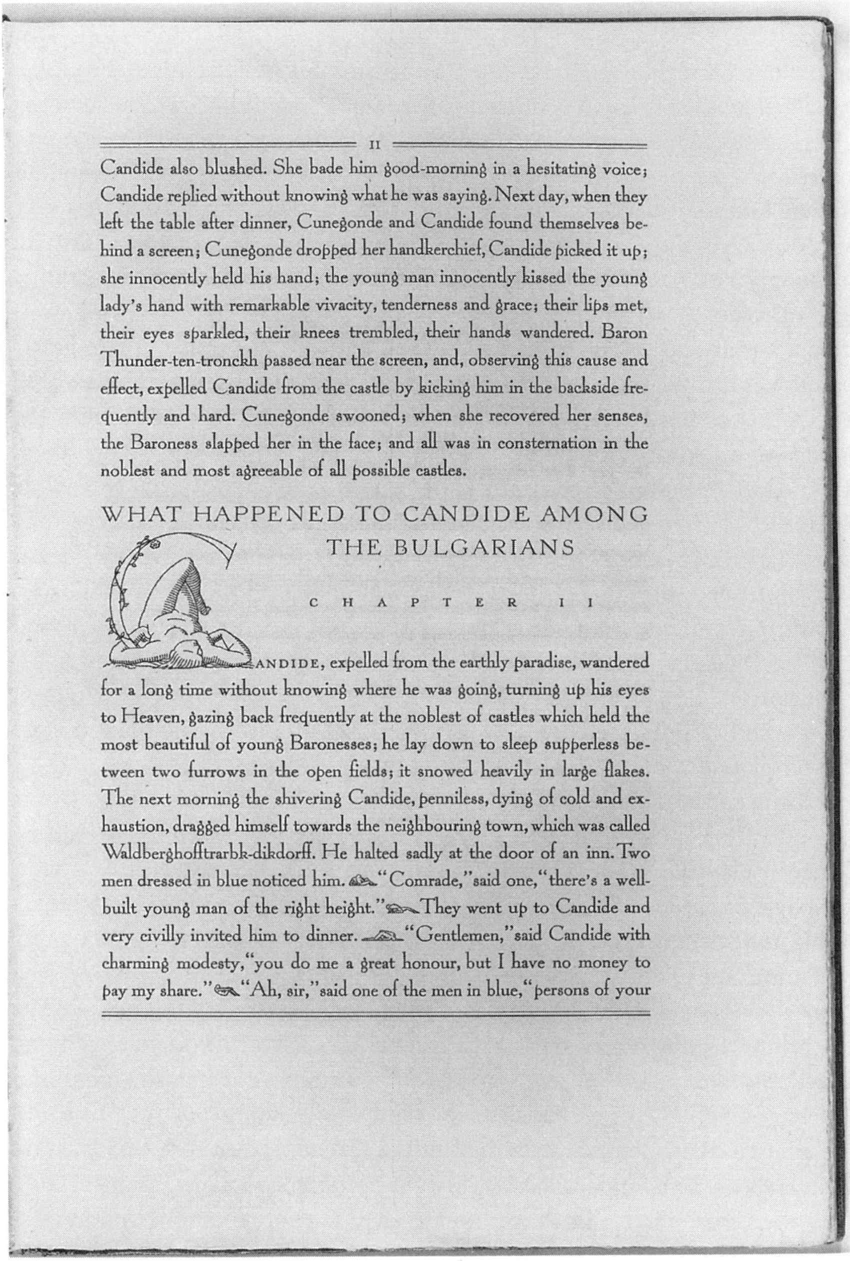

Candide also blushed. She bade him good-morning in a hesitating voice; Candide replied without knowing what he was saying. Next day, when they left the table after dinner, Cunegonde and Candide found themselves behind a screen; Cunegonde dropped her handkerchief, Candide picked it up; she innocently held his hand; the young man innocently kissed the young lady's hand with remarkable vivacity, tenderness and grace; their lips met, their eyes sparkled, their knees trembled, their hands wandered. Baron Thunder-ten-tronckh passed near the screen, and, observing this cause and effect, expelled Candide from the castle by kicking him in the backside frequently and hard. Cunegonde swooned; when she recovered her senses, the Baroness slapped her in the face; and all was in consternation in the noblest and most agreeable of all possible castles.

WHAT HAPPENED TO CANDIDE AMONG THE BULGARIANS

CHAPTER II

CANDIDE, expelled from the earthly paradise, wandered for a long time without knowing where he was going, turning up his eyes to Heaven, gazing back frequently at the noblest of castles which held the most beautiful of young Baronesses; he lay down to sleep supperless between two furrows in the open fields; it snowed heavily in large flakes. The next morning the shivering Candide, penniless, dying of cold and exhaustion, dragged himself towards the neighbouring town, which was called Waldberghofftrarbk-dikdorff. He halted sadly at the door of an inn. Two men dressed in blue noticed him. "Comrade," said one, "there's a well-built young man of the right height." They went up to Candide and very civilly invited him to dinner. "Gentlemen," said Candide with charming modesty, "you do me a great honour, but I have no money to pay my share." "Ah, sir," said one of the men in blue, "persons of your

Figure 15. Voltaire, *Candide* (New York: Random House, 1928). Illustrated by Rockwell Kent; designed and produced by Elmer Adler, Pynson Printers. Photo courtesy of Special Collections Division, University of Washington Libraries.

Type was the designer's foremost expressive tool. Each typeface offered a unique blend of historical and cultural associations as well as visual characteristics of color or quality of stroke (firm, bold, vigorous, delicate, fragile, and so on). Astute designers developed keen sensibilities concerning these typographic qualities: for example, Elmer Adler chose for the Dunster House edition of Archibald MacLeish's *Nobodaddy* the modern French Cochin as a typeface that was sufficiently "robust" albeit "a bit self-conscious," while Bill Dwiggins insisted on "warm-blooded" Original Old Style (similar to Caslon) rather than Scotch roman for an edition of Poe's *Tales* — "I'm after a warmer, more 'romantic' page," he explained.[22] Each designer began with type selection when crafting an interpretive presentation, and each used it with a distinctive touch, or personality.

Despite his misgivings about Dwiggins's *Jekyll and Hyde* design, Elmer Adler was not wedded to conservative or grandiose typography. The books he designed were often deftly personable, even playful, as in the edition of Christopher Morley's *The Palette Knife* Adler produced for the Chocorua Press in 1929 (see figure 8). A more famous example of Adler's inventiveness is the edition of *Candide* that he produced to debut the Random House imprint in 1928. Typically, the book is valued primarily for Rockwell Kent's copious artwork, more than seventy half-page illustrations and dozens of pictorial initials that open each chapter, but Adler's typography is no less remarkable; Bruce Rogers called it a "delightful" work in an "ultra-modern" style.[23] The text was handset in the new Bernhard roman, which was "modern" in that it did not recreate a historical face; its "x-height" (the height of lowercase letters like *a*, *e*, and *x*) is small, so that capital letters loom tall in the line. The resulting "open" and light page accords well with Kent's pen and ink drawings. Each type page forms a neat rectangle, because new paragraphs are not indented. Instead Adler simply inserted a small stylized human figure, contorted into one of several postures, and continued the text on the same line (see figure 15). The design captures the levity and wit of Voltaire's text in a fresh, engaging way.

Rockwell Kent was the premier bookmaking personality between the wars. His skills were hailed particularly in the massive three-volume edition of *Moby Dick* that he designed and illustrated for R.R. Donnelley's Lakeside Press over a four-year period culminating in 1930 (figure 16). He ruminated on Melville's novel as the book's typography slowly took shape in his mind: "Moby Dick is a most solemn, mystic work," he wrote to Lakeside's production manager, William Kittredge. "Each chapter is in itself a poem, and should be presented with all the seperate [*sic*] distinction and dignity possible. The whole book is a work that should be read slowly, reflectively; the large page

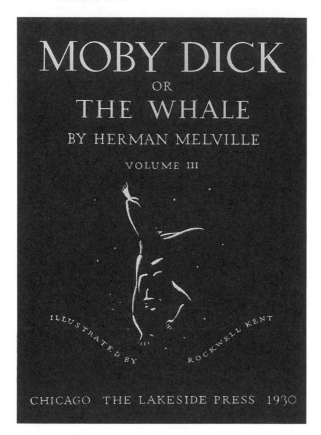

Figure 16. Herman Melville, *Moby Dick* (Chicago: Lakeside Press, 1930). Illustrated and designed by Rockwell Kent; produced by William Kittredge. Photo courtesy of Special Collections Division, University of Washington Libraries.

and type [he was considering fourteen-point Caslon] induce such reading. The character of the type should be homely, rather than refined and elegant, for homeliness flavors every line that Melville wrote." His ideas for illustration emerged similarly from his sense of the text, which he characterized above all as "*homely* and *rich.*" "Its prose is ample, voluminous, rich, warm; it is above all not refined, not studied; it blunders through to triumphant success by the dramatic intensity of the visionary mind it serves. It is literary woodcutting, not engraving." Of one thing he was certain: dominating the edition would be "the midnight darkness enveloping human existence, the darkness of the human soul, the abyss, — such is the mood of Moby Dick."[24]

Kittredge encouraged Kent to design the new edition according to that deeply personal experience of the text. He urged Kent to immerse himself in the text, to work "as though you were Melville and Melville you; that, as you engrossed your book, you charted, illuminated, and illustrated it — such a book as you might do if there were only to be one copy, entirely done by your own hands." This approach, which unabashedly placed designer/illustrator as mediator between text and reader, was so effective that the edition remains known as the Rockwell Kent *Moby Dick*. Contemporaries were so enthralled with Kent's interpretive artistry that when Random House published a trade reprint edition in 1931, it was so eager to display Kent's name on the cover that it inadvertently omitted Melville's.[25]

A final example of interpretive typography hailed in its day is the 1930 Grabhorn Press edition of *Leaves of Grass* produced for Random House (figure 17). One of the book's most striking features was its bold type. Ed Grabhorn later explained that after the publishers had announced it as "the finest book to be published in America," the printers felt compelled to use "the finest type & the finest type was the latest type." They ordered a thousand pounds of a new face from Holland named Lutetia, but after a succession of unsatisfying proofs they realized with despair that the type was too pretty, too delicate for the job. Grabhorn recalled with rhetorical bravado that his "eyes lighted upon a dusty case of type" already in the shop, Frederic Goudy's semiarchaic Newstyle, tried a page in it, "and Lo! He saw . . . strength: he saw the strong, vigorous lines of Whitman, born of the soil, without grass. . . . He saw strong, vigorous, simple printing — printing like mountains, rocks and trees, but not like pansies, lilacs and valentines; printing that came from the soil and was not refined in the class room."[26] Grabhorn's sense that the book demanded strength and vigor, not some typographical equivalent of pansies and violets, was well expressed in the final production. The book was large (about nine by fourteen inches), bound in mahogany boards, and as imposing visually as it was physically.

Sometimes personality meant showcasing a distinctive typographic talent or taste. Several printers developed a trademark stylistic feature: Rogers and Frederic Warde earned reputations for adroit constructions of type ornaments, and Dwiggins preferred handlettering to type for titles, but the best example of a trademark style was John Henry Nash's proclivity to encase texts in grids of rules, usually printed in a second color. This feature was hailed for its technical virtuosity, because it required precise mitering of the rules as well as meticulous make-ready to ensure that the rules did not print too heavily and score the paper. Nash used rules in most of his books, including his magnum opus, the four-volume 1929 edition of the *Divine Comedy*. The practice added

[BOOK XXII.] MEMORIES OF PRESIDENT LINCOLN

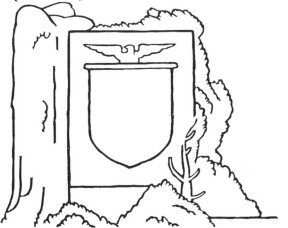

WHEN LILACS LAST IN THE DOORYARD BLOOM'D
1. When lilacs last in the dooryard bloom'd,
   And the great star early droop'd in the western sky in the night,
   I mourn'd, and yet shall mourn with ever-returning spring.

   Ever-returning spring, trinity sure to me you bring,
   Lilac blooming perennial and drooping star in the west,
   And thought of him I love.

2. O powerful western fallen star!
   O shades of night—O moody, tearful night!
   O great star disappear'd—O the black murk that hides the star!
   O cruel hands that hold me powerless—O helpless soul of me!
   O harsh surrounding cloud that will not free my soul.

3. In the dooryard fronting an old farm-house near the white-wash'd palings,
   Stands the lilac-bush tall-growing with heart-shaped leaves of rich green,
   With many a pointed blossom rising delicate, with the perfume strong I love,
                                    260

Figure 17. Walt Whitman, *Leaves of Grass* (New York: Random House, 1930). Illustrated by Valenti Angelo; designed and produced by Edwin and Robert Grabhorn. Photo courtesy of Special Collections Division, University of Washington Libraries.

historical luster to his typography by evoking the medieval manuscript tradition of ruling pages to guide the scribe's placement of text columns, gloss material, and so forth.[27] Design moved beyond expertise into art, and as art, these designers' books were valued for that distinguishing mark more than for a particular text.

One particular strategy of interpretive designers was to create pictorial or decorative arrangements of rules and fleurons to echo the text's themes or subject matter. Here design preempted illustration. Perhaps because he preferred to work with sole authority, Bruce Rogers initiated and dominated work in this vein. When Crosby Gaige decided to publish Joseph Conrad's unfinished novel *The Sisters* in 1928, he enlisted Rogers to transform the relatively slight manuscript fragment into a book. Given its brevity, Rogers chose to add not only extra leading between the lines of Scotch roman type but also a series of typographic decorations to stretch the text to a respectable number of pages. Although he found "not much in the text upon which to hang ornamental suggestions of it," Rogers labored to construct appropriate "illustrations." A text reference to "a beast from the jungle," for example, prompted Rogers to assemble "a strange animal, some bushes, a stretch of rule simulating grass, and two little ornaments like pagodas to convey the hint of the East." Rogers admitted that "these are perhaps rather tenuous connections between text and ornament, but they are more interesting (and also more time-consuming) to produce than a repetition of meaningless borders or combinations."[28]

This playful strategy relied on imaginative use of prosaic punctuation marks, abstract fleuron components, and so on. For the opening page of the 1925 Rudge edition of *Joseph Conrad: The Man,* Rogers constructed a scene of dolphins leaping across waves, flanked by palm trees (presumably to suggest the nautical themes of Conrad's writing), entirely from punctuation: parentheses, commas, periods, and so on. For the acting version of Michael Arlen's *The Green Hat,* Rogers used ornament and punctuation to suggest an elaborate stage setting for the title page (figure 18). Others also tried their hands at this form of design showmanship. The Grabhorns produced James Branch Cabell's *Sonnets from Antan* for the Fountain Press with a title page assembly that formed a view of a rising (or setting) sun through an arch between two towers. Combined with swash Lutetia italic type, the visual effect is lush and exotic, much like Cabell's poetry. Adler produced at least two noteworthy specimens of this variety of design as well, Elinor Wylie's *Trivial Breath* for Knopf in 1928 and Aldous Huxley's 1931 *Music at Night and Other Essays* for Fountain Press.

The pictorial approach to ornament stemmed from a long typographic tradition of presenting important text — usually the title page — within an elaborate border of assembled fleurons and rules. This practice was intended only to decorate the page, however, not to supplement meaning via constructed images. Similarly, modern printers sometimes used abstract ornament simply to add beauty, in part to alert the reader to the fact that this was no ordinary book. One woman thanked Elmer Adler for his gift of an ornamented book with a blushing confession that her "first impulse was to return the book and say I can't accept gifts of jewelry from gentlemen."[29] Bruce Rogers's title page for W. H. Hudson's *Ralph Herne* (published by Knopf in 1923) features an ornate fleuron frame surrounding the type, which is chosen and arranged with equal care: the author's name appears in all italic capitals except for the final *N,* which is a semiswash roman (figure 19). Adler's elaborate border of

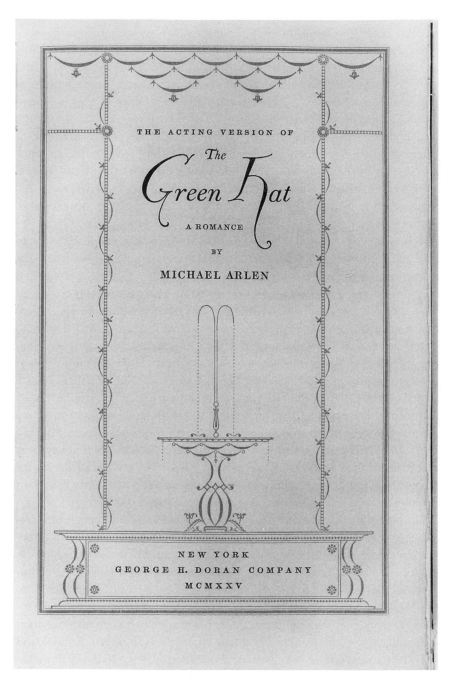

THE ACTING VERSION OF

The
Green Hat

A ROMANCE

BY

MICHAEL ARLEN

NEW YORK
GEORGE H. DORAN COMPANY
MCMXXV

Figure 18. Michael Arlen, *The Acting Version of the Green Hat, a Romance* (New York: George H. Doran, 1925). Designed by Bruce Rogers; produced by William E. Rudge. Photo courtesy of the Bancroft Library of the University of California.

RALPH
HERNE

By W. H. HUDSON

B R

New York
ALFRED A. KNOPF
1923

Figure 19. W. H. Hudson, *Ralph Herne* (New York: Alfred A. Knopf, 1923). Designed by Bruce Rogers; produced by William E. Rudge. Photo courtesy of the Bancroft Library.

fleurons for Knopf's 1924 edition of *The Work of Stephen Crane* also illustrates this traditional yet performative style of typography.

Brand Name Book Design

Interpretive or expressive design left no doubt as to the hand — or more accurately, the eye, brain, and will — governing a fine book's presentation. This aspect of design reinforced the new authority and status granted to those designers who displayed the requisite knowledge, taste, skills, and compelling personality. Expressive typography created a star system of brand name bookmakers, an elite world of celebrity designers that repudiated lesser printers who might aspire to a share of the glory.[30] Ordinary printers were to produce books for ordinary readers — for which invisible clarity and sober, humble adherence to convention were demanded. Fine printers seemed all the more exceptional when bad typographers were defined less as ignorant than as pretentious.

Fine printing enthroned the professional typographer as a kind of monarch whose authority reigned absolute. A young and starstruck Frederic Warde reported in 1921 that at the William Rudge Company, Bruce Rogers's will prevailed uncontested in virtually all aspects of his projects. "Mr. Rogers detests doing anything excepting the thing that occurs to his own individual tastes and interests," Warde wrote, in full sympathy with his idol's temperament. Rogers's creative achievements were in fact the result of rigorous demands he placed upon the workers who executed his designs. The fabulous arrangements of ornaments for which Rogers was so heralded had to be shaved and mitered with extreme accuracy in order to hold together long enough to be electrotyped, because the form would collapse immediately if printed.[31]

Fine printers underscored the fundamental superiority in "taste and talent," as the litany ran, that authorized their judgments. Despite conventional business maxims, preferences of neither client nor customer were to be tolerated, much less accommodated. Clients quickly learned that they had no choice but to defer to the expert's superior knowledge in typographic matters. When the Lord & Taylor clothing company preferred another designer's plans to Adler's for one of its advertisements, Adler refused to produce the work using a layout he considered unacceptable. "We must maintain our standards," he informed the company. The paper he had already purchased for the job was appropriate only for his own "fifteenth-century idea." He added, "Of course we shall be glad to work with you whenever you feel enough confidence to permit us to design and execute work in the field where we have achieved and maintained our position." Consumers' judgments were even less entitled to prevail. When a Minnesota judge who had purchased Knopf's 1924 edition of Sterne's *Sentimental Journey*, designed by Adler, returned his copy because he found its cover "unappealing," Knopf and Adler immediately blamed the rejection on the man's inferior taste, reassuring each other that "we're not in business to do business with Mr. Flaherty." As Rogers explained, a master printer labored for those few individuals able to detect and understand the nature of his mastery, not for the average reader. "The average reader will not see [a fine book's] rather obscure points, and will not care," he noted, "but it should not be for the average reader that a designer elaborates his work."[32]

This elite world depended on vigilant preservation of the self-bestowed privileges of "masters" and artist-typographers. Toward the end of the 1920s, typographic critics began to warn of an industrywide epidemic of "too many typefaces" and "too much freedom" in their use. In part, this alarm echoed a broader cultural call for discipline and restraint (explored in Chapter 1). But it also mirrored the need to clarify and preserve cultural hierarchy, to uphold the perquisites of the typographic saving remnant. The renaissance of historical typefaces made possible largely through the efforts of Monotype and Linotype companies was thus a mixed blessing: the new faces added all-important historical breadth to fine printing's design palette, but they were also available, cheaply, to any printer with a mechanical composition system. The lament over "too many books" was echoed in complaints of design profligacy enabled by "too many types." Fine printers feared that unschooled printers would indulge a taste for the novel, the decorative, or the trendy in selecting type. Carl Rollins keenly regretted Bruce Rogers's decision to allow Monotype to issue a version of his Centaur type, for example, rendering it "available to those who don't know how to use it." "The poorly educated printer thinks he must have many new faces," Rollins mourned, thanks to the "silly democratic idea that everyone can or should have everything." The result was a "universal mauling of Centaur by unintelligent users," he fumed.[33] "The unrestricted usage of type-faces by the many unblessed designers who are permitted, through some circumstance or another, to design and supervise work, is very distressing," wrote L. J. Ansbacher of the Viking Press. His standard for separating the few skilled designers who used type judiciously from those who used it recklessly or ignorantly was high; he praised Rogers and Dwiggins but damned the work of other fine printers as "preposterous dissonance." "The typographic impertinences which a great many American designers use basely for self-expression are to be resisted. Taking advantage of a people who should but do not know better, they should at any rate be laughed at by those who do. Until they either change their vocation to something more suitable or give themselves some rudimentary schooling and do some disavowing, we can do no more, but also no less, than make plain our disrespect for them."[34] If Elmer Adler and Frederic Warde could be guilty of "typographic impertinence," how much more so were these words meant to chasten the expressive impulses of ordinary printers across the country?

In particular, foolhardy printers without the necessary credentials of education and taste were discouraged from even attempting to use fleurons. Updike cautioned that "to use intelligently these typographic 'flowers' . . . requires knowledge of the dates of their first appearance, and the types with which it was intended they should harmonize, and in some cases their appropriateness in design. To build up typographical ornaments into a picture — save for men with taste and talent — is a dangerous business." Only historicized authority could sanction what might be seen as a relapse into Victorian "frills" and "clutter." Updike warned that if ornamentation were carried too far, "ingenuity replaces taste, and the results resemble sad specimens of Victorian wool-work."[35]

Even accomplished practitioners understood that ornaments could easily be used poorly — which meant gratuitously, ignorantly, or carelessly. Frederic Warde warned in 1928 that ornamentation was a "most charming and dangerous diversion"; only the few dare attempt it. The frequency of warnings about its hazards indicates, however, the popularity of ornament in postwar typography, especially in books that aspired to be special in some way. In 1929 Beatrice Warde attempted to explain its appeal, contending that ornament "tempers the mysterious with reassuring elements. . . . Decoration in books keeps the subconscious at peace while the intellect is busy."[36] She emphasized its superficial, undemanding contribution to the page that entertained the eye without competing with the text for meaning. This condescending theory was a bit facile, a maneuver to accommodate ornament within her larger ethic of invisible printing. In reality, ornament was a lively, highly visible, and widespread form of interpretive typography.

Book Monuments

Late in his career, Bob Grabhorn readily admitted that many bought Grabhorn Press books for reasons other than to read them. Referring to their 1930 production of *Leaves of Grass,* he explained that "of course you're not going to read [it]. You can buy a pocket book. But if Whitman's your favorite author, you like a monument to him."[37] If he sounded a bit exasperated and defensive, it was because he was right. Many postwar fine books were objects of art, created and purchased for their design, illustration, or production. A good number were explicitly iconic; their material form was intended to invest value and prestige in the books' symbolic nature no less than had special books hundreds of years before, encrusted with jewels and ornately gilded, painted pages. Informed and justified by this hallowed historic tradition, modern iconic bookmaking similarly relied on lavish uses of extravagant materials and labor in an unabashed construction of books that functioned as cultural icons.

The most immediate source of grandeur was the paper. Anything other than handmade would be foolish because economy was hardly a concern for bookmaking in this vein. Yet handmade paper bestowed only minimal extra value in itself. Distinction was achieved by exploiting special watermarks, or images visible in the sheet when held up to a light, formed where patterns stitched to the mould created a thinner pulp layer. Papermills typically offered a variety of watermarks, sometimes two or three in each mould. To go one step further, fine printers commissioned handmade papers with custom watermarks, usually their own initials or those pertaining to a particular book project. Vojtěch Preissig, for example, commissioned papers watermarked with his initials for the two monumental books he produced for Random House, editions of Ben Franklin's *Way to Wealth* and Walt Whitman's *Salut au Monde.* The most steadfast user of personally watermarked paper was John Henry Nash; in many of his books a large *JHN* dominated the blank pages. Crosby Gaige tried a different twist in his search for distinction in paper, issuing nine otherwise undistinguished copies of his books on a special colored handmade paper. This capricious practice infuriated collectors and his distributor, Random House, which protested bitterly.[38]

The prominence of special paper is apparent in the excessive number of blank leaves that commonly preceded and followed the text pages. A few blank leaves are common, of course, to protect the first and last printed pages from soiling, particularly during the binding process, or to fill out a gathering of printed pages. But bibliophilic books frequently included a more generous allotment of blank leaves front and back. They both added heft to the book and provided a succession of pages devoted to the beauties of the paper itself, its watermark(s), its irregular deckles, and so forth. Bruce Rogers discouraged the practice, calling it "an ostentation to be avoided." He contended that "one or two [blank leaves] in front and the same number at the back are sufficient."[39] Nash was particularly extravagant with blank leaves of his personally watermarked handmade papers: his productions of Robert Louis Stevenson's *Silverado Squatters* for Scribner's in 1923 and of Hugh Studdert Kennedy's *The Visitor,* which he published himself in 1930, feature a total of thirteen and twelve blanks (twenty-six and twenty-four pages), respectively.

The height of extravagance surpassed paper itself. On rare occasions part of a fine edition was printed on vellum. This appealed especially to the San

Francisco printers; both Nash and the Grabhorns produced vellum copies of a few of their books, perhaps because their clientele was readily at hand and could more reliably be expected to accept (if not vie for) the more expensive copies. Because it represented the pinnacle of sumptuous bookmaking and radiated ultimate historical evocations, the use of vellum measured the ambition of a bibliophilic undertaking. Vellum copies were planned for *Leaves of Grass,* for example, even though they were never made. After urging Ed Grabhorn to look into ordering "special paper for the 'Leaves of Grass' with both your own and the Random House water-mark on it" (adding shrewdly that "if this is possible, we must be sure to make some mention of it in the prospectus"), Cerf further clarified: "you will make 12 additional copies in full vellum. Of these 12 copies, one each is to go without charge to Edwin Grabhorn, Robert Grabhorn, Valenti Angelo, Elmer Adler, Donald Klopfer and Bennett Cerf, and the other 6 copies will be priced so as to cover the entire cost of the 12 vellum copies."[40]

Extravagant materials distinguished bindings, too. Beyond their obvious structural purpose, bindings were the most immediate, constantly visible expression of a book's importance to its maker and owners. More than any other aspect of a fine book, its binding was what one displayed or admired in passing or at a distance. Even so, bindings of most fine editions did not usually feature individual artistry in the ways that interiors did. Generally they shunned any hint of the advertising efforts that dominated trade book covers; fine books were virtually never offered in dust jackets, which were derided as a marketing tool — a slipcase sufficed for extra protection.[41] A slipcase added overall substance and an implicit importance to the book as well, presuming a permanent place on one's shelf. Like most books published in the 1920s, fine books were usually casebound in rigid paper boards covered with paper, cloth, leather, or some combination of those conventional materials. Color and pattern were important, but the effect was almost always subdued and decorative — not commercialized in any way.

In his "decalog for the making of fine books," Otto Ege declared that bindings should ideally — that is, historically — accord with the book's text: "Paper-covered boards give a friendly aspect to a book and should be used for poetry, fiction, informal essays; cloth presents the idea of service and seriousness and suggests text-books — it should, therefore, be used for scientific works and serious essays; leather bears an air of aloofness, an aristocratic tone, and is appropriate for metaphysics and classics; and vellum . . . radiates an air of luxurious and consecrated quality that should be reserved for the most precious of intellectual achievements, epic poems, religious works and lofty essays."[42] Postwar fine editions, however, suggested no correlation between subject matter and binding material. Bindings simply imparted "aristocratic tone" and even "consecrated quality," virtually regardless of text. "Taste" and luxury were the key.

Sometimes that luxury was achieved through elaborate decoration, but more common was the use of extravagant materials.[43] Twice the Grabhorns had their books bound between mahogany boards, for example, with a leather spine. Leather was an obvious prestigious choice, but its high cost was usually prohibitive as an edition binding (applied to all copies) for all but the grandest and most carefully financed undertakings: its expense would both require a major capital investment and limit the number of buyers. More often, fine books were bound in quarter (spine only) or half (spine and outside corners) leather. These bindings, distinctive and decorative without the expense of full leather, satisfied bibliophiles whose tastes exceeded their fortunes (see table 2).

Proportions are another key clue to the generic material difference in fine books. Especially when status was an explicit consideration, these books tended to be large. Porter Garnett scoffed at the notion that small, "handy" books were necessarily better than large ones. "There are those who, undeluded by pragmatism and undebased by false ideas of efficiency, may still, in the seclusion of study or library, find pleasure in the leisurely perusal of, let us say, *The Golden Legend* [a Kelmscott masterpiece], in folio, nobly enthroned upon its lectern." Morris contended that large books were the naturally felicitous result of using handmade papers; for an ideal book's pages to turn smoothly and "lie quiet" during reading, only larger dimensions allow the stiffer, thicker handmade papers to relax when the book is open. "A small book seldom does lie quiet," he wrote, "and you have either to cramp your hand by holding it, or else put it on the table with a paraphernalia of matters to keep it down, a table-spoon on one side, a knife on the other, and so on, which things always tumble off at a critical moment, and fidget you out of the repose which is absolutely necessary to reading; whereas, a big folio lies quiet and majestic on the table, waiting kindly till you please to come to it, with its leaves flat and peaceful, giving you no trouble of body, so that your mind is free to enjoy the literature which its beauty enshrines."[44] According to Morris, a book's size derives from structural considerations; ideally, the use of handmade papers dictates that a book's dimensions be large enough to allow the paper to behave properly.

Bob Grabhorn had a more mundane explanation for why fine books were frequently large, reaching eight to ten by fourteen to fifteen inches, or even bigger (see table 3). He explained that big books simply sold better than small, that people would rather buy an eight-page folio than a forty-page duodecimo. His brother put it more graphically, admitting that they made so

Table 3. Dimensions and Proportions

	1920–26	1927–28	1929	1930	1931–32	All	% of Known
Total books	61	67	65	66	41	300	
Page dimensions							
H & W 10″ or more	5	0	2	4	3	14	5.7
H or W 10″ or more	17	14	12	20	15	78	31.6
Height 7–10″	27	45	36	23	14	145	58.7
Height under 7″	1	1	5	2	1	10	4
Not known (17.7%)	11	7	10	17	8	53	
Foot margin as % of page height							
31% or more	4	4	5	3	1	17	9
26–30%	15	14	10	12	8	59	31.4
21–25%	18	23	16	18	11	86	45.7
16–20%	4	4	5	4	5	22	11.7
Less than 15%	1	0	1	1	1	4	2.1
Not known (37.3%)	19	22	28	28	15	112	
Text type size							
16 point or more	7	2	9	10	5	33	17.6
14 point	11	4	7	8	8	38	20.2
12 point	19	26	11	16	9	81	43.1
Less than 12 point	3	12	11	4	6	36	19.1
Not known (37.3%)	21	23	27	28	13	112	
Leading as % of text type size							
60% or more	1	4	7	6	4	22	12.2
36–59%	8	10	7	9	8	42	23.3
20–35%	15	13	12	5	4	49	27.2
Less than 20%	16	17	9	16	9	67	37.2
Not known (40%)	21	23	30	30	16	120	

many big books because "it was a matter of price. You print a little book and put a lot of work into it and the most you can get for it is three dollars. You print very big books, even if they have only half a dozen pages, and you can justify twenty, twenty-five dollars for the price."[45] Their largest book of the decade was a 1926 edition of *The Book of Job* (twenty-five dollars), just thirty pages long but measuring eleven by seventeen inches. The Grabhorns and Nash account for a disproportionate share of the monumental fine bookmaking in the 1920s and early 1930s, but they were hardly the sole purveyors of large books.

Grand size conveyed exactly what many bibliophiles sought in their books: "Stateliness of form imparts dignity," Garnett asserted. "Stateliness of form implies stateliness of content, and vice versa." Ed Grabhorn recalled that once he and Cerf had decided that their edition of *Leaves of Grass* would be "the finest book to be printed in America," he knew that "it had to be a folio in size, because for One Hundred Dollars you had to get a folio." Similarly, when Maurice Firuski of the Dunster House Bookshop commissioned the Pynson Printers to produce a fine edition of Archibald MacLeish's *Nobodaddy* in 1925, he envisioned offering the book in two sizes, printed on different hand-made papers. Because only a part of the edition would be signed by MacLeish, Firuski wanted to ensure through its larger dimensions that the signed edition (50 of 750 copies) "should seem substantially more, even in appearance."[46]

A book's size connoted much about how one was to interact with it: large books required a special facility for reading and storage. They were emphatically not transportable, not meant to be curled up with or tucked into a pocket for private reading on a park bench. When Bruce Rogers began designing the New Oxford Bible in 1930, he privately expressed dissatisfactions with the book's design, remarking that "size is its only merit as typography." He recognized that the book's dimensions alone, twelve by sixteen inches, amply accomplished the primary design agenda, which was to create a book of unmistakable grandeur and preeminence.[47] It was to be a lectern bible, destined for the finest cathedrals in England and America — an icon to inspire awe and reverence. Others also acknowledged, often wistfully, the power of sheer size to suffice for fineness; Carl Rollins welcomed deliberately small fine books (four by six inches or so) as a refreshing contrast to the market's penchant for "Great Big Tomes, which have only their size to commend them." Rollins urged printers and collectors to look with greater favor upon smaller "gem-like" books, arguing that "the big book demands a big subject — wanting that, it is a failure."[48]

The tendency for fine books to be large was so pronounced that those who defied it either provoked objections or felt compelled to supply an explicit defense. Bennett Cerf vigorously rejected an overture from Cecil Johnson proposing that the Windsor Press produce a series of small-format ("sixteenmo") books for Random House. "I loathe 16mos," Cerf declared with uncharacteristic vehemence. He dismissed them as "hackneyed knickknacks" that exploited the allure of fine bookmaking by dispensing it in shamelessly small doses. When Dwiggins began to design the Lakeside illustrated edition of Poe's *Tales*, he anticipated Kittredge's qualms by conceding, "the size of the book as it shapes up to me is so much smaller than the usual grand edition that it may strike you as odd. Its (relatively) small size is somehow a feature of it with me, I picture it as a quite personal volume — quite handy and intimate — and not one of the usual kind of limited edition affairs. I think we can make it rich enough to be quite desirable to the fancy without depending on area. I see it as a compact and quite rich package."[49] The book's elaborate gold tooled covers helped compensate for its modest size.

Upon the page, scale was proportionately grand as well. Printers often re-created the generous formulas for margins employed in medieval and Renaissance bookmaking (typically 1.5:2:3:4 or 1:1:2:4 for inner, head, outer, and foot margins, respectively). On folios this might mean a foot margin of three or more inches. The Cheshire House edition of Dante's *Inferno,* which measured twenty-six by thirteen inches, included a foot margin of nearly five inches. More telling than raw measurements, however, is the proportion of the page's total height occupied by its foot margin. Although conscientious designers rightly hesitate to pronounce rules about ideal margins, in most well-designed trade books today the foot margin occupies between 10 and about 18 percent of the page's height.[50] Fine editions regularly exceeded these trade norms, and a significant number featured foot margins of more than a fourth, and even as much as a third, of the book's height (see table 3).

Type would be scaled correspondingly large too. A large page needed a large text type to maintain comfortable and attractive proportions. Books for adult readers are usually considered best composed in nine-, ten-, or eleven-point type, depending upon the typeface and line length, but fine editions seldom used text types smaller than twelve-point, and were often composed in four-teen-, sixteen-, eighteen-, and even twenty-four-point type (see table 3).[51] Large text type may also have helped to signal hand composition, because machine composition often could not exceed twelve-point output.

A final consideration of proportion is the amount of space between each line of text, or leading. While leading also defies definitive norms, in general it should be proportionate to the size of the type, modified slightly depending on the length of the line. Ten- or eleven-point type is usually set with one or two points of leading, and twelve- and fourteen-point type generally need two points of leading, according to typographic authority Marshall Lee.[52] Converted to ratios, these proportions recommend leading that ranges from 10 to 20 percent of the type size. In fine book composition, that ratio tends to be much higher; it was not unusual to compose fine books with leading that was more than 35 percent of the type size (see table 3).

Because the artistry and resources invested in a fine book's physical features ostensibly signified bibliophilic values, excesses were inevitable. Printers and patrons alike grew tempted to focus on grand size, opulent materials, or typographic artistry per se, overshadowing the book's functional or textual identity. Donald Friede cringed later to recall the colossal vanity of the 1929 Covici-Friede edition of the complete works of Rabelais. Totaling more than thirteen hundred pages, thirteen by ten inches in size, and illustrated by Jean de Bosschere "in all the colors of the rainbow plus a lavish use of gold leaf," the edition was massively ambitious. "Even in those free and easy days, when anybody could sell anything for any price, we came close to coming a cropper on this book," Friede admitted. "We had planned it for three volumes, bulked as all limited editions were bulked then, and solidly boxed in cardboard. But the books . . . weighed a total of fully twenty-five pounds, and no cardboard known to man could contain them without breaking. . . . The worst thing about this edition was that . . . the first volume ran to well over six hundred pages and weighed almost fifteen pounds. . . . It was a physical impossibility to hold the first volume, let alone read it, and the booksellers threw up their hands in horror when they saw it."[53] Although they managed to sell about half the copies themselves and eventually wholesaled the rest to a mail-order dealer, the episode illustrates both the rewards and risks of extravagant fine publishing. Its increasingly material preoccupations had two immediate and contradictory consequences: they were greeted by an acquisitive bibliophilic clamor on one hand, and by critical scorn on the other. The market pulled fine printing in one direction, and its ideological imperatives pulled it in the other.

Some critics felt that the iconic qualities of a fine book betrayed its functional qualities. The most withering contemporary criticism of fine books' "sybaritic gaudery" was leveled in 1931 by Henry Hazlitt in the pages of *The Nation*. "A book too exquisite to be read is as preposterous as a house too exquisite to be lived in," he protested. "As soon as an edition de luxe becomes so luxurious that it becomes a desecration actually to handle it, to read it, its taste has become doubtful, even, at bottom, vulgar." He mocked the Boni and Liveright fine edition of Eugene O'Neill's *Strange Interlude* as a book "with about six times the weight and cubic displacement of the trade edition of the same play, . . . and with a white and gold binding that it seemed a sacrilege for human hands to touch." And as for the Rogers-designed edition of the *Boswell Papers:* "Those gorgeous Venetian-red covers must literally be handled with gloves or a handkerchief; they take a thumbprint that would have made the late M. Bertillon squeal with delight; the type and margins are extravagantly large, and the books are built to stand upright only on the bookshelves of a Brobdignagian."[54]

Even bibliophiles sometimes scorned bookmaking that seemed to have lost all connection to its ostensible purpose. In 1927 Frederic Warde forswore the superficialities he saw in American fine printing that diverted typographic talents toward gimmickry: "No pastries, jacks-in-the-box, no whimsical tricks, no paper flowers, no graveyard decorations: I am sick of them. I want to see examples of typography in which the types have been used almost as effectively for their purpose as are the little wheels in a Swiss watch." Warde raged with vicious sarcasm against the corruptions of "the so-called 'precious' book — the limited edition printed from type which has been specially made and baptized with more talk than work, or all this or that rubbish about so-and-so-many copies on this kind of paper and some other kind of paper or vellum. By Jove, if I had my way once about all this I *would* print an edition in just such a precious manner, and I would print all the copies on human skin ripped from the backs of all these dribbling fancy idiots." In a milder vein Oscar Lewis, San Francisco patron of fine books and long-time officer of the Book Club of California, regretted that printers occasionally succumbed to the "most obvious temptation" to pursue elaborateness for its own sake. "There are too many $50 books," Lewis conceded, "and not enough $5 ones." Publishing industry analyst O. H. Cheney declared bluntly that "too wide a vogue" existed for books that were "beautiful but dumb."[55]

In a host of ways — including grand proportions, rich materials, and performative typography — fine book design venerated the material book as a traditional cultural object. Fine books also, however, reflected the social and cultural ambitions of those who made and bought them. Together these two realities pursued the peculiar iconic agenda at the heart of postwar American fine book design. Fine bookmaking became an end in itself as much as a means of restoring dignity and respect for the printed word. More accurately, the material extravagance of postwar fine bookmaking highlighted its growing service to a different and more ideologically problematic end, that of signaling social and cultural distinction.

5

Classics or Cabbages?
The Question of Content

In October 1928 Bennett Cerf scolded Ed Grabhorn as sternly as he dared: "get that respected bean of yours to work on the Whitman." His telegram warned the California printer that he would not "cease hounding" him until *Leaves of Grass* was started, and that he "might as well give in as gracefully as possible." The problem exasperated Cerf no end; Grabhorn's previous book for Random House, Nathaniel Hawthorne's *Scarlet Letter*, proved a great success and Cerf was eager to keep the partnership going. But Grabhorn was notoriously lackadaisical about plans and commitments, and even about answering urgent letters and telegrams. That August Cerf had urged Grabhorn to "please plan definitely to do Whitman's 'Leaves of Grass' after you have finished 'The Scarlet Letter,'" but by late December Grabhorn still had not agreed, so Cerf wired him a few other ideas: "would you prefer *Moby Dick* or something by Ambrose Bierce?" The following day Cerf wrote again, tenaciously pursuing a deal to produce *something*. Although he still leaned heavily toward *Leaves of Grass* as the next book, Cerf this time suggested Melville's *Billy Budd* as an alternative. Cerf's letter was in the mail before he received Grabhorn's long-awaited reply, by telegram: "Moby Dick four hundred cc will make dummy." "I will stick to you and give you some good books," Grabhorn tersely assured the anxious publisher.[1]

Cerf must have yowled in distress to learn that Grabhorn, at last agreeing to produce another book for Random House, had chosen *Moby Dick*. He had just learned that Rockwell Kent was completing a *Moby Dick* for Donnelley's Lakeside Press. "Seems both foolish and ungracious to compete," he quickly wired Grabhorn, again suggesting *Billy Budd* instead. This time his wait for a reply was not so excruciating. By early January 1929 Grabhorn wired back in his laconic, offhand way, "Whitman elected if you want it," and the matter of the next book was at last resolved.[2] The *Leaves of Grass* regarded by many as the greatest masterpiece of American fine bookmaking, produced at the peak of the golden age of fine editions, might as easily have been *Moby Dick, Billy Budd,* or "something by Ambrose Bierce."

By the end of the 1920s, the material attractions of fine books increasingly clashed with a fundamental imperative of the enterprise — that a fine book's design be devoted to the greater glory of its text. Throughout the boom market, publishers struggled to select texts that might warrant the special raiment of a fine edition, even as they were aware that most consumers would purchase books for the raiment more than the text. Editorial considerations of content were situated precisely at the troublesome intersection of culture and commerce, an especially treacherous crossroads in the realm of fine books.

By definition, fine publishers invested greater care and resources in the material than the textual nature of their books. Random House emphasized that its mission was to issue "books of typographical merit," for example, and when Frederic Warde launched his short-lived Pleiad Press imprint he announced that its texts would be chosen for their "typographic opportunity" as well as for their "literary interest." Leo Hart, a fine printer in Rochester, New York, cheerfully confessed that he was not "a great reader," but that his love for fine printing spurred him to begin publishing bibliophilic editions in the early 1930s. Even so, a fine book was expected to have a fine text. "Only excellent writings on topics of permanent value ought to be considered," solemnly proclaimed one enthusiast, "for shoddy, transient or racy writing has no right to the painstaking care that must go into the formation of the Ideal Book."[3] The whole enterprise rested on the premise that the text itself held a certain cultural or literary stature. Too often, however, texts not only failed to contribute value but actually weakened or undermined the bibliophilic ambitions that encased them. For virtually all fine publishers, in fact, the ability to choose and acquire appropriate content was something of an Achilles heel.

Critic Ben Ray Redmond asserted that fine editions could be divided into two classes: "those that are really worth making beautifully in limited numbers and those that are simply over-priced booby-bait." The epithet of "booby-bait" hung ominously over the content of many postwar fine books. "A cabbage gilded is still a cabbage," one critic pronounced, while another declared that "fine feathers, even in bibliophily, do not make fine birds." A 1926 *Publishers' Weekly* editorial welcomed the growing typographic care and sophistication among printers, but it warned that "famous printers" tend to produce "too high a percentage of ephemeral material or material that does not deserve the distinction of so beautiful a format" and urged them to select "permanently valuable material for their efforts." Three years later, when interest in typographic excellence had turned into a veritable boom in fine publishing, *PW* initiated a monthly column devoted to "Limited Editions" with the hope that the expanding markets would nudge fine publishers beyond the conservative, "rather unimportant material" they had thus far tended to publish.[4]

What, precisely, did bibliophiles want to find upon the pages of their fine books? Although fine printers were aware that the text should be worthy of special treatment, few had the editorial skills or inclinations to make subjective judgments about textual merit. They knew that, despite the cavils, many bibliophiles were not seriously concerned if their list of beautiful books included yet another edition of the *Rubaiyat* or *Sonnets from the Portuguese* or even President Calvin Coolidge's 1926 speech to the American Association of Advertising Agencies.[5] Publishers and patrons alike preferred to think in broad, fairly lax categorical terms when assessing content. The text had to contribute status or value to the production, and its overall character was expected to harmonize with the larger appeal of bibliophilic books as such. Accordingly, the most suitable texts invoked or were sympathetic to the elite cultural values that fine printing embraced.

The interplay of textual and typographic priorities is most evident in the treatment of the two fundamental categories of books: established texts by authors from an earlier era, and new or recent work by contemporary authors. These categories corresponded roughly to two styles of fine publishing: editions of the former tended to subordinate textual content to artistic and typographic performance, while editions of the latter typically exhibited interpretive restraint, focusing on relatively conventional typography but luxurious materials or production processes.

Classics

At the Grabhorn Press, as Bennett Cerf learned so dramatically, the printers focused primarily on making beautiful books; they didn't expend much careful thought on which books. If a lull developed between projects commissioned by other publishers, they simply commenced making a fine edition of whatever struck their fancy. Wrapping up one project, Ed might ask Bob if he had any ideas. As one worker recalled, the younger brother wouldn't hesitate. "Sure, do the Robin Hood. That's a swell book. I was just reading it over last night." At this a nearby typesetter would pause and growl, "What do you want to print that bunk for? Rats! Why don't you print something that isn't so dead it smells? There's a lot of stuff with a real kick in it that you could print." Press artist Valenti Angelo would immediately see the sort of neomedieval possibilities he relished. "Listen, Jack," he'd chide the typesetter, "what do you know about it? Did you ever read the book? I think it's a good idea. Bob, I could make some illuminated initials and we could use that Klingspor black-letter." Pressmen had opinions too: "Why don't you print something by Thackeray?" "How about *Alice in Wonderland?*" Ed would listen as ideas floated by, then end the discussion as abruptly as it had begun. "Hand-set it? Why, we might as well set the Bible. Say, that's not a bad idea, either. Something like *The Book of Ruth.* I always liked that."[6] And that was that.

They were in safe territory, and they knew it. Loosely termed "classics," reprinted texts of a former era (sometimes not very distant) that were presumably respected by critics as well as readers, were squarely compatible with everything one expected in a fine book. Classics emerged from a passively canonical understanding of literature, identified by generations of teachers as the "best" works from the European literary heritage. George Macy defined them as those "fundamental books — always the same books — [that] lie at the base of our culture, and form part of our spirit's very texture." Classics, however, were "not necessarily the most grave and solemn works," Macy continued; they were generally not highbrow, esoteric, or even particularly profound, qualities that risked alienating many modern bibliophiles. Macy assured prospective members of the Limited Editions Club that "obscure 'literary items,' hitherto unpublished work, or works requiring a high degree of literary sophistication" would not be tolerated by the Club's editorial policies.[7] Preferred authors included brand names like Chaucer and Shakespeare and familiar favorites like Robert Louis Stevenson and Edgar Allan Poe. Classics encompassed works that one presumably had read and grown to love and that one could easily and happily read again, but that neither required nor (in many cases) particularly rewarded strenuous intellectual engagement.

Classics ranged from biblical and ancient texts to works by such then-recent authors as Thomas Hardy and Oscar Wilde. Offering a tremendous range of historical periods, subject matter, style, and tone, they showcased designers' or illustrators' talents. It did not much matter that the text was already in print, as it usually was (in fact, that was often something of a relief). A fine edition offered not merely *A Christmas Carol,* for instance, but a notable designer or illustrator's rendition of it. In fact, an old adage advises book collectors to have at least three copies of any favorite text: one to admire, one to read, and one to lend to friends. As one bibliophile explained to a puzzled pragmatist, he often bought multiple copies of the same books because "just as we like to see our beloved in different clothes, so does a favorite book gain charm in varied dress."[8]

Publishers well understood this benevolence toward editorial selection. As long as they remained within the generous parameters of classics, they were more or less free to choose a text according to its bookmaking opportunities. Reprinting classics was a safe editorial course, especially for fine publishers with relatively little interest in or special insight into editorial matters. It was the course fine printers — the Grabhorns, Nash, Richard Ellis, and the Johnson brothers — usually followed when they ventured into publishing. Because they were familiar texts, fine editions of classics were not expected to be much read; their central value lay in expressive presentation, which need not be scrupulous about legibility. In short, classics offered a perfect stage for typographic and artistic performance, for what Bob Grabhorn called monumental bookmaking. When asked "How to Print a Classic," Bruce Rogers confided, "The classic itself is relatively unimportant; in fact, you can make any reasonable piece of literature a classic for book collectors . . . merely by printing it in an acceptable and, if possible, an unusual or luxurious style. It is, however, my conviction that the classics of literature, when printed in a luxurious or unusual style, are fated to live mostly in glass-fronted bookcases and are taken out only occasionally, to be shown to a fellow-collector. The real student of literature prefers to read them in more ordinary editions. But I doubt if they are very widely read at all! Many of them are dull and outmoded to the modern reader, and many of them must have been dull reading when first published."[9]

Within this realm of classics, editorial selections usually reflected the typographic interests of the designer. Some turned an allusive eye to texts of a favorite historical period: Richard Ellis chose work by Goldsmith, Pope, and others to indulge his appetite for eighteenth-century English design, while Valenti Angelo could resist nothing medieval. But most selections were unpredictable, and fine publishers' lists reflected those casual and even arbitrary impulses. Random House initiated its imprint with *Candide* solely because it was what Rockwell Kent wanted to illustrate. When Cerf assessed what the infant company would publish next, the list of possibilities was based on printers' and artists' inclinations rather than any focused editorial policies. Had each title materialized, the 1928 Random House list would have been eclectic indeed: poems by William McFee designed by Updike, a new Homer by Bruce Rogers, *Manon Lescaut* designed by Tom Cleland, Castiglione's *Book of the Courtier,*

Joseph Conrad's *The Sister,* and Robert Louis Stevenson's *Dr. Jekyll and Mr. Hyde,* designed and illustrated by Dwiggins.[10] Similarly, when Cerf traveled to London in the spring of 1930 to scout out possible new Random House productions, he was delighted to take, if he could get it, whatever text a sought-after designer or illustrator wished to produce. He worked particularly hard to acquire the edition of Euclid that Bruce Rogers had been "fooling with" and to secure at least part of a new edition of La Fontaine's *Fables* illustrated by premier English wood engraver Stephen Gooden.[11] Cerf's acquisitional energies focused on securing work of prestigious designers and artists more than on publishing particular texts per se.

Cerf certainly earned his editorial stripes trying to steer the working relationship between Random House and the Grabhorn Press—or even to discern its course. After the immediate success of the first Grabhorn book to bear a Random House imprint—the *Voiage of Maundevile*—Cerf shrewdly recognized the eager market for books made by the Grabhorns. He promptly commissioned them to produce an edition of *The Scarlet Letter,* which sold out almost entirely in advance. Anxious to continue the successful collaboration, Cerf led the often ambivalent printers through a sporadic dance of editorial ideas, initiatives, and inspiration over the next four years. Even as he mailed Ed a formal agreement outlining terms of the *Leaves of Grass* edition in mid-May 1929, Cerf blazed ahead. Probably summarizing conversations during his recent visit to San Francisco, Cerf clarified that "future possibilities for Grabhorn Press-Random House books are 'Two Years Before the Mast,' Marlowe's 'Hero and Leando' [*sic*], and 'A California Diary.'" In October he declared himself eager to do *The Overland Journey,* which Grabhorn had expressed a desire to print, and added, "Don't you think it might be fun to get hold of one of the first Nick Carter stories or something of that sort and bring it out in an appropriately gaudy fashion?"[12]

Grabhorn's silence, stretching for months at a time, no doubt taught Cerf to let the printer finish one book before taking up definite plans for another. The Whitman book proved a greater undertaking than expected, and it was not finished until mid-1930 (to Cerf's helpless anguish). That May, however, the Random House prodding began again in earnest: "What do you say about the Benvenuto Cellini?" Klopfer asked Grabhorn, proposing an edition of the *Autobiography.* In August Cerf eagerly responded to Grabhorn's suggestion about doing an edition of Crane's *Red Badge of Courage,* but warned of an impediment—the book was still governed by copyright: "This would be a marvelous book for us to do if I could possibly worm the necessary permission out of Appleton, who own the copyright." Cerf pronounced Appleton an exceedingly obstinate firm, "with their president, a fat poop named Hiltman, winning all prizes for nastiness. . . . However, I will beard the lion in his den and try to buy, borrow or steal permission to do the Red Badge in a small but worthy edition." In the meantime, Cerf continued, "let's let the Cellini hang fire. In the event that there's nothing doing on the Red Badge, we can take up the question of old Benvenuto again. Another alternative for Cellini, if we *must* do a long book, would be Pepys' Diary. What do you think of that one?"[13]

By December 1930, permissions matters resolved, Cerf spelled out to Grabhorn his preference that they proceed immediately with the *Red Badge,* to be followed by the Cellini and Hawthorne's *House of the Seven Gables,* a title not mentioned previously but that Cerf envisioned as a "natural successor" to the 1928 *Scarlet Letter* and "an absolute cinch to sell out." In the several months that followed, however, economic conditions cooled both men's bibliophilic ambitions. In November 1932 Cerf welcomed the "deliriously satisfying news" that Grabhorn had not even begun to work on the Hawthorne book, gladly forfeiting the advances he had paid toward its and the Cellini's expenses, because both books would have been difficult to sell during the depths of the Depression.[14] Their erratic, exasperating collaboration had effectively come to an end. The meandering editorial course of the Grabhorn–Random House partnership serves as a map, however, of the expansive territory of "classics" deemed safe for fine editions.

Classics provided fine editions with respectability and of course subject matter and character; equally important, their dead authors readily deferred to the artistic performance of designer or illustrator. Cerf was gleeful that Rockwell Kent chose *Candide* for the first Random House edition. It was a popular, well-known classic and, best of all, there would be no need to pay a royalty to "poor old Voltaire; he was in the public domain — the kind of author it's easy to deal with — dead for centuries."[15] In this and other instances the illustrator enjoyed premiere status in virtually every aspect of the book's making, from editorial selection through design and production to marketing, essentially supplanting the author. Illustrator, not author, supplied marquee value and commanded handsome fees if not actual royalties. The absence of an author both freed the publisher from scrupulous attention to textual accuracy (no author would be checking proofs or badgering the editor with revisions and so on) and shifted the spotlight to what was new and interesting about the edition, its visual and material presentation.

Rockwell Kent enjoyed this authorlike status more than any other artist during the postwar boom in fine books, but he was not alone. Dwiggins, Angelo, Thomas Cleland, Donald McKay, Edward O. Wilson, Wharton Esherick, Rudolph Ruzicka, Alexander King, Jean de Bousschere, and a few other artists similarly commanded varying degrees of top billing status. Elmer Adler acknowledged this star quality by showcasing the work of the few most accomplished illustrators. The first major book published by Adler's Pynson Printers (which normally produced fine books only for other publishers) was *The Decorative Work of T. M. Cleland,* published in 1929 after some six years in the making. The book featured nearly one hundred color plates of Cleland's artistry, primarily commercial work commissioned for advertisements, brochures, labels, and so on. In the twenties, the first great era of modern advertising, first-rank artists were hired for commercial enterprises, yielding a new genre of art that many, including Adler, admired. In fact, he hoped to publish a series of books featuring contemporary illustrators. After broaching the subject to Cleland and finding him "quite receptive" to the idea, Adler wrote to Dwiggins about a similar book that "should have Dwiggins for subject and author." But Dwiggins was unenthusiastic, if not downright appalled, at the idea. He exclaimed that the scheme "doesn't hit me at all, at all!" and that the prospect of a compilation of his commercial work for the Strathmore Paper Company and other clients "forms up as a very stupid affair indeed!" Although he tried briefly to formulate an alternative approach, he could not overcome his initial distaste for a book showcasing his commercial illustration, and the project was soon abandoned.[16]

Other major artists of the day shared this ambivalence to commercial work, helping to make book illustration an attractive, though less lucrative, option. Although its rates could not rival the fees paid by corporate clients, book illustration offered better opportunities for more expressive and dignified work. When approached by William Kittredge about designing and illustrating a literary classic to promote the fine printing capacities of R.R. Donnelley's Lakeside Press, for example, Dwiggins welcomed it as a "chance to do something beside waste-basket stuff." "I am rather fed up on spinning myself out for no other purpose than to be promptly thrown away!" he explained. He plainly wished to illustrate one of the special books, but he clarified the trade-off: "I take it that your illustrator-cooperators will have to take a part of their pay in terms of fame and general satisfaction with the product," he noted, which "means that they will have to have subjects that they have always longed to do, and that they will be willing to spend themselves on without much care for the money returns."[17] In exchange for artistic freedom, featured status, and significant editorial prerogatives, more than for money, top illustrators lent their talents to fine book productions.

Dwiggins's reputation empowered him to call the editorial shots. He accepted projects only when the text's illustrative possibilities tempted him. He told Kittredge that he hankered to illustrate Stevenson's *New Arabian Nights,* but—restricted to American classics—he proposed *Knickerbocker's History of New York* or something by Ambrose Bierce: "I want 'em a bit whimsical and a bit grotesque, you see." He subsequently accepted Kittredge's counteroffer of Poe's *Tales,* as well as the "sacrificial" (relative to commercial rates) fee of two thousand dollars. Dwiggins held the same editorial privileges with Random House. In April 1929, as their edition of *Dr. Jekyll and Mr. Hyde* drew to completion (which he had illustrated for a thousand dollars), Dwiggins wrote to Klopfer of his desire to illustrate *New Arabian Nights,* whose stories he commended as "corking subjects for a fantasia" worth considering "if it strikes you to take another whirl at Victorian texts." Klopfer replied the next day that he would prefer something by a different author, "but as long as you're so enthusiastic we definitely want you to do it. We are interested in any book that you want to do," he assured the prized illustrator.[18]

The illustrator's celebrity status was most evident in Rockwell Kent's *Moby Dick* for the Lakeside Press in 1930. Kent was already one of the country's leading book illustrators, noted particularly for the 1928 Random House *Candide,* but the Lakeside *Moby Dick* exceeded his previous work not only in scope (three volumes and nearly three hundred drawings) but in the powerful imagery kindled by the Kent-Melville "collaboration." Kittredge was nearly beside himself with excitement as the project neared completion. "I am scared to death an automobile will run over you," he confessed to Kent early in 1929. "You know when you are associated, even three times removed, with what you think is going to be the greatest book done in this generation, and all you can do is sit and wait and not even push—well, it's a good deal like sitting in the next room waiting to see if it's a boy or a girl." Two months later his nervous joy escalated as another batch of drawings arrived: "We will all go jump in the lake if this book is not the greatest illustrated book ever done in America," he crowed. Kent no doubt relished Kittredge's pleasure, but he demurred at Kittredge's request that he write the introduction to the edition. "I feel that for the illustrator to obtrude himself beyond the bounds of his art, would be in bad taste," he explained. Especially with a title "so established in the world of literature," Kent felt that any introduction would be out of place. Even so, as illustrator Kent catapulted to a prominence that rivaled if not exceeded Melville's. His work so caught the public's attention that his *Moby Dick* illustrations were rendered into wallpaper patterns, just as his illustrations for the Boni Brothers 1929 fine edition of *The Bridge of San Luis Rey* had been adapted for chintz curtain fabric by the Waverly Company. Rockwell Kent was proof that an illustrator could be the star of a bibliophilic book.[19]

The importance of illustration to fine editions of classics is difficult to overstate.[20] When Ed Grabhorn agreed to produce the Random House *Leaves of*

Grass, he understood that its hundred-dollar price tag demanded the inclusion of illustrations. Just as the printers spent months finding a suitably "strong" type, discarding as too weak the Lutetia they had purchased with the advance money from Cerf, so illustration possibilities evolved by trial and error. San Francisco artist Maynard Dixon, who was in the shop when Cerf's go-ahead cable arrived, clamored to illustrate the book. Grabhorn recalled that Dixon hurried out of the shop "and came back the next day with some of the funniest illustrations I ever saw in my life. He took lines from Whitman — 'I loaf and invite my soul[.]' Then he made a picture of Maynard Dixon on the top of a hill with the sun shining on his face, his hat over his head — he was loafing and inviting his soul. The next one he picked out was, 'I sing the body electric.' Then he had a man and woman standing on a rope over a chasm and they had sparks going out of their bodies. They were the funniest thing I ever saw. I'd have been the laughing stock of America if I had used them. They had on coarse knit underwear."[21]

Despite Dixon's entreaties, the task of illustration fell to Valenti Angelo. He worked spontaneously and largely by instinct, trusting that once the right combination of art and typography was struck, he and his colleagues at the Grabhorn Press would all recognize it. For "nine long months," Angelo recalled, they drifted along. "I was given pages set in different kinds of type. For each page set I endeavored to draw a decoration that would be in harmony with the type, after which everyone in the shop was asked his opinion. There were days when I thought I was employed in a lunatic asylum — for all the pros and cons that followed each trial page. . . . Finally I designed and cut a few decorations on plank maple wood. Lo and behold, everyone agreed this idea was well worth considering. Up to this period in experimenting, most of the type used in the trials proved too weak to be in harmony with the strong woodcuts. . . . It was not until a new face cut by Frederic Goudy was found and proofs taken that I began to see a harmony between the art work and the type."[22]

Angelo's account suggests that his woodcuts, carved directly without preliminary designs, preceded and perhaps led the way toward the discovery of the Goudy Newstyle type that was finally used for the book. Bob Grabhorn, however, recalled that once they had decided upon the type, they composed it leaving a space for a very large opening initial for each new poem. After typesetting much of the book, "we decided it would look like an alphabet book. And then we had the spaces there and we had to fill them up." According to Grabhorn, Angelo came to the rescue, substituting "those decorative things, woodcuts" for the large initials originally planned.[23] The illustrations are in fact one of the book's weakest features, but they added a crucial ingredient of art to complement and reinforce the stature of the edition.

Although it was no secret that fine editions of classics served primarily as artistic platforms, discontent grew apace with evidence of a yawning ambivalence toward all but the most rudimentary editorial concerns. Classics were safe, but a safe selection was rarely an applauded one. By the early thirties many felt fine publishing was mired in an editorial rut of overdone classics. O. H. Cheney, in his 1930 report on the state of the publishing industry, complained that although classics constituted only 3 percent of American reading, they were "overabundant" among in-print editions. He lamented that new editions of classics diverted resources from the publication of a more diverse range of contemporary titles. That same year Paul Johnston encouraged fine publishers to choose texts that might invite at least cursory interest in themselves: "It should be obvious that there would be more vitality in an activity concerned with contemporary letters and contemporary book design than in one devoted exclusively to the reprinting of books of another period."[24] Several fine publishers chafed at this criticism that content served merely as an excuse for bibliophilic bookmaking. They sought alternatives to classics, looking for texts of interest in their own right.

Flowers for the Living

When theater impresario and bibliophile Crosby Gaige decided to enter fine publishing in late 1926, he snubbed the usual editorial formulas for fine books. Editions of "well-known contemporaries," he recalled, "seemed to me to be a much more interesting and useful form of limited-edition publishing than the practice of eternally issuing reprints of the classics in new dress. I have always thought flowers for the living, and in this case the living author, more graceful and fragrant than garlands for the dead."[25] Others shared his predilection, especially those who were primarily publishers, not artisans or printers. Even many trade publishers issued fine editions of contemporary work by prominent or critically recognized authors. Alfred Knopf led the way, publishing fine editions by several of his major authors, including Willa Cather, Joseph Hergesheimer, and Elinor Wylie. Other trade publishers similarly splurged in fine editions for their "star" authors: Edna St. Vincent Millay for Harper Brothers, Edwin Arlington Robinson for Macmillan, Eugene O'Neill for Liveright, Robert Frost for Holt, and so on. Fine editions enhanced the author's reputation, connoting literary stature, and enabled both author and publisher to capitalize on the higher prices readily paid for fine books.

A few fine publishers concentrated more or less exclusively on new or un-published work by living authors. Most notable among them were Pascal Covici and Donald Friede of Covici-Friede, James Wells and Elbridge Adams of the Fountain Press, and Crosby Gaige. Although he described himself as only a "desultory reader," Gaige was lured by the adventure, prestige, and profit of fine publishing. He published the work of primarily British writers, including Siegfried Sassoon, Liam O'Flaherty, and Thomas Hardy, in fairly conservative, dignified editions designed and produced by the best-known American fine printers. When he tired of the venture within a few years, claiming that by early 1929 the enterprise "had become more of a business than a pastime as more commercially minded men than I took it up," Gaige's list was taken over by James Wells and Elbridge Adams, who changed the imprint to the Fountain Press.[26] Wells and Adams continued Gaige's editorial policies, adding more American authors to the list.

Publishing contemporary authors brought fine publishers all the editorial headaches and editorial satisfactions of trade publishing. In many respects working with contemporary authors was the livelier path, more engaged with serving and shaping modern literary tastes and talents than reprint-only pro-grams. Unlike the world of classics, whose parameters seemed fixed by canoni-cal assessments (and fine publishers had little interest in challenging those boundaries), the contemporary field remained wide open, full of opportunities for literary contribution. Astute editorial judgments could bring to light the era's finest works — the classics of future generations. Given fine publishing's commitment to texts of permanent value, for those working with contempo-rary texts editorial judgments were as crucial as design and production deci-sions. These fine publishers risked more, certainly, but they also likely stood to gain more — especially in prestige among their publishing peers and within the larger literary and bibliophilic communities. Just as a fine format asserted a text's importance, an important text justified the care of its presentation. As long as the text could plausibly warrant a fine edition, the publication of living authors yielded broader cultural influence than any other editorial strategy.

If a publisher could produce authorized *first* editions of new work by note-worthy writers, the value of the text almost certainly contributed handsomely to the value of — and prices paid for — the edition. Typically such first editions were also signed by the author, providing an endorsement of the edition and adding the value of a prized autograph. In 1929, for example, Bob Grabhorn and San Francisco bibliophile Oscar Lewis formed a partnership as the West-gate Press, an imprint devoted to fine editions by "the most eminent names we could think of," authors like Lewis Mumford, Sherwood Anderson, Virginia Woolf, and Havelock Ellis. Lewis explained that "it occurred to us that there are a number of writers in this country and England who are not 'collected' to any great extent, but who are fully as important as many who are, and that a series of signed first editions by these would interest enough people to sell out small editions." That the books would be printed at the Grabhorn Press was assurance enough of their typographic merit; the Westgate editorial plan reflected the partners' ambition that their books' content would appeal as much as their form, "that these could be sold on their merits and not as examples of typography alone."[27] In theory, first editions of new work by important — or at least reputable — contemporary authors represented an ideal achievement to fine publishers who sought editorial as well as typographic distinction.

Significant difficulties arose, though. The greatest challenge was to identify and secure worthy texts. Most contemporary authors had not yet achieved undisputed acclaim, and each new text was subject to independent scrutiny. Whereas a classic had already been winnowed from its author's corpus, a new work stood yet to be judged — by editor and publisher, by critics, and especially by consumers. The risks that a book's content might be deemed unequal to its form, rendering a misappropriation of fine bookmaking that could discredit the larger enterprise, plagued publishers who plied these editorial waters. Sometimes they relied on others' advice or mere hunches. Bob Grabhorn recalled the cavalier naiveté with which he and Lewis commenced their Westgate Press. "We started out by Oscar selecting magazine articles by what we thought were collected authors."[28] They claimed neither editorial ambition nor talent; they simply looked for short work by authors whose names they recognized as "hot." But they knew that popularity alone was not a sufficient virtue, and that it often signaled qualities of "mass-ness" that bibliophiles found repugnant. The most read authors of the nineteen twenties — including Zane Grey, Bruce Barton, and Emily Post — were notably not honored with fine editions.

Fine publishers of modern writers found themselves seeking the editorial balance between merit and marketability that all publishers seek. They did so more obliquely, however, bound by a professed disdain for commercial concerns. Ideally, fine printing adorned texts of indisputable merit, as determined by cultural reputation or astute critical judgment. Most postwar fine publishers conveyed this impression as they eschewed conventional bookselling strategies in cover design and other advertising techniques. But in reality most recognized the tenuous relationship between the quality of an author's writing and the success of his or her fine editions; they squirmed a bit to think that modern writers who sold well in fine editions might be regarded years later as second-rate. Adler asked Henry Seidel Canby to address this issue in an article for *The Colophon,* a quarterly for book collectors that Adler founded in the late 1920s. "Are collected authors the 'best'?" Adler wondered, adding — perhaps hoping for some editorial guidance — "What English literary master-pieces are overlooked or undervalued by collectors?"[29]

Behind the scenes, fine publishers worked hard to find and acquire work by modern writers that their patrons would deem both legitimate and desirable. The extensive correspondence between Bennett Cerf and Crosby Gaige, then James Wells, dealing with the Crosby Gaige and Fountain Press list of titles offers a fascinating view of these editorial deliberations. Because Random House was the exclusive distributor of the Gaige/Fountain books, and so was expected to purchase each book's entire edition at a significant discount, Cerf increasingly intervened in the publishers' editorial decisions. Initially, how-ever, the agreement with Gaige stipulated that Random House would "have nothing to say about the editorial content, . . . but specifications for the format of the books, the prices and the sizes of the editions are to be approved by Random House, before a definite order for the manufacture of any book is placed."[30] As distributor, Random House was concerned only that Gaige books uphold its typographic and bibliophilic standards. When several of Gaige's books failed to sell well at the prices Gaige set for them, however, Cerf took a more active role in Gaige's editorial affairs. Not wishing to be saddled with unsellable copies of overpriced editions of mediocre literature, Cerf fre-quently offered Gaige advice about what to publish, which the latter was obliged to receive if he wanted Random House to sell his books. In particular, Cerf objected strenuously that Gaige's books were overpriced for the value of either their content or their typography.

Gaige's initial list of prospective books was impressive. It included poems by Siegfried Sassoon and A. E. (George Russell) and fiction by Walter de la Mare, Liam O'Flaherty, and James Joyce. When the proposed books failed to mate-rialize as envisioned, however, or to appeal to American bibliophiles, Cerf dispatched Gaige on an editorial mission to Britain with specific advice about items "worth breaking one's neck for, (particularly yours), while in London." He urged Gaige to secure "anything at all, if signed" by Bernard Shaw or Rudyard Kipling, as well as work by Lytton Strachey, Aldous Huxley, James Stephens, or Norman Douglas.[31] Gaige returned triumphantly with manu-scripts from Strachey and Stephens and Thomas Hardy's widow, as well as Virginia Woolf's *Orlando,* and the list seemed off to an auspicious start.

Gaige was a wealthy and restless cultural dilettante. He admired and col-lected beautiful modern editions and prided himself on the impeccable bibli-ophilic pedigrees of the books he published, but he was not especially inter-ested in fine bookmaking. Neither was he an avid student of contemporary literature. He relished eccentric meetings with literary characters like Strachey and Stephens, but was put off by more seriously modernist writers, both in person and by their texts. He published *Orlando* because he knew Woolf's book would distinguish his list, but he thought little of the work, shrugging it off as "baffling and elusive." He outright disliked the "squalid, unhandsome confusion" of both Joyce's prose and his Paris apartment, where he felt he "was gazing upon the twilight of a very minor god." Regardless, Gaige published a short piece from what would become *Finnegans Wake, Anna Livia Plurabelle*. "O tell me all about Anna Livia! I want to hear all about Anna Livia," the work began. Gaige was unimpressed. "Anyone who wants to know more about Anna Livia has my permission to buy the book," he yawned.[32]

The scramble to produce fine editions of new work by important contemporary authors was fueled in part by the almost frenzied market for signed first editions among postwar book collectors. The prized status of these editions virtually ensured, however, that abuses would occur. Publishers (and authors) sometimes exploited the gullibility of buyers by asserting first edition status of work that had been previously published, usually in a slightly altered form. On at least three occasions Cerf felt cheated by publishers or authors who tried to pass off published material as new, complete with the high prices attending first editions. As distributor, Random House bore the brunt of booksellers' and consumers' ire when such discoveries were made, and Cerf promptly redirected the anger. In August 1928 he fumed to Gaige that the fine edition of James Branch Cabell's *Ballades from the Hidden Way* was not the original material he had been led to believe it was. Cerf shuddered at the expensive scam in which he had unwittingly participated: "When you mentioned this item to me you quite neglected to tell me that it was simply another collection of poems from The Hidden Way, and that the thing you were doing was offering the public, for a total sum of $40.00, a number of poems that had appeared, every one of them, in a volume that was and still is obtainable for $2.00 a copy."[33]

A few months later Random House was again compelled to apologize to the trade for misrepresentation of a Gaige fine edition. This time the culprit was a short play by Irish poet James Stephens, *Julia Elizabeth*. Random House issued an announcement that the playlet "is in effect little more than a copy of a short story written by Stephens many years ago, and now put into play form." To control damage to its credibility, Random House explained that it and the publisher "feel that the book was offered under false pretenses" and urged booksellers to return all copies for full credit and reimbursed expenses. Within three months 150 of the book's 450 copies had been returned. Later that year Cerf proposed to Wells that they lure Stephens to a nearby lake and "duck him six or seven times, charging the credit to the account of 'Julia Elizabeth.'"

Other Gaige/Fountain Press titles caused similar outrages, notably the phony "first edition" of Thomas Hardy's short play *The Three Wayfarers,* originally published in 1893.[34]

These fiascoes stemmed from desires to exploit the keen postwar market for first editions as well as to make beautiful and significant books. Particularly by the end of the decade, the two markets — one in signed and "limited" first editions for collectors, who often bought for investment value, and the other in finely made books for bibliophiles, who bought for a more culturally complex variety of reasons — dovetailed, even as they diverged in significant ways. Many if not most first editions were limited only in that they claimed to be so, and many bore a copy-specific number and an author signature, but usually that was the extent to which they resembled fine editions. Hence the distinction, murky at times but critical here, between limited editions and fine ones. All fine books were limited — usually explicitly and proudly, for reasons ostensibly imposed by features of their design and production — but many limited editions were not fine in any but the most superficial and even deceptive senses. Books published by Crosby Gaige, Fountain Press, and other imprints devoted to fine first editions tried to appeal to both markets, but those markets' divergent priorities often made that difficult, and perhaps inevitably disappointing to both audiences.

By the time Gaige completely lost interest and sold the troubled list to Wells late in 1928, Cerf was taking no chances with the new young publisher. He clarified which authors he could proudly and easily sell: Joyce, Stephens, A. A. Milne, John Galsworthy, and American poet Edwin Arlington Robinson. Conversely, Cerf made it equally clear "that we will not consent for a moment to any more such authors as Liam O'Flaherty, Richard Aldington or John Drinkwater." Furthermore, in agreeing to distribute Fountain Press books as it had handled Gaige's, Cerf was more demanding in terms of editorial privileges: "Random House is not only to see [each book's] manuscript, but is to authorize the publication of that book with the price and the exact size of the edition in writing, before manufacture of the book is begun."[35]

The correspondence between Cerf and Wells over the next few years documents an ever-spiraling exasperation in their relationship. Notes flew back and forth across Manhattan as the two men sparred over the editorial wisdom of almost every title contemplated, and over the appropriate prices and edition sizes for each. Invariably Cerf's estimation was less sanguine than Wells's. Cerf could muster little enthusiasm for a prospective book by D. H. Lawrence, he wrote to Wells in March 1929, but in the same letter he regarded a new G. B. Shaw item as "a horsie of a different color. If you let that slip through your fingers, young fella," he warned, "you will not only have me to answer to but an old man with long red whiskers who peddles lead pencils outside of Gimbel Brothers, and looks very much like G.B.S. himself." In June Cerf approved the possibility of Virginia Woolf's *A Room of One's Own* as "a neat addition" to the Fountain list, but he nixed a collection of Sinclair Lewis short stories as "the cheapest kind of 'pot boilers,'" having "about as much distinction as a Reuben bologna sandwich, and . . . about as much right to be perpetuated in a limited edition as has the Wells-Cerf correspondence. Less even!" A month later Cerf returned the manuscript of Arthur Symons's *Confessions* to Wells, pronouncing it "very anaemic fare. . . . If you are going to insist on bringing out stuff of this nature, more poems by Humbert Wolfe and unimportant essays by people like Ellen Glasgow, your Fountain Press imprint will soon be absolutely worthless."[36]

The bickering continued throughout the fall. In October Cerf refused to distribute an edition of "Tree in December," a poem by Melville Cane, after consulting area booksellers and confirming that "not one of us has ever heard of Melville Cane." Wells's reply conveys the tone of much of the men's business transactions: "Except for a feeling of sadness it is relatively unimportant to me what S. Moss or Drake [New York booksellers] or yourself know or hear of Melville Cane. It is too late in life for me to undertake the education of either Moss or yourself, nor have I the patience to attempt it. If we were to offer . . . Christ's own memoirs, signed by him, there would be someone in this wide land who would come back with the statement that he was not known to them."[37] Wells's insinuation that he heeded literary merit while Cerf was governed by pecuniary market considerations is largely bluff. Both men understood that fine books were obliged to honor, or at least pursue, both criteria. Both also were well versed in contemporary writing and reasonably shrewd judges of editorial merit. As distributor, however, Cerf was more alert to market considerations — which in fine publishing depended on reputation more than merit alone. Fine editions confirmed an author's reputation; they were not well suited for "discovering" an author, however brilliant.

Editorial Problems and Challenges

TEXT VERSUS TYPOGRAPHY

Tensions frequently arose between design priorities and concerns for the text. When producing work by living authors, fine publishers negotiated the same gamut of relationships with authors, from collaborative to combative, that trade publishers faced. In most instances authors cooperated, becoming involved only in the traditional ways: finalizing text copy, correcting proofs, and so forth. Occasionally, however, authors devoted exceptional attention to a text to be finely printed, fussing with it to the exasperation of the printer. Archibald MacLeish intervened in the production of his play *Nobodaddy* after work was well under way, for example, confessing to Dunster House publisher Maurice Firuski that upon seeing proofs he "skittishly" found it "unworthy to print." MacLeish proceeded to revise the short play extensively, even though it meant bearing the costs of resetting the type himself.[38]

More common were struggles over textual accuracy and over which interests — textual or typographic — would take precedence. At times printers went so far as to alter a text to achieve a more attractive typographic page. In designing the fine edition of Elinor Wylie's *Trivial Breath* for Knopf in 1928, for example, Elmer Adler trimmed words and punctuation in his quest for the page beautiful. Wylie's response to the proofs was anything but trivial, Adler later wrote. He also rearranged the order of the poems to suit his concerns for visual balance, prompting Wylie's husband, William Rose Benét, to protest that all such decisions should be cleared with Wylie first. MacLeish similarly implored his publisher to make sure that "no one changes my rhythms as they were changed in the first proofs" of *Nobodaddy,* a book also made by Adler's Pynson Printers.[39]

Although authors of classics were usually long dead and unable to tinker with their texts in proofs, or to resist another's tinkering, contemporary translators and editors of fine editions of classics frequently entered into such squabbles. When Updike designed the Random House edition of Whitman's novel *Franklin Evans,* he relegated much of Emory Holloway's editorial work to the back of the book, contending that "too much apparatus diverts the reader from the story and upsets the typographical illusion" sought by the nineteenth-century design scheme. Holloway proved to be a "very fussy fellow" in guarding the interests of his work, but he accepted his demotion to the back matter, possibly because he had serious misgivings about the production. As he had earlier warned Cerf, he could not muster much praise for the book in his introduction since even Whitman had reprinted the story as "juvenilia" mainly to prevent others from doing so.[40]

Authors, editors, and translators sometimes claimed or sought authority over the typography as well. Just as fine printers understood their craft as a means of shaping textual value and meaning, savvy authors also recognized typography's interpretive power. At times the result was happy, as when Willa Cather received from Adler a preview copy of Knopf's fine edition of her 1922 *April Twilights* (accompanied by a bouquet of roses). She declared that his work had revived her interest in the poems and that the occasion marked a new threshold of "relations between writer and printer." More often, however, writers were unwilling to defer to printers when typographic decisions undertook aggressive interpretive roles. Even Cather grew wary of Adler's work later in the decade; in 1927 he chafed when Knopf granted the prized author approval power over her books' design. As critic Jerome McGann has explored, the fine printing revival begun in the 1890s "encouraged writers to explore the expressive possibilities of language's necessary material conditions." In ways not unprecedented but freshly envisioned, many modern writers recognized that careful and deliberate typography "foreground[ed] textuality as such, turning words from means to ends-in-themselves."[41] Power over a text's presentation was no less critical than power over its linguistic content.

When writers took a keen interest in the typography of their work, they often pitted their ideas against the designer's. Bruce Rogers recalled that for the Rudge edition of *Roderigo of Bivar* author T. Sturge Moore had made a type ornament of a fish to indicate pauses and to fill out short lines in the brief drama, set in medieval Spain. Rogers balked at the sight of Moore's plan for the first page, thus ornamented with seventeen fish. He complained that "at the very first appearance of the ornament, at the end of a line of stage directions, the line was made to read: 'As the curtain rises Martin's voice from within the trellis on the right cried: [fish].' . . . the whole book would have been peppered with fish. This might have been well enough in *The Compleat Angler,* but not in a Spanish tragedy."[42] Rogers's indignant will prevailed, and no fish appeared in the edition.

Authority over content and form was nowhere more hotly contested than in the 1932 Random House *Beowulf,* illustrated by Rockwell Kent (see figure 20). The edition was suggested to Kent by George F. Richardson, a *Beowulf* scholar whose new translation impressed both Kent and Cerf. Random House advisors disliked the translation, however, preferring either a "popular" translation or the original Old English text. Richardson was incensed. He freely admitted that "it is Mr. Kent's drawings, . . . not my translation nor anybody else's, that will sell the book," but scorned "the brilliant idea of wasting Rockwell Kent drawings on the Old English text—presumably without notes or glossary—which not more than one man in a million could read easily and completely." He exclaimed, "Good God, to wrap up the Old English in Kent drawings would be like embalming a corpse in good ale—for which there are better uses." He dismissed the translation of William Ellery Leonard, which the press eventually used, as a failed effort at popularity. "To put the *Beowulf* into galloping ballad couplets is about as inappropriate as to give the 'Star

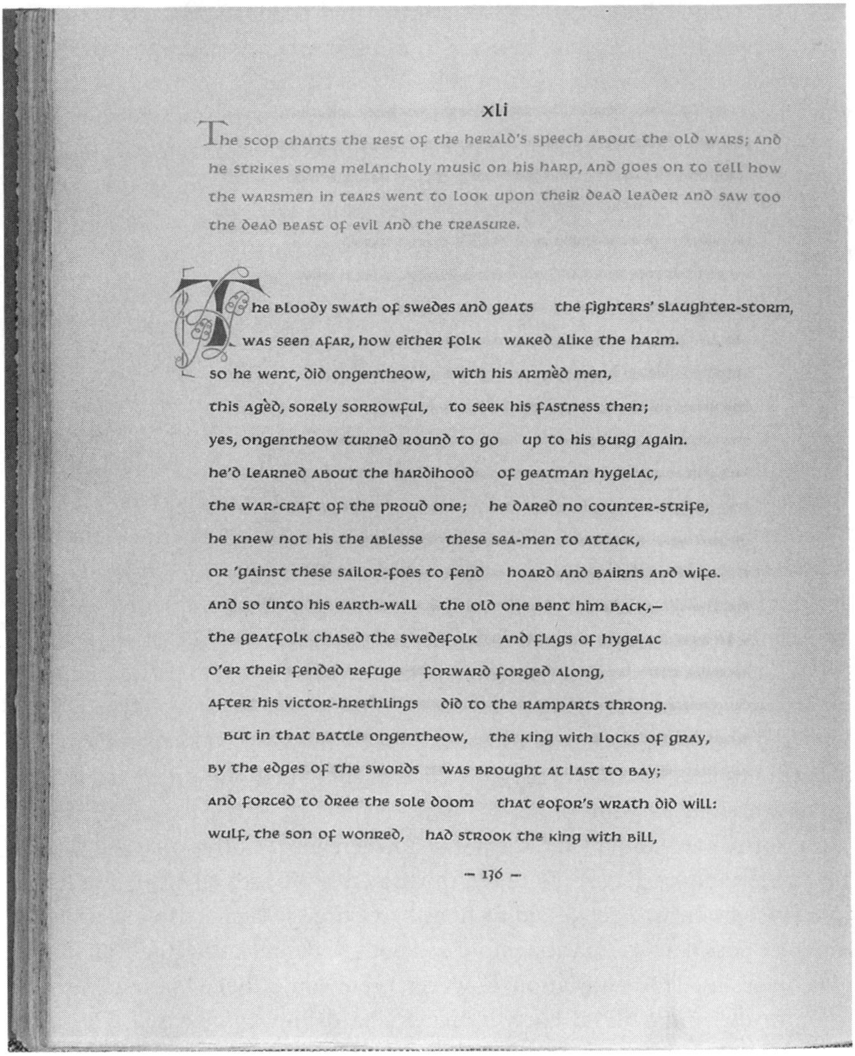

xli

The scop chants the rest of the herald's speech about the old wars; and he strikes some melancholy music on his harp, and goes on to tell how the warsmen in tears went to look upon their dead leader and saw too the dead beast of evil and the treasure.

The bloody swath of Swedes and Geats   the fighters' slaughter-storm,
was seen afar, how either folk   waked alike the harm.
So he went, did Ongentheow,   with his armèd men,
this agèd, sorely sorrowful,   to seek his fastness then;
yes, Ongentheow turned round to go   up to his burg again.
He'd learned about the hardihood   of Geatman Hygelac,
the war-craft of the proud one;   he dared no counter-strife,
he knew not his the ablesse   these sea-men to attack,
or 'gainst these sailor-foes to fend   hoard and bairns and wife.
And so unto his earth-wall   the old one bent him back,—
the Geatfolk chased the Swedefolk   and flags of Hygelac
o'er their fended refuge   forward forged along,
after his victor-hrethlings   did to the ramparts throng.
    But in that battle Ongentheow,   the king with locks of gray,
by the edges of the swords   was brought at last to bay;
and forced to dree the sole doom   that Eofor's wrath did will:
Wulf, the son of Wonred,   had strook the king with bill,

— 136 —

Figure 20. *Beowulf* (New York: Random House, 1923). Illustrated by Rockwell Kent, designed and produced by Elmer Adler, Pynson Printers. Photo courtesy of Special Collections Division, University of Washington Libraries.

Spangled Banner' the rhythm and tempo of 'Hot Time.' Incidentally," he added, "do you think the *Beowulf* could ever be popularized with any but a high class of the intelligent?"[43]

Perhaps Richardson's ire was appeased when the book finally appeared. Leonard pronounced Kent's drawings a travesty, his interpretations so "ridicu-

lously conventional and inadequate (indeed, inaccurate)" as to constitute a "swindle." Leonard's role also had been badly mangled; he coolly pointed out to Adler that in the book's preface his translation had "been reduced to a *transition*" and his "authorship of the English to the work of an *editor*." Leonard had earlier conceded to the publisher's request that, "since it is to be a very fine book," the notes be omitted.[44] In the end there was little pretense that the edition was much more than a vehicle for Kent's art. Both translators, representing textual authority, considered themselves victims of a bibliophilic agenda that sacrificed content to form.

THE HO-HUM DEPARTMENT

With a yawn, in 1927 Carl Rollins commenced his biweekly "Compleat Collector" column on fine publishing in the *Saturday Review of Literature*. He wryly confessed, "we can only record with mournful boredom the arrival of yet another edition of Fitzgerald's "Rubaiyat," . . . Referred to the ho-hum! department." By the late 1920s growing discontent over reprinted classics gave way to an even sharper complaint, that fine editions offered little variety even among the classics. Joseph Blumenthal understood this as he considered launching his Spiral Press. Not interested in turning out "still another *Sonnets from the Portuguese* or a *Rubaiyat of Omar Khayyam*," he turned instead to lesser-known works of eighteenth- and nineteenth-century American literature. Paul Johnston urged fine publishers to extend their editorial vision even further. "When the different makers of fine books come to a point of printing the same titles over and over again," he contended, claiming a preponderance of such titles as *Gulliver's Travels*, Sterne's *Sentimental Journey*, works of Chaucer, and the *Book of Ruth*, "the natural suggestion is that they ought to turn their attention to contemporary literature." Johnston's point is valid, but he might have selected better examples. Fine publishers seemed to find most tempting the works of Voltaire, a handful of American writers — Ben Franklin, Washington Irving, Nathaniel Hawthorne, Edgar Allan Poe, and Walt Whitman — and especially Robert Louis Stevenson. Arguably the single most popular "author" of postwar fine editions was the Bible; buyers seemed never to tire of new fine renditions of the *Song of Solomon*, the *Book of Ruth*, and so on.[45]

The practice of returning too often to a well-regarded author was hardly limited to classics, however. Overpublication of some living writers was just as tempting, resulting in what Cerf termed "overdone" authors. At least twice Cerf discouraged publishers from pursuing a particular title for this reason. Early in 1929 he warned James Wells that Random House would not distribute the proposed Fountain Press edition of Humbert Wolfe's *Homage to Meleager*. He did not dispute its "high literary merit," but pointed to the recent poor sales of Wolfe's *Craft of Verse*, published by Gaige in 1928, as evidence of too many Humbert Wolfe editions in the past twelve months.[46] Similarly, Cerf cautioned publisher Joseph Leventhal of the Chocorua Press that his planned edition of Christopher Morley's *Trade Winds* was likely to suffer because, as Cerf put it, "Morley is overdoing this limited edition thing."

Leventhal conceded that the Morley market was "on its last legs," but he clung to his conviction that *Trade Winds* "will go on its own merits, despite the Morley slump."[47]

Although complaints about yet another *Rubaiyat* or *Sonnets from the Portuguese* were a fashionable if facile cliché, the problem of exploiting a particular author was more serious in the contemporary arena. Of the authors whose work appeared in multiple fine editions throughout the decade, most were still living. Both British writers — notably, Virginia Woolf, Aldous Huxley, and George Moore — and American writers — including Robert Frost, James Branch Cabell, and Willa Cather — enjoyed a considerable cachet among postwar bibliophiles.

BOOKEENS

Another problem that surfaced more often with modern texts was the tendency to create a book from a very short text, usually in an attempt to stretch work (ideally new) from a sought-after author into several small books rather than to offer it as one more substantial publication. In 1930 the Fountain Press issued as a fine book Aldous Huxley's fourteen-line poem *Appenine*, and Westgate published Virginia Woolf's eight-page essay *Beau Brummel*. Rudge published John Drinkwater's sixteen-page poem *Persephone* in 1926, and the Grabhorns published a nine-page edition of Homer's *Hymns to Aphrodite* in 1927, to mention a few other examples. Authors sometimes had slightly more scruples about this than publishers did: James Stephens assured James Wells that although the original manuscript of his essay "On Prose and Verse" was only six pages long, he had mustered "extra matter of ten pages" so that "the bookeen will be of quite respectable size."[48] Publishers, however, seemed more inclined to calculate just how little text would suffice. Cerf recognized as "first rate stuff" T. S. Eliot's poem *Ash Wednesday*, but he expressed reservations to Wells that because it was "very slender" the market might not bear the steep ten-dollar price Wells had in mind. Cerf encouraged Wells to "have a fine little book made out of this item," but cautioned him to keep its price accordingly modest.[49] When Elmer Adler planned a fine edition of Thornton Wilder's new *Bridge of San Luis Rey* for Albert and Charles Boni, he worried that the text seemed "too slight to become a classic." Despite his qualms, Adler conceded that "the book may be worthy of a special handling but to me it appears even more necessary that everything possible be put into the book if the edition that we are to make is to stand on its own feet."[50]

Adler's strategy of compensating materially for brief textual content was common. Several hallmark features of bibliophilic bookmaking were at least partially rooted in the need to stretch out a slight text into a reasonable number of pages to warrant production as a book. These techniques included generous illustration when the budget allowed (as in the Boni Brothers edition of *The Bridge of San Luis Rey,* with six full-page color lithographs by Rockwell Kent), extravagant margins, numerous blank leaves, thick papers, and unusually large type sizes and generous leading. Conventionally books are composed in ten- or eleven-point type with one or two points of leading, depending on length of the line and the particular typeface used. (This norm is based on legibility requirements for comfortable sustained reading. It is not as beholden to economic considerations as norms on margins, dimensions, and so forth.) By contrast, fine editions of skimpy texts were often composed in noticeably larger types—eighteen-point or even twenty-four-point—and heavily leaded with as much as ten or twelve additional points. Although this strategy yielded additional pages, it violated a basic precept of revival typography—the preference for close, even dense, word spacing and minimal leading to achieve visual unity. This discrepancy between theory and practice is no small irony; it reflects an unspoken but widespread willingness to sacrifice aesthetic principles to publishing expedients.

The need to bulk out a slim text also drove decisions to add elements— editorial commentary, supplementary essays, and so on. Especially when the primary text was a reprint of some familiar literary work, it was virtually essential that the edition include something new to justify the publication. Sometimes these extras matched or exceeded the text itself in length, as in John Henry Nash's edition of Addison's essay *The Trial of the Wine-Brewers,* which occupied only eight of the book's eighteen text pages. Random House's edition of *The Way to Wealth,* an eleven-page excerpt from Ben Franklin's *Almanac* was accompanied by an eleven-page essay about it, and Johnck and Seeger's 1926 edition of Gray's *Elegy Written in a Country Churchyard* filled only nine of the book's twenty-one text pages. When possible, the author could be enlisted to generate more material.

TYPOGRAPHIC PICTURES

"What Is Fine Printing?" the small-town Pennsylvania printer Horace McFarland queried skeptically in the trade journal *Printing Art* in 1922. He had received a copy of Porter Garnett's fastidiously designed brochure announcing the new Laboratory Press, but he claimed he could "barely decipher" the neomedieval type chosen for the title (see figure 21). He found the brochure condescending in its lengthy and esoteric colophon and its studied historicism that "subordinates everything to decoration." Confessing to "iconoclastic impulses," McFarland challenged the fineness of printing "supposed to be reverenced by us poor dubs who still cling to the idea that the primary function of printing is to convey thought."[51]

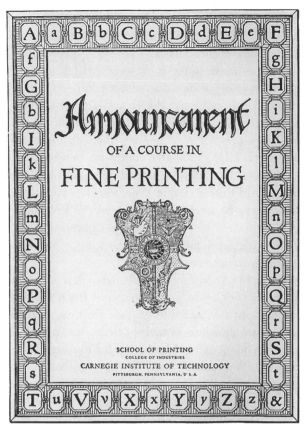

Figure 21. Announcement of fine printing course,
Carnegie Institute of Technology, Pittsburgh, 1923.
Designed by Porter Garnett.

In truth, sometimes bibliophilic priorities not only subordinated content but actually obscured it. When fine editions rendered their texts inaccessible to readers, sacrificing legibility to larger aesthetic aims, they betrayed the most basic publishing function. The Grabhorns' proprietary typeface, for example, was a neomedieval design by Frederic Goudy that they named Franciscan. They heard grumbling from customers each time they used it, but Ed Grabhorn persistently dismissed as "ridiculous" complaints that it was difficult to read. The objection made sense if one assumed that the book was meant to be read, but the Grabhorns understood that the texts were usually familiar — Bible selections, fables, and so on — and could be read easily in other forms. Even when the press's bibliography, compiled in 1940 by David Magee, was composed in Franciscan and met the same complaints, Magee contended that the type's handsome design compensated for its illegibility. Because the book was a reference tool, not meant to be read at any long sitting, Magee assured, its owners could "endure" the unfamiliar type for the "five minutes" they would likely spend reading it on any single occasion.[52]

John Henry Nash was even less abashed about the occasional sacrifice of legibility to typographic art. In 1929 he produced an ornate edition of *Psalms of the Singer David* composed in a decorative gothic (blackletter) type called Priory Text. The book's colophon explained that Nash made the book as a gift to his "Jewish friends of San Francisco" in tribute to "their distinguished patronage of music, art, and letters." He anticipated confusion, however, and clarified his purposes: "About this Gothic printing of the *Psalms,* it will doubtless be said by critics that it is hard to read. I agree; the book has been done with the hope that it will prove to be a typographic picture."[53] Everything about the book — its size (about sixteen by nine and a half inches), the three colors of printed text, its handmade paper, and its stylized, archaic type — was intended to create a beautiful object, not a readable book.

Although they rarely stated so in public, most fine printers knew well that legibility was not a top priority. They could and did espouse the prevailing dogma of invisibility, of typography's mandate to provide clear, unimpeded access to the text, but they seldom practiced in their fine editions what they preached for books in general. When Random House decided to issue a trade edition of *Candide,* reproducing the Rockwell Kent illustrations that had so enthralled buyers of the fine edition, Adler made certain to use a different type for the text. In part this was to preserve the distinctive character of the fine edition, to protect its rarity and value, but it was also to make the trade version a "much more readable book." "A popular-priced book should be a reading book," he explained to Cerf, "in contrast to the collector's item that the original edition is likely to become."[54]

Legibility was not often a serious issue, because it was not a prime source of the value of fine books. Criticism from within the bibliophilic world tended to be mild or muted, and few outsiders had occasion to observe and so to evaluate the readability of fine books.[55] Occasionally, however, blistering resentment was expressed when formal and material ambitions were achieved at the outright expense of the text. Even if one did not primarily intend to read a finely printed text, one should at least be able to if so inclined, critics protested. As McFarland's objections revealed, there was a growing disparity between editorial and typographic ambition in much of postwar fine publishing. While conscientious typography purported to serve content — even to exalt it — needs of the text often threatened to compromise the desire for distinguishing cultural goods that in fact powered the market for fine books. In matters of text as well as form, fine books were not intended for Horace McFarland or any other "poor dubs" simply seeking to read a text.[56]

Characteristics of Content

Texts chosen for fine editions reflect the cultural and sociological impulses that propelled two, often intermingled, strands of postwar literary thought. One embraced the social and cultural canons loosely associated with gentility. A notoriously slippery term then as now, *gentility* in literary contexts of the day emphasized moral and ethical idealism and deference to aesthetic standards established in western European and New England cultural traditions. The other represented revolt against the puritanical strains of that American gentility, urging a more sophisticated openness toward sensuality and other "real" rather than ideal aspects of human nature and refusing to subsume American literature within a superior Anglo-European tradition.[57] Those who produced and bought fine books in the 1920s shared sympathies with both attitudes toward the nature and purpose of literature, and so did the books' content. It also highlighted a pair of shared values that transcended the differences: defense of cultural elitism and regard for a relevant past.

AN ELITE WITHIN THE ELITE

Fine editions tended to feature "literary" texts well outside the mainstreams of popular contemporary reading material. Although texts and authors of fine books were often well known, their merit was established by critical rather than popular success. Most had no claim to mass readerships, which would have been an incidental (if not damning) credential to fine publishers and their audiences. Volumes by acclaimed contemporary poets such as Edwin Arlington Robinson, Carl Sandburg, and Robert Frost were published in fine editions, for example, but none of the work by the more popular poets Edward Guest or Robert Service. The few authors of fine editions who were among the decade's best sellers (such as Thornton Wilder, John Galsworthy, and A. A. Milne) were deemed likely to transcend ephemeral popularity and achieve an enduring readership.

The belletristic genres of poetry, drama, and the essay represent a much higher proportion of postwar fine editions, relative to fiction, than was common in mainstream trade publishing of the twenties (see table 4). Poetry and drama accounted for roughly 10 percent of trade titles of the day, but, together with essays, they were the most common genres featured in fine editions. By contrast, each year some 14 to 21 percent of trade titles published in the twenties were novels (defined as a single work of fiction of at least one hundred pages), between 60 and 75 percent of them new titles; only a small portion of fine editions offered fiction, however, and the great majority of those texts were reprints.[58] In part, the emphasis on publishing poetry, drama, and essays was pragmatic: their shorter or easily divisible texts enabled publishers to

Table 4. *Genre*

Genre	1920–26	1927–28	1929	1930	1931–32	Total
Poetry, verse, songs	17	22	19	16	14	88 (29.3%)
Drama	3	3	5	2	1	14 (4.7%)
Essay	5	4	6	9	6	30 (10%)
Short fiction	6	11	9	10	6	42 (14%)
Novel	4	5	7	7	7	30 (10%)
Tales, legends, scriptures	5	1	1	2	2	11 (3.7%)
Letters	0	1	1	2	1	5 (1.7%
Other nonfiction	17	16	16	18	4	71 (23.7%)
Unknown	4	3	1	1	0	9 (3%)
Total	61	66	65	67	41	300

focus attention and resources on design, illustration, and materials. Even so, the unusually high proportion of belletristic literature helped to attract elite audiences.

Sometimes subject matter helped to attract this rarefied audience by evoking interests and occupations redolent, occasionally in strikingly anachronistic ways, of aristocratic lives of leisure and cultural preeminence (see table 5). Suggesting past eras of privilege, privacy, and refinement, such subjects created literary oases amid the modern commercial and industrial societies in which bibliophiles lived and worked. The best example is the spate of "sporting" titles devoted to fox hunting, fly-fishing, equestrian subjects, and the like. Several titles were reprints of classic eighteenth- and nineteenth-century essays, accompanied by illustrations or reproductions in the style of the original engraved illustrations, such as Rudge's decorative 1930 edition of John Gay's *Rural Sports* (figure 22). The Huntington Press made its 1930 debut with a fine illustrated edition of *A Remedy for Disappearing Game Fishes* by no less prestigious a figure than President Herbert Hoover, an avid fisherman. At least one fine publisher, Derrydale Press, was devoted exclusively to sporting titles. Founded and run by Eugene V. Connett III, son of a wealthy New Jersey manufacturing family, the Derrydale Press issued elegant editions of such titles as *Hounds and Hunting Through the Ages* and *Gentlemen Up,* stories and illustrations of steeplechase riding.[59]

The elitism of fine book content was not limited to vaguely aristocratic textual realms, however. Many leading modernist or avant-garde authors also sought fine editions for their work. They recognized the critical distinction accorded work produced in fine editions, and they welcomed the distance from

Table 5. Notable Subjects

Author, Title	Illustrator	Publisher	Date
Sports			
Boker, *Legend of the Hounds*	Gordon Ross	Rudge	1931
Gay, *Rural Sports*	Gordon Ross	Rudge	1930
Higginson, *As Hounds Ran*	Aldin & Edwards	Huntington Press	1930
Higginson, *Letters from a Sportsman*	Lionel Edwards	Doubleday, Doran	1929
Hoover, *Disappearing Game Fishes*	Harvey Cimino	Huntington Press	1930
Munroe, *Grand National, 1839–1930*		Huntington Press	1930
Somervile, *The Chace*	J. & T. Bewick	Doubleday, Doran	1929
Walton, *The Complete Angler*	W. A. Dwiggins	Goodspeed	1928
Books and Printing			
Blades, *Words on Caxton*	Julian A. Links	Windsor Press	1926
Bonnardot, *Parisian Bibliophile*	Jose Longoria	Northwestern U	1931
Bullen, *Nicholas Jenson*	1478 leaf	Nash	1926
De Vinne, *Plantin-Moretus Museum*		Grabhorn Press	1929
Dearden, *Leaf from the Bible*	1782 leaf	Howell	1930
Dürer, *Dürer's Roman Letters*		Dunster House	1924
Johnson, *Press of the Renaissance*		Windsor Press	1927
Johnston, *Biblio-Typographica*		Covici-Friede	1930
Lone, *Noteworthy Firsts*		Lathrop Harper	1930
Newton, *A Noble Fragment*	1455 leaf	Gabriel Wells	1921
The Diary of Roger Payne		Harbor Press	1928
Pollard, *Cobden-Sanderson*	leaf	Nash	1929
Rollins, BR, *Typographic Playboy*		Georgian Press	1927
Updike, *In the Day's Work*		Harvard UP	1924
Winship, *Leaf of 1663 Bible*	1663 leaf	Goodspeed	1929
Illustrated "Polite Erotica"			
Balzac, *Droll Stories*	Ralph Barton	Liveright	1928
Balzac, *Droll Stories, Second Decade*	Jean de Bousschere	Covici-Friede	1929
Bible, *Song of Solomon*	Wharton Esherick	Centaur Press	1927
Boccaccio, *Decameron*	Jean de Bousschere	Covici-Friede	1930
Delteil, *On the River Amour*	Alexeieff	Covici-Friede	1929
Douglas, *Paneros*	Robert Rutter	McBride	1932
Flaubert, *Salammbô*	Alexander King	Brown House	1930
Huxley, *Leda*	Eric Gill	Doubleday, Doran	1929
Louÿs, *Satyrs and Women*	Majeska	Covici-Friede	1930
Works of Rabelais	Jean de Bousschere	Covici-Friede	1929
Rachilde, *Monsieur Venus*	Majeska	Covici-Friede	1929
Shakespeare, *Venus and Adonis*	Rockwell Kent	Hart	1931
Works of Villon	Alexander King	Covici-Friede	1928
Wilde, *Salome*	Valenti Angelo	Grabhorn Press	1927

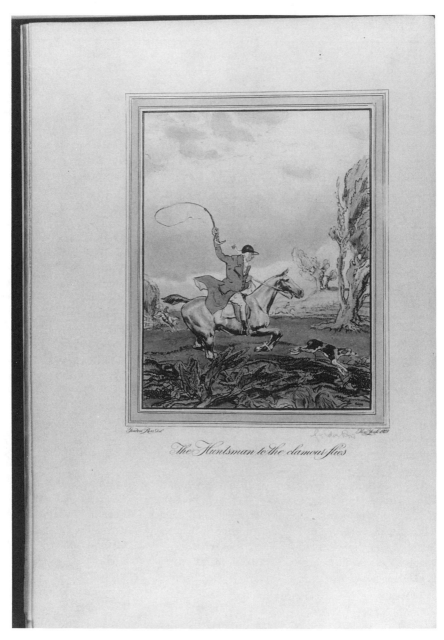

The Huntsman to the clamour flies

Figure 22. John Gay, *Rural Sports* (Mount Vernon, NY: William E. Rudge, 1930). Illustrated by Gordon Ross; designed by Frederic Warde. This copy hand-colored. Photo courtesy of the Bancroft Library at the University of California.

RURAL SPORTS

together with

The Birth of the Squire
and
The Hound and the Huntsman

By
JOHN GAY
Author of
THE BEGGAR'S OPERA

Pictures by
Gordon Ross
with an introduction by
Owen Culbertson

New York
William Edwin Rudge
1930

popular or mass readerships. Consequently, American publishers produced fine editions of several major serious writers of the era, including Crosby Gaige's fine first edition of Virginia Woolf's *Orlando;* Boni and Liveright's fine editions of Eugene O'Neill's drama; and the Fountain Press editions of James Joyce's *Haveth Childers Everywhere,* an excerpt from his yet-unpublished *Finnegans Wake,* and T. S. Eliot's *Ash Wednesday.*

The fact that landmark modernist writers like Eliot, Woolf, and Joyce appeared in fine editions highlights the complex nature of modernism and the dangers of equating the aims and assumptions of postwar literary modernism with those of its typographic cognate. While typographic modernists repudiated the past and idealized democratized, industrialized society, Anglo-American literary modernism retained a sense of the need for an aesthetic elite, an anchoring sense of history, and an authoritative cultural tradition, even as it confronted a postwar world largely severed from those once-stabilizing forces.[60] As Lawrence Rainey discusses in his study of the publication history of *The Waste Land,* fine editions well suited a modernist writer like Eliot, who valued both their classically dignifying forms and their limited, noncommercial distribution. Rainey points to Yeats's Morris-influenced practice of publishing his work in two stages—a handcrafted bibliophilic edition produced by his sisters' Dun Emer (later Cuala) Press, followed by a standard trade edition by Macmillan—as the model for writers who sought to distinguish their work from the conventional. "The limited edition established a kind of special productive space insulated from the harsh exigencies of the larger marketplace. It bypassed a broad public receptive to standardized products ... and instead it addressed a prosperous minority with a luxury good that emphasized innovation and was produced in small quantities. . . . It enacted, in other words, a return to an essentially precapitalist economic structure, an artisanal economy producing luxury goods in limited quantities for aristocratic consumption. By the early 1920s it had become a routine step in a tripartite publishing program—journal, limited edition, and public or commercial edition—that was now normative for the avant-garde."[61]

Through his friendship with Conrad Aiken, whose *Priapus and the Pool* was produced in a fine edition (designed by Bruce Rogers) by Dunster House in 1922, Eliot learned of one attractive option for the limited edition publication he sought for his poem. Aiken immediately wrote to Maurice Firuski, proprietor of Dunster House, warning him that Eliot "seeks a publisher who will produce [his poem] nicely, and in America, and in a small edition. Firuski! cried I, and there you are. When I elucidated, mentioning Rogers and 450 copies and two years exclusive rights and a possible hundred dollars and a beautifully produced book, his eyes glowed with a tawny golden light like fierce doubloons, his hands took on singularly the aspect of claws, his nails tore the table-cloth, and he took your address."[62] Within a fortnight Eliot did write to Firuski, admiring the fine edition of John Freeman's *Two Poems* (*The Red Path* and *The Wounded Bird*) that Firuski had recently published; it had been printed on handmade paper and designed by Rogers. He inquired about the terms Firuski might offer to publish a similar edition of *The Waste Land*. "It is, I think," Eliot explained, "much the best poem I have ever written, and I think it would make a much more distinct impression and attract much more attention if published as a book."[63]

Significantly, however, Eliot had already made arrangements for the poem's publication as a book, with New York trade publisher Horace Liveright. Rainey sees Eliot's overtures to Firuski as evidence that the poet was anxious also to secure the elite, ostensibly acommercial presentation of a fine edition. "Eliot, it is clear, wanted his poem to be successful, yet not too successful. For the prospect of immediate publication by a commercial firm raised prospects that were largely unimaginable within the logic of modernism." Eliot rejected an offer from *Vanity Fair* to publish his poem because it "represented a degree of commercial success and popular acceptance that would have undermined the very status of the work that he was trying to establish." In characterizing the Rogers-designed *Two Poems* that enticed Eliot to approach Firuski, Rainey captures the qualities of postwar fine books that attracted so many discerning authors and bibliophiles of the day: "inspired by rather classical models of typography and design[,] it suggested a tone of genteel decorum, a distinctly Harvardian note, and yet sounded that tone with even greater subtlety, as if to hint at an elite within the elite, or select and more reflective minority with discriminating taste, a minority lodged within the wider elite that unreflectively assumed its privileges solely on the basis of class, money, and inherited status."[64] Postwar fine publishing was indeed ideally predicated on an "elite within the elite," a reflective and historically informed minority community of taste and social privilege within which fine books were both produced and distributed. Many American fine printers and publishers thus shared with literary modernists an ambition to assert authoritative new criteria by which aesthetic, intellectual, and cultural excellence in the modern world was to be judged. For both communities, those criteria were imbedded in critical relation to tradition, and they were best described by the elite few who could perceive, articulate, and model them for others.

The elitism of fine editions also sometimes revealed a disdain born of sophistication rather than aristocratic affectation. This form of separatism grew from the rebellion against puritanical morality as mocked by Sinclair Lewis, H. L. Mencken, and others. While polemicists like Mencken are noticeably absent from fine editions, those who shared a vaguely cosmopolitan and cynical attitude toward human nature were well represented in fine editions. These writers reflected modern "enlightened" attitudes toward sex, religion, Freudian psychology, socialism, and so on, which put them at odds with the conservative, even reactionary, mainstream of American society in the 1920s characterized by a resurgent Ku Klux Klan, the Scopes trial, and Prohibition. Writers such as James Branch Cabell, Pierre Louÿs, and Michael Arlen welcomed elite editions not because they wished to assume cultural leadership but because they had little wish to address a general population they regarded as Babbittlike — repressed, boorish, and dull.

This vein of elitism defied conventional moral codes by mocking them, usually through satire or exotic fantasy. Such editions included contemporary writing, such as Christopher Morley's humorous sketches and essays in *Born in a Beer Garden,* Lytton Strachey's *Elizabeth and Essex,* and Llewelyn Powys's *Now That the Gods Are Dead,* and older satirical work, such as Mark Twain's *Burlesque Autobiography,* Voltaire's *Candide,* or John Skelton's bawdy sixteenth-century ballad of *Elynour Rynnynge.* Often droll, these editions played on traditional, even archaic, literary, linguistic, and typographic forms. They were inside jokes shared by an educated elite that debunked or at least twitted the religious and social mores cherished in mainstream society. Even when tongue-in-cheek or whimsical, fine book content cultivated an elite audience.

This slightly decadent form of elitism helped fuel the brisk market for what Donald Friede discreetly termed "polite erotica." "By sacrificing taste in content, and often in illustrations as well," he dryly recalled, Covici-Friede quickly established itself as a leader in this highly profitable niche market. It offered fine (often marginally so) reprints of the *Song of Solomon,* the *Satyricon,* the *Decameron,* and the like, their texts either unexpurgated or newly translated into a "racy contemporary American idiom," as Covici-Friede boasted of its extravagant new edition of the works of Rabelais. Risqué work by more modern writers, such as Balzac's *Droll Stories,* Oscar Wilde's *Salome,* Norman Douglas's *Paneros,* and the tales of Pierre Louÿs (see table 5), also thrived in fine editions. Virtually all located their subjects in exotic, ancient, or mythological times and places, fantastically remote from contemporary society and seemingly exempt from present-day prudishness. When George Macy's Brown House published Flaubert's *Salammbô,* for example, Macy praised the novel's "passionate exoticism, its grotesque and savage characterizations of the political and martial bigwigs of Carthage, their concubines and wives," which were given "perfect embodiment" in Alexander King's stylishly erotic illustrations (see figure 23).[65]

Usually the most titillating aspect of these editions was not the text but the illustrations. They typically incorporated nudity and erotic subject matter, but seldom if ever could be considered pornographic. Sometimes it was their thoroughly jaded and cynical style that bibliophiles found so scandalously thrilling. Among the most sensational illustrators was the young Alexander King, whose "cold disdain for human beings," expressed in macabre and bleakly expressive drawings, Donald Friede took particular pleasure in championing. "King seemed to hate everything and everybody," Friede explained of the artist's success, "and all decent feelings were his very special target."[66] These editions were implicitly destined for the private libraries of affluent bibliophiles who would admire and value the sensual Rockwell Kent drawings or lithographs as much as the mildly erotic literary content.

Expensive fine editions enabled publishers to circulate among well-heeled buyers texts that were rigorously censored in trade markets. Fine formats implied a literary stature that gave books immunity from moral scrutiny. Not intended for general audiences, fine editions thus successfully evaded censorship; their texts were deemed unlikely to encounter, and so corrupt, the nation's youth and other vulnerable readers. Cheney scolded publishers for sanctioning controversial or erotic work under the guise of classic literary status: "Does labelling a book with 'Elizabethan gusto' or 'Restoration wit'—either by an advertising writer or a critic—make it clean? The idea that a 'sex book' is bad if it is new or by a new author and good if it is 'classic' or by a 'great artist' is stupid, dishonest and destructive of any standards of literature, taste and publishing. . . . The idea that a book in a $25 limited edition is clean while the same book at $1 is dirty is also destructive of standards. The $1 book may be more harmful because it reaches more people—but it is no dirtier." The strategy was too alluring to resist, however. It worked beautifully when Covici and Friede scored a major coup by outbidding rivals (by offering a 20 percent royalty) for the rights to publish the American edition of Radclyffe Hall's sensational new novel of lesbianism, *The Well of Loneliness,* after Knopf decided to drop the controversial book. Covici-Friede promptly bought the "sizeable number" of copies that Knopf had already printed (on very fine paper, Friede noted), "printed a new title page, numbered the copies, called it a pre-publication limited edition, and sold out the entire edition overnight at ten dollars a copy."[67]

HISTORICISM AND NATIONALISM

Fine book content is also marked by a strong historicism and deference to Western cultural traditions. Fine publishing's emphases on serious, enduring texts fostered the sense that it preserved legacies of time-honored cultural

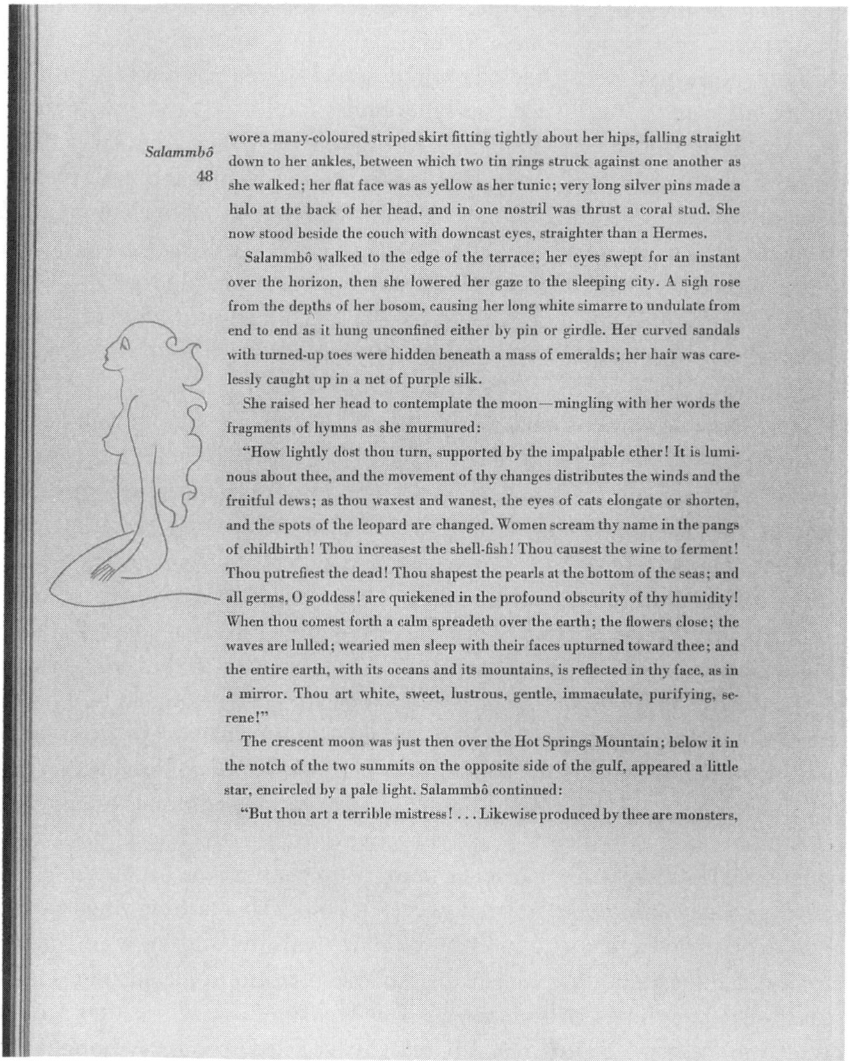

Salammbô
48

wore a many-coloured striped skirt fitting tightly about her hips, falling straight down to her ankles, between which two tin rings struck against one another as she walked; her flat face was as yellow as her tunic; very long silver pins made a halo at the back of her head, and in one nostril was thrust a coral stud. She now stood beside the couch with downcast eyes, straighter than a Hermes.

Salammbô walked to the edge of the terrace; her eyes swept for an instant over the horizon, then she lowered her gaze to the sleeping city. A sigh rose from the depths of her bosom, causing her long white simarre to undulate from end to end as it hung unconfined either by pin or girdle. Her curved sandals with turned-up toes were hidden beneath a mass of emeralds; her hair was carelessly caught up in a net of purple silk.

She raised her head to contemplate the moon—mingling with her words the fragments of hymns as she murmured:

"How lightly dost thou turn, supported by the impalpable ether! It is luminous about thee, and the movement of thy changes distributes the winds and the fruitful dews; as thou waxest and wanest, the eyes of cats elongate or shorten, and the spots of the leopard are changed. Women scream thy name in the pangs of childbirth! Thou increasest the shell-fish! Thou causest the wine to ferment! Thou putrefiest the dead! Thou shapest the pearls at the bottom of the seas; and all germs, O goddess! are quickened in the profound obscurity of thy humidity! When thou comest forth a calm spreadeth over the earth; the flowers close; the waves are lulled; wearied men sleep with their faces upturned toward thee; and the entire earth, with its oceans and its mountains, is reflected in thy face, as in a mirror. Thou art white, sweet, lustrous, gentle, immaculate, purifying, serene!"

The crescent moon was just then over the Hot Springs Mountain; below it in the notch of the two summits on the opposite side of the gulf, appeared a little star, encircled by a pale light. Salammbô continued:

"But thou art a terrible mistress! . . . Likewise produced by thee are monsters,

Figure 23. Gustave Flaubert, *Salammbô* (New York: Brown House, 1930). Illustrated by Alexander King. Photo courtesy of the Bancroft Library of the University of California.

merit in the face of contemporary ambivalence and volatility. As unprecedented numbers of Americans completed high school and proceeded to college, alarms sounded that the influx would sweep Babbittlike tastes and utilitarian objectives into the once-hallowed halls of academe. Many saw the fate of liberal arts, serious literature, and the classics in particular as a bellwether

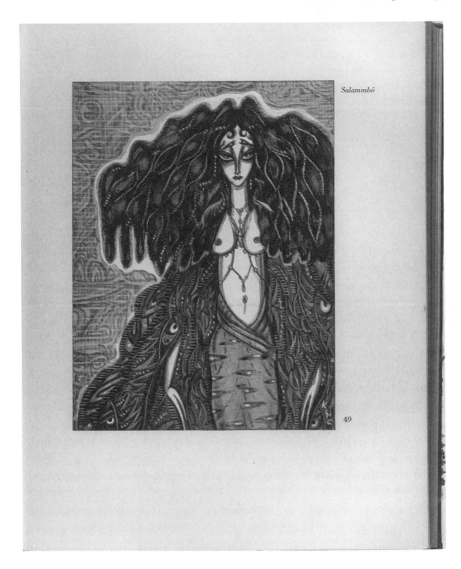

Salammbô

49

of shifts in larger cultural values. "Are the Classics Dying Out?" a *Publishers'*
Weekly forum wondered, concerned by the soaring sales of heavily advertised
but short-lived works that threatened to lure the public away from books
"established by the test of time."[68] Fine printers of "timeless" texts — both new
and established — staunchly resisted the ephemeral, fickle, and popular. They

Table 6. Date of Text Origin

Date of origin	1920–26	1927–28	1929	1930	1931–32	Total
Before A.D. 500	5	2	1	3	3	14 (4.7%)
500–1499	3	5	1	2	3	14 (4.7%)
1500–1699	1	3	4	3	5	16 (5.3%)
1700–99	3	9	6	4	2	24 (8%)
1800–99	13	9	14	15	15	66 (22%)
1900–19	7	6	8	7	2	30 (10%)
New as book	29	33	31	32	11	136 (45.3%)
Total	61	67	65	66	41	300

infused bibliophiles with a sense of cultural heritage and stewardship in a postwar era marked by both iconoclasm and sedulity. This allegiance is evident in the unusually high proportion (approximately half) of fine editions of texts from earlier eras, a considerably higher proportion than the 12 to 18 percent of trade books published in the 1920s that were reprints of earlier work (see table 6).[69]

Yet the desire to locate and reify a distinguishing cultural heritage was frustrated by an ambiguity surrounding the roles of Americans within that tradition. It seemed a shame that many buyers flatly preferred English writers; as Crosby Gaige remarked, "our American poets were too close to us to assume their real importance." This often led to a deliberate nationalist slant on the classics editorial strategy. As Bob Grabhorn put it, "we got the idea, since we are American printers, we'd better use American classics." Others shared his impulse: only the English outnumbered Americans as authors of classics editions.[70]

The emphasis on American literature stemmed from two opposing impulses. To some, the inclusion of American titles among the classics was a gesture of national pride that helped to bolster their status, to establish them as equal if not superior to their English and European counterparts. Convinced of the importance of indigenous literature, Joseph Blumenthal devoted his Spiral Press imprint to fine editions of "unavailable and unusual" American literary titles. More than any other fine publisher, Blumenthal gave serious care to editorial selection and treatment; he enlisted noted scholars to edit and introduce each text, and Howard Mumford Jones agreed to edit the series, which Blumenthal envisioned as including six titles a year. His ambition was impressive. He planned fine editions of *The Poems of Edgar Allan Poe, The Day of Doom* by seventeenth-century New England Calvinist Michael Wigglesworth, a volume of *Selected Poems of Herman Melville, The Philosopher of the Forest and Other Essays* by eighteenth-century writer Philip Freneau, a collection of tales by Ambrose Bierce, the poetry of Anne Bradstreet, two sermons by Jonathan Edwards, Fanny Anne Kemble's *Diary on a Georgian Farm,* sonnets of Longfellow, and other largely overlooked works of American literature. Only the Poe and Wigglesworth were published, however; the market proved less than keen for such material. Cerf counseled Blumenthal in early 1930 to take heed from the Random House experience: "Our venture into Americana with Mary Jemison, Parson Weems, and Franklin Evans has not yet conclusively demonstrated whether or not we can get away with this sort of thing, but early returns do not make me unduly optimistic."[71] Yet Blumenthal remained undeterred on his editorial course; he was determined to help elevate American work to the ranks of universal literary achievement.

The impulse to enhance the status of American literature by including it among the classics contrasted with the impulse to diminish the vaguely off-putting eliteness of strictly European literary masterpieces. By turning to less daunting American authors for classics and literary chestnuts (as the Grab-horns called them), some fine publishers sought to deflect accusations that their editions served only to cultivate snobbery and pretense. They viewed American classics as more natural, logical choices to inhabit American home libraries. These publishers, proud of the American power and vitality that had prevailed in the recent war and in world economic markets and industrial achievement, wished to enact a similar triumph of American literature over what they regarded as its aging and increasingly irrelevant European ancestors. R.R. Donnelley president George Littell, for example, stipulated that Lakeside Press fine editions were to feature "books of American literature that were interesting to read to the normal business man, as apart from those classics in England and the United States that have already been published a great many times, and which people look at and admire, but do not read. . . . we have picked books anyone of us would be glad to sit down at night and read for amusement, and I think that is where our idea differs entirely from that of other publishers of limited editions, and I think we should stick with it."[72]

Undisguised national pride and even "boosterism" loomed behind the insistence that the classics include American titles. To showcase the insights and talents of American printers and illustrators, Littell insisted that only American texts would do. For the Lakeside "Four American Books" project, which were to feature "definitive" illustrations by American artists, Littell approached about a dozen illustrators and gave them a list of possible titles they might choose to work on, titles he had prescreened to ensure they both merited an "exquisite" production — as the Lakeside books aspired to be —

and had not yet been produced in an illustrated edition. Suggested titles included Twain's *Huckleberry Finn* and *Tom Sawyer,* Owen Wister's *The Virginian,* Jack London's *Call of the Wild,* Hawthorne's *Scarlet Letter* and *House of the Seven Gables,* Joel Chandler Harris's *Uncle Remus,* George Cable's *Creole Days,* Henry James's *The Portrait of a Lady* and *Daisy Miller,* Bret Harte's *Tales,* Frank Norris's *Lady Letty,* Crane's *Red Badge of Courage,* O. Henry's *The Four Million,* Washington Irving's *Sketch Book,* George Ade's *Fables in Slang,* Cooper's *Last of the Mohicans,* and Melville's *Typee* and *Moby Dick.* The latter was selected, along with Poe's *Tales,* Richard Henry Dana's *Two Years Before the Mast,* and Thoreau's *Walden.* All options were prose fiction, only two were by living authors, and all were written by men except for Willa Cather's *My Antonia.*[73]

Yet even within the context of their own national literary production, past and present, many postwar Americans struggled with a sense of cultural ambiguity rooted in the nation's multiple ethnic heritages. While some defined national character in ways that encompassed that diversity, others longed to affirm a place within a fixed and superior Western cultural tradition, as traced roughly from classical Greece and Rome through western European and particularly English aristocratic social, political, and religious institutions. The ethnic demographics of fine edition authors clearly associate American bibliophilia with the latter impulse. White, Protestant men of northern European extraction overwhelmingly predominated among American authors of fine books.[74]

The dichotomy in attitudes toward American literature — some viewing it as less lofty and so a more palatable alternative to Anglo-European classics, and others aspiring to assert its place within, if not at the head of, that older tradition — was further reflected in notions about how it should be presented. That is, the politics of nationalism in editorial decisions was apparent in design and production decisions as well. To those like Littell who found in American literature a refreshing, readable change from the European great books, American books invited more "democratic" and unpretentious forms. Rudolph Ruzicka, who illustrated Lakeside's edition of *Walden,* welcomed Littell's American-only scheme as an antidote to the sacralizing "precious de looks" approach common to most bibliophilic publications. Others, such as the Grabhorns and Cerf, used monumental bookmaking to signify that American literature deserved no less honor than that bestowed upon Shakespeare, Dante, and Chaucer. Admittedly, few openly discussed these decisions in such terms, but their overtones were apparent to at least one critic. Carl Rollins noted the disparity between material stature and literary merit in American fine editions, demurring that "in the absence of masterpieces (and a democratic civilization perhaps does not induce *editions de grand luxe,* although it may provide *expensive* books for its millionaires), perhaps the smaller, gem-like book may have its day." He called the Grabhorn–Random House edition of *The Red Badge of Courage* "far too large," a book whose content failed to justify its form. He deemed only two productions, both landmark texts in English culture (the Random House *Beowulf,* illustrated by Rockwell Kent, and *The Book of Common Prayer,* produced by Updike), truly worthy of their monumental bibliophilic form.[75]

Not all bibliophilic celebrations of past cultural glories were literary, however. The most explicitly historicized material was the specialized type of publication known as a "leaf" book, so called because it included a single leaf of an important rare book in printing history (taken, presumably, from an incomplete copy). The tipped-in leaf was typically accompanied by a short essay explaining the original book and printer's significance. The most grand and costly leaf book of the era was *A Noble Fragment,* featuring a leaf from the Gutenberg Bible. Although its price of one hundred and fifty dollars hardly rendered it a book for everyman, this leaf book expanded manyfold the number of enthusiasts who could own at least a part of the most celebrated printed book in Western history (only six copies then existed in the United States, most of them held by institutions unlikely to part with or break apart their copies).[76] Other postwar editions featured a leaf from a book printed in 1478 by Nicholas Jenson in Venice; a 1663 leaf of the famous "Indian" Bible, translated by John Eliot into the Algonquin language; a 1782 leaf from the first English Bible printed in the American colonies; and a leaf printed by T. J. Cobden-Sanderson at the Doves Press.[77] Leaf books enabled prosperous Americans to own at least a piece of the esteemed past, housed within an edition that recreated the style and stature of older aristocratic books.

Other, usually less expensive attempts to provide links to a revered past include reprints of historical texts, often featuring facsimiles of documents, old maps, and so on. Rudge's lavish eighteen-volume edition of the newly discovered James Boswell papers included reproductions of deeds, wills, and letters, complete with binding seals and other details that approximated the original materials (figure 24). The Bowling Green Press edition of William E. Barton's *Lincoln and the Hooker Letter* featured a full-size foldout reproduction of the letter, accompanied by Barton's essay on its significance. These editions tended either to literary subjects — such as the Boswell Papers or John Howell's edition of Robert Louis Stevenson's *Baby Book* — or to travel and exploration histories.[78] These books clearly strove to recreate articles of the past as well as inform readers about a historical subject.

In this realm, too, American historical texts were prominent: memoirs, the Family. All this was done upon the nineteenth day of October in the year of our Lord one thousand seven hundred and sixty seven years, in presence of James Boswell Esquire my eldest Brother and Heir of the Family, the Reverend Mr. John Dun Minister at Auchinleck, and the Reverend Mr. Joseph Fergusson Minister at Tundergarth, Chaplains appointed for the occasion I departing for Valencia in Spain there to settle as a Merchant. Also in presence of Mr. James Bruce Overseer at Auchinleck and Alexander, John, Andrew and James Bruces his sons, all present having with one voice wished the continuance and prosperity of the ancient Family of

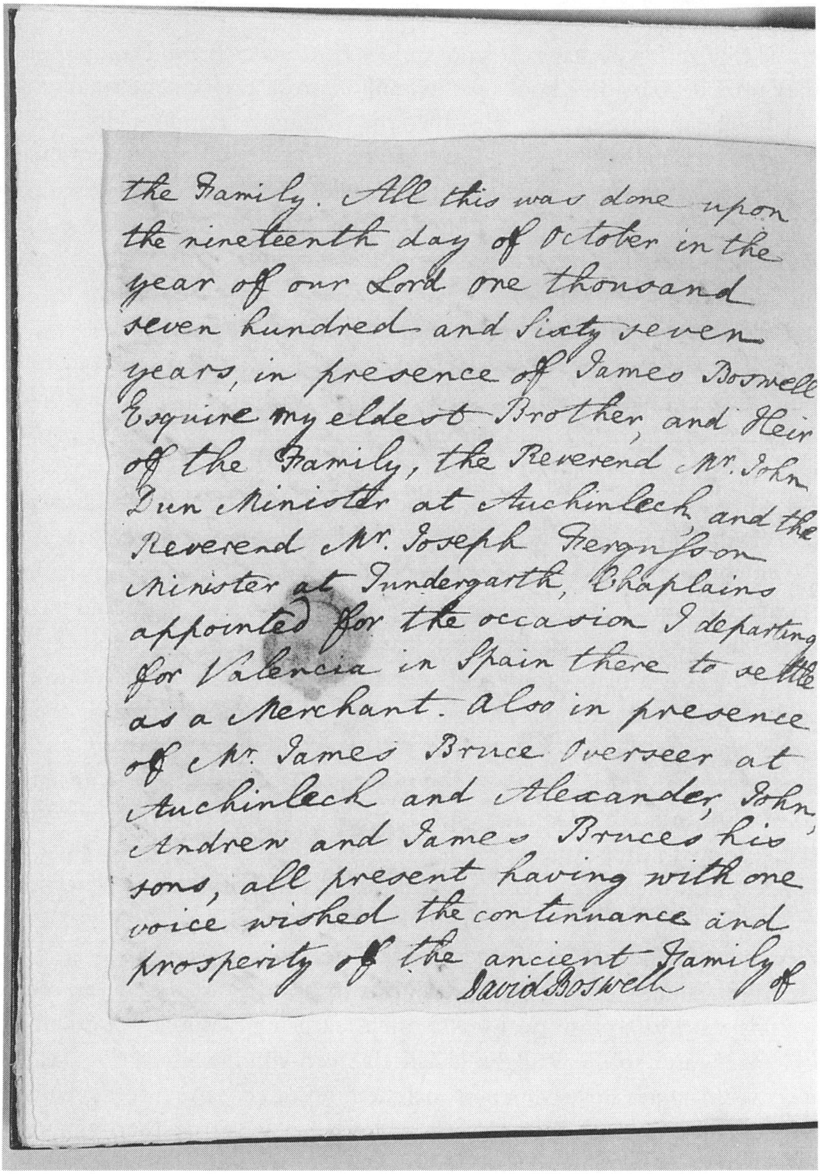

David Boswell

Figure 24. Tipped-in facsimile document in *The Private Papers of James Boswell from Malahide Castle*, vol. 1 (Mount Vernon, N.Y.: Rudge, 1928). Designed by Bruce Rogers. Photo courtesy of Special Collections Division, University of Washington Libraries.

of Auchinleck, and that the Family of
Bruce might ever flourish there. In
testimony of which I now subscribe these
presents, and seal them with the
seal of my investiture, they being
written by the said James Boswell Esqr.
and subscribed on the twenty seventh
day of the said month and in the said
year of our Lord. Amen.

David Boswell

James Boswell Witness.

John Dun Witness

Joseph Fergusson witness

Jas Bruce witness

After an absence of near thirteen years I the said David Boswell
being now returned from Valencia in Spain where, on account
of the prejudice of the inhabitants of that country against
old testament names, I assumed the name of Thomas in
honour of the first laird of our family, and being about

travel journals, treatises, and similar works of nonfiction. Both geographic centers of American bibliophilia (and wealth), New England/New York and California, generated a particular canon of regional favorites. Such books were especially popular in California, where printers often turned to bits of Californiana — pioneer memoirs, gold rush diaries, and the like — and to work by writers associated with the area, especially Robert Louis Stevenson, Bret Harte, Jack London, and lesser-known locals such as Hildegarde Flanner and Ella Young. Regional Americana appealed to patrons' desires for rare or unusual materials pertaining to a local subject or author. It also combined a celebration of the past with an avocational kind of scholarship, melding art and knowledge. Often these editions reprinted obscure but important titles long out of print, making available texts that had been accessible only in libraries and the private collections of wealthy collectors. At least one critic applauded this strategy as a healthy and productive alternative to "the morass of reprinted classics."[79] Printers also relished the opportunities for allusive typography such texts provided.

The pervasive historicism of fine editions helped give substance to bibliophilic cultural ambitions; the books embodied a sense of cultural cohesion and continuity. Fine editions of classics and historically important texts invoked a seamless heritage of Western civilization, aligning prosperous Americans with centuries of elite European culture. Classics of Western, particularly English, literature served to culturally anchor those Americans who felt beleaguered and adrift in a society whose population grew increasingly diverse — racially, ethnically, and linguistically. Coupled with the historicized physical forms that distinguished them, the contents of these editions provided a bridge between postwar America and past centuries' elite worlds of education and book ownership.

6

For the Joy of Doing
The Business of Anticommercialism

"Lovers of fine printing will be interested in the opening of a printing office at 47 Kearny Street," read the leaflet that fluttered through the mail slots of a hundred of San Francisco's most prominent business and professional addresses in January 1920. With this handsome flyer, typeset by hand and printed in two colors on a special paper known as Japan vellum, Edwin and Robert Grabhorn announced their arrival in town, fresh from Indianapolis. Flanked by neoclassical, slightly mischievous-looking figures, the message was clear (see figure 25). The new Grabhorn Press promised to "strive to impart more of a personal and less of a commercial air in its work."

The publishing business has always uneasily straddled the worlds of commerce and culture, and the truism is no more apt than in fine publishing. There was something inherently contradictory between a commitment to reinvigorated standards of typographic quality, unsullied by the modern impulse toward cheap, standardized, mass-made goods, and the commercial activities of pricing, advertising, and selling books that embodied that commitment. In this dilemma, however, postwar fine publishers found a ready mentor in William Morris and his Kelmscott Press. He modeled a way to price and sell his work without unduly compromising the anticommercial, even anticapitalist, principles of his bookmaking enterprise.

By adapting Morris's practices, postwar fine publishers preserved at least

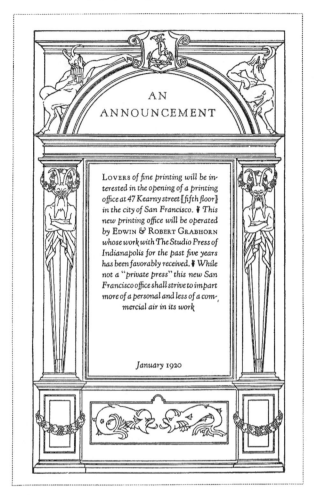

Figure 25. Announcement of business services,
Grabhorn Press, San Francisco, 1920.

the appearance of cultural and artistic integrity while engaging in a patently
for-profit enterprise. They managed this by sustaining two broad assertions —
often myths — about their work. First, they distanced themselves from the
profit motive, publicly embracing instead the artisanal or genteel rewards of
"joy" and intrinsic satisfaction of superior work. Second, they characterized
those who bought their books as appreciative, discerning patrons of fine typography, as colleagues who shared their cultural commitments, rather than
as anonymous, merely acquisitive customers.

Although by the 1920s the fulsome neomedievalism of Kelmscott books had lost much of its appeal, Morris's legacy remained vital for demonstrating how private press standards and principles could be financially supported in the public marketplace without compromise. In 1929 Alfred Pollard described the economic dimension of Morris's work in terms that conveyed exactly what most postwar fine publishers wanted to believe about their work as well. "Morris made no profit from the Kelmscott books as a publisher; could allot himself no payment for all the magnificent decorative work which he put into them with his own hands. He got nothing from his venture save the joy of achievement and pleasure of giving copies to his friends. But he proved the existence of a public willing to pay for the cost of print and paper, even when both print and paper were the best which money could buy."[1]

Pollard's statement encapsulates what fine printers and publishers asserted about their commercial activities: profits were irrelevant or incidental; the venture was motivated by the "joy of doing," as John Henry Nash frequently exclaimed, and by the pleasure of providing beautiful books to a select, appreciative community; the monies paid for the books directly reflected the necessarily high costs of their production; and those who bought the books valued them for their superior quality of bookmaking. These assertions were pronounced, publicized, and purportedly enacted with gusto throughout the postwar bibliophilic book trade. But the reality of fine publishing frequently belied its anticommercial rhetoric. Unlike Morris, postwar fine printers and publishers depended upon the sale of books for their livelihood. Although they could not afford to run truly private presses, wherein sales income merely mitigates some of the expenses involved, they were ideologically bound to eschew conventional business sensibilities. As a result, they repeatedly pronounced or established antibusiness principles. Paradoxically, that aversion to "business" was one of their most lucrative products for sale.

Ideological Knots: Principles and Profits

All the central players in postwar fine bookmaking publicly proclaimed a concern for quality above profit, as when Elmer Adler commenced operation of the Pynson Printers in 1922 by announcing that they would "do no work in which quality must be sacrificed to the exigencies of time and cost." No one, however, was more dramatic in expressing contempt for financial considerations than Porter Garnett. His stance was most aggressively stated in the colophon of *That Endeth Never,* a short story written by Hildegarde Flanner for Garnett and produced in a fine edition under his direction at the Laboratory Press in 1926. Garnett ferociously warned, "Because this story, in manuscript form, was a *gift;* because the printed copies are also to be gifts; because this book, done in the fifty-fifth year of my life, is the first to be composed in type entirely by my own hands; and because the making of it has been a labour of love, — it is my wish that NO COPY OF THIS BOOK SHALL EVER BE BOUGHT, SOLD, OR BARTERED either separately or as part of a collection or library. Whosoever impelled by that most contemptible of human passions, the desire of gain — shall, *at any time,* purchase, sell, or exchange a copy of this book, will brand himself forthwith as *without conscience or honour,* and upon him, upon his children and his children's children shall rest, for ever and ever, my MALEDICTION." There followed a lengthy curse invoking mythological gods to rain upon "the mercenary wretch" who attempted to buy or sell the book an assortment of disasters specially formulated to cause bibliophilic suffering. Despite the note of self-parody, his aversion was serious.[2]

Garnett's animosity toward commercialism was a luxury of working within a fully subsidized institutional setting. Others had to support themselves with their craft and could not adopt Garnett's prohibitive policy, but they could vigorously embrace its wariness toward venal corruption of art. Adler's Pynson Printers manifesto left no doubt as to his resolve that "the printer should be primarily an artist — a designer and a creator rather than a *mere manufacturer.*" The shop, with its chandeliered library and exhibition gallery, was in business to serve only those for whom "quality is the first consideration." John Henry Nash similarly attested that he bestowed his finest efforts on magnificent printed pieces to be distributed gratis to friends and associates. As one admirer marveled, Nash unselfishly produced work "whose recompense has been found in the joy of his labor, and whose reward has been derived from the sincere appreciation of his friends." Another treasured such work all the more because "these precious printings . . . of course have put no money into Nash's purse."[3]

Fine printers' sincerity was commonly measured by their disregard for money. R. Critchell Rimington declared Richard Ellis "an artist, and once a manuscript is in his hands, such mere matters as costs, sale price, etc., are over the hills and out of sight." While Ellis's devotion to typographic excellence might at times exasperate his clients, Rimington admitted, nothing less could render the superior work wrought at the Georgian Press. William Kittredge exalted Frederic Warde to the same rarefied circles when he testified that Warde "was too much of a poet and philosopher to be much at home in the business world, and the necessity of earning a living was a great bore to him." Ed Grabhorn similarly insisted that "money as money never interested me." A local writer recalled that Grabhorn's "idea of properly running the accounts and the financial side was to have a box outside the door in which you put the money that he owed to others, and they could come and take it. He didn't want to be bothered with anything else." The press hired a financial manager only briefly during its lifespan of over forty years, and Ed fumed at the accountant's presence the whole time he was there.[4] A fine printer was an artist, servant only to inspiration and insight, not a mere tradesman or manufacturer.

DISASTERVILLE! PRINTERS' AVERSION TO BUSINESS

Fine printers refused or seemed unable to conform to standard practices that promoted economy and efficiency. Most commonly this meant failing to work reliably within budgets and schedules and to monitor, much less control, costs. Adler and Ellis refused to submit bids for prospective work: as the Pynson Printers policy unequivocally stated, "we believe that the practice of competitive bidding encourages the awarding of contracts to the bidder most willing to sacrifice quality to cost. Consequently we will have no part in this system." Both printers made it known that they never solicited work, that prospective clients would have to come to them in hopes of retaining their services, and that thereafter costs and fees would take secondary importance to typographic achievement. When Adler produced a small edition of *Twin Peas in a Pod* for its author, Earnest Elmo Calkins, and the bill reached a sum more than double Calkins's budget, Adler admitted that he had exceeded instructions. He explained, however, that in his efforts to make an "exceptional book," he hadn't counted costs until the book was finished. In virtually all cases, in fact, final charges for Pynson Printers work exceeded either Adler's estimates or clients' budgets. The most regular, and regularly annoyed, of those clients, Bennett Cerf, recalled that Adler "turned out beautiful work that was only about eight times what it should have cost."[5]

The Grabhorns gained special notoriety for their nonchalant, "artistic" approach to their work. Ed remarked that—had he cared solely about making money—he could easily gross forty thousand dollars a year from setting ads. While the figure may be exaggerated, it is plausible—especially for the early 1920s, when the press secured such clients as the H. H. McCann advertising agency, which brought a stable of affluent accounts such as Standard Oil and the Bank of California. Despite the regular and flush income, however, Ed was anxious to wash his hands of ad work because, he explained, "you had nothing to show for it at the end of the year, except money. I decided I'd rather print a book."[6] Fine bookmaking offered independence and artistry; ordinary printing, bound to a client's specifications and budget, offered only income.

The Grabhorns' design process was accordingly unhampered by plans or agendas; it proceeded by trial and error, by whim and hunch. They would compose a few pages of a book in three or four different typefaces, print up proofs, and then as likely as not start over with new types or a different size or line length. Ed Grabhorn admitted, and others confirmed with undisguised admiration, that he would often abandon a project when it was half-finished and begin again if he decided it was "too silly" or otherwise not to his liking. After contracting to sell the *Voiage of Maundevile* to Random House, Grabhorn's message of reassurance — "I expect the book to be completed easy by June, yet I am going to make this the best I can if takes the rest of my life" — proved a harbinger of the printer's schedule-defying priorities.[7] Illustrations and decorative elements were incorporated just as intuitively, and just as imperviously to budget and schedule considerations.

This chaotic production process plagued the Random House edition of *Leaves of Grass*. After finally agreeing in early 1929 to print the book for Cerf, who envisioned releasing the book in time for the peak Christmas sales season, the Grabhorns tinkered for months with ways to make the book live up to its monumental price. They tried different types and different styles of decorations and even experimented with green papers. Although the result was hailed as a masterpiece, its see-as-we-go design and production delayed the book's completion until well into 1930. By that time, economic retrenchments had eroded the book's advance orders, and the edition did not sell out upon publication. Cerf recalled the book's lateness with a shudder: "Disasterville!" Ed Grabhorn, who felt harassed by Cerf's schedule anxieties, claimed with some vindictive pleasure that at least a few copies were remaindered in the mid-thirties for ten dollars apiece.[8]

The notion that fine printers could not be bothered by budgets and schedules is not only a featured theme of contemporary accounts but much celebrated in subsequent memoirs and fine printing lore. This notion, intended to create exactly that impression, is often deceptive. In truth, fine printers were not so much ambivalent about income and profits as insistent that others value their work for its quality rather than for its economy. That value was measured in cost. This priority led, ironically, to an acute preoccupation with earnings. Virtually all felt exploited and underpaid, even though they tended to characterize the shortfall as a slight to their professional and artistic dignity, not to their bank accounts. In one remarkably candid outburst, Frederic Warde fumed that "I should like to chuck printing. There is no money in it. . . . I mean to have money and all I want of it." Warde's usually lofty view of printing as a soul-saving art faded as he vowed to "refuse any more commissions unless I am paid very handsomely."[9]

Adler felt perennially exploited in his intimate and manifold dealings with Random House. His correspondence reverberates with feisty exchanges with Cerf contesting the charges for Pynson Printers work. Cerf's protests, and his growing inclination to hire other printers for Random House projects, infuriated Adler, who accused the publisher of "cheapening" the imprint's prestige. "My first interest is in the making of books that might be a credit to me and would help to build up [my] reputation," he declared, and "your first interest is in possible profit."[10] But Adler's bills were exorbitant, judging from the astonishment and dismay that usually greeted them. Those protests were frequently met with Adler's cool reply that not only were true taste and quality expensive — which, he would add, a discerning clientele ought to understand — but the Pynson Printers had made little or no profit on the work.

This refrain echoes throughout Adler's business dealings. He repeatedly insisted that the Pynson Printers "never made a profit" even as he took pride in cultivating the elegant, monied atmosphere of his shop. The paradox rested in semantics, and in an accounting trick. As Paul Johnston described it in 1931, no doubt carefully guided by Adler's own explanation, the Pynson Printers "has not made money, . . . but it has returned, and does return a fair profit on the money invested." When Will Ransom reported that within seven years the shop's original investment had been "repaid and multiplied by six," he concluded exactly as Adler wished others to believe, that the Pynson Printers' success offered a "direct contradiction of the well-founded belief that ideals and prosperity are incompatible."[11] As long as a return on investment was not considered profit, Adler could both honor his anticommercial ideals and maintain a visibly prosperous personal and professional countenance.

Ed Grabhorn is another telling example of this contorted stance toward income and profits. He acquired a legendary reputation for nastiness in his business relationships, suspecting and often accusing clients (many of whom were friends and colleagues) of cheating him by paying too little for his services. David Magee, a prominent San Francisco bookseller who was also a loyal friend and client, described this as a "persecution complex," a "piteous . . . and almost continuous" cry that no one ever paid him fairly.[12] On one hand, Ed Grabhorn was an artist who despised cost accounting and financial organization, while on the other hand he zealously measured his income and forever found it insulting. He resented and disdained money matters yet brooded over them constantly.

The Grabhorns never felt properly paid for their labor on *Leaves of Grass*, for example, even though Cerf paid them as agreed at the outset: forty dollars per book, or sixteen thousand dollars. Even a generous bonus of another one thousand dollars did not smooth their ruffled feathers. Their grievance is somewhat perplexing. Although no surviving records detail their expenses for this book, both brothers described its making during oral history interviews decades later. Ed recalled that he spent about two thousand dollars on the paper for the book, and roughly fifteen hundred dollars for the binder's services. The brothers used a type already in the shop for the text, and other labor costs would have been limited to printing and typesetting — a large portion of which was their own work — because they employed no editors or proofreaders.[13] Overhead costs (notably, one hundred and fifty dollars per month for rent and one hundred dollars per month for the illustrator's salary) would have been shared with the several other major projects also in press during these months — much to Cerf's frustration. The money paid seems to have generously covered not only the book's expenses but a healthy profit. The Grabhorns' dissatisfaction likely stemmed more from a feeling that they should have received a larger share of the hundred dollars paid for each book than from any rational accounting of their costs and profit margin. Regardless, Ed complained bitterly to Cerf, who tried his best to console and appease the printer. In August 1930 Cerf stated things as bluntly as he knew how: "One thing is definite. On the next book that the Grabhorns do for Random House, *the Grabhorns are going to make money*. I have begged you time and again to set a figure high enough to cover all possible costs and to leave you with a more than fair margin of profit. What in hell can I do to *make* you make money on the books that you produce for us?"[14] Grabhorn felt unwilling to put a price on his work at the outset, finding the correlation both repugnant and restricting, yet he apparently felt that others should express their pleasure in cash, not mere praises.

BEOWULF OR BUST: PUBLISHERS' BUSINESS POSTURES

"Our new motto is going to be Beowulf by June 1st or bust!" exclaimed an exasperated Donald Klopfer to Rockwell Kent, trying to hasten the artist's work on the overdue edition for Random House.[15] Publishers often found themselves at odds with the laconic, unbusinesslike production environment that artists and fine printers cultivated, and tension soon emerged between producers' anticommercial principles and the economic necessities (and opportunities) of for-profit publishing. In fact, the anticommercialism of fine printing virtually mandated an adversarial posture toward the commercial nature of publishing. This adversarial stance aggravated the working relationships between publishers and printers, to be sure, but it also subtlely and paradoxically enhanced the perceived value of the resulting book: the more a book was felt to have emerged from an artistic rather than commercial context, the more consumers valued it. The fortunes and prestige of both fine printers and publishers benefited from the perceived conflict between them.

Publishers, typically more alert to and untroubled by the lucrative market for fine books than printers, could to some extent embrace (or at least genially tolerate) printers' ostensible distaste for good business practices. Sometimes this helped to blur the fully commercial realities of fine publishing, as when Adler described the newly formed Random House as a *"private* press established to further interest in well printed books," even though it had never been conceived as anything but a clearly commercial venture. At other times publishers simply accepted that they were more or less helpless; if they wanted fine books, they would have to take them on producers' terms, which meant erratic schedules and costs, despite contracts and sworn promises. In instances when original plans were long abandoned, Cerf even sat back and had a bit of fun with the unpredictability, wagering on final publication dates, ultimate costs, and even sales of books. He won a hundred dollars from Pascal Covici when the Covici-Friede *Canterbury Tales* failed to appear by January 1930, and merrily accepted the more modest, if "idiotic," bet from a New York dealer that the Random House *Jekyll and Hyde* would not sell a thousand copies when it finally appeared.[16]

In fact, just as fine printers claimed they were not motivated by money, so publishers distanced themselves rhetorically from the pursuit of profits. Bennett Cerf, who hardly shied away from healthy profits, later claimed he "didn't expect great money" from Random House fine editions, that he was only after some "excitement and fun on the side" while his other imprint, the Modern Library, sold steadily.[17] Cerf would have it thought that Random House fine editions were issued primarily for the joy of it, suggesting distance from the capitalist world of ordinary publishing and casting a carefree, even altruistic and culturally "pure" light over the enterprise.

Cerf's claim misrepresents, or at least obscures, the economic truth of the business. While it was not uncommon for a fine publisher to also publish trade books, few fine editions were underwritten by more profitable trade publications. At Covici-Friede, in fact, fine editions provided the bedrock sales, supporting the riskier trade titles. It bears stressing that fine books were priced and sold to sustain a livelihood, not merely to cover expenses. As Cerf wrote to Ed Grabhorn in August 1928, urging him to set production charges for the Random House *Scarlet Letter* high enough to make a "decent profit": "It's all very well to publish good books for the glory of the thing, but I am getting a little fed up on that line of procedure and hope to cash in a little on some of our future publications." Months later Cerf again pleaded with Grabhorn to figure costs for making *Leaves of Grass* to ensure himself "a very decent profit. . . . I want this to be something we'll all make darn good money on."[18] The fact that fine publishing withered as profit opportunities dried up with the changing economy of the early 1930s further testifies to the business's truly commercial nature.

Table 7. *Publishers' Unit Costs and Income*

Title	Publisher/Printer	List Price	Avg. Net Income	Unit Prod. Costs	% of Net Income	% of List Price
Cabellian Harmonics	Random House/Ellis	$ 4.00	$ 2.64	$ 1.07	41	27
The Kasidah of Haji Abdu	Knopf/Adler	5.00	3.30	1.47	45	29
Amy Lowell: A Mosaic	Rudge/Rudge	4.00	2.66	1.55	58	39
Music at Night	Fountain/Adler	10.00	4.75	1.86	39	19
Beowulf	Random House/Adler	25.00	16.50	10.00	61	40
Candide	Random House/Adler	20.00	13.20	10.73	81	54
Salammbô	Brown House/Southworth	20.00	13.13	12.00	91	60
Silverado Squatters	Scribner's/Nash	30.00	20.00	15.00	75	50
Dec. Work of Cleland	Pynson Printers/Adler	20.00	13.40	15.00	112	75
When I Was Very Young	Fountain/Adler	10.00	4.70	2.22	47	22
Yokohama Garland	Centaur/Adler	10.00	6.33	2.28	36	23
Nobodaddy	Dunster House/Adler	6.00	4.00	2.57	64	43
The Palette Knife	Chocorua/Adler	20.00	9.00	3.00	33	15
The Time Machine	Random House/Taylor	12.50	8.25	3.33	40	27
Poor Richard's Almanac	Rimington & Hooper/Kittredge	8.00	3.79	3.75	99	47
Franklin Evans	Random House/Updike	10.00	6.66	4.29	64	43
Poems of Robert Frost	Random House/Blumenthal	15.00	10.00	4.75	48	32
Voiage of Maundevile	Random House/Grabhorn	70.00	52.50	40.00	76	57
Leaves of Grass	Random House/Grabhorn	100.00	66.66	42.50	64	43
Dr. Jekyll and Mr. Hyde	Random House/Adler	10.00	6.66	5.28	79	53
Scarlet Letter	Random House/Adler	15.00	10.00	6.00	60	40
Song of Solomon	Centaur/Adler	15.00	10.00	6.10	61	41
Tom Sawyer	Random House/Adler	20.00	13.30	6.48	49	32
Red Badge of Courage	Random House/Grabhorn	15.00	9.90	6.00	61	40
Average		$ 19.77	$12.97	$ 8.63	67	44

Source: Data used for calculations in Tables 7, 8, and 10 are derived from documents located in publishers' and printers' archives, as

Financial Realities: Income and Expenses

Both printers and publishers needed to cover expenses with income from the sale of labor or books. Although most postwar fine printers were also involved to varying degrees in publishing, economic aspects of the two functions are best considered separately. What follows is a necessarily general and simplified introduction to the basic economic dimensions of fine book production and publishing. Because few financial records have survived in archives, the data tends to be anecdotal or incomplete, and generalizations should be regarded cautiously. I was able to locate financial information detailing publishers' direct expenses and income for only twenty-four fine editions (see table 7), and those records are rarely complete or fully reliable (estimates, for example, instead of final invoices, and sales orders instead of receipts). Even so, they shed valuable light on the ways in which fine printers and publishers characterized the economic nature of their work.

PUBLISHERS' INCOME

Fine publishers' income derived almost wholly from the sale of books. Sales income was determined by three factors: price, discounts offered to retailers, and the number of books available to sell. This simple formula pertained to trade publishing as well, but, according to Cheney, there price structure was "based essentially on low margins and high hazards rather than the cost of the books."[19] Cheney's 1930 economic analysis of the industry was among the first to argue what has since become widely accepted: the notorious financial riskiness of trade publishing (only about two or three books in ten yield a profit) stems not from high production costs but from unreasonably low prices that allow only about a 6 percent margin for profit or "error" — miscalculation of a book's sales. Given the seemingly inscrutable nature of the public's taste in reading matter (publishing's "high hazards"), Cheney contended, trade book prices were simply too low to protect publishers from losses. He denounced as untrue and unsound the conventional wisdom that low prices encourage sales. He blamed the industry's chronic economic woes on a financial structure that began with a ceiling on prices, then struggled to produce its goods and remain solvent within that self-imposed restriction.

In fine publishing, finances ostensibly began with the costs of making materially distinguished books. Prices were accordingly considered a direct reflection of production costs. Because fine publishing was understood as a kind of professional service — producing books that embodied the values book lovers sought to express and support — high prices were deemed the necessary consequence of high production standards. Paul Johnston accepted as fact that "fine books have been usually, and almost necessarily, expensive. . . . The better grade of materials and workmanship that have been applied to fine books are naturally costly and must be paid for." Bruce Rogers insisted that there was nothing "particularly heinous" about high price tags "if expense is a legitimate factor in their production. We often hear it said that it costs no more to produce a fine piece of printing than it does an ordinary one; but I assure you that is not true. . . . Practically every book I have made could have been made better had I more money to spend on its production." Bennett Cerf announced to booksellers and patrons that Random House prices "are based *not* on [the books'] scarcity appeal nor on 'what the traffic will bear' principle, but on the actual cost of their editing and manufacture, plus a fair and reasonable profit."[20] Distancing Random House from others' exploitive corruptions of limited edition publishing, Cerf anchored his pricing philosophy in the ideologically acceptable realm of production costs. As such, the high prices of books from Random House and other "sincere" fine publishers were deemed fair and reasonable, as was the resulting profit. Both parties in the sales transaction were able to separate the exchange of monies from more distasteful notions about commercialism.

Such a view preserved the anticommercial ethic so essential to the world of fine books, but it obscured the real factors that determined a book's price. In truth, price was tied primarily to the perception of the prospective book's value. Usually this was a function of the felicity or success of the book's design, related to but not strictly dictated by the amount of money that had gone into its making. Savvy publishers, including Cerf, determined a price that consumers would likely be willing to pay for a fine edition of the text at hand, estimated the size of that particular audience, then derived a production budget accordingly. James Wells figured that he could sell about a thousand copies of A. A. Milne's short story *When We Were Very Young* at ten dollars, for example, but he urged Adler to confirm with Cerf the number of copies that Random House would take (as North American distributor for Fountain Press books); only then, he explained, could he "figure out what we have to spend on the printing and so on."[21] Decisions about price thus dictated production costs, not vice versa.

As Cerf and others well understood, the successful sale of a fine book at any price — however high — depended utterly on the perceived value of its material form. San Francisco publisher-bookseller John Howell maintained, "if a man could afford to buy a $300 book as well as you or I could afford to buy a $10 book, then let him pay $300 for it but give him full value." Full value meant significant and readily apparent features of bibliophilic bookmaking: hand labor, handmade materials, extra colors, illustration, and other visible evidence of typographic quality—scaled somewhat to the literary and cultural merits of the text so bedecked. Hence, some developed informal rules of thumb regarding minimum production expenditures to warrant fine book status, and prices. Adler felt that at least 25 percent of any fine book's retail price should be invested in its manufacture. Similarly, when Random House agreed to distribute the fine edition of Franklin's *Poor Richard's Almanac* published in 1928 by Rimington and Hooper, it stipulated that the latter must spend not less than $1,000 to produce the three hundred and fifty copies—a minimum per-copy expenditure of $2.86, or 36 percent of its $8 retail price.[22]

What prices proved justifiable to postwar bibliophiles? In a decade when 90 to 95 percent of all trade fiction sold for $2.50 or less, and 87 percent of trade nonfiction was priced under $5, and when the average *annual* per capita expenditure for books was only $1.80,[23] a fine edition cost on average between $15 and $20. The twenty-four fine editions whose financial records were analyzed cost buyers an average of $19.77 (see table 7). This figure alone is only slightly useful, however, because it does not distinguish between a four-hundred-page folio printed on handmade paper, for example, and a palm-sized twelve-page edition of a single poem. A more useful calculation is the average price per ten pages of text, although this calculation does not consider page dimensions or the amount of text on each page. This figure ranges from $16.67 ($20 for a book of twelve text pages) to 40 cents ($10 for two hundred and forty-eight text pages); the average was $2.14 (see table 8). By contrast, the average cost per ten-page increment of a trade book at the time was approximately 8 cents. One must be wary of this statistic as well, however, because it does not account for other bibliophilic features that determined much of a book's perceived value. The twelve-page book that sold for $20, for instance, was the Chocorua Press's edition of Morley's *Palette Knife,* each copy of which was illustrated with six original watercolors by René Gockinga.

Rarely, however, did publishers receive the full retail price paid by consumers. Although fine books were sometimes sold directly to individual customers, they were more commonly sold like ordinary books: wholesale to booksellers, who in turn sold the books at list or retail price to consumers. Fine books were rarely sold through regular trade bookstores, however, but by dealers or shops that specialized in fine, rare, or particularly expensive goods. Like their trade counterparts, then, fine publishers typically received only *net* income—the discounted price paid by the bookseller, not the retail price paid by the consumer. Most fine publishers allowed a discount of about one-third off the retail price, a rate little different from that of trade books. Cheney noted that in 1930 bookstores on average paid 62.5 cents on the dollar for their merchandise.[24]

Table 8. *Production Cost and Price*

Title	List Price	Unit Prod. Costs	No. Text Pages	10-pg. Unit List Price	Comp. Method	Paper
Cabellian Harmonics	$ 4.00	$ 1.07	96	$ .42	Machine	Machine
The Kasidah of Haji Abdu	5.00	1.47	94	.48	Hand	Handmade
Amy Lowell: A Mosaic	4.00	1.55	28	1.43	Machine	Machine
Music at Night	10.00	1.86	139	.71	Machine	Machine
Beowulf	25.00	10.00	146	1.71	Hand	Machine
Candide	20.00	10.73	111	1.80	Hand	Handmade
Salammbô	20.00	12.00	345	.58	Machine	Machine
Silverado Squatters	30.00	15.00	99	3.03	Hand	Handmade
Decorative Work of Cleland	20.00	15.00	112	1.79	Hand	Machine
When I Was Very Young	10.00	2.22	26	3.85	Hand	Handmade
Yokohama Garland	10.00	2.28	64	1.56	Machine	Handmade
Nobodaddy	6.00	2.57	67	.90	Hand	Handmade
The Palette Knife	20.00	3.00	12	16.67	Hand	Handmade
The Time Machine	12.50	3.33	83	1.51	Machine	Machine
Poor Richard's Almanac	8.00	3.75	144	.55	Machine	Machine
Franklin Evans	10.00	4.29	248	.40	Machine	Machine
Poems of Robert Frost	15.00	4.75	350	.43	Hand	Machine
Voiage of Maundevile	70.00	40.00	156	4.49	Hand	Handmade
Leaves of Grass	100.00	42.50	420	2.38	Hand	Handmade
Dr. Jekyll and Mr. Hyde	10.00	5.28	161	.62	Hand	Machine
Scarlet Letter	15.00	6.00	368	.41	Hand	Machine
Song of Solomon	15.00	6.10	48	3.13	Hand	Handmade
Tom Sawyer	20.00	6.48	132	1.52	Machine	Machine
Red Badge of Courage	15.00	6.00	142	1.06	Hand	Handmade
Average	$ 19.77	$ 8.63	150	$ 2.14		

Because several fine publishers in the twenties were small businesses, some-times with only a few employees (Fountain Press, Dunster House, Chocorua, and others), they were ill-equipped in personnel, expertise, warehouse facili-ties, and capital to undertake sales and distribution of their books. These publishers often sold entire editions to a larger house specializing in fine edi-tions — usually Random House or Doubleday, Doran — at a deep discount in exchange for handling all responsibilities and expenses of advertising, dis-tribution, and sales. The discount ranged from 50 to as much as 60 percent, but was usually 53 to 55 percent. In effect, this arrangement transferred the financial risk from publisher to distributor. The publisher received certain, immediate income, incurring little more than manufacturing and editorial expenses, and the books presumably received better exposure and better sales when handled by a well-known larger organization with established trade contacts among booksellers. The distributor shouldered most costs of marketing and sales, as well as the risk that copies might not sell at all. Cerf described the arrangement in detail to Crosby Gaige at the outset of their contractual relationship: "Mr. Gaige is completely protected and guaranteed against loss, since before going to press he can estimate the costs and know exactly what his receipts are going to be. The entire risk of the transaction is borne by Random House, and while the directors of Random House feel that in most cases this risk will be negligible, it must be borne in mind that there are several titles on the list that will be sold out only after much difficulty — with the strong possibility that some copies will never be sold. Another thing that must be considered is that while Random House pays cash on delivery, many of its largest accounts are notoriously slow-paying."[25] Any publisher, whether it entrusted an edition to a distributor or sold books to retail booksellers directly, therefore received only a portion of the monies paid by consumers. Its income was significantly affected by the costs involved in the commercial sale of goods.

Along with price and discounts, edition size was key to determining a book's earnings. Ensuring that the number of copies printed would be small, relative to trade conventions, was essential. In theory, fine editions were inevitably limited because only a small number of people would appreciate and value fine bookmaking, and because careful craftsmanship and high-quality materials were thought to naturally cap the number of copies that could be produced. Both assertions mingled economic and ideological purposes.

Fine editions were in fact limited to a quantity usually slightly under the publisher's estimate of the number of prospective buyers. This differed little from trade practice, where edition sizes were also scaled to anticipated demand. Significantly, however, trade publishers printed slightly more copies than expected demand (both to reduce unit costs and to be prepared in case sales exceeded predictions) while fine publishers aimed low, hoping instead to sell out quickly. A quick sale not only enhanced the imprint's prestige and strengthened the claim that edition sizes were not calculated for maximum profits, but also yielded the distinct financial rewards of immediate income and spared marketing expenses. Fine publishers thus strove to maximize earnings through astute calculations of quantity no less than did trade publishers. In several instances, they revised edition size in light of early indications of demand, notably advance orders. James Wells assured Cerf that "if you get a couple of hundred orders from the west" — that is, he clarified, "all points west of Fifth Avenue" — for the Fountain Press edition of Virginia Woolf's *A Room of One's Own*, a print run of 500 copies "will be a pretty sure thing." As usual,

Cerf was skeptical, replying that because they had sold only 350 copies of *Orlando*, "surely we can expect to do no better with the very much less important" *Room*. He set 300 as a limit, but later agreed to distribute 350 copies. Planned edition sizes went up as often as they went down: as publicity and excitement spread about Rockwell Kent's artwork and Adler's design for the Random House *Candide*, for example, its edition size grew from an initial plan of 1290 copies, including 50 special hand-colored copies, to a final count of 1635 copies, including 95 deluxe copies.[26]

At times edition size was increased to offset growing expenses. Although author George Henry Sargent resisted William Rudge's plea that the fine edition of his *Amy Lowell: A Critical Essay* be printed in 500 copies, preferring that it remain limited to 350 copies, Rudge ultimately authorized the printing of 450 copies. After the books were completed, Rudge explained to the peeved Sargent: "It was necessary to increase the size of the edition in order to make the little book come out on the right side of the ledger as Mr. [Bruce] Rogers spent considerable time with it but I am sure it was all worth while[;] as you say it is a fine little book and I think will be a credit to the author."[27]

The assumption that fine editions were naturally limited by anti-industrial production methods was largely a convenient fallacy. Not only were many fine books produced using methods little different from those used to produce trade books, but historical precedents challenged any correlation between hand labor and edition size. For hundreds of years printers had produced massive books in large editions when demand warranted, with materials and processes requiring more manual labor than those used in the 1920s. A far more relevant limitation was the fact that fine editions usually required greater material investments than their trade counterparts; limited capital was more likely to restrict edition size.

Decisions about edition size were rooted primarily in marketing and sales considerations. Markets for "limited" editions, ranging from a few hundred to a few thousand copies, were sometimes not much smaller than those for ordinary trade editions. In 1929 nearly 46 percent of trade nonfiction books sold fewer than a thousand copies, and more than 30 percent of lower-priced fiction titles sold fewer than two thousand copies.[28] Fine books were produced in smaller numbers than trade editions, to be sure, but the difference between trade and limited editions was not as great as it seemed.

PUBLISHERS' EXPENSES

Carl Rollins once grumbled that "the damned traders have discovered the possibility of getting fifteen dollars for a four dollar book, and now the middlemen are trying to hog *all* the profits — witness the grotesque absurdity of a book designed by Rogers, printed by Rudge, published by Crosby Gaige, and distributed by Random House, and retailed by the book stores! In this case they say they should charge fifteen dollars to break even (that is, give everyone his rake-off)!" It seemed unfair that, as Bob Grabhorn complained, unless you are the publisher, "you find yourself printing a thirty-dollar book for ten dollars, and it must still look like a thirty-dollar book."[29] The considerable costs of publishing were least understood and most resented by printers who perceived the difference between production costs and retail price as easy profit. By the mid-twenties, when demand for fine editions was beginning to seem insatiable, several fine printers entered the publishing field, lured by readily identifiable audiences and escalating prices: Adler's Pynson Printers undertook a colossal publication of *The Decorative Work of T. M. Cleland,* a project nearly six years and eighteen thousand dollars in the making which nearly bankrupted the small shop; Frederic Warde initiated his brief Pleiad Press; Richard Ellis produced a few titles under his Georgian Press imprint; and the Grabhorns, Nash, and the Windsor Press directly cultivated the ready markets of wealthy California bibliophiles.

Most were dismayed, however, to discover that from a publisher's point of view design "is more than anything being a bookkeeper. You have to realize what the book's going to sell for and how much you can afford to spend on its manufacture, and work within those limits," as Bob Grabhorn ruefully put it. This involved marshaling and carefully monitoring one's capital resources and calculating the size, taste, and expendable income of a prospective market — tasks not altogether savory to craftsmen who were concerned primarily with making beautiful books. David Magee observed that the Grabhorn brothers soon grew to hate "the mechanics of publishing"; they hated "the wrapping and the billing and that sort of thing. It bored them to death." Bob Grabhorn admitted that by the late twenties he and his brother "didn't want to be bothered with the collection and bookkeeping and all that stuff."[30] They felt exploited by publishers' pricing structures, but they could not bring themselves to engage in the mundane, time-consuming, and financially risky business of publishing.

They discovered that a publisher bore risks and financial burdens that diminished considerably the lure of garnering full retail price with each sale. In addition to receiving only net, not list, income, publishers encountered a host of major expenses that printers only vaguely anticipated. As Cheney calculated for the trade industry, average manufacturing costs — including the often-significant fees paid to an illustrator or designer that were not necessarily covered in the printer's charges — represented only about a third of a publisher's expenses (see table 9). Other major expenses included author

Table 9. Distribution of the Trade Publisher's Dollar

Manufacturing	$0.357
Editorial costs	0.021
Royalties	0.173
Selling	0.067
Advertising	0.121
Shipping	0.019
Overhead	0.183
Other items (bad debt, losses, and profit)	0.059
Total	$1.00

Source: O. H. Cheney, *Economic Survey of the Book Industry, 1930–1931* (New York: National Association of Book Publishers, 1931), p. 188.

royalties (averaging 17.3 percent of a publisher's receipts), editorial expenses (2.1 percent), all costs of marketing and sales (approximately 20.7 percent), and general business overhead expenses (18.3 percent) for rent, salaries, equipment, taxes, interest payments, and so on. Only the scant remaining 5.9 percent of a publisher's receipts, gathered under the rubric of "other," offered an opportunity for profit, after covering bad debts, losses on unsold copies, and other fiscal misfortunes. Fine publishing also operated within this larger commercial environment, but although some of its practices consequently differed little from trade norms, others sometimes diverged considerably, yielding a fairly anomalous financial picture.

Like their trade counterparts, fine publishers had to secure and edit manuscripts and promote, distribute, and sell books as well as produce them. In trade publishing the primary factor affecting sales is the text itself — author, particular title or subject, or genre. Sales occur after some exposure to the book's existence — a review, an ad, a copy displayed in a bookstore window, a neighbor's remark. Each book sells on its own mixture of textual appeal and publicity exposure; book buyers feel little brand name loyalty to a particular imprint. Financial success in fine publishing, by contrast, relied less on textual content than on material form, and less on broad publicity efforts than on a discreet, selective, "informational" ethic of marketing and sales. These differences provided the alternative economic realities that made postwar fine publishing fiscally viable.

Between 12 and 22 percent (averaging 17 percent) of trade publishers' income covered editorial expenses, primarily author royalties; the corresponding expense in fine publishing was much lower.[31] Because so many fine editions reprinted copyright-free texts that required no royalty, average costs directly pertaining to the text were modest. When fine publishers did pay author royalties, however, they rarely offered less than the standard industry rates, 10 percent of retail price. If anything, fine publishers erred on the generous, even extravagant side. At least twice Crosby Gaige bestowed thousand-dollar advances on struggling authors he wished to help — or dazzle. He paid Richard Aldington such a sum for his slim collection of *Fifty Lyric Poems,* blithely terming it an "encouragement, moral and financial."[32]

It was more common to pay authors a flat fee for permission to publish their work. This appealed to authors because the small, fixed edition sizes limited opportunities for royalties, and a flat fee meant payment at the outset, unaffected by a book's sales. Conversely, this practice sometimes posed a financial burden for publishers. When Lewis and Grabhorn set out to publish Westgate fine editions by contemporary authors, for example, they offered $750 to authors of magazine articles or stories they admired: $250 for rights, and $500 for signing the copies. "We obviously offered these people too much money," Grabhorn recalled, because all the authors they approached — including Sherwood Anderson, Virginia Woolf, and Lewis Mumford — "jumped" at the offers.[33] Conventional royalties would have netted each author only $500: 10 percent of the $10 retail price paid for each of five hundred copies.

Because a fine book's featured content was often artwork more than text, artists sometimes commanded compensation equal to if not exceeding what a premium writer might earn. Rockwell Kent's authorlike status earned him the standard 10 percent author's royalty for illustrations to *Beowulf* (Random House, 1932): $2,500 for six lithographs, a title page, and a colophon page. He earned the same royalty on two other books also published by Random House, books with no text at all: his *Birthday Book* (1930) and *The Bookplates and Marks of Rockwell Kent* (1929). Each artist of the Lakeside Press's "Four American Books" project — Dwiggins, Rudolph Ruzicka, Edward O. Wilson, and Kent — was paid $2,000 per volume (Kent received $6,000 for the three-volume *Moby Dick*), for example, averaging slightly more than 10 percent of the edition's retail income. Similarly, Alexander King was paid $1500 to illustrate the Brown House edition of Flaubert's *Salammbô,* approximately 9.4 percent of prospective retail earnings.

Few printers understood the significant extent to which marketing and distribution costs also burdened a publisher's budget. When Cerf outlined for Gaige the terms of their distribution contract, he documented a rare glimpse of those costs:

The average discount that Random House will allow will probably amount to over 35%; in other words, if the total retail value of the twenty-one books on the list submitted is $120,000, its receipts will be about $78,000. Mr. Gaige will receive $54,000. This $22,000 differential must pay the following:

Salesmen's commissions (approximately $6,000)
Overhead
Advertising
Cost of carrying accounts[34]

Although Cerf did not detail average expenses involved in the latter categories, probably because they pertain generally to the business itself and so could not be attributed specifically to particular titles, his point was well taken. All marketing and sales and distribution costs, as well as the risk of failing to sell copies at all, had to be covered in that negotiated difference between the discount at which Random House bought the books and the discount at which it sold them.

The most striking difference between fine and trade publishing fiscal norms lies in the proportion of earnings absorbed by production costs. In any basic publishing economic analysis, the ratio between a book's manufacturing cost and its selling price, both retail and net, offers a fundamental reference point. According to Cheney, a book's production cost typically ranged from 15 to 25 percent of its retail price or 25 to 40 percent of its net price. Because trade book prices were so stable, seldom exceeding $2.50 for fiction and $3 for nonfiction, manufacturing costs were limited to a per-copy expenditure between 37.5 and 75 cents for all but a very few trade books. These figures provide useful benchmarks when examining the relationship between a fine book's production costs, its other costs, and its price.

Because fine publishers sought to base a book's price on its material cost, they devoted exceptional care and expenditure to design and material production. Of the fine editions whose manufacturing costs are known, the per-copy proportion of a book's cost to its eventual earnings ranges from a low near the trade industry average of 36 percent (for the Centaur Press's edition of *Yokohama Garland*) to the disastrous 112 percent registered by the Pynson Printers' edition of Cleland's *Decorative Work*.[35] The books' production costs averaged $8.63 a copy, or 70 percent of their net earnings (see table 7). These costs would have been immediately ruinous had the books been destined for the conventional trade market, of course, but because special, even extravagant material features were so intrinsic to fine books they were deemed an essential perquisite for success. Those features not only dramatically drove up the prices of fine books but rationalized them, hence providing the most compelling source of perceived value.

No simple equation can correlate a book's price with a specific material ingredient; the complex blend of factors — material and otherwise — that influenced pricing decisions precludes easy isolation of a single feature. Even so, prices must be considered in terms of the several production variables that attributed perceived value to a fine edition. Did fine books' prices directly reflect bibliophilic features, as publishers asserted? Table 8 correlates production costs with two such features (handmade paper and hand composition) for the twenty-four titles for which records survive. The fifteen composed by hand averaged $11.37 per copy to produce (45.4 percent of their average list price of $25.07), while those machine-composed averaged $7.61 in production costs (50.6 percent of their average $15.05 list price). Ten titles were both printed on handmade paper and composed by hand; they cost their publishers an average of $14.30 each to produce (41.3 percent of list) but garnered a list price averaging $34.60. By contrast, eight titles sported neither feature, yet their unit manufacturing costs averaged $4.66 (29.8 percent of list), and they sold for an average of $15.61.

These figures suggest that the prices of fine books were indeed the consequence of more expensive materials and hand production processes, ostensibly yielding greater material value. Most striking about the figures, however, is not the ratio between cost and price but the high production costs themselves. Why would fine books composed by machine and printed on machine-made paper — exactly like trade books — cost on average between six and twelve times more to produce ($4.66 each, compared to 37.5 to 75 cents)? The answer lies partly in other design and production features, such as use of color, illustration, large dimensions, and elaborate ornamentation. The prices also reflect fine printers' artisanal business practices and the anticommercial refusal to "compromise" with cost-reducing strategies of efficiency, planning, and competitive bidding. Particularly for Adler's Pynson Printers, Ellis's Georgian Press, and John Henry Nash, the notion that "quality costs more" was beyond axiomatic: it seems to have discouraged the reduction or containment of costs because lower charges for production might signal inferior quality.

Fine books' high manufacturing costs also represented, to some extent, expenses that might otherwise be budgeted for book promotion. Typically, fine publishers regarded a healthy and visible investment in production as a key marketing tool. Cerf urgently advised Crosby Gaige to "put every last cent into your first five or six books," to assure customers that quality of bookmaking was foremost to the new imprint. "Skimping would be fatal," he warned —

prophetically, as it turned out.[36] Cerf's insistence on the utmost standards of production quality reveals his shrewd grasp of the peculiar business in which generous, even extravagant production expenditures were in fact a solid investment that paid off in a reputation for quality and anticommercial ideals that sold books, swiftly and profitably.

A significant investment in material production helped develop a clientele of buyers who recognized the caliber of bookmaking a particular designer, printer, or publisher sought to achieve, regardless of the specific text. That awareness eased the need to promote individual titles, because the books' primary feature was the artistry or craftsmanship of their making, enabling publishers to spend more on production and less on marketing per se. Limiting edition sizes theoretically eliminated or at least minimized the speculative nature of book editions. That is, fine publishers could avoid the common practice of printing an ample number of copies so that, should promotional tactics prove successful, there would be plenty of copies available to meet demand. Trade publishers often skimped on production quality in order to purchase more copies, then relied on marketing and luck to sell the books. Fine publishers, by contrast, limited their editions partly to limit the effort and cost of selling them. Again, this strategy tacitly served both ideological and economic ends.

It seems, then, that fine books' high prices were indeed based on extraordinarily high production costs. Before those costs are examined, a glance at typical production costs for an ordinary trade book of the day offers a helpful context. According to a contemporary analyst, a typical 325-page novel of a standard size (seven by five inches), printed in an edition routinely set at 5,000 copies, would cost its publisher approximately forty-five cents to manufacture. Of that total cost, paper would account for eight cents (17.7 percent), printing would cost nine cents (20 percent), binding would add another twenty-two cents (48.9 percent), and a basic dust jacket would cost 2 cents (4.4 percent). The final four cents per copy (10 percent) would be allowed to cover the cost of both printer's wastage and copies not for sale—those intended to be given away for review and other promotional purposes.[37] This hypothetical average book would be printed in black ink only on machine-made wood-pulp paper in a ten- or eleven-point machine-composed typeface with one or two points of leading and narrow margins, it would include no illustration, and it would bear no special features.

Of the twenty-four fine editions whose production costs are known, unit production costs range from $1.07 for the machine-set, *Cabellian Harmonics* (one hundred and three pages) to a whopping $42.50 for the monumental, hand-composed Grabhorn/Random House *Leaves of Grass* (see table 8). Detailed breakdowns of publishers' specific manufacturing costs are rare. I found only one such set of computations in the Pynson Printers archive, for example: an informal, pencil-written preliminary calculation that Adler worked out before submitting a single-figure estimate to the publisher. It outlines Adler's plan for the manufacture of Archibald MacLeish's *Nobodaddy,* published by Dunster House in 1926. In August 1924 Adler estimated that seven hundred and fifty copies of the book would cost $1,320 to produce: $200 for hand-made paper (27 cents per copy), $240 for the cloth binding (32 cents each), $480 for hand composition of the book's sixty-seven text pages ($7.16 per page), and $400 for printing. After adding $100 to hire an artist (Dwiggins) to produce a vignette for the title page and rounding up the total, Adler submitted an estimate of $1,500 to publisher Maurice Firuski.

Most striking here are Adler's labor charges. Records suggest that he figured one hundred and twenty hours of labor for composition and one hundred hours for printing, both charged at four dollars an hour. If so, this means he charged the publisher roughly four times what the workers earned. It also represents either an exceptional devotion of skilled labor to the typesetting and printing of sixty-seven moderate-sized pages (measuring seven and seven-eighths by five inches), or a deliberate inflation of this cost variable to ensure ample profit. That is, Adler's typesetters composed about three typewritten pages in a day; if each of the printed text pages represents two typescript pages (a generous equivalency), the book would have been typeset in about forty-five hours, not the one hundred and twenty Adler estimated.[38]

Had these initial figures accurately predicted the book's expenses, the seven hundred and fifty copies of the slim book would have cost $2 per copy to manufacture — or 50 percent of the net receipts earned on the $6 book. In truth, the book proved to be a fiscal debacle for both printer and publisher. Spiraling design ambitions and unsatisfactory results that required reprinting and rebinding portions of the edition drove up Adler's costs to $2,433.06, although he charged Firuski only $1,833.06. With some fanfare he assured the panicked publisher that he would shoulder the difference as "advertising expenses" for the Pynson Printers, explaining that the additional expense was incurred to satisfy his high standards of workmanship, by which he hoped to secure future clients who valued exceptionally fine work. Even with Adler's seemingly magnanimous gesture, the finished book cost its publisher $2.44 per copy to produce — 64 percent of its $4 net income.

PRINTERS' EXPENSES

On what were these manufacturing costs based? Extant records indicate only what *publishers* paid for design and production; seldom if ever were *printers'* per-title expenses — for paper, composition, printing, and binding — monitored and recorded, at least in any surviving documents. To further complicate analysis, no consistent practice governed what expenses were included as "manufacturing" or production costs. Illustration costs, shipping, and binding were commonly subcontracted and paid for separately. Despite the vague nature of the information, however, a closer look at fine printers' costs is instructive.

Fine printers incurred three general kinds of expenses. First, they bore the immediate costs directly related to design and production. For any given book, direct materials costs included paper and plates, if any, while direct labor costs included typesetting and printing. Depending on the length and special needs of the book, composition or printing could also be subcontracted to other shops better suited to meet particular requirements. Illustration costs included not only the artist's fees (sometimes paid by the printer but more typically paid directly by the publisher) but also the cost of making plates and, if necessary, of having the illustrations printed elsewhere, as was required for photography or lithography. For hand-composed books, the cost of type was included in overhead expenses, along with rent, other equipment, publicity, and other costs incurred in the general operation of the shop.

Paper was usually a printer's single greatest material expense. In trade printing, paper averaged just under 18 percent of total costs, while in fine printing that percentage often ran much higher.[39] When the Pynson Printers produced *The Palette Knife,* for example, handmade paper represented two-thirds of the book's total manufacturing cost. Although papers used for trade books were fairly consistent in quality and price, paper costs for fine books varied considerably: handmade paper was generally more expensive than mouldmade, which in turn typically cost more than machine-made. Other variables influenced costs dramatically: the weight of the paper, its imported or domestic origin, the quantity purchased, and the size of the sheet. Sometimes printers ordered a large quantity of a particular paper that became a sort of house stock, such as the "BR Rag" used extensively by Rudge; this lowered cost but also diffused direct paper costs for a specific book into general overhead expenses.

Printers were usually responsible for binding expenses as well, even when books were subcontracted out to a commercial bindery.[40] Binding expenses were also determined primarily by materials. Trade bindings typically ran to nearly half of all manufacturing costs. Bindings of fine books were typically more expensive, in part because the smaller edition sizes of fine books led to higher per-copy costs, but chiefly because more lavish material was used. High-quality cloth, specially decorated paper, and sometimes leather used for part or all of the book's binding could increase cost dramatically.

Labor costs are also difficult to determine. One skilled typesetter recalled that when he started work at the Grabhorn Press in 1929 he accepted a salary of $35 a week, which was somewhat lower than Nash had recently paid him. (The Grabhorns did not employ union members, which reduced their labor costs.) On the East Coast, a skilled worker at Rudge's shop was paid $50 for a forty-four-hour work week in the late twenties. This suggests an hourly wage of a little more than $1 an hour. By comparison, the Pynson Printer's total wages (excluding office and management salaries) expended during a typical one-month pay period at that time averaged $574.41 per week, which presumably covered the services of the twelve workers (nine compositors and three pressman) Adler employed at the time. If each worked a standard forty-four-hour week, their earnings averaged $1.06 per hour.[41] Adler often boasted of the long-term stability of his small workforce, so one may infer that his employees considered themselves well treated and fairly paid.

A fine printer had to cover these and all overhead expenses, as well as his own salary, with charges billed for work produced. A book's manufacturing costs, as paid by a publisher, thus exceeded the printer's direct costs (except for binding done out of house, whose cost was simply passed along). A rule of thumb, then as now, was to charge roughly double the direct costs in order to cover indirect and overhead expenses. It is not safe to surmise that a fine printer's actual costs were approximately half of what was charged to a publisher, however; bound ethically if not legally to a preproduction estimate, printers bore most of the additional expense if costs exceeded an estimate. On the other hand, Adler routinely computed labor costs at four to five dollars an hour, considerably more than twice the wages he apparently paid.

To Serve Our Special Friends: Marketing and Sales

Because fine books signified a disdain for mainstream American consumerism, marketing had to be conducted along a more discreet, dignified avenue. To conceal their own commercial selling activity, fine publishers sought to obscure the nature of their consumers' buying. Promotional rhetoric and tactics stressed three themes, each of which distanced — through overt aversion or implicit ambivalence — the world of fine books from the consumer climate of postwar commerce. First, instead of making overtures to the general public, fine publishers appealed to a collegial community of knowledgeable bibliophiles, "insiders" who supported the historical and ideological endeavors that animated fine bookmaking. Second, they stressed that fine books offered broad cultural and social distinction, a means for expressing allegiance to fine things of quality and taste. Third, they contended that fine books constituted stable and enduring value — in contrast to the volatile world of goods that one merely consumed, or used and gradually depleted.

In each of these ways, marketing messages assured that the purchase (and consequently the sale) of fine books differed from ordinary material consumption, reflecting the blend of privilege and responsibility embodied in the cultural stewardship of postwar America. That is, antibusiness postures veiled fine publishing in a pair of paradoxes. They sustained the myth that sales transactions were more pure, more centered in cultural and artistic patronage than in material acquisition, and they enhanced one of the central attractions of fine printing, its eliteness. That this eliteness was ostensibly grounded in cultural sensibilities and tastes rather than mere wealth made it both more palatable in a democratic society and more compelling, more selflessly noble. Adler praised millionaire bibliophile Frank Altschul for his "patronage" of Random House's first book (Altschul bought Kent's original illustrations, ensuring that the artist was handsomely paid for the work), assuring him that his "intellectual interest and support make possible the creation of a book like Candide." Marketing rhetoric thus shrewdly implied refusal to compromise a standard of clientele quality — the restriction of sales to "those capable of *appreciating,* and paying for, the quality of the product" — that matched heralded commitments to material and design quality standards.[42] These themes are apparent in both book content and the methods of marketing and sales overtures.

Promotional materials conveyed dignity and restraint; they were portrayed as a *service* in that they offered information about the book and the opportunity to secure a copy. Promotions were circulated as "announcements" rather than as "advertisements" — in the twenties, the latter term often connoted manipulation, pandering to common or mass tastes, and dissembling if not deceit. The announcements typically took the form of a prospectus profiling the coming work and its special features. Distributed to potential buyers, either directly or through booksellers, the prospectus described salient aspects of the book's making and usually previewed its design or illustration in some way.

Prospectuses were not as matter-of-fact as they purported to be, however; carefully crafted to entice buyers, they showcased the bibliophilic delights that awaited the books' owners. When Adler sent Dwiggins a dummy of the prospectus for Random House's 1929 edition of *Dr. Jekyll and Mr. Hyde,* Dwiggins's candid critique reveals his astute understanding of the task at hand. First, he noted, "It is a little page. The prospectus might make a bigger dent if you gave them a bit more paper." He continued: "Prospectuses . . . of limited edition books that I get always make me want to see a trifle more of the inside. Why show them the title-page? Why not better save that so that they get a thrill when they get their copy. The chapter heads are a bright and cheerful feature of this celebrated edition: why not show them a chapter head? I have a hunch it would have more sting than [the] title-page. I also have a hunch that you ought to sell Random House as well as the edition—I mean get R. H. strong in the page 1 bang: a R. H. title-page to the *prospectus* rather than the title-page of the book. More active merchandising." He then outlined what he believed the prospectus should entail: "a prospectus title-page featuring R. H. edition; 3 pp. of book—opening of a story, a text page, an illustration page; a 'come on, clip the coupon,' page at the end."[43]

The prospectus often went hand in hand with a personal, direct method of promotion and sales, an effective selling technique for retail fine booksellers and occasionally for publishers themselves. A direct approach worked for fine editions more than for trade books both because the market was relatively easy to identify and because the chief appeal of fine books was easier to spotlight. In general, trade booksellers were difficult to excite with news of a publication. Cheney skeptically described publishers' efforts to "sell to the trade," noting that the "various 'pep' letters and telegrams of diverse degrees of peppiness" that publishers sent out reached only "a de-pepped and non-peppable bookseller who is more worried about selling what he has than about ordering more."[44] But fine books rarely circulated through ordinary bookstores, which could seldom afford to tie up capital in expensive stock that relatively few, if any, of their customers would be able or inclined to buy. Fine editions were therefore usually sold through quasi-private channels, which only enhanced their prestige.

As prominent Los Angeles dealer of fine and rare books Jake Zeitlin explained in a 1930 *Publishers' Weekly* article sharing tips about "Developing Interest and Sales in Books of Fine Presses," "our books are sold to the individual and never to the general public." Zeitlin urged others to follow his practice of sending out personal letters enclosing a prospectus provided by the publisher. For example, "as soon as the first Random House announcements are made," he wrote, "I request about 100 copies from them and send these out with a carefully worded letter in which I make my own selection. These always bring results. It is often easier to sell a book in advance of publication than when you have it in your hand. The imagination has such a grand way of surrounding a description with glamor that it always works for us in our customer's mind. . . . We always book up most of our sales before the books are published." Booksellers specializing in high-end merchandise typically developed an intimate sense of their clientele's preferences and tastes, acting more as brokers than as sales agents per se. They often prepared chatty newsletters describing new or forthcoming books, but learned that "letters pull better than printing," as Connecticut bookseller A. Leland Ziglatzki confirmed when he made only four sales from a printed brochure listing his stock that was mailed to fourteen hundred clients.[45] Personal letters, usually on finely printed stationary and often supplemented with a prospectus, brought best results: not only more sales, but sales that left little commercial taint to the transaction.

Publishers sometimes used similar methods to sell their books directly. When editions were small and the market easy to identify, this strategy was both manageable and effective. Printer-publishers — notably Adler, Nash, and Rudge — enjoyed good results when they sent personal letters to their many bibliophilic acquaintances. Although direct sales entailed considerable clerical labor, a secretary's small salary was more than recovered with even modest results because this technique garnered retail rather than wholesale income (less the handling, postage, and general inventory costs). It also further obscured the commercial nature of the business when publishers could reassure their customers that "we are offering the book to special friends" and "not selling through dealers at all."[46] Direct sales also focused attention on a book's design and manufacture, encouraging bibliophiles to attribute a key part of a book's value to its printer. Although he published only one title in the twenties, Elmer Adler fostered such brand name status for his work by buying at wholesale quantities of books produced in his shop and retailing them directly to clients. In effect, he conducted a side business as a book dealer, though his motive was not income but the opportunity to market the books as Pynson Printers work.

Letters soliciting sales allowed printer-publishers to guide perceptions of their enterprise as artistic (as opposed to profit-driven), in the revered vein of the great William Morris and other famous predecessors. John Henry Nash was most rhetorically audacious. Under the signature of his secretary-librarian, Nash sent out letters portraying him as a solitary artisan devoted to his craft and depicting the prospective customer as a patron who, in supporting Nash, would help sustain the noble cultural endeavor at which he labored. About a year before his monumental four-volume folio edition of Dante's *Divine Comedy* (priced at $200) was ready, for example, Nash sent out hundreds of letters seeking advance sales. Each began: "John Henry Nash has always dreamed of producing a great classical work which would fully express his ideals as a printer. The work is now well under way and in the course of another year Mr. Nash's edition of THE COMEDY OF DANTE ALIGHIERI OF FLORENCE will be issued. The work on this production has been going forward for four years, not without those difficulties that hamper a printer who works with his hands for his livelihood. That is to say, it has cost a great deal of money and progress had to stop at times when money was not available. Perhaps for this very reason it will be a better book than otherwise, since difficulties overcome enrich all products of craftsmanship."[47]

Although direct marketing often proved effective, selling one copy at a time could be tedious and drain energies needed for the myriad other tasks involved in publishing. Publishers occasionally purchased advertising space in periodicals to reach more prospective customers, but they did so with considerable caution. Because fine publishers sought to distance themselves from the public marketplace, fine book ads were restrained in their rhetoric, striving to reflect in prose the elegant, dignified effect that the typography usually achieved. They emphasized bibliophilic features and the book's limited availability. When Covici-Friede published *The Canterbury Tales* with illustrations by Rockwell Kent, for example, its full-page ad in *Publishers' Weekly* heralded the date of the book's arrival and advised retail dealers to order copies immediately because, they claimed, it seemed certain that both editions ("regular" at $50 and "deluxe" in full leather binding with extra illustrations at $250) would be heavily oversubscribed before publication. Although advertising in *Publishers' Weekly* was directed to the trade, not retail consumers, the emphasis on informational service rather than "hype" again predominated.

When the occasional fine book was advertised beyond the trade, it was promoted only to readers of judiciously selected forums. Joseph Blumenthal advertised his Spiral Press editions in the *Saturday Review of Literature, American Literature,* and the *New England Quarterly,* hoping to attract buyers to their literary as well as bibliophilic merits (see figure 26). The *Saturday Review* was an astute choice, given Carl Rollins's regular review column; other periodicals deemed suitable included the *American Mercury* (affiliated with Random House), the *Atlantic Monthly,* and *Vanity Fair.* Each magazine prided itself on a discerning and sophisticated, elite readership. *Vanity Fair* was unabashed in characterizing its readers as the "mental aristocracy of America" who have the "taste, intelligence, and sensibility" as well as the "discernment and money to buy fine books." The *New York Evening Herald* boasted to Random House of "the finest class of readers" in the city, linking them to membership in prominent clubs and "our finer Park and Fifth Avenue apartment houses," where one could most readily locate "people of acknowledged wealth" who most appreciate fine books. Such reassurances helped to allay fears that advertisements might demean an imprint's exclusive reputation by seeming to appeal indiscriminately to general audiences. When Adler agreed to place an advertisement for the Pynson Printers in the *Fleuron,* a small English periodical devoted to fine printing, he expressed a few qualms about the quality of the company such an ad would keep. He urged the *Fleuron*'s advertising

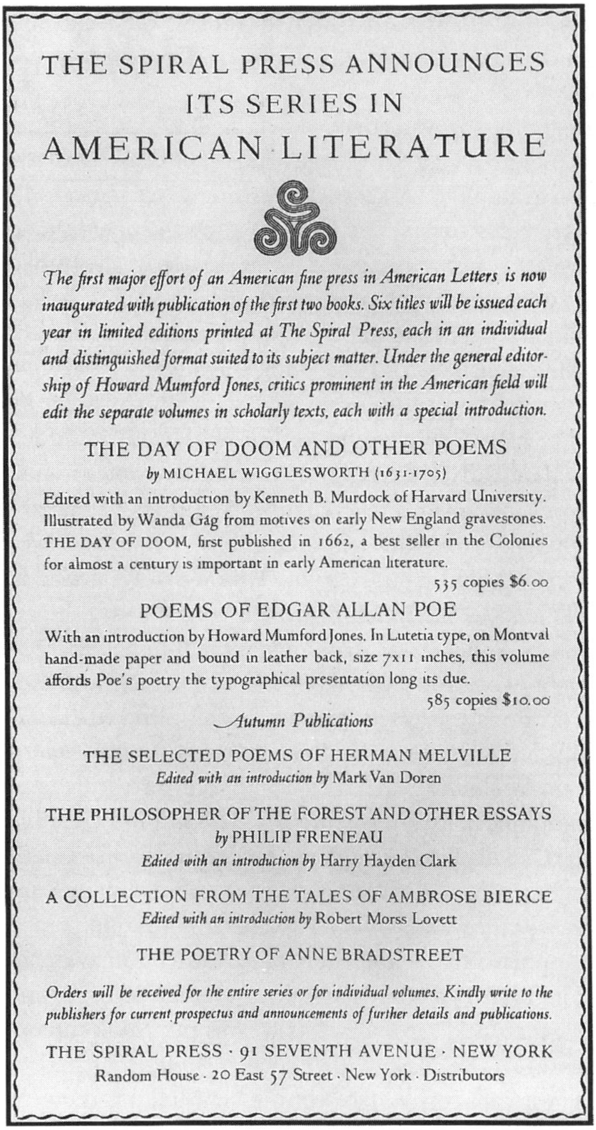

THE SPIRAL PRESS ANNOUNCES
ITS SERIES IN
AMERICAN·LITERATURE

The first major effort of an American fine press in American Letters is now inaugurated with publication of the first two books. Six titles will be issued each year in limited editions printed at The Spiral Press, each in an individual and distinguished format suited to its subject matter. Under the general editorship of Howard Mumford Jones, critics prominent in the American field will edit the separate volumes in scholarly texts, each with a special introduction.

THE DAY OF DOOM AND OTHER POEMS
by MICHAEL WIGGLESWORTH (1631-1705)

Edited with an introduction by Kenneth B. Murdock of Harvard University. Illustrated by Wanda Gág from motives on early New England gravestones. THE DAY OF DOOM, first published in 1662, a best seller in the Colonies for almost a century is important in early American literature.

535 copies $6.00

POEMS OF EDGAR ALLAN POE

With an introduction by Howard Mumford Jones. In Lutetia type, on Montval hand-made paper and bound in leather back, size 7x11 inches, this volume affords Poe's poetry the typographical presentation long its due.

585 copies $10.00

Autumn Publications

THE SELECTED POEMS OF HERMAN MELVILLE
Edited with an introduction by Mark Van Doren

THE PHILOSOPHER OF THE FOREST AND OTHER ESSAYS
by PHILIP FRENEAU
Edited with an introduction by Harry Hayden Clark

A COLLECTION FROM THE TALES OF AMBROSE BIERCE
Edited with an introduction by Robert Morss Lovett

THE POETRY OF ANNE BRADSTREET

Orders will be received for the entire series or for individual volumes. Kindly write to the publishers for current prospectus and announcements of further details and publications.

THE SPIRAL PRESS · 91 SEVENTH AVENUE · NEW YORK
Random House · 20 East 57 Street · New York · Distributors

Figure 26. Advertisement for the Spiral Press, 1929, designed by Joseph Blumenthal. Photo courtesy of Special Collections Division, University of Washington Libraries.

representative to "not get too many printers. For the value of the advertising will be very much dependent upon the quality of your clientele and it is most important that it be kept up to a high plane."[48]

Because they were not intended to appeal to general audiences, fine editions were typically not reviewed in mainstream media. Except for notices and reviews in Rollins's and George M. Troxell's "Compleat Collector" column in the *Saturday Review* and a few other forums that specialized in fine editions, reviews were a backup promotional device, pursued after other marketing tactics had failed to sell out the edition. As Cerf explained to Elbridge Adams, who was uncertain about how many review copies of Fountain Press titles to set aside: "On our own Random House books, we send out sometimes as few as six copies and in other cases as many as 30 review copies, depending largely on how general the appeal of the book is, and to an even greater extent on how many copies there remain unsold." He suggested that about twenty-five copies would be ample.[49]

If the text bore special literary interest, such as new work by a contemporary author, however, fine editions were sometimes reviewed in media targeted at a general audience. But this could be risky: reviews by critics not versed in fine printing often revealed the inadvertent, even ironic, hazards that attended the presentation of new literature in bibliophilic form. When a text was packaged in noticeably luxurious or special form, there was some danger that a critic's attention — and hence readers' — would be distracted by that form. Three reviews of *The Music from Behind the Moon,* a fine edition of poems by James Branch Cabell and wood engravings by Leonard Musser published by John Day in 1926, illustrate the tensions. While a *New Republic* reviewer praised the book as "an artistic achievement for publisher as well as author," another wrote in the New York *World Book World,* "That it will add a cubit to Cabell's stature we doubt. There is not a new note in it. The book is presented as a collector's item rather than as a contribution to contemporary literature." A third reviewer contended that "with all due respect to Mr. Cabell, the outstanding things about this volume are the eight wood engravings and the excellence of the bookmaking."[50] Because such reviews revealed that fine publishing's typical subordination of content to form was as likely to diminish regard for the text as to enhance it among mainstream critics and readers, fine publishers approached most book review media cautiously.

Fine publishers' marketing strategies most often fell under the broad guise of "educational" and even missionary-like endeavors to cultivate among select audiences an appreciation for fine books in general, as well as for particular editions. This meant not only spreading the word about fine printing within appropriate communities but also solidifying fine printers', publishers', and dealers' perceived expertise and authority in the subject. As Zeitlin observed, "we can only sell our customers what they are ready to buy. They can not appreciate nor want what they have not been prepared to appreciate and want and I have therefore sent them books about books and spent hours talking printing and thumbing pages and chanting over and over to them the words of Cobden-Sanderson and telling them of the lasting delight there is in beautiful type and good paper and in rich and durable bindings." Fine printers and publishers sometimes sponsored exhibits that stimulated interest in their work, as when the Lakeside Press mounted a major exhibit of important illustrated books in conjunction with the publication of its "Four American Books." Adler used the Pynson Printers gallery space to showcase fine printing and related graphic arts. The social teas hosted by Adler and Richard Ellis at the Georgian Press, and the graciousness with which fine printers like Nash, Rudge, and Updike welcomed visitors to their luxurious libraries, similarly mingled business with pleasure, commerce with enlightenment. Adler also occasionally conducted evening courses in book collecting, offering tips on how to discern the ways in which fine printing exceeded the quality of ordinary printing. As he reminded Blanche Knopf, this activity was not altruistic: "The real purpose of this, you will appreciate, is to stimulate the book publishing business," he explained candidly.[51]

A related productive strategy was the semipublic lecture. It underscored the cultural importance of fine printing and offered an opportunity to convert new enthusiasts and customers. Zeitlin happily exploited such occasions: "Whenever I am invited to speak, my topic is always something like 'The Book as a Work of Art.' In the past year I have spoken about ten times before university groups, art clubs, women's clubs and informal home gatherings. The phrases of William Morris and the golden words of Cobden-Sanderson have been the material and inspiration for these talks. Every time I speak I take with me some fine example of the printed book and try to make my audience see that a beautiful book is a work of art with a tradition and a history behind it." Zeitlin encouraged the listener to view him not as a bookseller but as a disinterested enthusiast: "He is made to feel that this is my hobby and he is sharing it with me."[52]

One of the most valuable sources of sales-generating publicity was the American Institute of Graphic Arts (AIGA) annual selection of the "Fifty Books" judged to be superior examples of bookmaking in the previous year. After struggling to sell out their edition of *Yokohama Garland,* David Jester and Harold Mason of the Centaur Press urged its printer, Elmer Adler, to submit the book in the AIGA "struggle for world supremacy." Adler promptly complied, assuring the anxious publishers that the hoped-for selection "will stimulate the sale of the book and perhaps speedily use up the remainder." His confidence was well grounded. As Zeitlin described his use of the AIGA competition, "As soon as the ["Fifty Books"] list is published in the *Publishers' Weekly* we rush a copy of it through on the multigraph and send it with letters and return order blanks to our complete lists [of customers]. It is news to them and they read it through and in many instances return the blanks filled in with from one to five items varying in price from $3.00 to $30.00. They are grateful for the information and they are again reminded of where they might drop in to browse."[53] The annual traveling exhibit of the Fifty Books further enhanced exposure and sales.

In the marketing of fine books under the pretext of informational service, colophons played a prominent (if not essential) role. In the editions of the typographic revival at the turn of the century, colophons had opened eyes to the significance of type and design in the overall character and quality of books, and postwar fine printers and publishers hoped to extend that awakening consciousness by sustaining this revival of an old custom. Alfred Knopf included a colophon in all books he published, not just his fine editions, a practice that the imprint continues to this day. Although Knopf's colophons usually named only the designer and printer and briefly described the text type and its origins, other fine publishers' colophons included a variety of additional information detailing the book's design and production. Such information identified the features that producers and, presumably, consumers found most valuable in a fine book.

Ostensibly educational, colophons struck many as contrived. Dwiggins felt that Knopf's colophons were merely "shop talk" added to "give the books tone." He contended, "I think it doesn't matter a damn one way or the other. All that shop detail is zero. [Readers] don't care to know and they don't *need* to know." Carl Rollins agreed. He disliked the increasingly lengthy and sometimes fulsome content of colophons, considering them "too colophony," and thinly disguised appeals to "the buyer's vanity." Too many colophons, he complained, are little more than "free advertising for the paper merchant, the edition binder, the man who cast the rollers, and the provenance of the pressman's pants."[54]

These grumblings point to the explicit use of colophons in marketing. Each bit of information was intended to heighten buyers' admiration and desire for the book. A colophon, then, reveals a great deal about not only a book's making but how value was ascribed to it. Most simply, colophons described or identified the materials and methods used in the book's making, such as imported papers and hand labor. They also highlighted other features that appealed to customers: names of the designer, printer, and/or illustrator if not otherwise indicated, size of the edition (including the number of the particular copy at hand), and value-enhancing signatures of author, illustrator, or even designer.

These latter categories of colophon content most overtly addressed marketing purposes. The tendency to view a fine book as the artistic creation of a particular designer, printer, or illustrator laid easy groundwork for marketing. As artistic presence grew increasingly prominent, attention focused on brand name book artists. When Random House issued a trade edition of the Lakeside Press *Moby Dick* with Rockwell Kent's famous drawings, for example, it was so eager to trade on Kent's fame that early advertisements for the edition neglected to include Melville's name. Similar enthusiasm catapulted Alexander King to prominence in promotions for editions he illustrated. When Boni and Liveright published a fine edition of Eugene O'Neill's *Emperor Jones* in 1928, the jacket copy crowed less about O'Neill's play than about King's illustration; O'Neill was mentioned primarily for his endorsement of King's artistic interpretations. Ads for George Macy's Brown House edition of Flaubert's *Salammbô* two years later similarly focused on King as illustrator (see figure 27). Hailing King as the most "astounding talent" to emerge "in this era of the renaissance of fine printing in America," the ad featured a photograph of the artist and a small illustration from the book — a female nude in the style of Beardsley and other fin-de-siècle artists. Flaubert's name appears only once, in the second paragraph of the ad's text.

Printers and designers gradually acquired star status as well. By 1924 William Kittredge noted that "the imprints of certain printers in a book in themselves inc ease the value of the book. I would venture to say that there are hundreds of collectors of the work of D. B. Updike and Bruce Rogers who care enough about the work of these masters to buy their books for their beauty alone." Shrewdly encouraging this inclination, fine printers often incorporated their logo in a book, usually on the title page or colophon page, and often gave it special emphasis with a contrasting ink color.[55] At the very least, the printer (and the designer if it were not otherwise obvious) was named in the colophon. After the edition size, this is the most commonly provided information in the fine books' colophons.

By far the most commodified fine printer was Bruce Rogers. No other printer developed a comparable celebrity status. Although his books varied widely in style, nearly every one featured Rogers's initials and his personal mark (a thistle), commanding unparalleled market value. Sometimes the "BR" was breathtakingly bold, as in the colophon to the 1926 edition of *Peronnik the Fool,* where the initials, printed in red, stand some two inches high and dwarf all other text (figure 28).[56] Usually the initials and thistle were more

ALEXANDER KING

ILLUSTRATES

SALAMMBÔ

AND TWO OTHER
LITERARY MASTERPIECES

in limited editions

for subscribers

Alexander King, born in Vienna in 1897, came to America before the war, sold some pictures to Otto Kahn in 1926, went to Africa on the proceeds, came back to America and drew corset advertisements for a living, attracted the attention of Eugene O'Neill with his African pictures, illustrated *Anna Christie* and other O'Neill plays, has now had several exhibitions at the Dudensing Galleries, has become one of the most-demanded illustrators of our day.

IN THIS era of the renaissance of fine printing in America, no more astounding talent has emerged than that of Alexander King. With most of his career yet before him, he nevertheless stands today already accepted by an enthusiastic coterie of collectors, perhaps as the most interesting illustrator of our time.

SALAMMBÔ, Flaubert's story of Hannibal's half-sister, considered one of the greatest of historical novels, has until now never been issued in a limited, illustrated edition in a satisfactory form. Its passionate exoticism, its grotesque and savage characterizations of the political and martial bigwigs of Carthage, their concubines and wives, find a perfect embodiment in the illustrations of Alexander King. There are eighteen full-page plates and more than one hundred small drawings in color. The printing is done by The Southworth Press, and the book is bound in full natural sheepskin by George McKibbin.

FOLLOWING *Salammbô*, Mr. King will illustrate for The Brown House *Tom Jones*, by Henry Fielding, and *The Brothers Karamazov*, by Dostoievsky. Of each book there will be only 800 copies, printed from type which will then be distributed. They will be sold only to subscribers. We will gladly send a prospectus upon request.

Illustration by Alexander King for Salammbô

To THE BROWN HOUSE, 1 EAST 45TH STREET, NEW YORK

☐ Kindly send me at once, without obligation, an illustrated prospectus of The Alexander King limited editions.

Name..

Address...

City and State...

If you wish us to reserve a subscription in your name, please indicate below, and enclose check for the amounts indicated.

☐ Salammbô ($20); ☐ Tom Jones (2 vols, $25); ☐ The Brothers Karamazov (3 vols, $30). *On subscriptions for all three, there is a discount of 20%.*

Figure 27. Brown House advertisement for *Salammbô*, illustrated by Alexander King, 1930. Photo courtesy of Special Collections Division, University of Washington Libraries.

discreet, incorporated into some larger decorative or whimsical theme. They even appeared on the title page, as in Knopf's 1923 edition of W. H. Hudson's *Ralph Herne* (figure 19). Because his mark was so coveted, Rogers invested particular creative attention in its presentation, delighting collectors with an unfolding variety of thistle designs and versions of *BR*.

In part because his reputation was well established by the 1920s (his career began before the turn of the century at Houghton Mifflin's Riverside Press

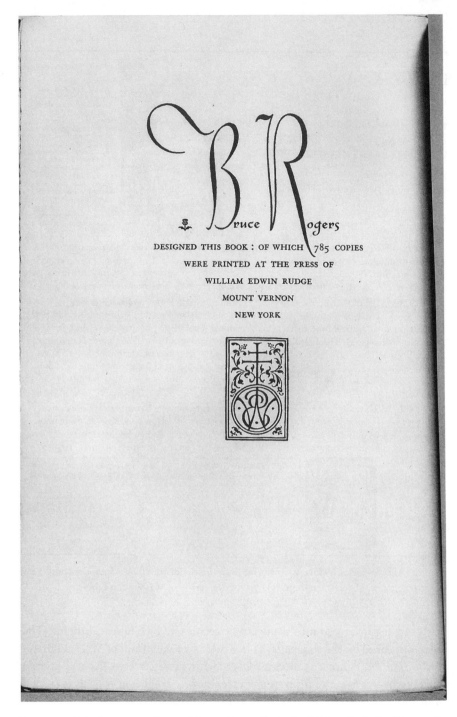

Bruce Rogers

DESIGNED THIS BOOK : OF WHICH 785 COPIES

WERE PRINTED AT THE PRESS OF

WILLIAM EDWIN RUDGE

MOUNT VERNON

NEW YORK

Figure 28. Colophon page, George Moore, *Peronnik the Fool* (New York: Rudge, 1926). Designed by Bruce Rogers; produced by William E. Rudge. Photo courtesy of Special Collections Division, University of Washington Libraries.

in Boston), Rogers came to personify American fine printing itself. Enthusiasts wisely recognized that as Rogers's work was venerated, so all fine printing gained stature. In 1927 Carl Rollins applauded a bibliophile's bequest of one hundred and sixty Rogers-designed books to Harvard as a "gratifying recognition of fine printing as a Fine Art." The gift was doubly significant, he continued, because it honored the memory of the university's former president Charles Eliot Norton, "who stands for culture in the purest and highest meaning."[57]

Rogers's exalted status was easily exploited, however. Rogers himself grew a bit cynical about the special value that immediately attached to just about anything he touched. After he had helped to design the *Monotype Bulletin* for the English Monotype Company, company officials insisted that Rogers's thistle mark appear in the publication, which — according to Frederic Warde — was "not worthy of it." Warde confided to William Kittredge that "Rogers wrote to them saying that if they insisted upon this (his mark), they would have to pay for it at the tune of $1,000 over and above the total cost of the entire production, and that he would at no time in the future do any more work for them along such lines. * * * * * * !"[58]

The bald equation of *BR* with instant prestige or profit offended some even as it impressed others. Mitchell Kennerley begged George Henry Sargent to choose some other designer for his fine edition bibliography of well-known book collector A. Edward Newton's writings: "Don't bring in BR! Let's have at least one book NOT designed by BR." Even Stanley Morison admitted in 1926 that he considered his friend's work "very much overrated." He confessed to Updike, "There is a little too much of the auction room influence at work in B.R.'s recent books to make them enjoyable to me — I mean a tendency to rely rather on the magic of his own initials than on any clear rationale." In 1935 Beatrice Warde reflected on the situation in an introduction to a new bibliography of Rogers's work, written as a letter to him. "There was a time, in the middle twenties, when some of us thought you were in danger of letting all your forces trickle away into mere typographic facetiousness," she mused. "Too many people were willing to be amused by what you alone could do with type ornaments and decorative conceits. But if we worried about you, we misunderstood the one most extraordinary fact about you, that you are not quite human in your ability to keep just beyond the corrupting touch of the world. You were doing those trifles for your own genuine amusement, and only secondarily because there was some clamor for them, particularly in America."[59] She thus added to Rogers's Olympian stature by concluding that his artistic integrity had remained intact, unsullied by the near frenzy for his work among postwar bibliophiles.

Unless Rogers was involved, however, the status of a book's maker was usually less central to a book's perceived value than its edition size. That information, along with an individual copy's number, came increasingly to be placed at the front of the book in a "limit statement," separated from the less influential information remaining in the colophon. This move ensured that no one overlook the book's exclusivity. It bears repeating that edition sizes were determined by ambiguous impulses: on one hand, fine printing was felt to be a craft-based enterprise of little interest to "mass" audiences and hence justifiably limited to small editions; on the other hand, small editions helped portray the book as rare, prestigious, and hence costly — and potentially profitable. In truth, as we have seen, fine publishers tried to calculate the maximum number of copies that could be produced and sold without jeopardizing either the edition's "necessarily" high price or its attractive exclusiveness. They touted a book's limited edition to underscore the elite (in matters of taste as well as wealth) company that one joined by buying a copy, yet they tried to maximize the potential sale that such an appeal would prompt. They discovered that hand numbering each copy gave it further prestige and a visible aura of craft, despite the fact that typically the task was consigned to a secretary or shop assistant.

Another prominent feature signaling extra value, also commonly placed at the beginning of the book, were the signatures that increasingly graced fine editions. A signature suggested an author's and/or illustrator's blessing upon the work, reminded buyers that the work was available only to a fortunate few, and added "autograph" value to the book's price. The latter aspect could be readily exploited. At least one bibliophile complained that everything Irish writer George Moore wrote seemed to be issued in signed limited editions bearing steep price tags: "Poor old Moore . . . seems to think his signature is worth about $2.50," he grumbled. Many writers were indeed eager to capitalize on the correlation between signed editions and higher prices — yielding higher royalty income for themselves.[60] Even editors sometimes tried to get in on the profits. Scholar Emory Holloway offered to sign the Random House edition of Walt Whitman's *Franklin Evans* that he had edited. William Ellery Leonard, translator of the Random House *Beowulf* illustrated by Rockwell Kent in 1932, boldly inquired: "Is there any point in having some of the copies signed by Mr. Kent and me — at a higher price with a small honorarium for author and artist? You see, I'm out to filch what I can from the idle rich." The book was eventually "signed" by Kent — via an inky thumbprint on the colophon page — but Random House declined Leonard's offer, as it had Holloway's.[61]

Ironically, high price also helped to sell fine books. Because they were portrayed as necessarily expensive — given the quality and care of their making —

their prices seemed to corroborate their fineness. This naive logic was tempting to exploit. Oscar Lewis admitted that when he and Bob Grabhorn commenced their Westgate Press in 1929, "people were saying you could sell anything provided only that you fixed the price high enough. We gave that theory a trial and it worked like a charm. It wasn't long before the customers were all but blocking the sidewalk in front of 510 Pine, all anxious to pay $7.50 for one of our handsome brochures."[62]

SALES

What came of these efforts to cultivate desire for fine books? Sales figures in publishing are notoriously elusive, and the archives of fine publishers are rarely more instructive concerning sales data than are those of trade publishers. Although publishers are quick and energetic in trumpeting stories of hugely successful sales — as when Harper's received so many orders for a new fine edition by Edna St. Vincent Millay that they dumped them all in a large hat and held a much-publicized drawing to select the fortunate recipients — publishers usually regard sales information as part of the marketing effort, subject to whatever discretion serves that larger purpose.[63]

In the twenties, not only were publishers loathe to disclose sales figures (even in-house, for fear of dampening the eternal optimism that sustains the industry), but available figures were often inaccurate. "Sales" usually referred to wholesale transactions, not to the eventual (one hoped) purchase by consumers, and even those were not necessarily final: sometimes booksellers were allowed to return unsold stock for refunds if the publisher felt obliged to share the burden of an unsuccessful fine publication. Even when publishers did reveal sales figures, they did not hesitate to distort the numbers to suit their purposes. The spring 1929 Random House catalogue listed two Crosby Gaige titles (Virginia Woolf's *Orlando* and Carl Sandburg's *Good Morning America*) as out of print, even though, as James Wells hotly pointed out as soon as he saw it, at least two hundred copies of each remained. Donald Klopfer coolly replied that the "error" was made deliberately so that book dealers and consumers would think the books were scarce and so "to stimulate interest" in them.[64] Announcements of sales figures, especially news that an edition was sold out, were part of publishers' repertoire of techniques to hasten sales or to burnish their reputation for producing desirable books.

According to in-house stock inventories, sales of the twenty-four fine titles for which information is available varied considerably. Given the disparity that sometimes developed between orders and actual sales, a more accurate sales tally derives from inventory figures a year after publication than from advance orders. As Cheney pointed out, virtually all sales occur within the first year, so

Table 10. Sales Performance Within One Year of Publication

Title	Publisher	Copies for Sale	Copies Sold	Percent Sold
Amy Lowell: A Mosaic	Rudge	450	417	93
Fifty Romance Poems	Crosby Gaige	909	759	83
Beowulf	Random House	1,000	818	83
Salammbô	Brown House	800	464	58
Julia Elizabeth	Crosby Gaige	600	460	77
Arabia Infelix	Fountain	300	150	50
Three Wayfarers	Crosby Gaige	500	380	76
Primitives	Spiral	350	100	29
Ballades from the Hidden Way	Crosby Gaige	831	703	85
Anna Livia Plurabelle	Crosby Gaige	800	791	99
Orlando	Crosby Gaige	800	328	41
Good Morning America	Crosby Gaige	750	365	49
At First Sight	Crosby Gaige	650	571	88
Bonnet and Shawl	Crosby Gaige	550	537	98
The Sisters	Crosby Gaige	935	923	99
Haveth Childers Everywhere	Crosby Gaige	300	75	25
Confessions of Symon	Fountain	500	300	60
Homage to Meleager	Crosby Gaige	450	310	69
The Fairy Goose	Crosby Gaige	1,190	690	58
Letters from Conrad to Curle	Crosby Gaige	859	674	78
Red Barbara	Crosby Gaige	600	433	72
The Birthday Book	Random House	1,850	1,662	90
Narrative of Mary Jemison	Random House	950	945	99
Tom Sawyer	Random House	2,000	1,960	98
Average		789	617	78

this calculation offers a reasonably accurate picture of an edition's full sale. Table 10 reveals the percentage of each edition that was available to sell (that is, minus review and promotional copies and other giveaways) that remained after one year. Sales performances ranged from near complete to as little as 25 percent of available copies. On average, 78 percent of the these editions' copies found buyers. (Notably, many of these titles were published by Crosby Gaige, an imprint troubled by questions of inadequate value, overpricing, authorial misrepresentations, and other headaches. Consequently, its sales figures may be more dismal than those enjoyed by the overall fine book market.)

CONSUMERS

One perennial mystery facing publishing historians is the identity of particular buyers of any given book. Because books are usually sold through retail outlets, individual consumers are difficult to trace. Limited editions and highly personal strategies for marketing and selling fine books, however, enable a more concrete glimpse into the nature and identity of these buyers, thanks to scrupulously maintained mailing lists. A good mailing list included names of all previous customers as well as members of bibliophilic or book-collecting organizations, particularly in the region. The effort to compile a good list was made easier as buyers increasingly competed to secure new work from a prestigious press like the Grabhorns' or Nash's or the Pynson Printers, or from a celebrated designer such as Bruce Rogers. Such prospective customers anxiously requested to receive announcements of forthcoming productions, or even placed a standing order. Because one's mailing list reflected not only careful and astute research but the fruits of one's particular prestige, it was zealously guarded. When R. C. Rimington was set to commence his new Rimington and Hooper imprint of fine editions in late 1927, he approached both Adler and Cerf about renting the Random House list for a direct mailing. Both men promptly rebuffed the request. As Cerf explained, it had been simply "too difficult to get together" and represented a precious resource they were hardly inclined to share with a new competitor. Three years later George Macy did lend his "remarkably valuable" Limited Editions Club membership roster to Cerf, but both men recognized the significance of the gesture—a peace offering between the two giants in the fine book field, who both knew they could survive only as allies in the post-Crash economic markets.[65]

The best sources of customers for fine books were the several bibliophilic clubs that flourished in the 1920s. The most prestigious and exclusive of these was the Grolier Club in New York, but other metropolitan areas supported lively and prosperous clubs as well: the Rowfant Club in Cleveland, the Caxton Club in Chicago, the Roxburghe Club and Book Club of California in San Francisco, the Zamarano Club in Los Angeles, the Carteret Club in Newark, the Quarto Club in New York, and the Club of Odd Volumes in Boston. These were important if not essential constituencies for fine publishers. As William Kittredge explained to Rockwell Kent, members of the Caxton Club specifically were invited to help celebrate the appearance of Kent's heralded illustrated edition of *Moby Dick* because they represented "considerable of the business leadership, wealth, and professional prestige of men in Chicago."[66]

When the Carteret Book Club published a register of its sixty-eight members in 1926, it included a brief profile of each member that provides demographic dimensions to the fine book market of the decade. All members were men (most of the clubs prohibited women from joining): thirty-three were professionals, including twenty-three lawyers; twenty-five worked in some book-related capacity (thirteen authors, eight publishers, four librarians, four professors or teachers, and one printer); and three were merchant businessmen. Other major bibiliophilic clubs have chronicled their histories, usually profiling membership. To commemorate its seventy-fifth anniversary in 1959, for example, the Grolier Club published *Grolier 75*, brief biographies of seventy-five of its most august or celebrated members. Similarly, Chicago's Caxton Club celebrated its centennial in 1995 by publishing a history of the club and profiles of one hundred eminent "Caxtonians." In both clubs, featured members were usually either leaders in the American book and typographic community (well-known designers, publishers, artists, librarians, or authors) or wealthy bankers, lawyers, physicians, industrialists, and others whose fortunes enabled them to develop impressive collections of valuable books.[67]

Skillful promoters like Nash were adept at creating new markets among those who perhaps had no previous interest in or even acquaintance with fine printing, but who enjoyed a high income and could be persuaded that cultural refinement ought to accompany wealth. Just as rare and fine book dealers shrewdly established their shops in metropolitan financial districts, so Nash and Adler, in particular, deliberately circulated in elite society.[68] Neither was shy about asking socially prominent clients for permission to approach their friends, to whom they would then write "at the suggestion of" that client offering advance opportunities to purchase books. Little wonder that Adler and especially Nash were seldom directly involved in the actual production of books issued from their shops; both were tireless salesmen, tirelessly laboring to expand and improve their clientele.

Nash's methods of cultivating new enthusiasts for fine printing and particularly for his own work were unexcelled. They centered on the practice, shared by the Grabhorns and others, of distributing complimentary typographically elaborate broadsides or booklets. Nash's description of the gift typically matched the extravagance of its production. One year he described his "Christmas card" (a large sheet of paper folded in half to make four pages) as "a book, magnificent in its proportions, truly wonderful in its conception and beautiful in typographical design and treatment. It is colorful too — at first glance there is an impression of two symmetrical type pages, surrounded by a wide floral border like a pictire [*sic*] in a frame, with a title in large Caxton initials and the whole a symphony in green, orange, and purple. The border is in the green, the title in the purple and the paragraph markers make spots of orange. The single page is eleven by sixteen and the type and border panel is marked by delicate rules" (figure 29).[69]

Produced "for the Joy of Doing," as Nash invariably emphasized in the colophons of complimentary promotional work, these pieces delighted their recipients, whose warm and admiring letters of thanks often provided quotes that appeared in subsequent Nash announcements. His proselytizing was selective, however. He sent complimentary work only to those he deemed good prospects for future sales. He once replied to a Milwaukee high school principal, who requested a copy of a broadside he especially admired, that no more copies were available, but he sent out at least two in the ensuing months. Astutely, Nash lavished bibliophilic attention on ostensibly ephemeral work, underscoring his promotional strategies. To announce the closing of his shop for a short vacation, for example, Nash distributed a four-color broadside printed on handmade paper. The effect was absolutely successful. As his biographer Robert Harlan wrote, these gifts, "the result of a deep desire to please and to impress, touched his contemporaries deeply. They were proud to know so eminent a man, but they were even more flattered that they should be the recipients of such remarkable works. . . . Many of these persons developed a respect and an appreciation for fine printing that had not existed before and a willingness to pay handsomely for it."[70]

Who, precisely, bought elite, bibliophilic productions? One contemporary observer described the market for fine editions as "people of exceptional intelligence and good taste," although of course this assessment begs the question.[71] Fortunately, fine publishers' careful monitoring and cultivation of markets help to identify consumers. Nash, for example, devoted inordinate care and energy to his mailing lists. One list of two hundred and thirty-five names surviving in his business archive at the University of California is particularly valuable because it is annotated with comments about professional or social credentials. This was not a typical mailing list of prospective patrons, however, because it had been compiled to offer suggestions for William Randolph Hearst's complimentary distribution of a lavish 1930 biography of his mother. The Hearst books were to be given away rather than sold, so the names likely reflect a bias toward enhancing and promoting Nash's and Hearst's status among their peers.

Despite its selective purpose, the list is instructive. The promotional nature of the book's distribution likely explains the inclusion of a pantheon of notable figures in the world of printing and publishing. Bruce Rogers, Elmer Adler, D. B. Updike, Alfred Knopf, Arthur Scribner, and Frederic Melcher (publisher of *Publishers' Weekly*) are only a few of the fifty-five names (23.2 percent of

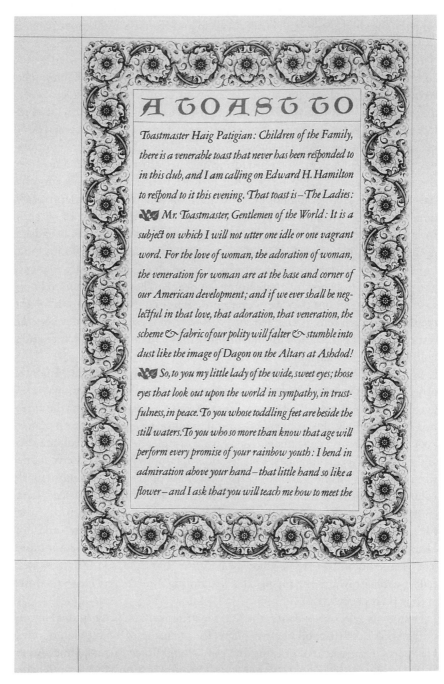

A TOAST TO

Toastmaster Haig Patigian: Children of the Family,
there is a venerable toast that never has been responded to
in this club, and I am calling on Edward H. Hamilton
to respond to it this evening. That toast is—The Ladies:
Mr. Toastmaster, Gentlemen of the World: It is a
subject on which I will not utter one idle or one vagrant
word. For the love of woman, the adoration of woman,
the veneration for woman are at the base and corner of
our American development; and if we ever shall be neg-
lectful in that love, that adoration, that veneration, the
scheme & fabric of our polity will falter & stumble into
dust like the image of Dagon on the Altars at Ashdod!
So, to you my little lady of the wide, sweet eyes; those
eyes that look out upon the world in sympathy, in trust-
fulness, in peace. To you whose toddling feet are beside the
still waters. To you who so more than know that age will
perform every promise of your rainbow youth: I bend in
admiration above your hand—that little hand so like a
flower—and I ask that you will teach me how to meet the

Figure 29. Edward H. Hamilton, *A Toast to the Ladies* (San Francisco: John Henry Nash, 1927). Photo courtesy of Special Collections Division, University of Washington Libraries.

THE LADIES

truth! ✦ *And to you milady of the cradle song: To you whose smile and courage lift the laggard oar when the wind is chill and the tide is running against the bow. To you, closer than any comrade, truer yet than friend. To you who have torn from your heart its holiest offering and placed it, uncomplaining, upon the burning altar of your land. To you who have made the name* Mother *the dearest word upon the tongues of men: I bend in adoration above your brow, and I ask that you will teach me how to meet the world.* ✦ *And to you milady of the silvered hair: To you whose worn, true eyes look out across that sea that seems to have no shore. I know from the halo that a golden hope has woven in your hair; I know from the look that Simple Faith has hallowed in your eyes—that beyond that sea you have seen a shore—and that on that shore there is a cross, a sanctuary, home. And so, milady, I huddle in veneration at your knee, and I ask, in childhood's confidence, that you will teach me how to meet my God. Gentlemen of the World—The Ladies!* ✦ ✦

the whole) that fall into this category (the Grabhorns were not listed). The peculiar purpose of the list may also account for the inclusion of a high number (fifty-eight) of writers, editors, educators, librarians, and others prominent in the academic and literary worlds, including Harriet Monroe (editor of *Poetry* magazine), H. L. Mencken, Christopher Morley, economist Jessica Peixotto, and numerous faculty, regents, and the presidents of Columbia, Stanford, Mills College, the University of Southern California, and the University of California. In addition, Nash suggested eight institutions and private clubs to which a copy of the opulent book might be sent. These included the Huntington Library, the Grolier Club, private preparatory schools, and other prestigious institutions whose members, faculty, or patrons were likely to admire fine printing. (Key personnel at other major institutions, such as the British Museum, Mills College, and the Bancroft Library, were listed individually.)[72]

On his list, Nash identified fifty-three individuals (22.6 percent) as eminent figures in business, law, banking, and industry. Included were J. Pierpont Morgan, William Andrews Clark, Jr., the presidents of several banks, Oscar Sutro of Standard Oil, railway magnate William Sproule, the Zellerbach brothers, California Senator James Phelan, and other notables. Another sixty-one names were described only as "collectors." Perhaps Nash assumed that — unlike those persons prominent in the book-related categories — Hearst would have known them personally. They might therefore be grouped with those representing the world of American wealth and power within which Hearst moved. Overall, 16 percent of those named were women and 90 percent were American, 56 percent of whom resided in California.[73] Despite its peculiar purpose, this list suggests the professional and demographic status of those who recognized and valued fine books, even if it does not necessarily identify those who regularly purchased them.

Fine publishers cultivated an aura of anticommercial idealism even as they exploited that aura to sell books. This contradiction colors virtually all financial and promotional aspects of the enterprise. It is a familiar theme, as fine printing emulated the style of private studios of gentlemen-printers while moving into a marketplace driven by eager, paying consumers. The ways in which fine printers and publishers negotiated between principles and profits illustrate the anxieties felt in the 1920s by bibliophiles and others who worried about the place of art and craft in a national culture driven by industry and big business.

7

Too Many Fine *Books*
Death of a High Tradition

When Bob Grabhorn launched his Westgate Press imprint in 1929 with partner Oscar Lewis, their first book was a fine edition of Lewis Mumford's essay *American Taste*. Did he pause self-consciously while hand-setting the following passage? "I doubt if any period has ever exhibited so much spurious taste as the present one; that is, so much taste derived from hearsay, from imitation, and from the desire to make it appear that mechanical industry has no part of our lives and that we are all blessed with heirlooms testifying to a long and prosperous ancestry in the Old World. Our taste, to put it brutally, is the taste of parvenus."[1] As Mumford so trenchantly recognized, even at its most elite reaches American taste was fraught with illusions — illusions that could be manufactured in material ways, and that many in the 1920s were eager to acquire. Fine publishers, striving to shape and sustain a part of American cultural identity, did so by manufacturing and selling those illusions — despite their occasional discomfort and denials. An uneasy theoretical and economic interdependence gnawed at the heart of the enterprise. It was chief among the forces that ended the fabled boom in fine books, forces in which culminated the energies that had both commercially propelled and ideologically eroded the role of fine books in postwar America.

To be sure, a changing economy was a major factor in the business's downturn in the early 1930s, but the enterprise was equally crippled by mounting tensions between theory and practice. The boom ended not merely because consumers could no longer afford to buy expensive books but because many who embraced the endeavor felt alienated from and betrayed by its success in the marketplace. Their dismay mirrored the concerns that reverberated behind the more general cry of "too many books" in the 1920s. Those proponents felt that the ideals of fine printing had been corrupted by a profusion of inauthentic, exploitive motivations for producing and owning fine books. This led, they believed, to an indiscriminate plenitude in the publishing of fine books and a corresponding laxness in production principles — evident in diminishing quality or mere pretension of quality. Elite fine books, they complained, were becoming neither elite enough nor fine enough.

It is easy to assume simply that the enthusiastic market for fine editions ended in late October 1929, when the stock market crash wiped out fortunes and abruptly ended the frivolous lifestyles of those who eagerly bought such luxurious books. This is how Bennett Cerf later recalled the end of the elite book craze, and historian John Tebbel reiterates Cerf's account when he declares that the "boom in luxury editions ended abruptly with the Crash." Just as the boom arose from a complex mix of postwar cultural anxieties and ambitions that included but was hardly limited to simple extravagance, however, it was brought to an end by more than economic retrenchment. In fact, the strong market in fine editions continued throughout 1930, carried by the momentum gathered in the heady economic climate of 1929. In late November 1929 Cerf wrote to Ed Grabhorn that despite the stock market collapse Random House was "enjoying a most successful year — business is flourishing." Seven months later when Cerf traveled to England to scout for new edition possibilities and to gauge the strength of markets there, he wrote home to Klopfer with giddy enthusiasm that "Random House should go places during the coming year! . . . [I have a] certain feeling that Random House stands absolutely ace-high all over England."[2]

In September 1930, nearly a year after the stock market collapse, Paul Johnston declared brightly that "the future of finely printed books is now as substantial as it has ever been." He argued that the new trade emphasis on cheaper books, culminating in a controversial strategy of increasing print runs to reduce per-copy costs so that prices could fall to one dollar, only enhanced the stature of fine books: "As huge editions for popular distribution increase, the standing of books that appeal only to a few people of good taste will be stronger than it has been, and the desirability of making such books attractive in form and appearance will increase." Johnston believed that cheap, mass-produced books highlighted the distinguishing qualities of fine editions and so were likely to "bring in new admirers." He contended that the audience for "substantial works in fine editions has not only failed to waiver but has actually increased in the past year."[3]

Cerf's and Johnston's optimism was not unfounded; many fine editions continued to exercise a powerful attraction among buyers. Donald Friede recounted the decision in late 1930 not to suspend the planned Covici-Friede fine edition of *The Canterbury Tales,* featuring more than fifty illustrations by Rockwell Kent. Friede and Covici proceeded with the plan to issue the book in two versions, a regular edition of fourteen hundred and fifty copies of the two-volume folio priced at $50, and a deluxe edition of fifty copies bound in full leather with extra illustrations for $250. Gambling that "there must be a few people in the country who were snobs enough to want to be able to boast that in this terrible year they could still spend two hundred and fifty dollars for a book," they even boosted the number of deluxe copies to seventy-five. To their bemused astonishment, they received one hundred and twenty-six orders for the deluxe edition, "and we actually had to cut the bookstore orders in order to allocate our seventy-five copies. And this with the Depression in full flower!"[4]

By 1931 and 1932, however, instances of frenzied competition for expensive fine editions were the exception rather than the rule. In May 1931 Cerf admitted that the "business of limited editions is very bad," and that Random House was having "great difficulty collecting on accounts with retail book-dealers." In November 1932 he declared bluntly that "obviously the expensive press book is completely dead." Friede considered more typical than the *Canterbury Tales* experience the fate that greeted Covici-Friede's $25 edition of *The Books of Cats,* a suite of poems and signed lithographs of cats by French artist Foujita published in 1931: "it was almost as unsaleable as a street corner apple at a dime. But they did make fine presents, and for years our friends, whether they loved or hated cats, would be solemnly presented with gifts of beautifully framed Foujitas." The boom markets were definitely over by 1933 as luxury consumption shrank dramatically. According to economist Stanley Lebergott, only about 28 percent of families with annual incomes exceeding $7,500 in 1929 still enjoyed such affluence in 1933.[5] Membership in the Book Club of California dipped from five hundred to three hundred members during these years. Clearly, by the early 1930s there were fewer buyers of fine books, and they were buying fewer and less expensive books.

Fine printing did not disappear completely, of course. It survived in the work of private presses, in books produced for the Limited Editions Club, and in occasional work by a few of the printers and publishers discussed here. The career of Bruce Rogers, for example, was unassailable. Rogers had turned sixty as the decade began. Despite a slowing pace, he continued to design majestic, expensive editions throughout the thirties (much of which he spent in England) and on until his death in 1955. In San Francisco the Grabhorn Press successfully weathered the Depression, a survival largely credited to the brothers' astute decision in the early thirties to publish a series of inexpensive but well-made editions of "Rare Americana" reprints, obscure but important texts in western and Californian history. The press was the unrivaled leader of a much smaller world of American fine printing into the 1960s, when age caught up with the brothers. In 1966 Bob retired and soon formed a partnership with Andrew Hoyem; Ed continued work on a few pet projects until his death in 1968. At Bob's death in 1973, Hoyem inherited the Grabhorn resources and their fabled reputation, and his Arion Press continues to publish expensive, elite editions on an ambitious scale.

On the whole, however, fine printing has never again circulated in the broadly visible circles or with the same compelling and heralded cultural connotations that it evoked in the 1920s. Publishers felt the downturn first and accepted the closure of the once lucrative field most readily. Least invested in the ideology of the craft, they found it relatively easy to locate the market's demise in economic change. Random House shifted to publishing ordinary trade books, for example; the Modern Library reprint series, priced at one dollar, continued to sell "magnificently" throughout the Depression, Cerf recalled, and helped establish the company as one of the country's leading trade publishers.[6]

Writing his memoirs in the late 1940s, Donald Friede not only let go of the dazzling fine book world of the twenties with little regret, but viewed the whole enterprise through a sober, even jaded eye. He regarded the decade as a fatuous time preoccupied with material pleasure, an era of escape and delusion. "We ran from reality," he wrote, from "the realization that our lives were empty and sterile and meaningless. We ran from the even more harrowing truth that we had become disillusioned with our own disillusionment and that we were suddenly faced with the probability that there was no point in doing anything at all." Friede saw desires to publish, sell, and own fine books as a symptom of postwar malaise, not as the remedy that others so fiercely claimed it to be. "The passion for possessions, which was such an important part of the life of the young aesthete of the twenties, long ago became a thing of the past. It began to die with the crash, when we first became aware of the impermanence of everything we had thought of as timelessly safe. It passed out of our lives completely in the hard days of the depression. . . . [I]t is hard to imagine any of us ever building our lives again around the importance of owning a mint copy of Richard Hughes's *Lines Written on First Observing an*

Elephant Devoured by a Roc, a four-page pamphlet printed for the author by the Golden Cockerel Press in an edition of twenty-five copies, numbered and autographed by the author."[7]

By contrast, most designers and printers struggled to reconcile themselves to the demise of their livelihood. Joseph FauntLeRoy, John Henry Nash's indispensable assistant, retired early in 1933, and demand for Nash's services steadily diminished. He continued to print throughout the decade, but he never regained the verve that propelled his career in the twenties.[8] Elmer Adler's Pynson Printers similarly continued operation well into the decade, finally closing its doors in 1938, but the final half dozen years were marked by precarious finances and sporadic, half-hearted attempts to adjust typographic ambitions to new realities. Adler launched *The Colophon,* a finely printed quarterly for book collectors in 1929, and the struggle to keep it afloat preoccupied him over the next several years. By 1930 D. B. Updike, then seventy years old, was ready to pass on leadership of the Merrymount Press to his longtime partner, John Bianchi. For Updike the thirties were marked by a few major exhibits and other occasions honoring his career. He died in 1941.

Others fared no better. When William Rudge died in 1931 at the age of fifty-five, his printing enterprise did not survive. Although his two sons inherited his heavily mortgaged plant, they were deemed too young to manage it. Noted book dealer and bibliophile Mitchell Kennerley was hired to manage the firm, but his ruthless style (he soon fired Rudge's sons) and ineptitude hastened rather than averted demise, and the company was dissolved in bankruptcy in 1936. Richard Ellis's Georgian Press thrived in the early 1930s, producing fine editions for Cheshire House, the imprint of wealthy young entrepreneur Walter Chrysler, Jr., until Chrysler tired of the venture in 1932, having "satisfied his publishing ambitions," and Ellis faced the same shortfall of work that confronted other fine printers. He was forced in 1933 to sell his business to George Macy, retaining only its name. Ellis took the decline badly, feeling it "a personal affront, a kind of betrayal."[9] In 1935 he was hired by the Haddon-Craftsmen, a large and respected commercial printing firm in Camden, New Jersey, where he worked as a designer for the remainder of his career. Carl Rollins continued to serve with distinction as production manager at Yale University Press until his retirement in 1948, but he still felt vaguely trapped by his work's prosaic requirements. In the early 1940s he confessed that he often thought despondently "of the fight against machinery which actuated the [Arts and Crafts movement], and of the apparent complete failure of Morris's struggle." Frederic Warde suffered the most abrupt and calamitous ending. Ever bitter and resentful of what he saw as failure to receive the recognition accorded others, he labored in Bruce Rogers's shadow at Rudge's until he lost his job when Kennerley took over operations. Warde floundered for a bit, then was hired as production manager for the Oxford University Press in New York in 1937. He died suddenly in 1939, two days after his forty-fifth birthday. Some claimed he took his own life, while others believed he had suffered a fatal heart attack on learning he had cancer.[10] His life remained enigmatic and troubled to its end.

Because fine printing and publishing provided so much more than livelihood to those who defined it, when it ended more seemed lost than mere income. They recognized the economic elements of the demise, of course, but most bitterly perceived — and ultimately blamed — a more insidious enemy. As late as 1930, Paul Johnston could still offer a sanguine appraisal of the market because he located its strength in the idealized notion that fine books were produced for and bought by people of "exceptional intelligence" and "good taste" who valued books enough to discern and pay for the highest standards of quality in their making.[11] This characterization, however, had from the start been largely a myth, sustained to reassure producers and patrons alike that their love for fine books was motivated by the right sorts of disinterested reasons. This myth wrapped fine book production and consumption in a quasi-genteel mantle of mingled cultural responsibility and privilege, worn by those able — in terms of both taste and wealth — to nurture the higher aspects of civilized living. The illusion helped to obscure the realities of publishers' practices in making and selling the books and of consumers' appetites in buying them. As success faltered, the myth died.

The disparity between this idealized understanding of the fine book market and the realities described throughout this study created troubling ambiguities that prosperity had only cloaked. In theory, fine editions embodied respect for and stewardship of the finest literary, cultural, and artistic traditions in bookmaking, uncompromised by considerations of economy or popular taste. They were deemed naturally expensive and elite, reflecting levels of care and taste that only the cultured few, society's "saving remnant," could appreciate. Yet, without the independent wealth to underwrite such a venture, fine publishers had to support themselves through sales. This dependence on consumers meant not only some need to accommodate market preferences in content and design but also a crucial, if somewhat contained, loss of control over distribution. There was no effective checkpoint at which potential buyers' tastes and motives could be authenticated and approved before a purchase. Thus evolved the myth described above, which begged the question by idealistically defining any buyer of fine books as a person with the requisite intelligence, taste, and disinterested values to appreciate fine books for their own sake.

Yet consumption had always been a problem. Pure, uncompromised fine bookmaking could only truly occur outside of the marketplace, when one could completely control distribution. As always, Porter Garnett exemplified this aversion to marketplace access. Nowhere is his contempt better expressed than in the printer's note that concluded his fine edition of *That Endeth Never.* He stipulated that three vellum and forty-nine paper copies of the book had been produced, and he specifically designated the recipients by their initials. This coy if cryptic gesture unequivocally established the elite community of individuals (and a few institutions) who were to receive a copy. Furthermore, Garnett's colophon prohibited recipients from ever selling or trading their copies, on pain of a protracted "malediction" composed largely of punishments suggesting the commercial enthusiasm for fine books that Garnett so loathed: "O good and beautiful Proserpina, . . . wrest away from the mercenary wretch who buys or sells or barters this book his health, body, complexion, strength, and faculties. . . . Suffer him to collect, at great cost, the worthless 'firsts' of ephemeral NOBODIES. . . . Suffer his 'rare items' to become drugs on the market. . . . Suffer his 'unique copies' to be stolen, his private press books, his 'limited editions' (ridiculous though such things be), and books, with highfalutin colophons and 'printer's notes' (such as this) to be destroyed by fire."[12]

Desire to maintain absolute control over distribution was most evident in the flourishing postwar trade in bibliophilic production "for hire." Sometimes breathtakingly extravagant, this so-called vanity fine printing was paradoxically both more idealistically pure and more commercially corrupt than work published in the conventional sense. Such work catered unabashedly to those wealthy patrons who alone could afford absolute fidelity to the highest standards of fine bookmaking, standards untempered by considerations of convenience, costs, efficiency, or audience. This extreme end of bibliophilia illuminates what might be ideal fine bookmaking, but it also illustrates the most overt and self-conscious use of fine books in pursuit of elite distinction.

By far the most prominent vanity printer was John Henry Nash. By the 1920s his career had reached its zenith; his clientele were the very wealthy and those who sought to associate with them. Although he did publish a few books himself as his own wealth grew, Nash produced books primarily for those who neither needed nor wished to offer their books for sale to the public. Regular clients included such legendary millionaires as William Andrews Clark, Jr., and William Randolph Hearst, who commissioned Nash to produce opulent private editions of favorite texts, family biographies, holiday gift publications, and so on.

For Clark, Nash printed many commissioned books, including several volumes cataloguing Clark's personal library of rare and valuable books. He also produced elaborate reprint editions of some of Clark's favorite selections from that library, which Clark then distributed to his friends as gifts. In 1929, for example, Clark commissioned Nash to print two hundred and fifty copies of Dryden's *All for Love* and paid him $37,500, or $150 per book, for the job. This dizzying sum both scandalized and enthralled the San Francisco fine printing community. Nash's vanity printing for Hearst was equally extravagant. In 1927 Hearst paid Nash $40,000 to produce a short biography of his mother. The book appeared two years later in stunning grandeur: each of the one thousand copies was printed on custom handmade paper bearing watermarks that read *Hearst* and *Nash,* bound in unbleached vellum hand-stamped and lettered in gold, and housed in a special green fleece bag to protect the creation. The announcement of the book, issued from Nash's shop, boasted that Nash's work "has every appearance of typographic immortality," and that it was indeed precisely what Hearst had set out to buy, the "best that money could produce."[13]

While Nash worked hard and skillfully to capture this market, others also capitalized on the popularity of opulent printing for wealthy private patrons. Certainly cynicism underlay much of the work; Ed Grabhorn once referred to himself as a "mortician among printers" for his lucrative business in printing memorial tributes for corporate executives mourning a departed comrade. Usually produced in a very small edition, sometimes printed on vellum, to be presented to the grieving widow (so she "wouldn't dump her stock," Bob Grabhorn surmised), the books were an extremely profitable genre. The brothers later claimed, perhaps not entirely facetiously, that they charged two prices for such work, five hundred dollars for a president and three hundred for a vice president.[14] On the East Coast, Elmer Adler pursued work in this arena as well, producing extravagant private publications for such millionaire patrons as Ralph Pulitzer, Frank Altschul, and Pennsylvania's Senator David Reed.

Prices for vanity work were often gauged to a perception of what the client could or would pay, compounded by possible costs in pride and reputation that association with the work might bear. A local bookseller/publisher remarked that Nash "charged so much that the rich people loved it," and Alfred Knopf recalled that one of Nash's best clients, William A. Clark, Jr., had told him in 1930—with little apparent resentment—that Nash had been nicknamed in some circles "John Henry Cash."[15] At first, Nash himself had been astounded at the willingness, even need, of wealthy patrons to pay prices that wildly exceeded standard rates. In a 1925 speech to the San Francisco Advertising Club he described with some pride the occasion at which he presented Clark the bill for one hundred and fifty copies of Poe's *Tamberlane,* his second (1923) Christmas gift book. "I remember that I only charged him $8,000 for the other book [the 1922 Christmas book, Shelley's *Adonais*] and got away with it so easy that I decided to boost up the price a little bit and finally made this bill out for $9,500. As usual, I delivered ten books to him. He took one of the books and looked through it for an hour or more, reading here and there in it. He put the book under his arm and went out into the garden. Finally he said, 'Did you bring the bill on this?' I thought something was wrong. I said, 'I am going to stay with you for a week and want to be happy while I am here so I am not going to give you the bill until I leave.' He looked at it and said 'I am very sorry about this. If you had made the bill $15,000 I would have been more than pleased.' "[16]

At some level, such expenditures functioned for the wealthiest patrons as a particularly satisfying, culturally sanctioned form of conspicuous and distinguishing consumption. In an age when more and more people were able and eager to acquire symbols of status and wealth, the price of true eliteness soared. Throughout the twenties many noted with contempt that several once reliable symbols of class privilege were now accessible to "everyone" — and so tainted by mass consumption. A telling example was travel to Europe, which millions of Americans undertook for the first time in the 1920s. Examples of dismay at this abound, from Anita Loos's satiric portraits in *Gentlemen Prefer Blondes* of Lorelei and Dorothy from Little Rock, agog at "devine" Paris, to Ernest Hemingway's scornful report in 1922 that "the scum of Greenwich Village, New York, has been skimmed off and deposited in large ladlesful on that section of Paris adjacent to the Cafe Rotonde. New scum, of course, has risen to take the place of the old, but the oldest scum, the thickest scum and the scummiest scum has come across the ocean, somehow, and with its afternoon and evening levees has made the Rotonde the leading Latin Quarter show place for tourists in search of atmosphere."[17]

Just as Hemingway and other writers and artists felt a need to distance themselves from the "scum" of prosperous Americans roaming the European landscape, so the most ostentatious reaches of bibliophilia represented territory into which others could not follow. Privately commissioned fine books were often aggressively blatant in their bibliophilic features that gestured difference from the popular and the common — even within fine printing itself. James Hart likened the typography of some of Nash's more sumptuous private work to "a savings bond suited to the taste of Oscar Wilde." Lush ornamentation appealed to the "frontier scions whom he attracted as patrons," Hart explained. "For the books they commissioned he often created monumental title pages bordered by line drawings simulating sculpturesque engravings that, had they been really three dimensional, would have been models for an appropriate niche in which to inter a pope."[18] Nash's ostentation in such

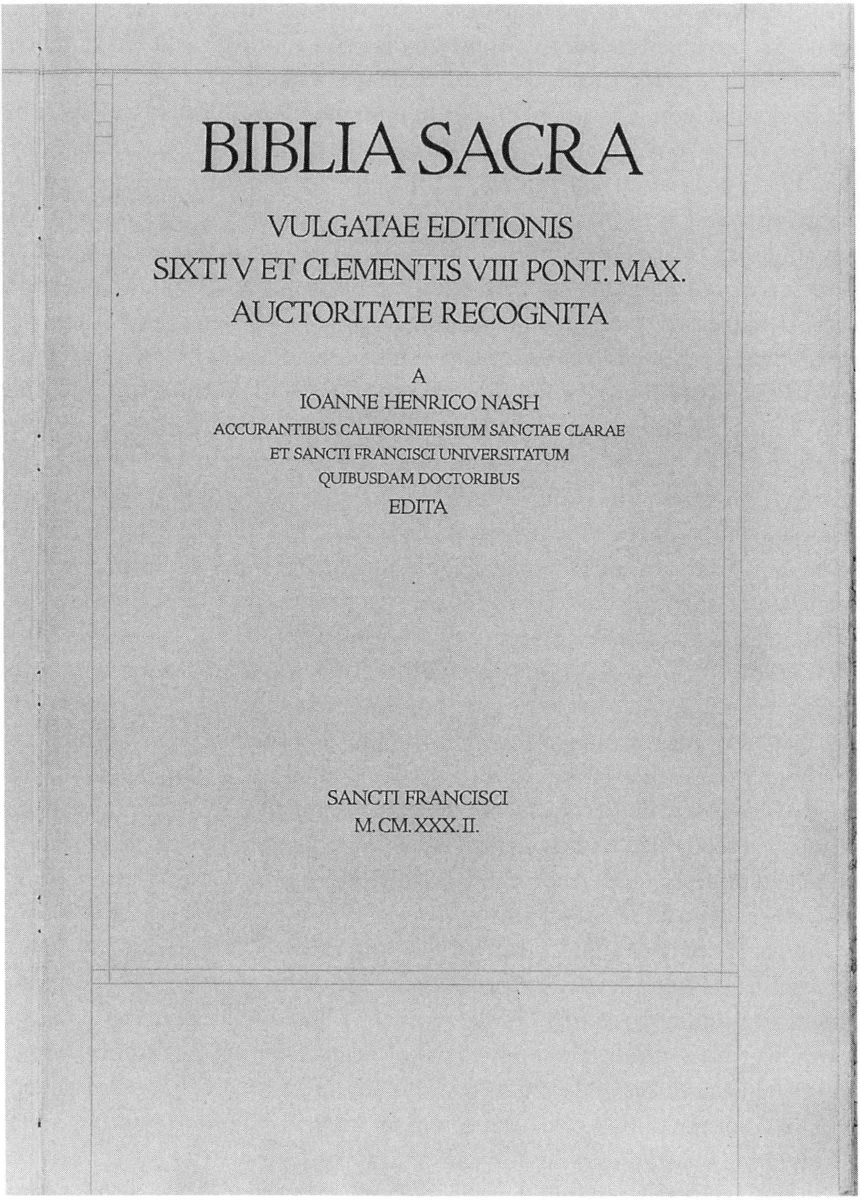

BIBLIA SACRA

VULGATAE EDITIONIS
SIXTI V ET CLEMENTIS VIII PONT. MAX.
AUCTORITATE RECOGNITA

A

IOANNE HENRICO NASH

ACCURANTIBUS CALIFORNIENSIUM SANCTAE CLARAE
ET SANCTI FRANCISCI UNIVERSITATUM
QUIBUSDAM DOCTORIBUS

EDITA

SANCTI FRANCISCI
M. CM. XXX. II.

Figure 30. Prospectus title page for *Biblia Sacra* (San Francisco: John Henry Nash, 1932). Photo courtesy of the Bancroft Library of the University of California.

work, which today mars his reputation, achieved the unbridgeable margin of difference that was worth the high price to his millionaire clients.

Nash astutely perceived, and to some extent shared, this need for eliteness that exalted form and price provided. This awareness is most evident in what was to have been his magnum opus had he been able to secure its financing. His greatest aspiration, as he expressed it with increasing conviction after the success of his Dante edition in 1929, was to produce a fine edition of the Vulgate Bible. Although he was not Catholic and could not read Latin, Nash was inspired by the challenge that "for five hundred years the Vulgate has not been done as a great typographic picture — not since Gutenberg produced his Vulgate, the despair of every emulating printer since the year of our Lord 1456." Therefore, as he explained in the prospectus of the book (figure 30), "it is my hope, conceived in reverence and humility, to give the world by way of our United States a Vulgate worthy to carry on the tradition that typography received from that great old printing shop in Mainz."[19] Nash hoped to adorn the book with the heights of sumptuousness. It was to be eighteen by twelve inches in dimension, printed on special handmade paper watermarked JHN and JOHN HENRY NASH, and available in a choice of bindings, full pigskin leather with silver clasps, or full vellum without clasps but gold-tooled. The price was to be one thousand dollars for the four volumes.

Nash widely promoted his plan through news releases and radio appearances, and he even considered arranging a public ceremony at which the archbishop of San Francisco would bless the type for the book. His ambition was breathtaking, and it might have succeeded five years earlier, before the Crash. But Nash failed to secure financing for the book, despite what seemed the promise of patronage by the wealthy Los Angeles widow Carrie Estelle Doheny. In the end Mrs. Doheny decided not to underwrite the production; Nash's efforts to persuade her instead finally offended her. He had proposed that her name be alternated with his as the paper's watermark, and that each volume begin with a dedication in Latin to one of her deceased family members. "There is perhaps no better means of leaving to posterity an enduring monument which time will not efface than by sponsoring and printing a fine edition of a great book," he assured her, but she found the prospect of such personal immortalization embarrassing rather than enticing.[20] The project revealed the limits of iconic vanity as well as those of bibliophilic splendor.

Vanity and patronized fine printing offer particularly clear glimpses into the world of extravagant cultural self-definition in the postwar era, glimpses that help to illuminate the nature of the kindred but market-mediated activity of fine publishing. That is, vanity fine book production was able to achieve what commercial fine publishing could only suggest by gesture and claim — in production standards, in editorial criteria, and in the nature of the audience to whom it was directed. Fine publishing sought to recreate, at least by inference, the same kind of unsullied and distinguishing work that acommercial vanity fine printing represented.

By the late 1920s, however, exasperation grew as more books called fine limited editions, with inflated price tags to match, bore only the most dubious if any evidence of fine production quality. Carl Rollins, Elmer Adler, Frederic Warde, and most other leading fine printing proponents were outraged at what they perceived as specious attempts to mimic the trappings of fine books. "Not all lambs are in Wall Street," exclaimed Rollins in his *Saturday Review* column, warning readers to beware of "semi-fraudulent offers for bedizened title-pages, meaningless 'limited edition' notices and gaudily decorated 'decorations.'" He happily passed along the satire he had spotted in Boni and Liveright's advertisement for a new book by Anita Loos, in which it was announced that the first edition was "strictly limited to 1,037,296 copies, most of which are for sale. The type has been distributed (after the making of six sets of plates), the paper is pure ragamuffin, coated (only in spots, we regret to say) by Ralph Barton." Rollins chortled, "Now there's candor for you!" Warde similarly claimed to detest the practice of limiting editions, declaring vehemently to William Kittredge that he would buy a copy of the books Kittredge was working on (the Lakeside four illustrated American classics) only if he could get one bearing the number "5,727 or 6,111 [or] any number higher."[21] Warde and Rollins directed their scorn at what they regarded as the inauthentic, transparently commercial practice of limiting and numbering copies simply to exploit snobbish instincts in book buying.

By late December 1929 Rollins summed up the problem: "I am afraid that the term 'limited edition' has suffered the fate of all words and expressions which start with a high and ambitious purpose, and then, in the sweat and hurry of the market, tend to lose their original and rather special meaning, and to take on new implications." In reviewing a batch of new so-called fine limited editions, Rollins conceded that they were "well printed," with "certain agreeable qualities." But they could not compare with truly fine work, he insisted: "The best printing demands more time in planning and execution, the use of better paper, of original engravings on wood or metal, and of much more imagination in design." Eighteen months earlier he had openly ridiculed a specious attempt by an unnamed publisher to characterize as fine an ordinary production of a newly translated tale of Solomon and his lover Sulamith: "The note preceding the title-page gives the whole thing away: 'Printed in 18-point Caslon on Villon antique laid paper. 1500 copies . . . issued for subscribers . . . type distributed after printing . . . illustrations especially designed.'

Bah! The type is *not* Caslon, the paper is ordinary book paper, the 'subscribers' are obviously those who happen to possess the price of copies, linotype slugs are never 'distributed,' and 'especially designed' illustrations is just salesman's bally-hoo."[22]

Ordinary publishers had discovered the lucrative appeal of limited and signed editions to the swelling numbers of status-hungry, affluent consumers in the late twenties, Rollins and others complained. They claimed that the greed of those unscrupulous publishers led them to shamelessly exploit and so threaten to corrupt a mode of publishing that had begun with "a high and ambitious purpose." They sputtered in protest at the increasing incidence of what they considered a travesty, soliciting orders for editions whose size would be limited to the number of advance orders received. Media such as the *Saturday Review* and *Atlantic Monthly* featured ads similar to those placed by William Morrow for its new edition of *Shakespeare's Songs,* hand numbered for subscribers only, the number of copies to be determined by the number of subscriptions placed by 14 November 1929. Alfred Knopf, for example, denounced as "largely hooey" a 1931 Dutton ad urging buyers to "order first editions now" of a new A. A. Milne novel.[23]

A prime target of skepticism was the Limited Editions Club, which debuted in fall 1929 after several months of vigorous efforts to enlist the fifteen hundred members who, upon paying an annual fee of $120, would receive the club's dozen fine editions for the year. Its advertising campaign, the voice of club president and publishing entrepreneur George Macy, reveals much about the avid market appeal of fine books in the late twenties.[24] The ads crystallized the message that fine books meant culture, culture that would impress one's friends and associates and prove to be an enduring investment, in the financial and professional sense of the term no less than the spiritual. "To own rare and beautiful books is the ambition of every cultured person," one ad announced, then proceeded to describe the advantages of the club's plan: relatively low prices ($10 per volume, roughly double the high-end price of most trade books, but below the $15 more commonly asked for comparable editions from, for example, Random House or Covici-Friede) and the regular arrival of preselected titles. Although the club was pitched in a manner similar to that of other book clubs, it encouraged its membership to buy books not in order to read the latest and best books but to acquire the social stature that accompanied ownership of aristocratic editions of classics. One of the club's most successful ads depicted a pair of men dressed in evening wear in an elegant home library (figure 31). "This man has fine books in his home," the caption read: "He is proud to show them to his guests. With the keen delight of the connoisseur in the rare and beautiful, he shares his book prizes with his

This man has fine books in his home....

H E IS proud to show them to his guests. With the keen delight of the connoisseur in the rare and beautiful, he shares his book prizes with his friends, and derives hours of enjoyment from them.

Good books, when they have been designed by master illustrators and typographers and *issued in limited editions,* are permanently valuable. Therefore, a collection of fine books is an investment for profit, as well as for pleasure. The longer you own them the more valuable they become. They are possessions that your children, and their children in turn, will be proud to own.

Figure 31. Advertisement for the Limited Editions Club, 1929. Photo courtesy of Special Collections Division, University of Washington Libraries.

friends, and derives hours of enjoyment from them. Good books, when they have been designed by master illustrators and typographers and *issued in limited editions,* are permanently valuable. Therefore, a collection of fine books is an investment for profit, as well as for pleasure. The longer you own them the more valuable they become. They are possessions that your children, and their children in turn, will be proud to own."[25] Macy wrote to thousands of book collectors seeking their subscriptions, but his acumen was revealed in his decision to reach out to "those men and women who have an appreciation of fine things, but who have never been book collectors before." A *Publishers'* *Weekly* editorialist admired the strategy, likening it to the "exploits of the most astute sales manager for a cosmetics or automobile factory."[26]

These advertisements — which distilled the value of fine books to their iconic nature and, more seriously, translated that essence into a marketplace commodity — offended many of the elite bibliophiles of the day. Bruce Rogers exclaimed to Elmer Adler in 1930 that "of all the worst printing and publishing schemes the 'Limited Editions Club' takes the prize — I never saw such disgusting books." He considered returning his copies of the first few books for a refund, but then threatened instead to "write my *exact* opinion of it in each volume and then put the complete set in the auction room or a bookseller's hand, and maybe come out of the deal with a profit."[27] This wry plan, which Rogers did not carry out, would have registered a "real" bibliophile's disdain for the club's overt commodification of fine bookmaking — even as it exploited Rogers's own brand name status.

Rollins expressed his misgivings about the club's scheme in his *Saturday Review* column, complaining that the books' textual content was patently ignored in the club's heavy emphasis on the books as desirable material objects. He quoted the club's promise that "no pains will be spared to achieve both perfection and beauty," then countered: "except, perhaps, in the matter of selecting the books to be thus glorified, but that is, presumably, unimportant since there is no suggestion anywhere of the subscriber sitting down placidly with his latest ten-dollar, Limited Editions Club product of Perfection and Beauty." Rollins effectively snubbed the club by separating its prospective membership into two camps, only one of which possessed the taste and other tools of discernment that distinguished true bibliophiles:

> For its support, such an organization must depend upon two groups, the assemblers of books who have to fill empty shelves in their book-rooms, and the collectors of either modern fine printing or illustrated books. The first class, although numerically large, need not be considered [they presumably did not read the *Saturday Review*], but the second has reason for bitter complaint. Why is it necessary to give space to volumes containing two of Stevenson's most hackneyed short stories, "Rip Van Winkle," Poe's "Arthur Gordon Pym," and Mr. Whittier's mosaic of rural folkways in Massachusetts during a snow-storm, simply because someone has had the novel idea of reprinting them elaborately, is beyond comprehension. . . . It is only extraordinary that the "Psalm of Life" and the "Rubaiyat" escaped attention for this year. . . . The author has been obliterated to make even more brilliant the apotheosis of the type designer and the illustrator. It is, perhaps, unnecessary to point out that the Limited Editions Club, Incorporated, in spite of its avowed alliance with

Beauty and Perfection, will scarcely disturb any real collector who continues to find his greatest pleasure in looking for what he wants without the kindly assistance of a publishing firm and the parcel post delivery service.[28]

The ease with which many other fine publishers reprinted familiar classics, however, made them as vulnerable as the Limited Editions Club to Rollins's contempt. Furthermore, the fine printers who scorned the club at its inception were either immediately or soon afterward actively involved in its operations. Rollins himself would design and print the edition of Whittier's *Snowbound* mentioned in his critique. Most fine book apologists were thus guilty of some complicity in the club activity they disparaged. Even Porter Garnett produced a book — an edition of *Daphnis and Chloe* — for the club in 1932. In its first year, for example, the club published the following fine editions: *Robinson Crusoe,* designed by the Grabhorns; *The Fables of LaFontaine,* designed by Updike; *The Surprising Adventures of Baron Munchausen,* designed by Kittredge; *Rip Van Winkle,* designed by Goudy; *The Narrative of Arthur Gordon Pym,* designed by Nash; *The Decameron,* designed by Cleland; *Tartarin of Tarascon,* designed by Dwiggins; *Leaves of Grass,* designed by Warde; *A Lodging for the Night,* designed by Hal Marchbanks; *Snowbound,* designed by Rollins; *Undine,* designed by John Fass; and *Gulliver's Travels,* designed at the Plandôme Press.

The spiraling prices charged for fine and less-than-fine editions triggered a different set of protests. Although the Limited Editions Club promoted the relatively reasonable ten-dollar price of its books, made possible by the "club" arrangement by which sale of copies was virtually guaranteed, other publishers were not so temperate in their pricing schemes. Again, commercial considerations — the nature and degree of buyers' desires — superseded the ideal production-based criteria for determining price. Critics did not hesitate to impugn publishers of books that were undoubtedly finely made, but overpriced. Rollins admired the "dignity and affluence" achieved by the sixteen-volume *Papers of Boswell,* designed by Bruce Rogers and published by Rudge, for example, but he protested the astronomical price:

> For the amount of material contained in each of the three volumes already issued (taking them as samples of the whole series) this is an outrageously exorbitant amount. It is as if the persons responsible for such a figure had looked at the current book market and decided that cost of production, even value of product, had nothing whatever to do with the price to be charged. The material in the first three volumes issued could well have been included in one, and not have exceeded the size of a stout folio. The binding of the volumes is merely casing of a transitory character; for $56 one is entitled to at least a full bound book.

I think that, however valuable may be the contents of these volumes, and of that there would seem to be no question, the publication at the fantastic figure of $900 for the sixteen volumes is a disservice to American publishing, and one likely to subject to ridicule and suspicion other and saner attempts at the publishing of *de luxe* volumes.[29]

A price deemed too outrageous, too detached from any plausible foundation in production costs, threatened to undermine a book's claim to fineness, however bibliophilic its design and material form. Throughout their stormy three-year business relationship, Bennett Cerf battled Crosby Gaige and then James Wells over the audacious pricing of Crosby Gaige/Fountain Press books. When Cerf first saw a copy of Gaige's edition of Richard Aldington's *Fifty Romance Poems*, which Random House was contractually obliged to promote and sell, he declared it "nothing short of a disgrace to its publisher. One or two more examples of flagrant over-pricing will give the name of Crosby Gaige a black eye among booksellers." Cerf fumed that the book "looks like a $1.50 text-book" and that, although the book had been advertised at fifteen dollars a copy, "$7.50 is the highest we dare charge for it." Cerf found similar fault with virtually every title Gaige published. Enclosing several letters of complaint from irate booksellers, Cerf pronounced Walter de la Mare's *At First Sight* a "disgraceful hold-up" at its fifteen-dollar price, evidence that Gaige was "not concerned with making the imprint stand for something in the publishing world."[30]

The refrain sounds throughout Cerf's correspondence with James Wells as well. Even though Cerf insisted on viewing proofs and production plans for all Fountain Press books, one after the other outraged Cerf for its minimal fineness at a steep price. He was "completely disappointed" by the edition of Yeats's *Winding Stair* (fifteen dollars), for example, and initially refused to release the edition of Joe March's *Lyrics* at the ten-dollar price Wells had assigned it.[31] He called the Fountain edition of T. S. Eliot's *Ash Wednesday* a "ridiculous looking pamphlet for $10" that would only "enrage the bookseller and collector." By mid-1931, their relationship sputtered to a fractious halt over Random House's reluctance to forward earnings to Fountain because the latter's books had cost Random House such ill-will among dealers and considerable losses in unsold copies. Cerf brushed aside Wells's ethical objections with the rejoinder, "I'd like to understand what code of morality governed your attempt to foist this item [Aldous Huxley's *Appenine*] on the public for $6.00 or anything like it."[32] Cerf was a shrewd businessman as well as a bibliophile; his concerns centered not on the production of finely made books for the marketplace, but on the necessity for fine publishers to deliver the

bibliophilic goods upon which their reputation rested. While Cerf was sometimes (if only privately) demeaned for his skill and energy in translating the
postwar enthusiasm for fine editions into a profitable commercial venture, he
recognized the sound expedience — if not ideological consistency — of making
books that were truly worthy of the fine printing mantle, and price tag.

Cerf's criticism is also noteworthy in that it focused responsibility for the
integrity of the fine book on its producer. While this may seem only reasonable, his voice was drowned out by more histrionic bellowing at the consumer
for lapses in bibliophilic integrity. Barton Currie argued that "jejeune collectors" prompted the late-decade profusion of "overpriced and shoddily pretentious" limited editions. Paul Johnston separated the fine book patron from the
collectors of limited editions by characterizing the latter as "newly intelligent"
buyers who foolishly "believe a book fine because it is expensive." Their ambition and ignorance, Johnston claimed, were what enabled "mountebanks" to
"prostitute good books" with their inauthentic fine editions. There was even
something insidious in buyers' voracious appetites for fine books, Beatrice
Warde implied when she consoled Porter Garnett in his battle to keep the
Laboratory Press free from any taint of commercialism. She noted the "cynical
satisfaction of machine-made wealth to subsidize what opposes it," suggesting
that powerful industrialists had coopted the integrity of his idealistic work at
Carnegie Tech by funding it.[33] These critics portrayed fine printers as victims
of the consumer. They blamed the dissonance between the theory of fine
publishing and its reality on the naive gullibility or bad faith motives of those
who bought the books. Patrons, once heralded as partners, slipped into the
dubious ranks of consumers, and finally to scapegoats.

Just as publishers who failed to exercise a modicum of anticommercial
restraint in their production and pricing practices were shunned by steadfast
advocates of "authentic" fine printing, so too were consumers who failed to
assume their presumed mantle of literary and cultural stewardship. They were
commonly denied identity either as true book lovers or as readers. As Rollins's
fellow columnist George Sargent insisted, those who fueled the craze for deluxe books were only gullible buyers. He and others insisted that "real" fine
book producers and patrons derived their primary pleasure and satisfaction
from what rare book dealer Gabriel Wells described as the ennobling opportunity "to get in touch with the forces of civilization."[34] They reiterated the
notion that the true function of fine books was a lofty and disinterested one: to
embody and preserve the increasingly fragile Western cultural tradition.

The almost immediate success of the Limited Editions Club made more urgent the critics' mission to distinguish true bibliophiles from those whose fine
book buying consisted only of facile and indiscriminate acquisition. Within a
few months of its inception, the club had reached its ceiling of fifteen hundred

subscribers, and throughout the 1930s it proudly maintained a waiting list of prospective members. George Troxell drew these boundaries when he addressed the phenomenon of "collector's madness." Offering a curious catalogue of stereotypes, Troxell readily conceded that "it is of no use to deny the inherent madness of collectors, the curious attitude of mind that induces men of business, physicians, distinguished professors of English literature, maiden ladies, lawyers, [and] Californians, to behave as if the universe, aside from their own respective daily occupations, were centered in the particular obsession of their leisure." Yet he defended these book collectors, however eccentric, as not only benign in their enthusiasms but ultimately laudable. "Their books are not dragged into conversation, . . . nor are they shown off to dinner guests in the fashion of recent advertising illustrations," he noted, scorning the proud collectors depicted in club ads. Troxell asserted instead that true book collectors are "trustees for posterity." Without their zeal, he warned, knowledge of the nation's literary and typographical heritage would be "made blank by all the mists of obscurity and ignorance."[35]

Many complained that club members and other superficially engaged buyers were interested in fine books merely as investments, and so felt none of the responsibility that ought to characterize fine book patronage. "Book collecting turned into good investments for its justification," wrote Troxell in disgust, "is merely another manifestation of the American craze for business for everything. . . . Cannot such persons be disposed of at the nearest stockbroker's, in order that books may be left to the few people who, quite romantically, love them for what they are? If all life is to be transformed into so many 'good investments' with stocks, bonds, and nicely illustrated prospectuses printed on thick paper, so that it may be made acceptable to standardized business men, the genuine collectors might better give up in despair." Disheartened by this intrusion of philistinism — confirmed by a 1930 report in *Publishers' Weekly* that 75 percent of limited edition buyers admitted they were motivated by resale values as much as or more than love of beauty — "genuine" bibliophiles, "who love [books] for what they are," felt their world disrupted by "standardized business men" in pursuit of investment income.[36] To maintain a sense of their own authenticity, "real" bibliophiles and fine book producers discredited and distanced themselves from the interlopers.

The other commonly cited evidence of bad faith motives among consumers was that they failed to read the books they coveted. "There is something fatuous in assembling books of a given press whether the contents interest one or not," sniffed Troxell, "it reminds one of books as furniture." He lamented that "reading used to be taken seriously," but as book collecting became fashionable in the late twenties it had been corrupted by those who "give themselves away by their ignorance of their books' contents." Ambivalence toward content only encouraged the production of insubstantial or overdone texts in expensive editions, because "lovers of fine books," as Troxell sarcastically described them, "feel excused, via price, from a more intimate acquaintance with their books."[37] Poet Walter de la Mare claimed that he found it "something of a mystery who buys limited and expensive editions of books [including his own] — since men of taste are seldom greedy of publicity; but it is even more of a mystery who reads in them." A Chicago businessman argued that such so-called bibliophiles are no true friends of books because they "love the package and not what's in it." He especially blamed "wives" for such superficial values, deeming them interested only in the decorative value of bindings.[38] Fine book producers, too, sometimes looked askance at consumers who valued their work for such patently material purposes. Rockwell Kent sarcastically blamed the nonliterary motives and tastes of "book lovers" for the ironic hierarchy of value that gave premium status to unopened copies — those whose folded outer edges had not yet been cut open. He cynically brushed aside editorial considerations for a fine book he was planning since "book lovers won't read it anyway." Bruce Rogers gently lampooned his admirers — and his own complicity — with a ditty he read after a 1938 dinner in his honor:

> O yes, I made this raft of books,
> I'm sorry now I med 'em,
> But I can tell you what, gadzooks!
> I'll bet you haven't read 'em.[39]

Many book lovers openly separated the reading function of fine books from an aesthetic, iconic one, however. At least two well-respected collectors not only dismissed literary interests as necessary for book collecting but deemed reading something of a hazard. A. N. L. Munby claimed that "reading one's books is hardly necessary" for the dedicated book lover. "I do read a few," he drolly admitted, "but mostly I just look at or take them down and stroke them from time to time. . . . Book collecting is a full-time occupation, and one wouldn't get very far if one took time off for frivolities like reading." Gabriel Wells explained that he collected hundreds of editions of Fitzgerald's translation of the *Rubaiyat*, for example, not to read them but to "delight in the variations" among the versions, much as one would prize different performances of the same piece of music. "An overfondness for reading," he continued, can actually spoil or impede the more immediate tactile, visual, and sensual pleasures of bibliophilia. Not reading one's books "is the oldest thing in the world," insisted cultural critic and avid collector Walter Benjamin, quoting Anatole France's answer to "a philistine who admired his library and then finished with the standard question, 'And you have read all these books, I suppose?' 'Not one-tenth of them. I don't suppose you use your Sèvres china every day?'"[40]

Indeed, the issue of reading fine books was something of a red herring. Producers and consumers alike realized, though seldom acknowledged, that fine books clearly served material and symbolic purposes more than strictly textual ones. In particular, Bruce Rogers was remarkably candid in private about his misgivings concerning the enterprise that so valorized his work. In 1931 he confessed that "the whole question of whether 'fine printing,' as such, has any real justification, is still (to my mind) an open one: — but as it would perhaps seem like burning the scaffolding on which my own work is erected, I am not going to argue it. Time alone will sift out the real from the pretentious — I mean, amongst my own books as well as others. I have made many merely pretentious ones."[41] Justly famous for his gift for puns, visual and literary, Rogers produced a hypothetical title page and colophon in 1929, at the height of frenzied demand for his work, that humorously mocked the conventions of fine publishing. *No Ado About Nothing,* he slyly implied, conveyed his opinion of all the commotion about deluxe books (see figures 32 and 33). Rogers's willingness to acknowledge some responsibility for the excesses that had become commonplace by the late twenties was rare, however. Most major players in the postwar fine book market blamed other publishers and especially consumers — and through them the broader American commercial marketplace — for the steady divergence from the principles and purposes with which the fine printing movement had so idealistically been launched.

"I aim at the idea and the ideal," mourned English revival fine bookmaker T. J. Cobden-Sanderson, "and never get beyond the 'collector.' " Kelmscott biographer William Peterson points out that William Morris might well have shared the lament: "The Kelmscott Press books, intended to symbolize a protest against the ethos of Victorian industrial capitalism, became themselves, in all their opulent splendour, an example of conspicuous consumption." By the mid-1930s virtually everyone who had shared in the preceding era's exultant confidence saw their ideals and their craft as victims of the fickle and unprincipled acquisitive appetites of the postwar mass society they had hoped to redeem. They shared Irving Babbitt's disdain for the "full-blown commercial insolence" they believed predominated in American cultural production and consumption. With Babbitt and other New Humanists of the day, fine printing apologists blamed the demise of the genteel function — in which their own was ideologically anchored — on what cultural historian Stow Persons calls the "hedonistic absorption in the pursuit of happiness" and the "spiritual indolence and philistinism of the mass man."[42]

Porter Garnett conveyed the dark spirit that subdued the fine printing community when, late in 1935, he wrote a long and impassioned letter to one of his devoted disciples. "There has been a marked and steady degringolade —

THIS EDITION

UNDESIGNED BY THE UNDERSIGNED

IS LOOSELY UNLIMITED TO

PRACTICALLY NO COPIES

OF WHICH THIS ISN'T NO.

1

BEFORE (IF EVER) IT IS PRINTED FROM REAL TYPE

THE PRESS WILL BE

destroyed

AND THE SHEETS WILL BE SPREAD UPON

THE BED OF THE RIVER BRONX

—against the Brydale Daye which ys not long,
Sweete Bronx! runne softly, or you'll end my song.

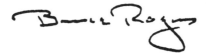

Figure 32. Mock colophon, "No Ado About Nothing" (1929), by Bruce Rogers.

distressingly conspicuous in some cases — that can be laid, I think, to that easy evasion of sedulity which now besets the world, a lack of resistance to the beguilements of the easiest way," he wrote. Even so, Garnett clung to the ideals that he had championed throughout the past fifteen years with the Laboratory Press. His sense of cultural mission was if anything more urgently kindled. As he explained, with the recent closing of the esteemed Ashendene Press, the last survivor of the great English revival private presses that had inspired fine printing in America, "we see a High Tradition folding its hands in preparation for death, thus beautifully exemplifying the *Ars Moriendi*. . . . the High Tradition *must not be allowed to die*. . . . I should like to *extend* the tradition. Let the press be called whatsoever it may be; let me be as inglorious and obscure as

No Ado About Nothing

A 'NO' DRAMA

NOT BY

Wm. Shakesphere, G^{ent.}

AUTHOR OF 'NO, NO, NANNETTE

WITHOUT WOODCUTS
BY GEORGE WOLF PLANK

Mount Vernon

UNPRINTED WITH INVISIBLE INK

neinteen twenty-nein

Figure 33. Mock title page, "No Ado About Nothing"
(1929), by Bruce Rogers.

was Emery Walker in the days of the Kelmscott and the Doves; but, for the love of St. John at the Latin Gate, LET THERE BE A PRESS! a press that will do in the coming years what *devout* printers have done in the past, and what, for all their vauntings, pedestrian printers have never done and never truly wanted to do."[43] Garnett affirmed the semi-spiritual nature of the responsibility that he hoped to shoulder, ministering to the "High Tradition" of fine printing. He vowed to remain faithful to the difficult and perhaps thankless work of a "*devout*" printer, to preserve the ideals that "pedestrian" printers—those who compromised with budgets, schedules, and popular taste—had betrayed. This declaration was among the last expressions of Garnett's lofty idealism; in 1936 he proposed to establish an "ideal press" at the new Colonial Williamsburg restoration project in Virginia. The idea came to naught, however, and Garnett retreated into quiet, sobered retirement until his death in 1951.[44]

The metaphor of death dominated another remarkable expression of the pall that enshrouded fine printers as their professional world collapsed in the early and mid-1930s. In 1932 John Henry Nash issued a finely printed broadside of the poem "A Printer Dreams a Terrible Dance of Death"; although credited to him, it was likely ghost-written by his associate Edward F. O'Day.

> I had a dream—it was a dreadful dream—
> Where Things were as they Are, not as they Seem.
> Methought a Holbein Dance of Death took life
> And all his skeletons in horrid strife
> To mournful strain and most funeral stave
> Did pirouet upon an antique grave.
> Of one nearby who watched in grief profound
> I begged that he this nightmare might expound.
>
> Quote he, "These are those printers of today
> Who have no souls to animate their clay.
> Wandered afar from standards of their craft,
> Their puny mind with money-making daft,
> They think of types as cost-accounting things,
> And spurn the work that no huge profit brings.
> Unto your vision, since you still can dream,
> They're offered as they Are, not as they Seem."
>
> "And whose the grave whereon with horrid din
> They dance this rout of ribaldry and sin?"
> My shadowy neighbor heaved a heavy sigh.
> "Alas," he said, "it is the tomb where I
> Was laid to rest some centuries ago—
> A place of rest no longer but of woe."
> "And you are——?"
>   "Gutenberg," he cried, and fled . . .
> The printers danced, not knowing they were dead.
>
> John Henry Nash, Printer[45]

The poem condemns those contemporary printers "who have no souls" and whose "puny minds" and preoccupations with profit led them to desecrate the noble craft of printing. There is no doubt with whom Nash aligns himself; like Gutenberg he is haunted and finally victimized by modern-day printing. With typical melodramatic flair, Nash epitomizes the almost martyrlike quality with which several leading postwar fine book printers characterized the desecration of their craft at the hands of modern commercialism and mass culture. Nash, Garnett, and others believed that the postwar fine book movement in America was undermined by economic retraction and by a pair of corrupting forces: unscrupulous publishers who exploited the superficial forms of fine book-making in order to extract maximum profits, and avaricious consumers who sought and used fine books for the "wrong" reasons, for their socially and culturally distinguishing powers.

Both notions are accurate in a strict sense, but disingenuous. Although economic depression was undoubtedly an important factor in the declining market for fine books, it was not the sole cause, and the corrupting forces ascribed to others' inauthenticity or cynicism were inherent within the move-ment itself. Those who made and published fine books were motivated by an intricate web of social and cultural convictions and ambitions no less than were those who bought the books. They keenly understood the iconic mean-ings of fine books — the capacity to embody elite traditional cultural values — but felt their ideological mandate crumble when the books came to com-modify those meanings, when the packages came to suffice for the qualities they were meant to honor. At heart, the tensions between ideology and prac-tice were located in the nature of a commercial enterprise in which the product for sale was defined in terms of its aversion to the marketplace. In its produc-tion, design, editorial, and business practices fine publishing enabled and en-couraged even as it was obliged to disdain the cultural and social purposes that fine books openly served. The enterprise thrived by cultivating in practice what in theory it could not condone.

More fundamentally, the ideal book, as it had been so righteously defined, could only be produced, not published. Offering books for sale to the public invariably entailed commercial and market considerations deemed anathema to the terms of the ideal. For those who insisted on maintaining the unsullied principles of "printing at its best," to share or spread those principles by selling them in any public venue meant to "compromise" them. By the early 1930s proponents of fine printing diverged: unwavering purists announced the death of the ideals they had labored for; most others streamlined and scaled back those typographic ideals (albeit not without regret) and offered them in service to the more modest and utilitarian but enduring world of trade publishing. They could no longer produce fine books, but they could work to produce better trade books, everyday books designed with more care and thought for how they would be used and valued. Bill Dwiggins, whose career shifted largely to designing trade books for Alfred Knopf, accepted in the thirties that the material book had shed most of its grand, perhaps inflated cultural meanings. The desires and anxieties it had provoked in the previous era now paled as new and larger, sobering realities prevailed. Dwiggins declared in 1939 that any book he designed would reflect a new ethic borne of new social and cultural conditions: it "will get down to the basics of realism — a handy, efficient, *cheap* tool for temporary use. Read it — throw it away. Who saves a book now? If you save it, where are you going to put it? In the car?"[46]

The world had changed, the way Americans lived had changed, and so must their books. By 1935 a promising young designer, Robert Josephy, declared with some relief that bookmakers "are developing a new idiom to suit new methods of production. We are finally trying to make the physical aspect of our books bear some relation to the culture of our own time. . . . In printing we are coming to realize that electrotyped plates, made from machine-set type and printed on wood-pulp paper on a perfecting cylinder press can produce a page quite as satisfactory, aesthetically, as the product of the hand-press. It is this new sense of values, born of respect for the machine and for what it can do if used with character, that must be the basis of the designer's attitude. If he is working with his fingers crossed, his work will show it."[47] The material book remained meaningful, to be sure, but the ambitions of those who produced it had settled back within the borders of legibility and integrity and general affordability, which meant working to make the best of, not merely to discredit, industrial realities. Shorn of its elite connotations, fine printing was quietly transformed into good printing, coming to rest at the heart of the principles that continue to govern book design today.

Epilogue

In the nearly hundred years since Henry Holt's jeremiad on the imminent death of the serious book, Americans have heard a dozen variations on the theme. Radios and movies, book clubs, mass market paperbacks, television, audio books, and now computers and the Internet have all loomed as executioners of the bulky, slow, and expensive traditional printed book. Never before, however, has the technology of the modern book changed so radically, or have its consequences been so volatile. Proponents find electronic forms of information and entertainment so obviously superior to print forms, they seem baffled that frightened "Luddites" or sentimental "humanists" cling to irrational preferences for print. Those who extol a printless future are so enthusiastic about what is gained with electronic technologies that they fail to recognize, or to accept as valid, objections about what is lost. Jay David Bolter's contention, for example, that "the book in any form is an intellectual tool, not a means of relaxation" not only dismisses as irrelevant the now trite (yet sincere) objections to the uncuddly qualities of electronic reading devices, but also confines the book to a startlingly narrow definition.[1] It is a familiar arrogance: books whose function is not primarily intellectual typically have been disparaged into otherness — as furniture, wallpaper, toys, talismans, and so on. Whatever they might be, critics sniff, they are not books.

Books are more than tools for intellectual inquiry and access to information. Books have always played multiple and complex roles in our lives, roles that transcend the business of delivering a text. Even though it has long been fashionable to devalue the spiritual, emotional, physical, social, and symbolic functions of books, those dimensions remain no less vivid and valid. Books help to shape a sense of personal and social identity, and they offer retreat, solace, and community as well as information and entertainment. Despite Bolter's denial, "curling up with a book" is about much more than gaining access to a convenient and lightweight power source, dealing with screen resolution and glare, and enjoying interactive reader agency. Books do still matter, most modern readers and writers stubbornly insist.

Books matter, that is, not simply texts. In the shift to electronic technology, of course, the physical form of the printed book would disappear: the textures, colors, odors, and heft of paper, ink, thread, glue, and cloth. Those elements are often inscribed in particularly evocative, storied ways: stains of a late-night coffee cup, the dank odor of a grandparent's trunk in the cellar, a child's first labored letters, images burnished by caresses or kisses, a scholar's exultant moments of insight. What would be lost is a fundamental, and fundamentally meaningful, quality of book culture, the inescapably sensual and personal encounters with an object that is at once tangible and symbolic, commercially specific and culturally boundless. Its finitude and particularity make each book a uniquely devoted thing. More than a window to another place, a book becomes that place — like other real places it shelters and sustains the meanings of what we experience there. Michel de Certeau has famously likened readers to poachers, roaming across another's property as they read, taking and using what they will but never owning it.[2] With electronic technology, readers remain forever visitors to another's text, however self-serving those visits might be. With print, however, the book itself — distinct from and in some senses encompassing that other's text — can be emphatically claimed as one's own.

If print impedes the informational function of books (certainly, many kinds of textual purposes are better served through digital technology), it often enhances the other ways in which we value and use books. The sensual experience of interacting with a material book is both powerful and compelling in its own right, and it is emblematic of the larger nexus of meanings and value that radiate from the heart of the book experience. Despite the tendency to value intellectual functions above experiential ones, subordinating form to content, the book has always engaged both realms of human sensibility. Consequently, in a society that clearly welcomes technological change in so many aspects of daily life, printed books remain (and, for some, have become more) vital and desirable today.

In the early decades of the twentieth century, amid similar technological, commercial, and cultural changes, fine books flourished because they expressed this potency of print with particular force. As I have argued throughout this book, fine books were produced and purchased primarily as complex (if sometimes clichéd or incoherent) material symbols of "bookness"; their textual function was secondary. They appealed precisely because that bookness was their most marked feature. It highlighted two assertions, both responses to anxieties about the unstable sense of the nature and future of the book. First, the "content" — the raison d'être — of a fine book lay in its form more than its text. By inverting the conventional priority of text over form, fine printers insisted that meaning emerges through, and is mediated by, material form. In foregrounding books' visual and physical presence, fine printers celebrated the inseparability of content and form, of textual and material meaning.

Second, fine books were patently iconic. For producers and consumers alike, a fine book signified more than a well-made or beautiful copy of a text. In every aspect — their modes of production and criteria for typographic excellence, the nature of their content (both textual and visual), and the means by which they were marketed and sold — fine books also delivered a host of culturally freighted abstract ideals. They were constructed to function as the kind of culturally charged objects that, as Hannah Arendt wrote in 1958, prevent drift and deterioration in one's sense of self and of the world.[3] As such, they distilled the emblematic appeal of books as such; they underscored the fact that we value books for what they say *about* us as well as *to* us.

What did fine books say about and to Americans in the 1920s and '30s? In part, they evoked a nostalgic dream of a golden age. Beatrice Warde pointed to this essential appeal of fine books when she tried to explain the rhapsodic, even fanatical praises that invariably greeted work from Bruce Rogers's desk. Warde explained to her old friend that "it is something very near to homesickness that you arouse in us. In this age of utter disintegration, we are homesick for that lost land from which you seem to come. . . . Do not expect us to be casual about the discovery that you can endow a printed page with all those qualities of our lost paradise: ease, merriment, striding tranquillity. It would indeed be a golden age again in which we could take such things for granted!"[4] With overt historicism in form and often content as well as through suggestions of preindustrial production methods, fine books offered tangible links to an idealized past, gestures of a "lost paradise," a refuge from the modern "age of utter disintegration."

Yet fine books signified much more than nostalgia. At their best, they posed an ideals-driven alternative to the anemic, ambivalent forms of ordinary books. In principles if not in particulars, fine books offered constructive models of the book at its best. They gestured opposition to industrialized mass production of cultural goods, exalted tradition as the soundest foundation for modern taste and values, and eschewed the postwar commercial marketplace. In each of these ways fine books resisted the "good enough" ethic of the cheap, plentiful, ordinary books made to satisfy the supposed tastes and values of the "masses." Fine books signaled a dissenting cultural framework that promoted the timeless, enduring, and "good" over the ephemeral, indifferent, and "ordinary."

Of course, much was lost in the translation of ideal into real, and in the transaction between producer and patron. The ideal book proved to be both elusive and illusive. Fine publishing was plagued with paradox as it reconfigured the old genteel essentials of intangible higher things into tangible, conspicuous new luxuries. The higher value that ostensibly set fine books apart from the commercial marketplace gave them a distinctive and pricey cachet within that market. Even as they repudiated the consumption-fueled, identity-anxious spirit of the 1920s, fine books embodied it. Yet in its fumbling and its flaws as well as in its most masterful achievements, the fine publishing enterprise offers a particularly compelling portrait of the cultural anxieties and ambitions that troubled many postwar Americans.

Today, as new but familiar doubts about the future of the printed book swirl around us, we are again drawn to locate, and measure, the meanings that books hold for us. Those meanings emanate from every aspect of their manifold nature. Perhaps a better understanding of the physical, textual, and commercial demeanor that rendered postwar fine books peculiarly attractive and meaningful may help us trace anew the shifting intersections between material and ideal, between function and value, that mark the complex world of modern cultural production and consumption.

Appendix

List of Sample Editions

The following list identifies the 300 editions analyzed for features and aspects of their content, design, production, financial arrangements, marketing, distribution, and sales. Many titles and some other entries are abbreviated. Asterisks indicate the 198 editions for which one or more copies were examined in detail. In some cases the words "Press" or "Publishing Company" have been omitted from the publishers' names. When a publisher is identified by a person's name, the surname either appears alone (e.g., Knopf) or is given first (e.g., Nash, John Henry). Author entries occasionally indicate the source (e.g., Bible) instead of an individual. Designers discussed in the text are identified by surname only; others are identified by full name at their first appearance. Prices are those charged at publication; when two or more prices are given, the latter refer to deluxe versions of the edition (e.g., with a leather binding, extra or hand-colored illustrations).

Publisher	Short Title	Author	Date	Designer	Retail Price
Adams, Ansel	Taos Pueblo*	Austin, Mary	1930	Grabhorns	$75
Apellicon Press	Tom O'Bedlam & His Song	Machen, Arthur	1930	Ellis	$8
Apellicon Press	All About Mother Goose*	Starrett, Vincent	1930	Updike	$7.50
Boni and Liveright	Emperor Jones*	O'Neill, Eugene	1928	Jacobs	$15
Boni Brothers	Bridge of San Luis Rey*	Wilder, Thornton	1929	Adler	$25
Bowling Green	Making of an Immortal*	Moore, George	1927	Hendrickson	$15
Bowling Green	The World's Lincoln*	Drinkwater, John	1928	Goudy	$10
Bowling Green	The Silver Cat*	Wolfe, Humbert	1928	Rogers	$15
Bowling Green	On Prose & Verse*	Stephens, James	1928	Warde	$10; $35
Bowling Green	Captive & Other Poems*	de la Mare, Walter	1928	Warde	$15
Bowling Green	Lincoln & Hooker Letter*	Barton, William E.	1928		$12
Bowling Green	The Spy*	Cooper, James	1929	Warde	$20
Brick Row Bookshop	Ballad of William Sycamore*	Benét, Stephen Vincent	1923	Rogers	$2.50
Brick Row Bookshop	Modred: A Fragment*	Robinson, Edwin A.	1929	Beilenson, Peter	$12.50
Brown House	Salammbô*	Flaubert, Gustave	1930	Macy	$20
Brown, Hubert R.	Night and Moonlight*	Thoreau, Henry David	1921	Rogers	
Burke, John	Dreams and Derisions*	Pulitzer, Ralph	1927	Adler	$30
Centaur Press	Song of the Broad-Axe*	Whitman, Walt	1924	Warde	$7.50
Centaur Press	Yokohoma Garland*	Coppard, A. E.	1926	Adler	$10
Centaur Press	Song of Solomon*	Bible	1927	Adler	$15
Cheshire House	The Inferno*	Dante	1931	Ellis	$60
Cheshire House	Erewhon	Butler, Samuel	1931	Ellis	$10
Cheshire House	Rime of the Ancient Mariner	Coleridge, Samuel	1931	Ellis	$10
Cheshire House	Legend of Sleepy Hollow	Irving, Washington	1931	Ellis	$10
Cheshire House	Shakespeare's Sonnets*	Shakespeare, William	1931	Ellis	$10

Publisher	Title	Author	Year	Designer	Price
Cheshire House	Scarlet Letter*	Hawthorne, Nathaniel	1931	Ellis	$12
Cheshire House	Fall of the House of Usher*	Poe, Edgar Allan	1931	Ellis	$12
Cheshire House	Through the Looking Glass*	Carroll, Lewis	1931	Ellis	$10
Cheshire House	Georgics of Virgil*	Virgil	1931	Ellis	$10
Cheshire House	Vigil of Venus*	Pervigilium Veneris	1931	Ellis	$7.50
Cheshire House	Christmas Carol*	Dickens, Charles	1932	Ellis	$10
Cheshire House	Maides Tragedy*	Beaumont & Fletcher	1932	Ellis	$10
Cheshire House	Bewick's Fables of Aesop*	Aesop	1932	Ellis	$10
Chocurua Press	The Palette Knife*	Morley, Christopher	1929	Adler	$20
Colophon	Summer Islands*	Douglas, Norman	1931	Adler	$6.50
Columbia UP	Bibliography of Masefield*	Simmon, Charles H.	1930		$7.50
Conde Nast	Robbins' Journal	Robbins, Archibald	1931	Douglas, Lester	$15
Covici-Friede	Letters of Byron*	Lord Byron	1930	Van Krimpen	$7.50
Covici-Friede	Works of Villon	Villon, François	1928	McMurtrie	$20
Covici-Friede	Rabelais	Rabelais, François	1929	Jacobs	$50; $125
Covici-Friede	Gabriel	Pushkin, Alexander	1929		$10
Covici-Friede	Droll Stories, 2d Decade	Balzac, Honoré	1929	Josephy	$12.50
Covici-Friede	On the River Amour	Delteil, Joseph	1929	Josephy	$12.50
Covici-Friede	Monsieur Venus	Rachilde	1929	Josephy	$12.50; $135
Covici-Friede	Canterbury Tales*	Chaucer, Geoffrey	1930	Jacobs	$50; $250
Covici-Friede	Love and the Luxembourg*	Aldington, Richard	1930	Warde	$10
Covici-Friede	Decameron	Boccaccio, Giovanni	1930	Josephy	$17.50
Covici-Friede	Book of Cats	Joseph, Michael	1930	Jacobs	$25
Covici-Friede	Biblio-Typographica*	Johnston, Paul	1930	Johnston	$7.50; $35
Covici-Friede	Satyrs and Women	Louÿs, Pierre	1930	Josephy	$15; $65
Covici-Friede	Circumference*	Taggard, Genevieve, ed.	1930	Jacobs	$6

continued

Publisher	Short Title	Author	Date	Designer	Retail Price
Covici-Friede	Fairy Goose*	O'Flaherty, Liam	1927	Hendrickson	$6
Crosby Gaige	Heart's Journey*	Sassoon, Siegfried	1928	Rogers	$10
Crosby Gaige	Mid-Summer Eve*	A. E. (George Russell)	1928	Rudge	$7.50
Crosby Gaige	Reminiscences of Andreyev*	Gorky, Maxim	1928	Warde	$10
Crosby Gaige	Fifty Romance Lyric Poems*	Aldington, Richard	1928	Rogers	$15
Crosby Gaige	Ballades from the Hidden Way*	Cabell, James Branch	1928	Dwiggins	$20
Crosby Gaige	Red Barbara	O'Flaherty, Liam	1928	Warde	$12.50
Crosby Gaige	Anna Livia Plurabelle*	Joyce, James	1928	Warde	$15
Crosby Gaige	Craft of Verse*	Wolfe, Humbert	1928	Adler	$15
Crosby Gaige	Conrad Letters to Curle*	Conrad, Joseph	1928	Rogers	$22.50
Crosby Gaige	The Sisters*	Conrad, Joseph	1928	Rogers	$20
Crosby Gaige	At First Sight	de la Mare, Walter	1928	Warde	$15
Crosby Gaige	Sonnets	Robinson, Edwin	1928	Dwiggins	$20
Crosby Gaige	Good Morning America*	Sandburg, Carl	1928	Dwiggins	$15
Crosby Gaige	Orlando*	Woolf, Virginia	1928	Warde	$15
Crosby Gaige	Bonnet and Shawl	Guedalla, Philip	1928	Warde	$15
Crosby Gaige	Elizabeth and Essex	Strachey, Lytton	1928	Dwiggins	$20
Crosby Gaige	Thomas Hardy*	Tomlinson, H. M.	1929	Adler	$10
Crosby Gaige	Old Mrs. Chundle*	Hardy, Thomas	1929	Updike	$15
Crosby Gaige	Julia Elizabeth*	Stephens, James	1929	Adler	$10
Crosby Gaige	Letters to Dujardin*	Moore, George	1929	Hendrickson	$15
Day, John	Gospel According to St. Luke*	Bible	1926	Rogers	$7.50
Day, John	Music from Behind the Moon*	Cabell, James Branch	1926	Musser, Fred	$6
Day, John	Peregrine Pickle	Smollett, Tobias	1929		$15
Doran	The Green Hat, Acting Version	Arlen, Michael	1925	Rogers	$25

Publisher	Title	Author	Year	Printer	Price
Doubleday, Doran	The Chace	Somervile, William	1929	Ellis	$20
Doubleday, Doran	Sarah Simon	Allen, Hervey	1929	Ellis	$10
Doubleday, Doran	Letters from a Sportsman	Higginson, A. H.	1929	Updike	$7.50
Doubleday, Doran	Leda*	Huxley, Aldous	1929		$7.50
Doubleday, Doran	Barefoot Saint	Benét, Stephen Vincent	1929	Reichl, Ernst	$7.50
Douglas, Lester	Gospel According to St. Luke	Bible	1930		$7.50
Dunster House	Two Poems*	Freeman, John	1921	Rogers	$3.50; $10
Dunster House	Priapus and the Pool*	Aiken, Conrad	1922	Rogers	$10; $25
Dunster House	Dürer's Roman Letters	Dürer, Albrecht	1924	Rogers	$5
Dunster House	Lucifer*	Santayana, George	1924	La Rose, Pierre	$10; $15
Dunster House	Nobodaddy*	MacLeish, Archibald	1926	Adler	$6; $10
Dunster House	Fragments	Brooke, Rupert	1925	Potter, Dick	$7.50; $75
Dutton	American Water-Colorists	Gallatin, A. E.	1922	Rogers	$6
Dutton	Gaston Lachaise*	Lachaise, Gaston	1924	Updike	$5
Equinox	Now That the Gods Are Dead*	Powys, Llewelyn	1932	Heins, John	$7.50; $20
Foundry Press	Born in a Beer Garden*	Morley, Christopher	1930		$10
Foundry Press	Apologia*	Morley, Christopher	1930		
Fountain Press	Sonnets from Antan	Cabell, James Branch	1929	Grabhorns	$12.50
Fountain Press	The Winding Stair*	Yeats, William Butler	1929	Warde	$15
Fountain Press	The Secret and Other Stories*	Milne, A. A.	1929	Blumenthal	$15
Fountain Press	Arabia Infelix	Huxley, Aldous	1929	Fass	$12.50
Fountain Press	New Forsyte Stories	Galsworthy, John	1929	Hendrickson	$15
Fountain Press	Fifteen Lyrics*	March, Joseph	1929	Wells	$10
Fountain Press	When I Was Very Young	Milne, A. A.	1930	Adler	$10
Fountain Press	Three Wayfarers	Hardy, Thomas	1930	Updike	$20
Fountain Press	Theme & Variations*	Stephens, James	1930	Simon, Oliver	$10

continued

Publisher	Short Title	Author	Date	Designer	Retail Price
Fountain Press	Brief Candles*	Huxley, Aldous	1930	Rollins	$10
Fountain Press	Haveth Childers Everywhere*	Joyce, James	1930		$20; $40
Fountain Press	Aphrodite in Aulis*	Moore, George	1930		$20
Fountain Press	Ash Wednesday*	Eliot, T. S.	1930	Simon, Oliver	$7.50
Fountain Press	Enchantment*	A. E. (George Russell)	1930	Hendrickson	$7.50
Fountain Press	Music at Night*	Huxley, Aldous	1931	Adler	$10
Fountain Press	Terry and Shaw	Terry, Ellen	1931	Updike	$30
Gentry, Helen	Aspen Leaves*	Foote, Elvira	1929	Gentry	$2
Gentry, Helen	Elynour Rymmynge*	Skelton, John	1930	Gentry	$3.25
Gentry, Helen	Tom of Bedlam's Song*		1931	Gentry	$5.75
Georgian Press	BR, Typographic Playboy*	Rollins, Carl	1927	Ellis	$7.50
Georgian Press	Civil Wars	Voltaire	1928	Ellis	$12
Georgian Press	Pastorals	Pope, Alexander	1928	Ellis	$12
Georgian Press	Mystery Revealed	Goldsmith, Oliver	1928	Ellis	$12
Georgian Press	Retaliation	Goldsmith, Oliver	1928	Ellis	$7.50
Goodspeed	Compleat Angler*	Walton, Isaak	1928	Updike	$12.50
Goodspeed	Leaf of 1663 Bible*	Winship, George Parker	1929	Updike	
Grabhorn Press	Book of Job*	Bible	1926	Grabhorns	$25
Grabhorn Press	Book of Ruth*	Bible	1926	Grabhorns	$17.50
Grabhorn Press	Hymns to Aphrodite*	Homer	1927	Grabhorns	$6
Grabhorn Press	Francis Drake*	Robertson, John	1927	Grabhorns	$15
Grabhorn Press	Salome*	Wilde, Oscar	1927	Grabhorns	$20
Grabhorn Press	Golden Touch*	Hawthorne, Nathaniel	1927	Grabhorns	$10
Grabhorn Press	Relation of Cabeça de Vaca*	Nuñez Cabeça de Vaca	1929	Grabhorns	$20
Grabhorn Press	Plantin-Moretus Museum*	De Vinne, Theodore	1929	Grabhorns	$5

Publisher	Title	Author	Year	Printer	Price
Grabhorn Press	Regulations for the Californias	Spain	1929	Grabhorns	$15
Grabhorn Press	Fables of Esope*	Aesop	1930	Grabhorns	$30
Grabhorn Press	Mines of California	Holmes, Roberta	1930	Grabhorns	$10
Harbor Press	Diary of Roger Payne*	Payne, Roger	1928	Fass	$5
Harbor Press	Narcissus*	How, Louis	1928	Fass	$12.50
Harbor Press	A Way Out*	Frost, Robert	1929	Fass	$7.50
Harbor Press	Flood	Moore, George	1930		$15
Harcourt, Brace	Steichen, the Photographer*	Sandburg, Carl	1929	Josephy	$25
Harper	Letters of Falstaff	White, James	1924	Adler	$7.50
Harper, Lathrop C.	Noteworthy Firsts*	Lone, E. Miriam	1930	Anthoensen	$8.50
Hart, Leo	Venus and Adonis*	Shakespeare, William	1931	Ransom, Will	$15; $75
Harvard UP	In the Day's Work*	Updike, D. B.	1924	Updike	$7.50
Harvard UP	Francesca Alexander	Alexander, Constance	1927	Pottinger	$7.50
Harvard UP	Between the Lines	Tomlinson, H. M.	1930		$7.50
Harvard UP	Pineapples of Finest Flavor*	Garrick, David	1930	Updike	$10
Heron Press	Le Voyage	Morand, Paul	1929		$7.50; $12.50
Heron Press	Prologue in Hell*	Kreymborg, Alfred	1930		
Heron Press	Epitaph*	Dreiser, Theodore	1930		$13; $15; $17
Holborn House	Reveries of a Bachelor	Mitchell, Donald G.	1931		$7.50
Holt	West Running Brook*	Frost, Robert	1928	Bianchi	$10
Houghton Mifflin	American Vignettes	Drinkwater, John	1931		$10
Howell, John	Diogenes in London*	Stevenson, R. L.	1920	Grabhorns	$10; $50
Howell, John	Ruth St. Denis*	Shawn, Ted	1920	Nash	$50
Howell, John	Dickens in Camp*	Harte, Bret	1922	Grabhorns	$7.50
Howell, John	Stevenson's Baby Book*	Stevenson, Margaret	1922	Nash	$20
Howell, John	Best Thing in Edinburgh*	Stevenson, R. L.	1923	Grabhorns	$10; $25

continued

Publisher	Short Title	Author	Date	Designer	Retail Price
Howell, John	Leaf from Bible of the Revolution*	Dearden, Robert	1930	Grabhorns	$17.50; $50
Huntington	Grand National, 1839–1930	Munroe, David	1930	Loos	$25
Huntington	English Dictionarie of 1623*	Cockeram, Henry	1930	Loos	$7.50
Huntington	Disappearing Game Fishes*	Hoover, Herbert Clark	1930	Fass	$7
Huntington	As Hounds Ran	Higginson, A. H.	1930	Updike	$25
Jonck and Seeger	Elegy Written in a Churchyard	Gray, Thomas	1928	Jonck, John	
Jonck and Seeger	To the Little Princess*	Young, Ella	1930	Jonck, John	$6
Jonck, Kibbee	Rubaiyat	Omar Khayyam	1926	Jonck, John	$15
Kennerley, Mitchell	Is Shaw a Dramatist?*	Henderson, Archibald	1929	Ellis	$4
Knopf	One of Ours	Cather, Willa	1922		$10; $25
Knopf	April Twilights*	Cather, Willa	1923	Teague, Walter	$7.50
Knopf	Presbyterian Child*	Hergesheimer, Joseph	1923	Rogers	$7.50
Knopf	Ralph Herne*	Hudson, W. H.	1923	Rogers	$7.50
Knopf	Fairfax*	Sternheim, Carl	1923	Goudy	$7.50
Knopf	Kasidah*	Burton, Sir Richard F.	1924	Adler	$5
Knopf	Edmund Burke*	Morley, John	1924	Rogers	$10
Knopf	Ornaments in Jade	Machen, Arthur	1924	Cleland	$10
Knopf	From an Old House*	Hergesheimer, Joseph	1925	Adler	$20
Knopf	Sentimental Journey	Sterne, Laurence	1925	Adler	$5
Knopf	My Mortal Enemy*	Cather, Willa	1926	Dwiggins	
Knopf	Trivial Breath	Wylie, Elinor	1928	Adler	$10
Knopf	The Aloe*	Mansfield, Katherine	1930	Ansbacher, L. J.	$5
Lakeside Press	Two Years Before the Mast	Dana, Richard Henry	1930	Kittredge	$20
Lakeside Press	Walden	Thoreau, Henry David	1930	Ruzicka/Kittredge	$15
Lakeside Press	Poe's Tales	Poe, Edgar Allan	1930	Dwiggins/Kittredge	$15

Publisher	Title	Author	Year	Printer	Price
Lakeside Press	Moby Dick*	Melville, Herman	1930	Kent/Kittredge	$52
Lantern Press	Hawaiian Hilltop*	Taggard, Genevieve	1923	Grabhorns	$1
Lantern Press	A Tree in Bloom*	Flanner, Hildegarde	1924	Grabhorns	$1.50
Lantern Press	The Modern Writer*	Anderson, Sherwood	1925	Grabhorns	$2.50; $7.50
Lantern Press	The Awakening*	Benson, Stella	1925	Grabhorns	$2
Lantern Press	For Whispers and Chants*	Zeitlin, Jake	1927	Grabhorns	$2.50; $8
Lantern Press	Poems from the Ranges*	Wood, Charles Erskine	1929	Grabhorns	$4; $12.50
Lantern Press	Speaking at Seventy*	Bulkley, Mary Ezit	1931	Grabhorns	$1.50
Liveright	Droll Stories	Balzac, Honoré	1928		$25
Liveright	My City*	Dreiser, Theodore	1929	Helmer, Werner	$35
Macmillan	The Brook Kerith	Moore, George	1929		$35
Macmillan	Matthias at the Door*	Robinson, Edwin A.	1931	Updike	$25
Marchbanks Press	Birth of Christ	Bible	1929		$10
McBride	Some of Us*	Cabell, James Branch	1930		$7.50
McBride	Paneros*	Douglas, Norman	1932		$5
Nash, John Henry	Sonnets from the Portuguese*	Browning, Elizabeth B.	1925	Nash	$35
Nash, John Henry	Jenson*	Bullen, Henry Lewis	1926	Nash	$30
Nash, John Henry	Divine Comedy*	Dante	1929	Nash	$200
Nash, John Henry	Cobden-Sanderson*	Pollard, Alfred W.	1929	Nash	$20
Nash, John Henry	The Visitor*	Kennedy, Hugh	1930	Nash	
Nash, John Henry	Trial of the Wine-Brewers*	Addison, Joseph	1930	Nash	$10; $30
Nash, John Henry	Life of St. Francis*	St. Bonaventure	1931	Nash	$20; $50
Newbegin, John J.	Legacy of Hours*	Arnstein, Flora J.	1927	Grabhorns	$3.50; $6
Newbegin, John J.	Journey to Oregon & California*	Damon, Samuel C.	1927	Grabhorns	$15
Northwestern Univ.	Parisian Bibliophile*	Bonnardot, Alfred	1931	Kittredge	$15
Oxford UP	Notes by Lady Louisa Stuart	Stuart, Lady Louisa	1928	Updike	$12

continued

Publisher	Short Title	Author	Date	Designer	Retail Price
Payson	New York	Cooper, James Fenimore	1930	Jacobs	$10
Peter Pauper	In Modern Dress	Morley, Christopher	1929	Beilenson	$3
Peter Pauper	Franklin on Marriage	Franklin, Ben	1929	Beilenson	$3.50
Peter Pauper	Twain's Burlesque Autobiography	Twain, Mark	1930	Beilenson	$3.50
Peter Pauper	Piratical Barbarity	Parker, Lucretia	1930	Beilenson	$4
Pynson Printers	Decorative Work of Cleland*	Cleland, T. M.	1929	Adler	$20
Random House	Candide*	Voltaire	1928	Adler	$20; $75
Random House	Voiage of Maundevile*	Mandeville, Sir John	1928	Grabhorns	$70
Random House	Scarlet Letter*	Hawthorne, Nathaniel	1928	Grabhorns	$15
Random House	Cabellian Harmonics*	McNeill, Warren A.	1928	Ellis	$4
Random House	Franklin Evans*	Whitman, Walter	1929	Updike	$10
Random House	Dr. Jekyll and Mr. Hyde	Stevenson, R. L.	1929	Dwiggins	$10
Random House	Mary Jemison	Jemison, Mary	1929	Adler	$6
Random House	Bookplates of Kent*	Kent, Rockwell	1929	Adler	$10
Random House	Skirmish with Jolly Roger*	Lawrence, D. H.	1929	Adler	$4
Random House	Worst Christmas Story*	Morley, Christopher	1929	Adler	$6
Random House	Leaves of Grass*	Whitman, Walt	1930	Grabhorns	$100
Random House	N by E	Kent, Rockwell	1930	Adler	$20
Random House	Tom Sawyer*	Twain, Mark	1930	Adler	$20
Random House	Poems of Frost	Frost, Robert	1930	Blumenthal	$15
Random House	Three Discourses	Weems, Parson	1930		$8.50
Random House	Shaw and Marx	Shaw, George Bernard	1930	Ellis	$10
Random House	Three Stories*	Irving, Washington	1930	Beilenson	$8.50
Random House	Gershwin Songs	Gershwin, George	1930	Beilenson	$25
Random House	Salut au Monde*	Whitman, Walt	1930	Preissig	$7.50

Publisher	Title	Author	Year	Printer/Designer	Price
Random House	Red Badge of Courage*	Crane, Stephen	1931	Grabhorns	$15
Random House	Birthday Book*	Kent, Rockwell	1931	Adler	$7.50
Random House	The Time Machine*	Wells, H. G.	1931	Dwiggins	$12.50
Random House	Descent to the Dead*	Jeffers, Robinson	1931	Hoffman, A. G.	$7.50
Random House	Idyll in the Desert*	Faulkner, William	1931	Fass	$3.50
Random House	Way to Wealth*	Franklin, Ben	1931	Preissig	$7.50
Random House	Beowulf*		1932	Adler	$25
Rimington & Hooper	Poor Richard's Almanac*	Franklin, Ben	1928	Kittredge	$8
Rimington & Hooper	Common Sense	Paine, Thomas	1928	Kittredge	$10
Rimington & Hooper	Gold Bug*	Poe, Edgar Allan	1928	Kittredge	$10
Rimington & Hooper	Punch and Judy*	Collier, John Payne	1929	Updike	$15
Rimington & Hooper	Zadig*	Voltaire	1929	Ellis	$10
Rimington & Hooper	Voyages of Companions	Irving, Washington	1929		$20
Rimington & Hooper	Travels of Capt. Smith*	Smith, John	1930	Ellis	$25
Rimington & Hooper	Beau Brummel*	Woolf, Virginia	1930	Dwiggins	$10
Riverside	Antigone*	Sophocles	1930	Josephy	$10
Rudge	XXVIII Sonnets*	Putnam, Elizabeth	1925	Rogers	$7.50
Rudge	Roderigo of Bivar*	Moore, T. Sturge	1925	Rogers	$6
Rudge	Conrad: The Man	Adams, Elbridge	1926	Rogers	
Rudge	Persephone*	Drinkwater, John	1926	Rogers	$12; $25
Rudge	Amy Lowell*	Sargent, George Henry	1926	Rogers	$4
Rudge	Glory of New York*	Pennell, Joseph	1926	Rogers	$75
Rudge	Peronnik the Fool*	Moore, George	1926	Rogers	$12.50
Rudge	Monmouth: A Tragedy	Stevenson, R. L.	1928	Rogers	$25
Rudge	Papers of Boswell*	Boswell, James	1928	Rogers	$56
Rudge	Two Singers	Towne, Charles Hanson	1928	Goudy	$6

continued

Publisher	Short Title	Author	Date	Designer	Retail Price
Rudge	American Conquers Death	Waldman, Milton	1928	Dwiggins	$5.50
Rudge	Songs for Annette	Allen, Hervey	1929	Rogers	$7.50
Rudge	Legend of the Hounds*	Boker, George H.	1929	Warde	$5; $25
Rudge	Music & the Cultivated Man	Gilman, Lawrence	1929	Warde	$5
Rudge	Rural Sports*	Gay, John	1930	Warde	$15; $35
Rudge	The Twelve	Blok, Alexander	1931	Warde	$5
Scribner's	Silverado Squatters*	Stevenson, R. L.	1923	Nash	$30
Scribner's	Soames and the Flag*	Galsworthy, John	1930		$15
Slide Mountain	Fortunatus*	Robinson, Edwin A.	1928	Grabhorns	$12.50
Small, Maynard	Journal of Madam Knight	Knight, Sarah Kemble	1920	Rogers	$8
Spannuth, J. E.	Doings of Gotham*	Poe, Edgar Allan	1929		$10; $25
Spiral Press	Primitives	Weber, Max	1926	Blumenthal	$7.50
Spiral Press	Phillida and Coridon*	Breton, Nicholas	1927	Blumenthal	$7.50
Spiral Press	Poems of Poe	Poe, Edgar Allan	1929	Blumenthal	$10
Spiral Press	Day of Doom*	Wigglesworth, Michael	1929	Blumenthal	$6.50
Spiral Press	Nature*	Emerson, Ralph Waldo	1932	Blumenthal	$10
U Chicago Press	Projects in Design	Szukalski, Stanislaus	1929	Blumenthal	$30
Washburn & Thomas	Psalms of David in Metre	Bible	1928	Rogers	$25
Wells, Gabriel	A Noble Fragment*	Newton, A. E.	1921	Rogers	$150
Westgate Press	American Taste*	Mumford, Lewis	1929	Grabhorns	$7.50
Westgate Press	Nearer the Grass Roots	Anderson, Sherwood	1929	Grabhorns	$7.50
Westgate Press	Marriage To-Day*	Ellis, Havelock	1929	Grabhorns	$7.50
Westgate Press	Hearn & His Biographers*	Lewis, Oscar	1930	Grabhorns	$15
Westgate Press	Street Haunting*	Woolf, Virginia	1930	Grabhorns	$7.50
Westgate Press	Norris of "The Wave"	Norris, Frank	1931	Grabhorns	$10

Publisher	Title	Author	Year	Printer	Price
Westgate Press	Last Adventure*	Benard de Russailh	1931	Grabhorns	$9
Westgate Press	Robyn Hode*		1932	Grabhorns	$7.50
Windsor Press	Cupid and Psyche*	Apuleius Madaurensis	1926	Johnsons	$12
Windsor Press	Aucassin and Nicolette		1926	Johnsons	$4.50; $6
Windsor Press	Words on Caxton*	Blades, William	1926	Johnsons	$15
Windsor Press	Letter of Columbus*	Colombo, Christoforo	1926	Johnsons	$8
Windsor Press	Lodging for the Night	Stevenson, R. L.	1926	Johnsons	
Windsor Press	Land of Heart's Desire*	Yeats, William Butler	1926	Johnsons	
Windsor Press	Marpessa*	Phillips, Stephen	1926	Johnsons	$4.50; $6
Windsor Press	Press of the Renaissance*	Johnson, James Sydney	1927	Johnsons	$15
Windsor Press	Legs of Sister Ursula*	Kipling, Rudyard	1927	Johnsons	$15
Windsor Press	Ballads of Villon*	Villon, François	1927	Johnsons	$15
Windsor Press	Nightingale and Rose	Wilde, Oscar	1927	Johnsons	$3
Windsor Press	Triumphs of Petrarch	Petrarch	1928	Johnsons	$25
Windsor Press	Medieval Student Songs		1928	Johnsons	$30
Windsor Press	Angel of Manfredonia*	Douglas, Norman	1929	Johnsons	$25
Windsor Press	The Ackymals*	Williamson, Henry	1929	Johnsons	$7.50
Windsor Press	Pierrot of the Minute	Dowson, Ernest C.	1932	Johnsons	$7.50
Yale UP	Old Houses of Connecticut	Trowbridge, Bertha	1923	Rollins	$25
Young Books	On Modern Gardening	Walpole, Horace	1931	Thompson	$8.50

Source Abbreviations

BCC   Bennett Cerf Papers; Rare Book and Manuscript Library, Columbia University

CPRY   Carl P. Rollins Papers; Arts of the Book Collection, Yale University Library

EAP   Elmer Adler Papers; Princeton University Library

FWG   Frederic Warde Papers; The Grolier Club, New York

FWN   Frederic Warde Papers; Wing Foundation Collection on the History of Printing; The Newberry Library, Chicago

GPC   Grabhorn Press Records; Bancroft Library, University of California, Berkeley

JHNC   John Henry Nash Papers; Bancroft Library, University of California, Berkeley

KN   William E. Kittredge Papers; Wing Foundation Collection on the History of Printing; The Newberry Library, Chicago

LPC   Laboratory Press Papers; Rare Book and Manuscript Library, Columbia University

NYPL   New York Public Library

PPNY   Pynson Printers Records; Manuscripts and Archives Division, New York Public Library, Astor, Lenox and Tilden Foundations

PPP   Pynson Printers Archives; Princeton University Library
PW   *Publishers' Weekly*
RHC   Random House Archives; Rare Book and Manuscript Library, Columbia University
SRL   *Saturday Review of Literature*

Notes

Preface

1. William Mitchell, *City of Bits: Space, Place, and the Infobahn* (Cambridge, Mass.: MIT Press, 1995).

2. Stephen H. Wildstrom, "A New Chapter for E-Books," *Business Week,* 2 November 1998; "Introducing the SoftBook Electronic Book," on corporate website: *www.Soft-Book.com;* "About the Rocket," on corporate website: *www.rocket-ebook.com.* For a discussion of the impact of new electronic technologies on traditional notions of intellectual property, see Charles Mann, "Who Will Own Your Next Good Idea?" *Atlantic Monthly,* September 1998, 57ff. For a description of the electronic paper technology under way at the MIT Media Laboratory, see J. Jacobson et al., "The Last Book," *IBM Systems Journal* 36, no. 3 (1997).

3. Bolter, *Writing Space;* Dugaid, "Material Matters," 75. See also Lanham, *Electronic Word,* and Landow, "Twenty Minutes into the Future" and *Hypertext.* Dugaid's essay offers a helpful discussion of the "demonization" of printed books.

4. Greco, "The Market for Consumer Books in the U.S.: 1985–1995," *Publishing Research Quarterly* (Spring 1997): 5.

5. Typical of this sort of doomsaying is Ken Auletta's "The Impossible Business," *The New Yorker,* 6 October 1997. See, however, Thomas McCormack's brief but brisk rebuttal in his "Cheerful Skeptic" column, "The Crisis — New Yorker Style," *PW,* 13 October 1997, 25.

6. A few highly varied examples of the many recently published tributes to the powers and values of the (printed) book are Sven Birkerts, *The Gutenberg Elegies,* Janice Rad-

way's *A Feeling for Books,* Nicholas Basbanes's *A Gentle Madness,* and Anna Quindlen's *How Reading Changed My Life* (New York: Ballantine, 1998). In addition, the 1990s witnessed the founding of the Society for the History of Authorship, Reading, and Publishing (SHARP), a fast-growing scholarly organization devoted to study of the history of pre-electronic book culture.

Introduction

1. "Dedicating a Printing Press," 33.

2. Garnett, "Making and Judging of Books," 605.

3. Cerf to E. Grabhorn, 26 February 1929, GPC. Cerf and his partners founded Random House to publish a "random" selection of books that would be noteworthy for their "typographical excellence," as Cerf recalled in his memoirs, *At Random,* 65, which is based on 1971 oral history interviews, "The Reminiscences of Bennett Cerf."

4. Wentz, *Grabhorn Press,* 42; Friede, *Mechanical Angel,* 74–75; Macy, "Club Is Organized," 1721. Macy's boast was somewhat hyperbolic, given that he was writing in part to solicit subscribers to his new Limited Editions Club. In fact, approximately two thousand names were listed in a 1928 register of American and Canadian book collectors, although not all were interested in contemporary fine editions, of course, and no doubt many enthusiasts were not recorded in that census. See *Private Book Collectors in the United States with Mention of Their Hobbies.*

5. Garnett, "Ideal Book," in *Books and Printing,* ed. Paul Bennett (1932), 128.

6. This is not an original notion, of course. A growing number of scholars are studying aspects of the physical book to better understand how readers interpret texts or how writers and publishers sometimes use those aspects to steer readers toward a particular understanding of the work. Literary critic Jerome McGann, for example, contends that the interpretive environments created by the typography and physical forms of a printed text, together with its commercial features — prices, advertisements, distribution channels, and so forth — essentially contribute to its meanings, *"whether we are aware of such matters when we make our meanings or whether we are not"* (*Textual Condition,* 12–13, emphasis in the original; see also *Black Riders*). Similarly, French cultural historian Roger Chartier relied upon the material aspects of inexpensive editions known as the Bibliothèque bleue — well-known texts peddled for more than two centuries throughout pre-Revolution France — for important evidence about how and why the popular little books were both produced and read. See "The *Biblioteque bleue* and Popular Reading," in *Cultural Uses of Print.* My focus here, however, remains on the more general meanings and significance of books' "materiality" per se. For extended theoretical explorations of the notion that the forms of cultural artifacts affect their meaning, see McKenzie, *Bibliography and the Sociology of Texts,* and Genette, *Paratexts.*

7. David Hall, for example, contends that fine books have enjoyed a disproportionate share of attention (and acclaim), to the neglect of more ordinary forms of print production. He urges book historians to recognize that in America "the press was in the service of utilitarian needs. Only incidentally were printers and booksellers responsive to any other patronage than that of the marketplace, or of institutions such as schools, churches, and political parties." Because he believes that fine books are produced privately, inde-

pendent of market or institutional patronage, he concludes that "fine books, fine bindings, and first editions do not loom as consequential" (*On Native Ground,* 20).

8. This reflects a sense that artistic integrity and for-profit sales (characterized as private and commercial objectives, respectively) are mutually exclusive. In 1961 John Carter, for example, described a press as private if "the printer is more interested in making a good book than in a fat profit. He prints what he likes, how he likes, not what someone else has paid him to print" (quoted in Cave, *Private Press,* xiii).

9. "Orchids from Pittsburgh," *New York Herald-Tribune,* 10 February 1925.

10. Ransom, *Private Presses.*

Chapter 1. Too Many Books

1. Canby, "Clear the Shelves," 411 (emphasis added).

2. Ibid.

3. Bennett, "What We Read and Why," 120. In addition to the Lynds' *Middletown,* see especially Gray and Munroe, *Reading Interests and Habits.* Middletown was the Lynds' pseudonym for Muncie, Indiana.

4. Gaskell, *Introduction to Bibliography,* 228.

5. Lebergott, *Pursuing Happiness,* 137. The high number of magazine and newspaper subscriptions has suggested to some that adult literacy was approaching universal proportions in the decade, although Carl Kaestle and others have pointed out that in 1930 approximately 12 percent of the adult population had not achieved more than a second-grade education. If those persons could read at all, it was likely only at rudimentary levels. See Kaestle et al., *Literacy in the United States,* 93. Moreover, new national levels of at least basic literacy should not be confused with transformed literary values or habits. As one social historian put it, "although Americans were reading in unprecedented numbers, they seemed to be moving their lips as they did so" (Perrett, *America in the Twenties,* 277).

6. *Recent Social Trends,* 902–904. One 1928 editorialist proclaimed the collective pursuit of the good life one of the nation's greatest intangible assets, an ambition that led naturally to prosperity and, consequently, to civic distinction and pride. See "Prosperity as a Habit," 30.

7. As Bennett Cerf put it in his inimitable way, before the twenties "most publishers were stodgy old poops who had no imagination at all" ("Reminiscences," 181). Although Cerf is central to this study as publisher of Random House's fine editions, he was also involved in the trade book business as publisher of the Modern Library reprint series.

8. Radway's *A Feeling for Books* is a thoughtful exploration of the impact and significance of the Book-of-the-Month Club. Chapter 3 of Rubin's *Making of Middlebrow Culture* also offers a valuable analysis of the club's cultural work.

9. On the emerging social and cultural distinctions between the parlor and the living room, see Halttunen, "From Parlor to Living Room."

10. Lynd and Lynd, *Middletown,* 230, 99–100; Donham, "Your Income and How to Spend It," 107; Johnson, "Alleged Depravity," 212.

11. U.S. Dept. of Commerce, *National Income and Product Account Data;* Claudy, "Books as Luxuries," 3111; Grover, "Why Not Professors of Books?" 2591.

12. *Recent Social Trends,* 905; Cheney, *Economic Survey,* 188–89; Duffus, *Books,* 4, 6.

13. Coolidge, "Books for Better Homes," 2.

14. O'Hagan, "Mary's Got a Book Already," 69; Van De Water, "Books for Babbitt," 68–71. I use the term *business class* to designate, as the Lynds did, those families supported by work in some commercial "business" enterprise—banking, sales, management, advertising, and so on. They are distinct from both the working class, whose livelihood derived from more or less physical labor, and the professional class, whose income was earned in various "service" industries—education, law, health care, and so forth. Although these categories are crude and far from perfect, they distinguish the so-called business class whose incomes were most expanded by the decade's prosperity.

Among those most intrigued by book-buying demographics was Maxwell Aley. His conservative estimate of the total book-reading public was 25 million, more than a quarter of approximately 90 million literate citizens. Figuring that an annual income of three thousand dollars was necessary to be able to buy books, Aley noted that the 1928 census tallied nearly 2.2 million incomes at or above that level. Sales figures of leading bestsellers suggested further parameters of the American book-buying population. Sinclair Lewis's *Main Street* (1920) sold more than 500,000 copies, primarily to readers with sophisticated literary tastes and reading skills, the traditional book-buying market. Yet the great popularity of Edith Hull's 1921 novel *The Sheik,* which sold more than 800,000 copies, and of H. G. Wells's *Outline of History,* also published in 1921 and which sold an estimated 1 million copies in the decade, indicated a sizable consumer audience beyond the traditional one. Aley concluded that "publishers and booksellers can count on a million habitual book buyers, a million more occasional buyers, and beyond that a vague but large number who buy one or two books a year" ("How Large Is Our Book-Reading Public?" 2691). Accurate sales figures of books are notoriously elusive, however, because publishers rarely reveal such data. Bestseller lists are commonly derived from reported sales at selected bookstores; intended to boost marketing efforts, they naturally warrant some skepticism. Figures cited here are those reported in *Publishers' Weekly,* the industry's trade journal, as compiled by Hackett, *70 Years of Best Sellers.*

15. John Farrar, quoted in Tebbel, *Between Covers,* 273; Allen, *Only Yesterday,* 145; Durant, "In Defense of Outlines," 8, 13.

16. Jones, "The Cult of Short-cut Culture," 14; advertisement quoted in Allen, *Only Yesterday,* 143.

17. Advertisement in *Collier's,* 1 January 1927, 36–37. Such messages touched a sensitive nerve in many households aspiring to business-class status. The Lynds reported that many Middletown adults expressed regret and anxiety that they "should read more," but were frustrated by the lack of energy, quiet, and time to do so. "I just read magazines in my scraps of time," one young mother lamented. "I should so like to do more consecutive reading but I don't know of any reading course or how to make one out" (*Middletown,* 235).

"Reading courses"—which laid out a series of texts to read on a selected subject, as determined by librarians, academics, and other experts—were not new in the 1920s, but they took on a more purposeful tone as subscribers saw them as useful, perhaps necessary, means to social and vocational ends. A study of more than 1,200 people who sought reading courses through the Milwaukee Public Library in 1927, for instance, found that the great majority were young adults between the ages of fourteen and thirty-five, with the single largest group (324) between twenty-one and twenty-five years old. Most had completed no more than a high school education. Although the sex of the participants was not recorded, the most frequently cited occupations of these readers suggest a preponderance of women: stenographers (122), housewives (107), students (103), office clerks (82), saleswomen (54), and so on. The most popularly enrolled subjects were literature, English, psychology, travel, and general studies. When asked about their reasons for participating, 24 percent explained that they sought to acquire general culture, while 20 percent named their hopes for improving career opportunities (Gray and Munroe, *Reading Interests,* 54–59).

18. Masson, "Domestic Bookaflage," 256.

19. Norris, "Infinite Riches," 101.

20. "Planning for Books," 110; Belk and Pollay, "Images of Ourselves," 894; "Books in Ads," 2073; Schauffler, "Mental Good Housekeeping," 88; Guthrie, "Decorative Value of Books," 139.

21. Garrison, "Bookcases," 123; Guthrie, "Decorative Value of Books," 139.

22. Post, *Personality of a House,* 356, 437; Garrison, "Bookcases," 158; Post, *Personality of a House,* 281–82; Duryea, "When Books Become Decoration," 45.

23. Post, *Personality of a House,* 438, 504. Another leading home decor writer of the 1920s, Montrose Moses, admitted that "books with distinctive backs are often like ladies at the opera — disappointing to talk to," but he too found pretty bindings a decorative tonic, even if he distanced himself from those whose "five-foot shelf habit" led them to regard books in what he considered such vulgarly superficial terms. See "Coming on Books Unexpectedly," 76; and "Books for the Guest Room," 86.

24. Doud, "Books for the Home," 538; Skinner, "What Well-Dressed Women Are Reading," 432–33.

25. Skinner, "Well-Dressed Women," 432, 433.

26. F. Warde to William Kittredge, 17 September 1922, FWN.

27. The simile is from Warde's typescript, ca. 1924, on American printing, FWG.

28. Warde feared that his poor education was apparent in his writing (Warde to William A. Kittredge, 2 June 1927, FWG). Although he gave others a variety of vague impressions about his education — including that he had attended medical school — little is known of his life before his 1920 marriage; there is no record of his education beyond high school in rural Minnesota. Both Frederic and Beatrice later admitted that she had written or substantially contributed to several of his early published essays.

29. "Fine Printed Books in the Princeton University Library," (1924), catalogue copy typescript, FWG.

30. "How the Middle Class Lives," 697; Persons, *Decline of Gentility,* 298.

31. Gerould, "Plight of the Genteel," 314, 317. Peixotto's study was prompted by faculty wives' complaints that a proposed new salary schedule was inadequate for those who sought "any material expression in her home of her love of comfort and beauty, or any intellectual or artistic quality in her daily occupations" (*Getting and Spending,* 211).

32. "How the Middle Class Lives," 696; Post, *Personality of a House,* 303.

33. Wiggam, *The Marks of an Educated Man,* 214; Mencken, "Lovely Letters," in *Selected Prejudices,* 115, 114.

34. Wright, "Buy Her a Book," 347; Sherman, "Mencken, the Jeune Fille, and the New Spirit," 3–4.

35. Edman, "American Leisure," 222–23. Outlines create only a "glaze of culture," Howard Mumford Jones declared, with their facile implication that "information comes without labor, and intelligence is formed without thought." He regarded the books' buyers as gullible victims of publishers' "ballyhoo" and "gorgeous advertising as noisy as a brass band" ("Cult of Short-cut Culture," 14).

36. Loos, *Gentlemen Prefer Blondes,* 28. Women were often blamed for the increasingly utilitarian attitudes toward books. Harold Stearns scorned the "extraordinary feminization of American social life" for causing an "intellectual anaemia or torpor" that had subordinated books to trivial domestic and decorative purposes, miring them in "stilted superficiality." He argued that American men, absorbed in the work of conquering a continent in the nineteenth century, had bequeathed to women the "unimportant things" of art, literature, and culture "to keep them busy." Things of the mind and the spirit had been feminized; they served "feminine" purposes of moral reform rather than masculine ones of disinterested contemplation or scrupulous introspection ("Intellectual Life," in *Civilization,* 135, 144). Karen Halttunen similarly notes that living room decor in the twenties usually expressed the resident woman's personality more than the man's; this contrasts with the typically masculine style dominating a home library. The two kinds of rooms thus not only represented opposing notions of one's relation to books, privately secluded or "invitingly" social, but also suggested a gendered understanding of books' purposes and value ("Parlor to Living Room," 177).

37. Fitzgerald, *Great Gatsby,* 45–46, 174.

38. Lewis, *Babbitt,* 15–16, 78.

39. Quoted in Tebbel, *Between Covers,* 276.

40. Huxley, "Outlook," 266, 268; Borsodi, *This Ugly Civilization,* 229; Edman, "American Leisure," 223.

41. After Bennett Cerf and Donald Klopfer bought rights to the Modern Library series in 1925, they replaced the books' fake leather bindings with cloth. See Cerf, *At Random,* 60–61; Hooper, *Country House,* 154.

42. Rollins, "The Artist: His Credo," in *Postscripts on Dwiggins,* 1:89. Updike's upbringing gave him cultural and intellectual advantages that "placed him on a level of superiority to nearly everybody with whom he had contacts"(Winship, *Updike and the Merrymount Press,* 6). Updike was also a distinguished autodidact scholar; his 1922 two-volume study *Printing Types: Their History, Forms, and Use* remains a landmark in typographic history and criticism.

43. Dwiggins to Rollins, n.d. (1923), CPRY.

44. Soule, "Rollins at Montague," 45.

45. Dwiggins, "Investigation," 143–44.

46. Ibid.

47. Ibid., 141, 142.

Chapter 2. On Sacred Ground

1. Bentley, "Bentley Remembers Garnett," 34.

2. Ibid.

3. B. Warde, "Inscription for a Printing Office, " in *I Am a Communicator,* 50; Levine, *Highbrow/Lowbrow,* 230.

4. Quoted in Ransom, *Private Presses,* 157.

5. An excellent recent study on modern experimental typography is Drucker, *Visible Word.*

6. See Stetz, "Sex, Lies, and Printed Cloth"; Brown, "Bodley Head Press"; and Stetz and Lasner, *England in the 1890s.*

7. Babbitt, *Democracy and Leadership,* 242.

8. Cole, *Influence of Fine Printing,* 34; Updike, "Essentials of a Well-Made Book," in *Some Aspects,* 29.

9. Tschichold, *New Typography,* 11, 28–29. Tschichold was not the first to formulate the tenets of modernist typography. Bauhaus faculty El Lissitzky and Lazlo Moholy-Nagy were earlier key proponents, but as Robin Kinross explains, both men were "artistic visionaries," while Tschichold "was the lucid practitioner, able to formulate and develop these visions in the ordinary world" (Kinross, introduction to the 1995 English translation of *Die Neue Typographie,* xvii). It is significant that Tschichold's work was not translated into English until nearly seventy years after its publication.

10. Ibid., 64–65, 29.

11. Rogers, *Pi,* 105; Cole, *Influence of Fine Printing,* 35; Updike, "Tendencies in Modern Typography," in *Some Aspects,* 46–48.

12. McMurtrie, "Modernism in Design," 89.

13. Zweig, *Old-Book Peddlar,* 23. On Americans buying European libraries, see Rosenbach, "Why Americans Buys England's Books," 452–59; and Schreiber, "Migration of European Collections," 845–47.

14. Bentley, "Bentley Remembers Garnett," 34.

15. Sedgwick, *In Praise of Gentlemen,* 35; Babbitt, *Democracy and Leadership,* 278.

16. Bourdieu, *Distinction,* 56; Garnett, "Ideal Book," 128.

17. Although a few women were among its most enthusiastic patrons, all of the major players in professional fine printing were men. A few wives — notably Bertha Goudy and Jane Grabhorn — participated in their husbands' enterprise, sometimes with great skill and insight, but the larger bibliophilic culture was distinctly masculine. Most major book clubs, centers of serious book collecting and scholarship, limited their membership to men, reflecting the traditional patriarchal society that bibliophilia evoked.

18. Adams, Jr., "Four Lives of Adler," 2–3.

19. Rollins to Adler, 10 January 1929, EAP.

20. The best survey of private presses active in the 1920s is Ransom, *Private Presses.*

21. Rogers, *Pi,* 116. On the function of gentility as an appreciative audience for culture and art, see Sedgwick, *In Praise of Gentlemen,* 39.

22. Cerf, "Reminiscences," 187; Duffus, *Books,* 44, 45; Earnest Elmo Calkins to Adler, 25 September 1925, PPP.

23. Johnston, "Fine Books in America," 77.

24. Rollins, "A Book in Every Home."

25. Morris regretted that books for the masses were necessarily cheap and ugly, but he conceded that, without broader social and political changes, "if they have not money enough to buy [fine books] they must do without." See "The Poet as Printer" (1891) in *Ideal Book*, 92.

26. Le Gallienne, "Philosophy of Limited Editions," 121, 122, 125. See also Sadleir's list of acceptable reasons in "Limited Editions," 299–302.

27. Jackson, *Printing of Books*, 27, 31; Huxley, "Typography for the Twentieth-Century Reader," 346–47.

28. In 1932, for example, the Lakeside Press sponsored a lavish exhibit featuring the "greatest" illustrated books in history. The exhibition was planned to help promote, and legitimize, its recent publication of "Four American Books" (*Moby Dick, Walden, Poe's Tales,* and *Two Years Before the Mast*), which it claimed were "definitively" illustrated. See Badaracco, *American Culture and the Marketplace.*

29. See, for example, McMurtrie, *The Golden Book* (1927); Orcutt, *Master Makers of the Book* (1928); and Johnston, *Biblio-Typographica* (1930). At least one person, Carl Rollins, expressed some doubts about the value of printing history per se for the lay audience, perhaps sharing Garnett's worry that to make it accessible to the common reader would diminish its scholarly import. Rollins did agree, however, that everyone should have at least a rudimentary sense of the role that printing has played in political and social history, of its key pertinence to "human progress" (*SRL*, 24 November 1928).

30. G. P. Winship to George Sargent, 14 September 1926, Sargent Papers, NYPL; Adler to Blanche Knopf, 12 November 1930, EAP.

31. Tebbel, *Between Covers,* 331. On the other hand, Rollins complained in his review of the 1928 show that market considerations seemed to take priority over purely aesthetic criteria in that year's selection: he called it a "confession of impotence to value expedience over high standards" ("Fifty Books of 1928," 900). A list of all AIGA Fifty Books winners is printed in the 1938 *Annual of Bookmaking.*

32. Garnett, *Documentary History,* 4.

33. E. Grabhorn, "Recollections," 29. The ascending status of fine printing is well measured in the honorary degrees awarded to recognize practitioners' cultural contributions. In addition to Nash, Updike received an honorary M.A. from Brown in 1910, Rogers received one from Yale in 1928, and Rollins accepted both an honorary M.A. in 1920 and an honorary doctorate in 1949. The Grabhorn brothers both received honorary doctorates from the University of California later in their careers. Only Nash, however, referred to himself as "Dr." after receiving the honorary degree.

34. Arguing that printing is a "learned profession," Carl Rollins urged Carnegie Institute of Technology to provide its students with "educational training not dissimilar to that for law or medicine" (Rollins to Robert E. Doherty, Carnegie Tech president, 17 May 1937, PPP). For discussions of the phenomenon by which many others "exchanged gentry status for professionalism" at the beginning of the twentieth century, see Persons, *Decline of American Gentility,* 297 and passim, and Galbraith, *Affluent Society,* 262–63.

The acclaimed fine printers of the twenties seemed to have come by their love for and prowess in creating tasteful fine books without external prompting or training. Several could point to a spontaneous "conversion experience" of sorts, a moment when they first saw a fine book and felt immediately compelled to study the craft. Rogers, for example, clearly recalled the first deluxe book he bought, Wharton's *Poems of Sappho,* which he promptly embellished in the style of medieval illumination (*Work of Bruce Rogers,* xliv–xlv). Bourdieu remarks that this ideological strategy of proclaiming supposedly "natural" taste is a chief way to establish hierarchical superiority: "it *naturalizes* real differences, converting differences in the mode of acquisition of culture into differences of nature; it only recognizes as legitimate the relation to culture (or language) which least bears the marks of its genesis, which has nothing 'academic,' . . . 'affected,' or 'studied' about it, but manifests by its ease and naturalness that true culture is nature—a new mystery of immaculate conception" (*Distinction,* 68).

35. Garnett, "Again What Is Fine Printing?" 573; Garnett, "Making and Judging of Books," 606, 608.

36. Garnett to John T. Morris, director, College of Industries, Carnegie Tech, 25 May 1923, LPC; Dill, "Garnett and the Laboratory Press," 671; Adler to Fred J. Hartman, National Graphic Arts Education Guild, 16 August 1937, PPP. This insistence that fine printing be kept "pure," the province only of those few with the right tastes and sensibilities, was ironically to cast an oppressive pall over many of the young men initiated into its inner circles through the Lab Press. As Carnegie Tech faculty member Glen Cleeton protested: "many of our former students who majored in the fine printing option [with Garnett] have found it difficult, and in some cases impossible, to adjust to commercial conditions existing in the industry" (Cleeton to Webster N. Jones, Carnegie Tech, director, College of Engineering, 10 June 1937, LPC). Letters to Garnett from his former students confirm this assessment; they repeatedly lament and seek his forgiveness for prostituting their fine printing ideals by working in the trade. See Benton, "Orchids from Pittsburgh," 48–52.

37. Jim Kibbel to Adler, 19 April 1932, EAP; Miers, "Ellis," 50.

38. O'Day, *John Henry Nash,* 13; quoted in Badaracco, *Trading Words,* 122.

39. Glick, *Rudge,* 32–33; Calkins, "Market Value of Good Taste," 2.

40. E. Grabhorn to E. Adler, n.d. [1923], PPP. Bob Grabhorn later recalled that Ed soon sold the prized books to buy a car, "a Stutz Bearcat, of all things!" Bob chuckled ("Fine Printing," 33). Nash admitted that the "$125,000 worth of monumental works" in his own elegant library were for him "typographic pictures" for visual study and inspiration only; like most of the others, he could not read the Latin in which most of the early texts were written ("Defense," 53).

Chapter 3. Man and Machine

1. Warde to Kittredge, 17 September 1922, FWN.

2. Ibid.

3. P. J. Conkwright to Will Ransom, n.d. [1940?], FWN.

4. Rollins to Fred Whiting, 11 January 1923, CPRY; Rollins, "Morris's Typographical Adventure," 31.

5. Rollins, manuscript annotation to a letter received from Updike, 12 May 1924, CPRY.

6. Filene, "Ethics of the Machine Age," 78; Frank, "Shall We Scrap Our Machines?" 412; Pupin, "Romance of the Machine," 136. A favorite example of the machine's emancipating capabilities derived from the struggle between labor and management that typically accompanied a print shop's transition to mechanized typesetting. Although New York City printers went on strike to protest the arrival of Linotype equipment at the turn of the century, Stuart Chase and others believed that their fears and objections had been foolish. Once installed, the machines meant fewer hours, better pay, better working conditions, and more challenging, stimulating work for their operators. Chase argued that the machine simply replaced human labor that was tedious, slow, expensive, and often flawed; it not only produced a better product, benefiting society at large, but lifted the worker "further than ever from the robot class" (*Men and Machines,* 150). In reality, it benefited the relatively few workers who were able to keep their jobs by learning the new system quickly and efficiently.

7. Borsodi, *This Ugly Civilization,* 149–50.

8. Russell, "Take Them or Leave Them," 174. Standardization was common in book publishing through popular "library" series — uniform, inexpensive reprint editions.

9. "Making of a Best Seller."

10. For a detailed description of the dramatic mechanization of the bookmaking trades in the nineteenth century, see Gaskell, "The Book: The Machine-Press Period, 1800–1950," in *New Introduction to Bibliography.* See also Steinberg, *Five Hundred Years of Printing,* and Thompson, *Morris and American Book Design,* chap. 1. Although modernists shared fine printers' contempt for the dreary look and structural "degeneration" of most modern trade books, they blamed the books' "corrupt" bourgeois forms rather than the machines that produced them. According to Jan Tschichold, machines had the power to produce goods and information economically and efficiently, thereby laying the foundation for a more equitable distribution of social and economic power. For him, machines engendered "a new kind of man: the engineer!" whose job was to unleash the machine's great creative force. Modernists thus championed precisely what American fine printers found most repugnant.

11. As William Peterson, Morris's foremost biographer, has pointed out, Morris was the first major artist since Blake to control every aspect of the printing of a book. See *Kelmscott Press,* 312. Morris's own writings about his "typographical adventure," as he called his work with the Kelmscott Press, are gathered in *The Ideal Book.* The English arts and crafts ideology bore distinctive progeny in America; see Thompson, *Morris and American Book Design,* and Boris, *Art and Labor.* I am indebted to John Roche for helpful discussions about the arts and crafts movement in America.

The neomedievalism so evident in fine book design was a prominent aspect of the arts and crafts philosophy. See Lears, *No Place of Grace,* chap. 4; Merz, "Twentieth-Century Medievalism," 228–36; Veblen's critique of Morris's cultivated archaism and obsolescence in *Theory of the Leisure Class,* 116–17; and McGann's analysis of Morris's historicized textual iconography in *Black Riders.*

12. Rollins to E. G. Gress, 19 December 1923, Gress Papers, NYPL.

13. Rollins, "Fifty Books of 1928," 900. The sight of Morris's "real printing" triggered Rollins's contempt for the "stupid gropings" and "witless concepts" of his own generation of printers. E. Grabhorn, "Recollections," 26.

14. Updike, "Educated Man in the Printing Industry," in *Some Aspects,* 3. Elsewhere Updike explained that what onlookers often interpret as a printer's joy is in fact mostly relief ("Essentials of a Well-Made Book," in *Some Aspects,* 39).

15. Blumenthal, *Typographic Years,* 60; quoted in Barr, *Presses of Northern California,* 198–200; J. and C. Johnson, "Regeneration of the Book," 406.

16. Rollins, "Printing at Its Best," 356–57; "Hand-Press Printing," 612; "Fifty Books of 1928," 900.

17. Bentley, "Bentley Remembers Garnett," 34. The handpress was a machine, of course, that imposed standardized precision on forms of the hand-copied manuscript book. Handpress printing remains the epitome of fine bookmaking today; for an authoritative treatment of its intricate details, see Rummonds, *Printing on the Handpress.*

18. Garnett, "Ideal Book," 120; Bentley, "Bentley Remembers Garnett," 34.

19. Nash, "In Defense of Finely Printed Books," 52. Adler to Magee, 12 May 1956, EAP; Adler to Marlowe Society, 7 December 1927, PPP.

20. Warde to Will Ransom, 20 July 1928, FWN; Macy, "Limited Editions Club Is Organized," 1722; Rollins, "Merrymount Press," 834; Rollins, "Printing at Its Best," 356; Kittredge to Dwiggins, 26 January 1927, KN; George Moore as paraphrased in Jackson, *Printing of Books,* 115. The edition of Poe's *Tales* that Dwiggins designed for Lakeside was one of the press's highly touted "Four American Books" — American classics designed and illustrated by leading book artists, primarily to demonstrate the company's capacity to achieve fine printing with machine production. The other selections were *Moby Dick,* illustrated by Rockwell Kent; *Walden,* illustrated by Rudolph Ruzicka; and *Two Years Before the Mast,* illustrated by Edward O. Wilson. See Badaracco, *American Culture.*

21. Even the Kelmscott Press relied in some ways on modern, machine-aided technology, notably in ink-making and type design. See Peterson, *Kelmscott Press.*

22. See Benton, "Orchids from Pittsburgh."

23. By 1924 the Grabhorns owned two Colts Armory presses, according to Wentz (*Grabhorn Press,* 34). A bill for repair in the Pynson Printers archive indicates that the shop included at least one 14 by 22 Style 5A Colts Armory.

24. Ransom, "Merrymount Press," 1617; Rimington, "Ellis," 2209.

25. Hart, *Fine Printing,* 25. Wentz, *Grabhorn Press,* 53. Grabhorn's remark is a pun on the fabled English bibliophilic practice of "destroying" type after it has been used exclusively for a special purpose, most dramatically by throwing it into the Thames. The phallic implications of a deep impression were not lost on bibliophiles. Several admired what was termed the deep, "masculine" impression that resulted when type is driven into "pliant, expectant" blank paper.

26. Virtually all books in the 1920s were printed letterpress, even though offset presses existed in an early stage of development. Edmund C. Arnold, writing in 1963, computed that offset accounted for only 18 percent of that year's total printing, and he noted that offset presses served primarily for newspaper printing (*Ink on Paper,* 226–70).

27. The long-standing resistance to recognition of photography as an art form reflects the same prejudices that discouraged its widespread use in postwar fine books. See Harris, "Pictorial Perils," in *Cultural Excursions,* 337–48; and Benjamin, "Work of Art," in *Illuminations,* 217–51. Modernists, not surprisingly, embraced the photograph; see

Kinross, *Modern Typography*. Meanwhile, the woodcut and the more graphically rough linoleum cut enjoyed a new vogue in postwar book illustration. A few artists, notably Lynd Ward and Frank Masareel, produced books whose only texts were sequences of narrative woodcut images.

28. Comparato, *Books for the Millions,* 42, 201–202.

29. It is worth noting that even foundry type, used for hand composition, was cast mechanically. Because hand typecasting is a highly skilled, laborious task, none of the postwar fine printers could cast their own type. Furthermore, only Carl Rollins argued publicly that handcast type was innately superior to machine-cast foundry type. See "Printing at Its Best."

30. Beatrice Warde (writing under the pseudonym Paul Beaujon), "Machine in Book Composition," 573. Historically derived typefaces were considered essential to fine printing. See Kinross, *Modern Typography,* 56–58, for a succinct account of the drive to produce historicist faces for machine composition. By mid-decade several were available. When Elmer Adler began planning the design of Willa Cather's *My Mortal Enemy* for Knopf in 1926, for example, he inquired of the Scribner Press, the production plant for Charles Scribner's Sons, about the Monotype composition it could offer. He was told that Scribner had Monotype matrices for Scotch Roman, Caslon Oldstyle, Garamont, and Suburban French as well as other faces "less desirable for high grade book composition" (Harold Cadmus to Adler, 6 April 1926, PPP). The book was composed in Monotype Scotch Roman.

31. Kittredge to Dwiggins, 26 January 1927, KN.

32. Rimington, "Ellis," 2208; Adler to Esherick, 25 July 1927, PPP.

33. E. Grabhorn, "Recollections," 45.

34. Kent reported that a worker could hand-color one page per day (completing all ninety-five copies), and he estimated that the coloring added about three months of extra labor to the deluxe edition's production, which cost $75 per copy more than the uncolored edition (Adler to Burton Emmett, 17 February 1928, PPP).

35. Morris, quoted in De Vinne, "Printing of Morris," 920–23.

36. Garnett, "Ideal Book," 127. Moulds for handmade paper could make only relatively small sheets, averaging about 20 by 25 inches. Machine-made paper is made in a wide, continuous roll that enables more pages to be printed at one time, reducing the cost of presswork. See Rogers, *Paragraphs on Printing,* 40. Others shared Garnett's disdain for mouldmade paper; Bernard Newdigate called its slight and even deckle edges an "impudent sham" ("Preciousness in Printing," 617).

37. Rimington, "Ellis," 2208–9. When Harper Brothers's production manager Arthur W. Rushmore proposed to produce a deluxe limited edition of Edna St. Vincent Millay's poems in 1930, he emphasized not only that the type of all six volumes would be set by hand but that the pages would be "printed from type" (composition estimates, Millay Collection, Columbia University). Twelve of the seventeen sample books bearing this phrase, however, were machine-composed.

38. Rogers, *Pi,* 117; Greenhood, "Book as an Aesthetic Object," 59; Edward Stone to Burton Emmett, 30 October 1929, EAP.

39. Wentz, *Grabhorn Press,* 42; R. Grabhorn, "Fine Printing," 75. Criticisms of presswork are fairly assigned only to the particular copy examined, however. Printing quality

can vary greatly throughout a press run, unless care is taken to regularly add ink, adjust impression, inspect for damaged letters and illustrations, and so on.

40. Veblen, *Theory of the Leisure Class,* 114, 115, 117.

41. "Literature and the Machine," 945.

42. Ibid.

43. Rollins, *Fine Printing and the Small Shop,* 8, 7.

44. Johnston, *Biblio-Typographica,* 3; Dill, "Ideal Book," 9, 18; F. Warde, untitled manuscript (1924), FWG, 6.

45. Adler to Doherty, Carnegie Tech, 14 June 1937, EAP; Garnett, *Documentary Account,* 99. Rogers, *Pi,* 110; Glick, *Rudge,* 22.

46. FauntLeRoy, *Nash,* 26; he recalled only one book that Nash composed, a 53-page essay on the life of Dante that he published in 1922. Harlan, *Nash,* 37; see Harlan's account of the employees and procedures on which Nash's "atelier" depended, 35–42. Peterson, *Kelmscott Press,* 312.

47. "Members of the Grabhorn Press," "Protest Against the Elevation of Printing," 405.

48. E. Grabhorn, *Fine Art of Printing,* 12.

Chapter 4. Gilded Goblets

1. B. Warde, untitled letter and speech, 23 October 1928, in *I Am a Communicator,* 8.

2. B. Warde, "Printing Should Be Invisible," 109.

3. Kinross describes a virtual "hegemony of invisibility" in modern Anglo-American book design (*Modern Typography,* 64).

4. Morison, "First Principles of Typography," 240; Johnston, "Books Should Look Like Books," 1594–95; Ansbacher, "On Fine Bookmaking Today," 953.

5. Bringhurst, *Typographic Style,* 19. In her study of European experimental futurist typography in the first two decades of the twentieth century, Johanna Drucker offers a useful distinction between what she calls marked and unmarked typography. She argues that futurists created highly marked work — its design aggressively demands attention and pushes the reader toward a particular response to the textual message. Such typography is openly manipulative; it "sells" a particular message, whether political, commercial, or bureaucratic. Drucker contrasts this with unmarked — invisible — typography, "the even, gray page of prose and poetic convention" that appears to "speak itself." This conventional "literary" page, she asserts, bears no signs of manipulation by author, printer, or publisher; its text seems neutral, natural, and so true. The text is simply "there, and the unmarked author [is] indeed the Author of the Text as pure Word" (*Visible Word,* 46, 95). For a broader sense of modern theoretical approaches to Western book typography, see Tschichold, *New Typography,* Tschichold, *Form of the Book,* Gill, *Essay on Typography,* Duncan, *Doors of Perception,* Spencer, *Pioneers of Modern Typography,* and discussions in the quarterly journal *Visible Language* and the irregularly published serials *Serif* and *Matrix.*

6. Heartened by revivalist rhetoric from England, eminent American printer Theodore Low De Vinne argued in 1892 for a return to what he called "masculine printing" and darker, bolder typefaces, rejecting standard contemporary types as spindly, weak,

and "feminine." He deemed them feminine not only because they featured fine, thin strokes but because they catered to the increasingly feminine masses of common readers. See De Vinne, "Masculine Printing."

7. Other acclaimed new types modeled on those from the fifteenth century were *Poliphilus* and its companion italic *Blado,* based (like *Bembo*) on early roman and italic types used by Aldus Manutius. *Centaur,* a roman typeface designed in 1915 by Bruce Rogers after type used by the earlier Venetian printer Nicholas Jenson, was paired with the *Arrighi* italic designed in 1925 by Frederic Warde and Stanley Morison after the work of Italian Renaissance calligrapher Ludovico degli Arrighi. The sixteenth and seventeenth centuries inspired a confusing welter of facsimile versions of types originally designed by French typecutter Claude Garamond (d. 1561) — Stempel Foundry's *Garamond,* issued in 1924, and Linotype *Granjon,* issued in 1928 — and versions of types designed by Frenchman Jean Jannon (b. 1580) but misattributed to Garamond: ATF foundry *Garamond,* issued in 1918; Lanston Monotype's *Garamont,* designed by Goudy and issued in 1921, and the English Monotype Company's *Garamond* of 1922. Many excellent studies discuss the forebears of twentieth-century type designs. Still among the best is Updike's 1922 *Printing Types.* Updike's scholarly assessment of typographic forms and history helped to educate his peers to the fine points of selecting and using type. For more contemporary treatments see Lawson, *Anatomy of a Typeface;* Bigelow, Duensing, and Gentry, eds., *Fine Print on Type;* and Bringhurst, *Typographic Style.*

8. Prospectus for *Shakespeare's Sonnets* (New York: Cheshire House, 1931).

9. Rogers, *Paragraphs on Printing,* 22; Rogers, "Address to the AIGA," in *Pi,* 104.

10. The other notable Bay Area neomedievalists were Cecil and James Johnson, who launched their Windsor Press in 1926 with four exuberant celebrations of fifteenth-century northern European typography. One, an edition of a 1493 letter from "Christoforo Colombo," was composed in a typeface called Inkunabula, lest anyone fail to note its historicism.

11. Sometimes Ellis's historicism was achieved via illustrations more than text. In 1931 he produced a stately edition (26 by 13 inches) of Dante's *Inferno* with copperplate reproductions of William Blake's memorable illustrations, and the following year he printed an edition of *Aesop's Fables* that reproduced Thomas Bewick's 68 famous wood engravings for the tales. Both books were published by Cheshire House.

12. Updike to Cerf, 19 November 1928, and 10 January 1929, RHC.

13. F. Warde, "On the Work of Rogers," 139. Altogether, 48 of the 300 sample editions illustrate allusive typography.

14. Teague, "Modern Style," 1568; Rollins, "Westgate Signed Editions," 120; Rollins, "Modernism in Practice," 702; Jackson, *Printing of Books,* 13. Updike to F. Warde, 27 September 1924, FWG.

15. Warde to Kittredge, 25 November 1926, KN.

16. Tschichold, *New Typography,* 11, 13–14.

17. Ibid., 66–68, 69. See also Kinross, *Modern Typography,* 87–90.

18. Tschichold, *New Typography,* 80; Kinross, *Modern Typography,* 88. Although Tschichold was the most effective articulator of modernist design ideals in the twenties and early thirties, he later recanted most of the radical and dogmatic positions described here. Early in 1933 he was briefly detained by the Nazi authorities on suspicion of "cultural bolshevism"; shortly after he emigrated to Switzerland. As the political climate

in Germany grew increasingly oppressive in the 1930s, Tschichold was drawn to the more moderate English typographic principles he had once disparaged. By the end of the decade his position had reversed completely, and he became what Kinross termed "one of [modernism's] most acute and sometimes acid critics" (Introduction, *New Typography,* xxxviii). In 1946 he defended his change of heart with the blistering charge that modernist typography's "intolerant attitude certainly corresponds in particular to the German inclination to the absolute; its military will-to-order and its claim to sole power correspond to those fearful components of German-ness which unleashed Hitler's rule and the Second World War" (quoted in ibid.). Tschichold emigrated to England, where he served as typographic director for Penguin Books, formulating the now famous typographic characteristics of those books.

19. Johnston, "Modernism in Book Design," 1126; Rogers, *Pi,* 105; Rogers to William Kittredge, 7 July 1932, KN. By the late 1920s, however, American printers could not altogether ignore modernist design. Typographic trade journals reverberated with varying opinions of the merits of modernism, most particularly the use of sans serif typefaces. Some articles were trenchant, as their titles suggest. See, for example, George Holden, "Shall Tradition Prevent the Adoption of More Legible Type Faces?" and Jairus Kemp, "In Defense of the Modern Movement — by a True Modernist." Will Ransom's 1930 query "Sanserif: Passing Fancy or Type of Tomorrow?" triggered an avalanche of letters from leading printers of the day, each taking a stand on the "newest band-wagon" of sans serif types, as Harry Gage, director of the Mergenthaler Linotype Company's typography department, called them. Type designer Oswald Cooper supposed that one might "learn to read sanserif lower case and to like it (as, for instance, we are learning to like broccoli)," and David Silve, an associate of the Pynson Printers, pronounced them "a sad lot," concluding, "I prefer my types with the serifs on" ("Type Designers and Printers Discuss Sanserif," 39–43).

One of the most spirited debates over the virtues of modernist typefaces and typography was prompted by a long and intelligent polemic by Jim Clarke entitled "Modernism Has Come to Stay: Dump the Classics in the 'Hell-Box,'" which occupied an entire issue of *Direct Advertising* in 1933. The title refers to the practice of consigning worn types to the shop "hell-box" so that their metal can be melted down and recast into fresh, sharp-edged type. The magazine devoted a subsequent issue to 64 responses to Clarke's assertions, which predictably ranged considerably. Most, however, argued strenuously that "the classics" should not be discarded. Clarke is "dead wrong," one respondent wrote. "The modern type is best for punch, push, and howl, but for the delicate refinement which many things require, it's not in the picture. . . . We are indeed living in an age of speed, but so much the worse for us. It's brought us to the brink of bankruptcy. And so will the sole use of modern type bring typography to the plane of a blacksmith shop" (Walton, "Modern Type Best for Punch, Push and Howl," 6–7).

20. Dwiggins to Adler, 23 November 1927, 7 January 1928, 30 June 1928, 4 August 1928, PPP.

21. Ege, "Decalog," 663; Morison, quoted in Greenhood, "Book as an Aesthetic Object," 58.

22. Adler to Firuski, 3 August 1925, PPP; Dwiggins to William Kittredge, 5 November 1926, KN.

23. Rogers to Emery Walker, 14 May 1928, EAP.

24. Kent to Kittredge, 11 November 1926, KN.

25. Kittredge to Kent, 30 December 1926, KN; Cerf, *At Random,* 72.

26. Grabhorn, *Fine Art of Printing,* 15–16.

27. Some found Nash's use of rules inauthentic and contrived. Ed Grabhorn grumbled that a mechanical (printed) simulation of a manuscript practice had "no feeling" to it, that it lost the "brilliance" and "nervousness" of the original handwork ("Recollections," 78). Also, because Nash neither cut and composed the rules nor printed them, presumably his skills were less admired than his bold design, which was difficult to execute successfully.

Some detected a characteristic style in regional fine bookmaking. By the end of the decade a stylistic as well as geographic polarity had developed between printers and designers on the East Coast (notably, Adler, Updike, Rogers, Warde, and Rollins) and those on the West Coast (essentially, the major San Francisco fine printers: Nash and the Grabhorns). The former group generally emphasized authoritative historicism and strayed less boldly from traditional typographic models. The westerners, although hardly alike in style, shared an unrestrained design exuberance. These differences accentuated an emerging rivalry as the fine book market grew, and snide remarks about the others circulated on both sides of the country. Updike quipped in private, for example, that the San Francisco printers "all print in rather a stilted style, and introduce a great deal of colour into their work. I remember saying once to a friend that I thought they put far too much red, blue and yellow in what they did; and he said it was the California climate — that I had only to look at their ties and shirts to perceive the effect of the brilliancy of the western coast on clothing, and that I must expect to find the same gorgeous effects in printing! . . . I suppose that in a land which looks like a tropical drop-scene, you have to have books that are equally theatrical" (Updike to Stanley Morison, 13 November 1923, in McKittrick, ed., *Selected Correspondence,* 76). Updike may have been referring to comments by Carl Rollins, who on other occasions voiced similar tongue-in-cheek theories about California's fine printing.

28. Rogers, *Paragraphs on Printing,* 166, 171, 176.

29. Peggy Joyce to Elmer Adler, n.d. [1932], PPP.

30. This need for elite authority bred rivalries and jealousies within the fine printing community and helped alienate that community from many rank and file printers. Adler assumed the role of "typographic advisor" for all printing done for Random House, for example. (His exact role was never clear to the three partners, and they squabbled constantly: Adler invariably felt his authority had been circumvented, while Cerf and Klopfer found Adler's complaints meddlesome.) He never hesitated to correct or advise other printers, often imperiously, when they were compelled to submit page proofs for his approval. He particularly criticized the work of William Kittredge on the Random House edition of *Poor Richard's Almanac* and Richard Ellis's plans for Random House's edition of *Cabellian Harmonics.* Both printers took umbrage; see, for example, Ellis's explanation to Bennett Cerf, 4 September 1928, RHC.

31. Warde to William Kittredge, 8 November 1921, FWN; Glick, *Rudge,* 20. Warde seemed to hunger for the power and authority Rogers enjoyed. He suffered anxieties about his professional stature, lying awake at night "thinking about how insignificant I am, and the same about my work" (Warde to Kittredge, 27 April 1922, FWN).

32. Adler to Lord & Taylor, 27 September 1927, PPP; Stephen Flaherty to Adler, 5 De-

cember 1925, PPP; Alfred Knopf to Adler, 15 December 1925, PPP. Rogers, *Paragraphs on Printing,* 176.

33. Rollins, "Centaur," *SRL,* 19 April 1930, 951.

34. Ansbacher, "Fine Bookmaking Today," 951, 953. His examples of inappropriate type selection included "Aristophanes and St. Luke set in sans serif [designed by Lester Douglas]; Whitman set in Estienne [by Warde], Voltaire set in Lucian Bernhard [by Adler], . . . "Tom Sawyer" printed on a lovely paper of a rich and delicate peach color [by Adler]" (953). This critique raises the obvious issue of subjectivity in expressive book design. Oddly, however, differences in taste or judgment were commonly seen as differences in authority or privilege. When Carl Rollins reviewed the Grabhorn Press's production of *Hymns to Aphrodite,* composed entirely in the italic form of the new Dutch face Lutetia, he attributed the resulting "thin and meagre effect" to the "preciosity in design resulting from the present oversupply of type varieties!" (*SRL,* 31 December 1927, 495).

35. Updike, *Some Aspects,* 33.

36. B. Warde, "Decorative Printing in America."

37. R. Grabhorn, "Fine Printing," 97.

38. Nash's egotism struck some as a matter of dubious taste. Although he did not refer to Nash by name, Stanley Morison likely had him in mind when he wrote to Updike, "I'm rather terrified of Americans whose taste runs to very deckle-edged handmade papers heavily watermarked with their own initials" (Morison to Updike, 23 September 1923, in McKittrick, ed., *Selected Correspondence,* 64). Gaige enjoyed the ruckus caused by the green-paper copies; he claimed that he issued them "for the befuddlement of book collectors" (*Footlights and Highlights,* 202). The practice of using specially watermarked papers was not limited to editions printed on handmade papers; manufacturers of mouldmade papers often provided the same service. Elmer Adler ordered paper for the Knopf edition of the *Works of Stephen Crane* with an *SC* watermark, for example, but the mark appeared upside down, so the paper could not be used (Adler to Alfred and Blanche Knopf, 13 July 1925, PPP). Several publishers — including Cheshire House, Rudge, Spiral, Random House, and Knopf — occasionally ordered mouldmade paper watermarked with their own monograms for fine productions. The Worthy Paper Company even made a mouldmade paper called, and watermarked, "BR Rag," which it sold commercially. Despite the implications, printing a book on this paper did not indicate that Rogers was involved with its design.

39. Rogers, *Paragraphs on Printing,* 102. At least 20 of the sample editions exceeded Rogers's recommendations; 9 included 16 or more blank pages.

40. Cerf to E. Grabhorn, 13 May 1929, RHC; formal book production contract, 13 May 1929, RHC. They did not print any vellum copies, perhaps because of the excessive cost of producing a dozen 430-page books, difficulties in procuring that much vellum, or simple failure to pursue the idea. Neither was the book's paper custom watermarked. Ed Grabhorn later recalled that he saved money by buying in-stock handmade paper directly from the English mill, which was no doubt cheaper than a custom watermarked order ("Recollections," 48–49). Perhaps the difficulty of printing on vellum was a factor as well. After the book was finished, Donald Klopfer thanked Ed Grabhorn for his labors and admitted that, although he was disappointed not to have the vellum copies, "what a hell of a time you'd have had" in printing them (5 December 1930, RHC).

41. Dwiggins begged Alfred Knopf to release him from any responsibilities for design-

ing dust jackets because, he wrote, "they have to be boobproof." He disliked working on overtly commercial materials intended to suit popular taste, preferring to work "where the object is to make a design good in itself, without an eye cocked in the direction of said boob" (Knopf, *Portrait,* 103). When Harold Mason of the Centaur Press suggested that the fine edition of *Yokohama Garland* be issued in a dust jacket that might offer an "advertising opportunity," Elmer Adler quickly squelched the idea. Dust jackets are "hard to make as dignified as a slip case," he explained, and offer "less protection than you might think." He steered Mason into ordering a slipcase for the book instead, which Adler claimed could be had for half the cost of a good jacket (Mason to Adler, 29 October 1926; Adler to Mason, 30 October 1926, PPP).

Bindings have always captured collectors' rapt attention. Lawrence Clark Powell, longtime director of the UCLA libraries, described the need he felt to see his own books every day: "Note that I said 'see' every day, not necessarily read. For next best to reading books is to sit at slippered ease and look at their backs. Each speaks in a different voice, each is fastened to my imagination by an invisible cord, and a mere glance nourishes me with the juice they hold. . . . Why should I waste the meager hours of my life staring at cinema or television, dealing in cards, fingering checker or chessman, when I can sit in the corner of my study and look with love at the backs of my books . . .?" (*Books in My Baggage,* 19–20).

42. Ege, "Decalog," 660–61.

43. Decoration usually meant silver or gold foil tooling. Dwiggins's design for the Lakeside edition of Poe's *Tales* included "lots of gold," for example. "I want to make the cover a gorgeous affair," he told Kittredge, "the person who gets the book wants to feel that he has in his hand a gift from the Rajah of Sakawak. The Tales warrant such opulence" (Dwiggins to Kittredge, 6 January 1927, KN).

44. Garnett, "Ideal Book," 117; Morris, *Ideal Book,* 72. Typically, a book's size is referred to in terms of its format, or the number and sequence of folds of a single "parent" sheet of paper that render the pages of a book. When a sheet is folded once it yields two leaves, or four pages, which is called a folio format. When a folio is folded in half again perpendicular to the first fold, the sheet yields four leaves and eight pages; this is called a quarto format. Succeeding folds create an octavo (eight leaves, sixteen pages), sexto-decimo (sixteen leaves, thirty-two pages), and so on. Because there is no universal standard size for parent sheets, however, format indicates only relative size.

45. R. Grabhorn, "Fine Printing," 97; E. Grabhorn, "Recollections," 80.

46. Garnett, "Ideal Book," 25; E. Grabhorn, *Fine Art of Printing,* 15; Firuski to Adler, 1 August 1925, PPP.

47. Rogers to John Henry Nash, in Carpenter, "BR to JHN," 36. Rogers's qualms must strike modern bibliophiles as ironic, because the Oxford Bible, published in 1935, is widely regarded not only as one of Rogers's masterpieces but also as one of the great bookmaking achievements in the twentieth century. Even when a designer determined to produce a book that could be both fine and functional for reading, the impulse toward significance through stature often prevailed. In planning the Lakeside edition of *Moby Dick,* William Kittredge reported to Rockwell Kent that the press management disliked Kent's plan to produce the book in three volumes, that they wished it to be a book "that one could with pleasure read in bed" (Kittredge to Kent, 9 December 1926, KN). The

book was in fact issued in three volumes, each measuring 11 1/2 by 8 1/2 inches, and each bearing a unique Kent title page — one of the features that made the edition so highly sought after.

48. Rollins, "Two Small Sets," 131; Rollins, "Survey of the Making of Books," 290. Rollins's qualms were less about large books per se than about books whose large, fine format was not warranted by the stature of its text. This was a recurring criticism of postwar fine books.

49. Cerf to Cecil Johnson, 3 October 1929, RHC; Dwiggins to Kittredge, 5 November 1926, KN.

50. Although three well-respected authoritative treatises on bookmaking provide no specific formulas or guidelines for determining optimal margins, their own pages sizes and foot margins averaged 13.1 percent of the pages' heights. The three sources consulted, and measured are: Lee, *Bookmaking*; *Chicago Manual of Style*; and Bringhurst, *Typographic Style*.

51. See Lee, *Bookmaking,* 91. Most determinations of these books' text type sizes are approximate, based on a measurement from the top of an ascender to the bottom of a descender in adjacent lowercase letters such as *ly*. This is the standard method of gauging the approximate size of type from its printed image. Similarly, calculations of leading are determined by measuring the distance in points from the baseline of one line of text to the baseline of the line below it.

52. Ibid., 93.

53. Friede, *Mechanical Angel,* 98–99.

54. Hazlitt, "In Dispraise of Fine Books," 559. Plenty of criticism was directed at particular editions as well, of course, but because those comments usually focused on the discord between a book's content and its design, they are discussed in Chapter 5.

55. Warde to William Kittredge, 2 June 1927, FWN; Lewis, "Field of Book Clubs," 665; Cheney, *Economic Survey,* 220.

Chapter 5. Classics or Cabbages?

1. Cerf to E. Grabhorn, 15 October 1928; Cerf to E. Grabhorn, 2 August 1928; Cerf to E. Grabhorn, telegram, 27 December 1928; Cerf to E. Grabhorn, 28 December 1928; E. Grabhorn to Cerf, telegram, 28 December 1928, RHC.

2. Cerf to E. Grabhorn, telegram, n.d. [late December 1928]; E. Grabhorn to Cerf, telegram, 9 January 1929, RHC.

3. See promotional literature in the Random House archives at Columbia University. "We have definitely set out to publish books of typographical interest," Cerf told James Johnson when he declined to publish Johnson's "Clown of the Cordilleras," "and we find ourselves with plenty of missionary work to do in this direction" (Cerf to Johnson, 3 December 1929, RHC). Warde to Will Ransom, 20 July 1928, FWN; Hart to Elmer Adler, 15 January 1930, PPP; Dill, "Ideal Book," 12.

4. Raymond, quoted by Bullen, "Open Letter," 724; Farquahar, "What's What"; Sadleir, "Limited Editions," 300; "Too Much Wisdom?" 668; "Growth of Limited Editions," 2756.

5. John Henry Nash produced an eight-page edition of Coolidge's speech for the

Pacific Coast chapter of the association. It measured 9 by 14 inches and was bound in blue boards with a white vellum back. Three copies were printed on vellum, including one presented to the president. The entire text was composed in italics, normally reserved for emphasis in modern typography. Nash, however, believed the speech to be "the most important expression ever given to the values of advertising," and therefore the text was italicized (O'Day, *Catalogue of Books,* 47).

6. Gregg Anderson, one of several aspiring young printers who apprenticed with the Grabhorns in the twenties, fondly recalled such dialogue in the shop (quoted in Wentz, *Grabhorn Press,* 44).

7. Warde, "George Macy," 36, quoted in Badaracco, *Trading Words,* 157; Macy, *Limited Editions Club,* 10.

8. Powell, *Books in My Baggage,* 53. Roughly a third of the 300 sample editions can be considered classics.

9. Rogers, *Pi,* 144–45. In several instances, content was selected explicitly for its ability to display some special typographic feature. When Joseph Blumenthal returned from Europe in 1932 with a thousand pounds of a new typeface of his own design, he chose to publish Emerson's essay *Nature* to debut the type—which soon bore the name of Emerson in honor of its inaugural use. He selected the essay, Blumenthal admitted, largely for its "long unbroken paragraphs that would show the type to best advantage" (*Typographic Years,* 58). Likewise, the Grabhorns sought a medieval text to use their new supply of Rudolph Koch's Bibel Gothic type, finally settling on *The Voiage of Maundevile* to showcase the distinctive type (Wentz, *Grabhorn Press,* 45). This inverted editorial process sometimes occurred with contemporary texts as well, as when Elmer Adler sought to produce a special edition of Katherine Mansfield's short stories because they offered an "exceptional opportunity of demonstrating the new Centaur type" soon to be available in Monotype (Adler to the Lanston Monotype Company, 30 August 1927, PPP).

10. Cerf to Adler, 12 December 1927, RHC. *Jekyll and Hyde* was the only title from this list that Random House in fact published. Rogers's Homer was produced for another publisher, Updike and Cleland became absorbed in other projects, and the Conrad novel was published by Crosby Gaige. Because Random House, like its clients, cared less about specific titles per se than about their production, Cerf felt no particular attachment to the titles considered, and he happily accommodated designers' other selections.

11. Cerf to Klopfer, 24 May 1930, RHC.

12. Cerf to Grabhorn, 13 May 1929, 21 October 1929, RHC.

13. Klopfer to E. Grabhorn, 19 May 1930; Cerf to E. Grabhorn, 4 August 1930, RHC. On 11 July Cerf had suggested to Grabhorn that they might "think of some smaller thing for next spring, a sort of filler between *Leaves of Grass* and another pretentious project."

14. Cerf to E. Grabhorn, 5 December 1930, 18 November 1932, RHC.

15. Cerf, "Reminiscences," 197.

16. Adler to Dwiggins, 1 June 1925, PPP; Dwiggins to Adler, 27 July 1925, PPP. Dwiggins had proposed a less "exploitive" approach, a series of short, straightforward ("NO FRILLS!" he insisted) monographs on premier designers that largely skirted commercial work and offered "a permanent and dignified *record* of a man's work, rather than an advertisement"(Dwiggins to Adler, 26 June, 1925, PPP). Adler promptly concurred. He

insisted that his aim was to "give the world an opportunity to find in one place a representative collection of these artists' work" and "to make some beautiful books." He worried a bit only about finding subjects "who would properly fit into such a group," tentatively considering Bruce Rogers, Rudolph Ruzicka, Allen Lewis, Rockwell Kent, and Rene Clark in addition to Cleland and Dwiggins.

17. Dwiggins to Kittredge, 20 September 1926, KN.

18. Ibid.; Dwiggins to Klopfer 29 April 1929; Klopfer to Dwiggins, 30 April 1929, RHC.

19. Kittredge to Kent, 8 January 1929, 28 March 1929; Kent to Kittredge, 4 November 1929, KN. Kent was in extraordinary demand in the late twenties. He agreed to illustrate an ambitious set of ten classics (the Iliad, the Odyssey, *Hamlet, King Lear, Faust,* Dante's *Inferno,* and "the finer books of the Bible") for Covici-Friede, but Elmer Adler balked at working with the publishers, perhaps because they specialized in mildly erotic material, and the series never materialized (Kent to Adler, 22 May 1929, PPP).

20. Elmer Adler — an ardent and knowledgeable art collector — recognized the importance of illustration early on, and always sought to incorporate art into books made by the Pynson Printers. Even when a book's budget precluded formal illustration, he turned to decorative or pictorial ornamentation, as with *Music at Night* or *Trivial Breath,* or attempted to provide a small drawing or two himself. In 1925, for example, Adler was reluctant to "bother" Rockwell Kent for a title page drawing for the Dunster House edition of *Nobodaddy* because the publisher could pay only one hundred dollars for it. Consequently, he came up with one himself and sent it to publisher Maurice Firuski for approval. Firuski replied simply that "your drawing makes me feel that the quality of New York gin is not terribly good," and suggested that Dwiggins would make an admirable second choice (Firuski to Adler, 5 August 1925, PPP). Adler complied without further mention of his own drawing, though noting that "it will require a contribution of a certain amount of good nature on [Dwiggins's] part to get him to carry it through" (Adler to Firuski, 7 August 1925, PPP). Dwiggins rendered the drawing for the fee named, and all parties seemed pleased with the resulting book.

21. E. Grabhorn, "Recollections," 56–57. Much of the long delay in the book's production has traditionally been blamed on this "discovery" that Lutetia was ill-suited for Whitman's poetry. The Grabhorns' tale of buying, then rejecting, this type for the Whitman edition is well known, often repeated in Grabhorn literature. It appears as early as 1933 in Ed Grabhorn's essay *The Fine Art of Printing.* He described his frustration in having composed "one thousand pounds of bright new type" that just "didn't look right." The account implies that the Grabhorns had been unfamiliar with Lutetia before investing significant money and time in it. However, they had printed books composed in Lutetia as early as 1927.

22. Angelo, "Art and Books," 102.

23. R. Grabhorn, "Fine Printing," 92.

24. Cheney, *Economic Survey,* 91–92; Johnston, *Biblio-Typographica,* 325.

25. Gaige, *Footlights and Highlights,* 201. See also Gunn, "Gaige Imprint," 1471–73.

26. Gaige, *Footlight and Highlights,* 203, 211.

27. Lewis, "How Not to Be a Publisher," 55; Lewis to Cerf, 21 May 1929, RHC. Of the eight titles that Westgate published in its two-year existence, however, only the first five

adhered to this editorial course. The final three books were reprints of historical material, two related to nineteenth-century California and one edition of *Robyn Hode and His Meiny,* in the archaic typographic vein of earlier Grabhorn productions like the *Voiage of Maundevile.*

28. R. Grabhorn, "Fine Printing," 26.

29. Adler to Canby, 30 July 1930, PPNY. Canby declined to write the article, pleading health concerns and a busy schedule.

30. Cerf to Gaige, 21 January 1928, RHC.

31. Cerf to Gaige, 19 April 1928, RHC.

32. Gaige, *Footlights and Highlights,* 204–205.

33. Cerf to Gaige, 8 August 1928, RHC. Five weeks later Cerf notified Gaige that more than one hundred copies had been returned because it was only a reprint. He regarded the books as unsalable since the "fiasco" and wished to return them to Gaige (17 September 1928, RHC).

34. Random House, open letter to booksellers, 14 February 1929; Klopfer to Wells, 5 April 1929; Cerf to Wells, 12 August 1929, RHC. On the Hardy fiasco, see Cerf to Wells, 23 January 1930; Klopfer to Wells, 3 March 1930, RHC.

35. Cerf to Gaige, 18 October 1928; Cerf to Wells, 22 November 1928, RHC. Cerf did not clarify his reasons for objecting to these particular authors. Most likely he considered them "difficult" — unreliable and demanding — or not sufficiently well known or critically acclaimed to warrant fine editions. Sales figures are not available for Gaige editions of the authors Cerf prohibited.

36. Cerf to Wells, 15 March, 21 June, and 26 July 1929, RHC. Wells and his partner Elbridge Adams protested, of course, particularly the assessment of the Symons book, which Adams considered "a very extraordinary human document." He continued testily, "When I compare it with some of the books which you have accepted, like [James Joyce's] 'Anna Livia Plurabelle' and [Philip Guedalla's] 'Bonnet and Shawl,' . . . I wonder if your literary taste has not undergone a decided change in the last few months" (Adams to Cerf, 31 July 1929, RHC). Fountain did publish the book, but not in a fine edition.

37. Cerf to Wells, 4 October 1929; Wells to Cerf, 7 October 1929, RHC.

38. MacLeish to Firuski, 28 October and 1 December 1925, in *Letters,* 172–73.

39. Knopf, *Portrait of a Publisher,* 1:16–17; Benét to Stimson, 8 March 1928, PPP; MacLeish to Firuski, 27 February 1926, in *Letters,* 177–78.

40. Updike to Cerf, 15 February 1929; Cerf to Updike, 12 March 1929; Holloway to Cerf, 17 January 1928, RHC.

41. Cather to Adler, 2 March 1923, PPP; Adler to Knopf, 3 June 1927, EAP; McGann, *Black Riders,* 20, 74.

42. Rogers, *Paragraphs on Printing,* 131.

43. Richardson to Cerf, 1 December 1928, RHC.

44. Leonard to Adler, 7 August 1933; Klopfer to Leonard, 20 June 1930, PPP.

45. Rollins, *SRL,* 31 December 1927; Blumenthal, *Typographic Years,* 15; Johnston, *Biblio-Typographica,* 235. Of the titles Johnston lists, no more than 2 fine editions had been produced for general sale. In addition to the Bible, source of 7 of the 300 sample editions, nineteen authors are represented by 3 or more editions. Of these authors, only seven had died before the 1920s: Voltaire, Washington Irving, Ben Franklin, and Nathaniel Hawthorne with 3 editions of their work; Walt Whitman with 4; Edgar Allan Poe with

5; and Robert Louis Stevenson with 6. Living authors with 3 or more fine editions included: Virginia Woolf, Willa Cather, Robert Frost, Norman Douglas, John Drinkwater, Rockwell Kent, and James Stephens with 3 each; James Branch Cabell, Aldous Huxley, Edwin Arlington Robinson, and Christopher Morley with 4; and George Moore with 6. Thirty-two additional writers, nineteen of whom were still living, were represented by 2 fine editions of their work.

46. Cerf to Wells, 30 January 1929, RHC. Fountain did publish *Homage to Meleager* but apparently not in a fine edition. Random House was not listed as its distributor.

47. Cerf to Leventhal, 3 December 1929; Leventhal to Cerf, 2 January 1930, RHC. This fine edition of *Trade Winds* was never published. According to the National Union Catalog, about seventeen sets of galley proofs were pulled and a few of them distributed, perhaps to gauge interest in the title, before the type was distributed and the project abandoned.

48. Stephens to Wells, 19 October 1927, in *Letters*, 358. Of the 300 sample editions, 39 consist of fewer than twenty pages of text.

49. Cerf to Wells, 13 September 1929, RHC. The fifteen-page book was published in 1930 and sold for ten dollars.

50. Adler to Rockwell Kent, 30 July 1928, PPP. In fact the fine edition of Wilder's *Bridge* was widely acclaimed for its exemplary bookmaking and illustration, which most critics applauded as a worthy complement to (not compensation for, as Adler anticipated) the text's merit. Illustration also helped to bolster the Fountain Press publication of A. A. Milne's story "When We Were Very Young." As Wells explained to Adler, "The Ms. such as it is . . . came in from Milne today [and] it looks as though there was enough text to make at least 32 pages of text matter. That, in addition to the illustrations, should make a book of almost respectable size" (9 August 1929, PPNY).

51. McFarland, "What Is Fine Printing?" 257. Another critic pronounced the fine editions of George Moore's books, designed by Bruce Rogers, "pompous" and "not friendly." He observed that their "ostentatiously hand-made paper and an unbending format tend to keep the reader at a distance. They are uncomfortable books, rather snobbish and, perhaps, a little meretricious" (Jackson, *Printing of Books,* 119).

52. E. Grabhorn, "Recollections," 43; Magee, "Bookselling and Creating Books," 13.

53. Quoted in Barr, *Presses of Northern California,* 75. Fine books for Nash were typically little more than typographic pictures. Several of the sample fine editions I examined for this study, originally belonging to Nash and now in the Bancroft Library at the University of California at Berkeley, remain unopened to this day. He had purchased or more likely received the books as gifts from other printers, but neither he nor anyone else cut apart the folded edges of the text pages; most have been opened only to reveal the title page and the colophon page. See, for example, the Bancroft Library's copies of Cheshire House editions of *The Scarlet Letter, Shakespeare's Sonnets,* and *Through the Looking Glass,* and *Night and Moonlight,* designed by Bruce Rogers.

54. Adler to Cerf, 2 May 1928, PPP.

55. Within the bibliophilic community, the most common and insightful criticisms addressed the larger typographic approach, asserting that the package was not suited to the material it presented. Except for complaints about "overdone" texts or authors, considerations rooted in textual matters per se were usually secondary.

56. The subordinate status of the text's legibility and accessibility similarly prompted

book dealer and Whitman specialist Alfred Goldsmith to decline to write the foreword to the Random House edition of *Leaves of Grass*. He observed that the book's price alone ($100) was prohibitive for those interested primarily in the text. "Instead of a fine edition of *Leaves of Grass*," he protested to Cerf, "you're publishing a magnificent specimen of printing and bookmaking" (Goldsmith to Cerf, 11 June 1929, RHC).

57. See Cowley, ed., *After the Genteel Tradition,* and Jones and Ludwig, *Guide to American Literature and Its Backgrounds*. See also Santayana, *The Genteel Tradition;* Sedgwick, "American Genteel Tradition."

58. Poetry and drama constitute 102 titles, or 34 percent, of the 300 sample editions, and another 10 percent (30 titles) are editions of essays. Only 10 percent of the sample are novels, and four-fifths of those are reprints. The best comprehensive compilation of trade book production by category is the study conducted by Palmer O'Hara and summarized in "Book Titles Published by Classes in the United States, 1880–1927," 276–77. He identifies an annual average of 730 poetry and drama titles published from 1920 through 1927; this compares to an annual average of 7,456 total titles published during the same period, according to John Tebbel's analysis (appendix A, *History of Book Publishing,* 3:681). For figures of trade fiction output compiled from annual *Publishers' Weekly* summaries, see Tebbel, ibid., 683.

59. See Connett, *Decade of American Sporting Books,* and Siegel, Marschalk, Jr., and Oelgart, *Derrydale Press*. Also pointing to the elite nature of postwar fine editions are the fifteen sample titles about printing and books themselves, ranging from reprints of classics such as Albrecht Dürer's sixteenth-century treatise on *The Construction of Roman Letters* to new historical studies of typography by or about well-known contemporaries such as Updike and Rogers.

60. Literary modernism encompassed a broad range of beliefs and styles, of course. Even so, a distinct strain of modernist thought shared significant ideological features with postwar fine book production. See, for example, Bradbury and McFarlane, eds., *Modernism,* especially chapter 1, "The Name and Nature of Modernism."

61. Rainey, "Price of Modernism," 114–15.

62. Aiken to Firuski, 15 February 1922, quoted in ibid., 116.

63. Eliot to Firuski, 26 February 1922, quoted in ibid., 117.

64. Ibid., 119–20, 119, 118. Dunster House did not publish a fine edition of *The Waste Land;* as Firuski tarried in his reply to Eliot, Liveright vigorously pursued the contract to publish a trade edition of the heralded work. Some ten months after Liveright's edition appeared in early 1923, Leonard and Virginia Woolf's Hogarth Press brought out a belated limited edition of the poem.

65. Friede, *Mechanical Angel,* 84, 98. Brown House advertisement, *SRL,* 19 April 1930, 976.

66. Friede, *Mechanical Angel,* 77. Of the several sample editions characterized here as "polite erotica," all are illustrated. Not all bibliophiles appreciated this vein of work; one woman returned her copy of *Song of Solomon,* designed by Adler and illustrated with some nudity by Wharton Esherick, because the friend she had intended to give it to was "far too conservative to . . . appreciate the cover and illustrations" (Jane Clark to Adler, 30 January 1929, EAP).

67. Cheney, *Economic Survey,* 94; Friede, *Mechanical Angel,* 94. Horace Liveright and

Covici-Friede, leading foes of postwar censorship, gained notoriety for publishing risqué titles in fine editions.

68. "Are the Classics Dying Out?" 574. See also, for example, Hazlitt, "Who Reads the Classics Now?" 449–51.

69. Tebbel, *History of Book Publishing,* 3:681.

70. Gaige, *Footlights and Highlights,* 211; R. Grabhorn, "Fine Printing," 82. Roughly 30 percent (31) of the 108 sample classics were written by seventeen American authors, while thirty-two English authors accounted for 35 of the classic editions. Thirteen of the "classic" editions were written by nine French authors; 6 were the work of a single Scotsman, Robert Louis Stevenson; 5 were by Italians, all Renaissance writers; 12 dated from ancient times; and Germany and Russia were represented by one author each.

71. Blumenthal, *Typographic Years,* 89–90; Cerf to Blumenthal, 17 January 1930, RHC. Blumenthal's editorial intentions are described in a series of letters written between 1928 and 1930 to Cerf, whom he kept well informed because Random House was the exclusive distributor for Spiral Press books. A desire to take American literary history seriously extended to minor work as well. Elmer Adler, who generally left Random House editorial selection to Cerf and Klopfer, urged that they publish a few American titles significant for their historical interest, including Whitman's early *Franklin Evans* and his own pet project, *A Narrative of the Life of Mary Jemison,* an 1823 account of a white woman captured by Indians. Adler bristled when Cerf tentatively grouped the books under the rubric "Curiosities of American Literature," suggesting instead the more dignified "Random House Reprints of Americana Classics" (Adler to Cerf, 18 October 1929, RHC).

72. Littell to William Kittredge, 17 January 1930, KN. Littell excluded poetry from his notion of what he felt Lakeside patrons "would be glad to sit down at night and read for amusement."

73. Badaracco, *American Culture and the Marketplace,* 32, 65. When Kittredge wrote to Edward O. Wilson about illustrating a book for the series, he explained that the book "should be handled from the point of view of 'the exquisite thing' and done with a good deal of finesse" (9 April 1926, KN). Wilson apparently did not understand the American theme. He felt that *Robinson Crusoe* should have been an option (Badaracco, *American Culture and the Marketplace,* 34).

74. Of the ninety-six American edition authors, all were evidently white, and only fifteen (16 percent) were women. Overall, of the 168 sample books written by non-American authors, 111 (66 percent) have British authors (sixty-four English, one Welsh, five Irish, and three Scots). The rest of Europe is represented by 28 titles written by twenty-four authors (eleven French, five Italian, three Russian, two German, two Spanish, and one Polish). The only non-European authors are medieval Persian poet Omar Khayyam and seven classical or ancient writers (including the Bible as a single composite "author").

75. Ruzicka to Kittredge, 3 February 1929, KN; Rollins, "Survey of the Making of Books," 290.

76. When bookseller Gabriel Wells published *A Noble Fragment* in 1920, with an introductory essay by E. Alfred Newton, only six of the forty-two extant copies of the Gutenberg Bible were located in America. Three were owned by J. Pierpont Morgan, one

by the General Theological Seminary in New York, one by the New York Public Library, and Henry Huntington had purchased one in 1911 for fifty thousand dollars, then the highest price ever paid for a book. See Norman, *Anniversary Pictorial Census*. The featured leaves were seldom bound into the book, both because they had been severed along the fold through which it would have to be sewn and because they were often later removed from the book and framed separately. This practice elicited some qualms from those who regarded the breakdown of a book into leaves as a violation of its integrity, which in turn diminished the beauty and significance of the isolated part. Beatrice Warde, for instance, confessed: "I always suspect the typographic enthusiast who takes a printed page from a book and frames it to hang on the wall, for I believe that in order to gratify a sensory delight, he had mutilated something infinitely more important" ("Printing Should Be Invisible," 112).

77. Henry Lewis Bullen, *Nicholas Jenson, Printer of Venice* (San Francisco: John Henry Nash, 1926); George Parker Winship, *The First American Bible*; a leaf from a copy of the Bible translated into the English language by John Eliot and printed at Cambridge in New England in the year 1663 (Boston: Goodspeed, 1929); Robert R. Dearden, Jr., and Douglas S. Watson, *An Original Leaf from the Bible of the Revolution and an Essay Concerning It* (San Francisco: John Howell, 1930); and John Henry Nash, ed., *Cobden-Sanderson and the Doves Press . . .* (San Francisco: John Henry Nash, 1929).

78. Fine editions devoted to reprint or facsimile editions of historical journeys include *The True Travells, Adventures and Observations of Captaine John Smith* (New York: Rimington and Hooper, 1930); Samuel Damon, *A Journey to Lower Oregon & Upper California, 1848–49* (San Francisco: John J. Newbegin, 1927); *Robbins Journal, Comprising an Account of the Loss of the Brig Commerce of Hartford* (Greenwich, Conn.: Conde Nast Press, 1931); and *Relation that Alvar Nuñez Cabeça de Vaca Gave of What Befel the Armament in the Indias . . .* (San Francisco: Grabhorn Press, 1929). Fine editions that offered facsimiles of historical documents, title pages, and so on, may also be linked directly to the interests of collectors; like leaf books, they in effect "shared" rare items owned by one collector. Stevenson's *Baby Book* is a good example; after San Francisco book dealer John Howell acquired the unique item, he commissioned John Henry Nash to produce a facsimile edition so that the many other collectors (located primarily in California) who shared his keen interest in Stevenson could enjoy the unusual materials he had acquired.

79. Rollins, review of *Relation of Cabeça de Vaca* (Grabhorn Press, 1929), *SRL*, 14 December 1929, 577.

Chapter 6. For the Joy of Doing

1. Pollard, "Trained Printer and the Amateur," 188–89.

2. Pynson Printers Announcement, 20 March 1922, reprinted in Johnston, "Adler," 1184; Garnett, "Printer's Note," *That Endeth Never*, reprinted in *Documentary History*, 104–105. Emphasis in the original.

3. Announcement in Johnston, "Adler," 1184; quoted in E. O'Day, *Nash*, 8–9. Others regarded Garnett as an ideological mouthpiece, able to express what their own professional conditions prevented them from asserting. Although Monotype publicist Beatrice

Warde, for example, was professionally obliged to decry the elitist implications of much fine printing ideology, she praised Garnett's elitist work at the Laboratory Press as the "lively leaven that counts enormously in our industry-ridden country" (Warde to Garnett, March 1928, LPC).

4. Rimington, "Ellis," 2211; Kittredge to Will Ransom, 7 January 1941, KN; E. Grabhorn, "Recollections," 26; Farquhar, "Comments," 91. See also Magee, "Bookselling and Creating Books," 42–43. Apart from this stressful interlude, the press's correspondence and business affairs were watched over by Oscar Lewis. He and others recounted with relish that the press's business was conducted from the proverbial "smallest room in the house," altered only to provide Lewis with a more dignified chair. The room's old clawfoot bathtub served as an open and fairly handy filing cabinet, "filled to overflowing with letters, bills, etcetera" (Magee and Heller, *Bibliography*, 64).

5. Quoted in Johnston, "Adler," 1184; Adler to Calkins, 16 December 1925, PPP; Cerf, *At Random*, 61. Adler enjoyed elite company in his budgetary defiance; Alfred Knopf recalled that when he invited Bruce Rogers to make a book "all [his] own way" for Knopf on the single condition that he inform Knopf in advance what it would cost, Rogers replied, "that's the one thing I could never tell you" (Knopf, *Portrait*, 15).

6. E. Grabhorn, "Recollections," 25.

7. Ibid., 75; E. Grabhorn to Random House, 31 March 1928, RHC. The books arrived in late July.

8. Wentz, *Grabhorn Press*, 54; Cerf, "Reminiscences," 199; Hart, *Fine Printing*, 28.

9. Warde to Kittredge, 2 June 1927, KN.

10. Adler to Cerf, 28 August 1929, RHC.

11. Johnston, "Adler," 1189; Ransom, *Private Presses*, 159. As an accountant pointed out in the shop's first year-end report, profits appeared in the significant discrepancy between labor charges billed ($2,167.26 in October 1922, for example) and wages and salaries actually paid ($1,037.26 for the same month) (Edward E. Knopping to Adler, 15 November 1922, PPP).

12. Magee, "Bookselling and Creating Books," 41. An especially acrimonious example is the dispute in 1930 with George Macy, director of the then-new Limited Editions Club. The Grabhorn Press had been enlisted to produce *Robinson Crusoe,* illustrated by Edward Wilson in New York, for ten thousand dollars. This figure was explicitly meant to cover the full costs of manufacture, as Macy reiterated throughout correspondence concerning charges for illustration plates, totaling some eighteen hundred dollars, which the club paid directly. When Grabhorn submitted a bill for ten thousand, and Macy paid only eighty-two hundred, he was livid. Macy made scrupulous efforts to explain the situation: "You intended to produce a book for us, at a profit to yourself, for less than $10,000. In order to do an even better job of it, you took a loss. Possibly other business will even this up for you. But . . . we must . . . stick to our budget, and buy the best books possible within its limits." This explanation, however, did nothing to assuage Grabhorn's fury. He refused to deal with the Limited Editions Club again, permanently alienating the press from the best-known bibliophilic organizations of the succeeding decades (Macy to E. Grabhorn, 5 November 1930, GPC).

13. E. Grabhorn, "Recollections," 49. Although the book was eventually set in Goudy Newstyle, a type they already owned, Grabhorn spent most of Cerf's advance payment on

a thousand pounds of new Lutetia, ordered from Europe, which he later decided did not suit Whitman's poems. Perhaps Grabhorn felt that Cerf should absorb the expense of this costly misjudgment.

14. Cerf to E. Grabhorn, 4 August 1930, RHC.

15. Klopfer to Kent, 11 February 1929, RHC.

16. Adler to C. C. Ronalds, 12 January 1927, PPP, emphasis added; Cerf to Friede, 9 October 1930, BCC; Cerf to Alfred F. Goldsmith, 19 January 1928, BCC.

17. Cerf, "Reminiscences," 196. "Distinction, not profit, was what we were looking for," Cerf insisted in retrospect (176).

18. Cerf to Grabhorn, 2 August 1928, 13 February 1929, RHC.

19. Cheney, *Economic Survey,* 188.

20. Johnston, "Fine Books in the Present Market," 950; Bruce Rogers, *Pi,* 115; Bulletin regarding "Current Prices," April 1931, RHC.

21. Wells to Adler, 9 August 1929, PPNY.

22. Howell, "Two San Francisco Bookmen," 23; Adler to Cerf, 23 June 1931; Random House to Rimington and Hooper, 9 December 1927, RHC.

23. Cheney, *Economic Survey,* 189; Kaestle, *Literacy in the United States,* 296. Cheney's figures are calculated before the so-called paperback revolution of the late 1930s, so the books referred to were typically bound in boards, covered with cloth or paper. They were, however, primarily new titles; reprint editions of previously published work (more comparable to the contents of many fine editions) were commonly priced at about one dollar.

24. Cheney, *Economic Survey,* 273.

25. Cerf to Gaige [1927], RHC. Although this statement clearly serves Cerf's interests more than Gaige's, his remarks about distribution risks were warranted. Delinquent accounts were a constant headache for Random House, the "most disagreeable feature of the publishing business" (Cerf to Charles A. Johnson, 17 September 1928, RHC).

26. Wells to Cerf, 21 June 1929; Cerf to Wells, 28 June 1929, RHC. The initial plan for *Candide* is detailed in a letter from Adler to Cerf, 1 February 1927, PPP.

27. Rudge to Sargent, 8 October 1926; 1 November 1926; 31 January 1927. Sargent Papers, NYPL.

28. Cheney, *Economic Survey,* 204–5. Of the 64 sample editions published that year, the 22 fiction titles averaged an edition of 804 copies, while the 21 nonfiction titles averaged 614 copies.

29. Rollins to Frederick Allen Whiting, 26 July 1927, CPRY; R. Grabhorn, "Fine Printing," 37.

30. R. Grabhorn, "Fine Printing," 85; Magee, "Bookselling and Creating Books," 37; R. Grabhorn, "Fine Printing," 26. In fact, although the Grabhorns coveted soaring retail prices, of the twenty-seven books printed by the Grabhorn Press in the 1920s that were offered for sale to the public, only seven were titles they published themselves. The remaining twenty were commissioned by other publishers, who gave them broad latitude in design matters, although usually with some budget parameters. Another fifteen books were produced for the Book Club of California, which sold books to its members for roughly 10 percent above what the Grabhorns received. This arrangement cut out the publisher's role, leaving both producer and consumers with a satisfied sense that the monies paid went into the right hands.

31. Cheney, *Economic Survey,* 140. Any rate higher than 10 percent of retail on the first five thousand copies or so was "unsafe," he warned, unless the author was particularly well known.

32. Gaige, *Footlights and Highlights,* 203. He also lavished this "extremely advantageous" advance offer on Lytton Strachey for his *Elizabeth and Essex* (204).

33. R. Grabhorn, "Fine Printing," 26.

34. Cerf to Gaige [1927], RHC.

35. Of the sample books whose production costs are known, one — *The Palette Knife,* printed by the Pynson Printers — registered an even smaller ratio of only 30 percent. This reflects only Adler's charges of three dollars per book for its manufacture, however; because the costs of René Gockinga's original watercolor illustrations are not included, the book's true manufacturing costs were certainly much higher than that modest proportion suggests.

36. Cerf to Gaige, 11 February 1928. RHC.

37. Duffus, *Books,* 42.

38. Adler to W. A. White, 4 November 1925, EAP.

39. Duffus, *Books,* 42.

40. The Grabhorns occasionally executed bindings in their own shop, incorporating labor and materials costs into their charges.

41. McDonald, "Reminiscences of the Grabhorn Press," 28; Glick, *Rudge,* 22. Pynson Printers figures are derived from bank statements and canceled checks for July 1929, PPP.

42. Adler to Altschul, 21 June 1928, Altschul Papers; Johnston, "Adler," 1189. Emphasis added.

43. Dwiggins to Adler, 16 August 1928, PPP.

44. Cheney, *Economic Survey,* 263.

45. Zeitlin, "Developing Interest," 2422; Ziglatzki to Elmer Adler, 13 November 1929, PPNY.

46. Adler to Harry Oppenheimer, 14 September 1929. PPNY.

47. Nash's "Librarian," to Frank Altschul, 28 April 1927, JHNC.

48. Blumenthal to Klopfer, 2 April 1929; E. Leeds to Random House, 6 April 1929; E. B. Fybush to Random House, 16 December 1930, RHC. Adler to Daniel Longwell, 31 August 1926, PPP.

49. Cerf to Adams, 4 August 1930, RHC.

50. The reviews appeared in *The New Republic,* 4 August 1926, 317; the New York *World Book World,* 5 September 1926, 4; and the *Independent,* 25 September 1926, 361. See Duke, *Cabell.*

51. Zeitlin, "Developing Interest," 2422; Adler to Blanche Knopf, 12 November 1930, EAP.

52. Zeitlin, "Developing Interest," 2422.

53. Jester to Adler, 13 January 1927; Adler to Mason, 8 February 1927, PPP; Zeitlin, "Developing Interest," 2422.

54. Dwiggins, "Investigation," 147; Rollins, "The Colophon," *SRL,* 12 April 1930; "About Colophons," *SRL,* 27 July 1929, 332.

55. Kittredge, "Better Printing," 108. Kittredge's good friend Frederic Warde expressed the cynical flip side to this growing enthusiasm for typographic celebrities. With not a

little jealousy, he remarked that he wished he could "become a definite personality and sling off beautiful books with my left hand and tell the world that such books are exceedingly efficacious stomachics for the typographical and printing appetites" (Warde to Kittredge, 2 June 1927, FWN). While the inclusion of their logos was to some extent historically authentic — for centuries printers had prominently featured their pressmarks in their books — the original purposes no longer pertained. In the past, when a book's printer was commonly also its publisher or retail seller, the mark alerted customers to where the book could be purchased and helped guide illiterate shippers to the printer's address.

56. Rogers once called the *Peronnik* colophon "the most immodest imprint I've ever put on a book" (*Paragraphs on Printing*, 113).

57. Rollins, "Books as Art," *SRL*, 26 November 1927, 359.

58. Warde to Kittredge [late 1921], KN.

59. Kennerley to Sargent, 2 November 1927, Sargent Papers; Morison to Updike, 2 March 1926, in McKitterick, ed., *Selected Correspondence*, 150; Warde, "Letter of Introduction" to Haas, ed., *Rogers Bibliography*, 4.

60. "Stelle" to George M. Sargent, 24 March 1929, Sargent Papers. Ninety-one of the sample editions were signed by their authors — including Moore, Virginia Woolf, Robert Frost, Theodore Dreiser, Willa Cather, and many other contemporary writers. The value of an author's signature is suggested by the difference in price between signed and unsigned copies of the same edition. Nine of the sample editions were sold in both versions: Christopher Morley's *Born in a Beer Garden* cost $7.50 unsigned but $20 signed; James Stephens's *On Prose and Verse* cost $10 and $35, respectively; James Joyce's *Haveth Childers Everywhere* was offered at $20 or $40; and so on.

61. Cerf to Holloway, 2 October 1929, RHC; Leonard to Donald Klopfer, 29 June 1930, RHC. Twenty-five of the sample editions featured their illustrator's signature; ten were also signed by the author. Those not signed by the author were almost always texts whose authors were dead.

62. Lewis, "How Not to Be a Publisher," 55.

63. Friede, *Mechanical Angel*, 75.

64. Wells to Klopfer, 3 April 1929; Klopfer to Wells, 5 April 1929; RHC.

65. Rimington to Adler, 28 November 1927, EAP; Rimington to Cerf, 29 November 1927; Macy to Cerf, n.d. [early November 1930], RHC.

66. Kittredge to Kent, 27 September 1930, KN. See Shaddy, " 'A Mad World, My Masters,' " whose appendix profiles prominent collectors, many of whom bought contemporary fine printing.

67. See *Carteret Book Club Register; Grolier 75; Members of the Grolier Club;* Piehl, *Caxton Club*. See also *Private Book Collectors;* Dickinson, *Dictionary of Book Collectors;* and Shaddy, "Mad World," appendix.

68. Howell, "Two San Francisco Bookmen," 15. Ward Ritchie recounted that Los Angeles fine booksellers were located where "doctors, lawyers, and business men" would "loiter and reconnoiter" in the shops after lunching at their clubs ("Forgotten Street of Books," 51).

69. Description of "A Toast to the Ladies" (1927), JHNC.

70. Harlan, *Nash*, 83.

71. Johnston, "Fine Books in the Present Market," 952.

72. No significant archival evidence supports the notion that fine publishers sought to sell books to libraries. Virtually all fine books seem to have been sold to individuals, most commonly through retail book dealers, rather than to institutions.

73. Untitled, undated (but late 1920s) clientele list, JHNC.

Chapter 7: Too Many Fine Books

1. Mumford, *American Taste,* 22.

2. Cerf, *At Random,* 77; Tebbel, *History of Book Publishing,* 3:168; Cerf to E. Grabhorn, 26 November 1929, RHC; Cerf to Klopfer, 28 May 1930, BCC.

3. Johnston, "Fine Books in the Present Market," 952, 951.

4. Friede, *Mechanical Angel,* 109.

5. Cerf to E. Grabhorn, 11 May 1931, 18 November 1932, RHC; Friede, *Mechanical Angel,* 100; Lebergott, *Pursuing Happiness,* 209.

6. Cerf, *At Random,* 78.

7. Friede, *Mechanical Angel,* 240, 238. The Golden Cockerel Press was a British fine press whose work was distributed in the United States by Random House.

8. According to Harlan, for Nash the 1930s was a decade of "depression and decline." See *Nash,* chap. 5.

9. See Glick, *Rudge,* 65–69; Harrington, *Praise Past Due,* 24–25.

10. Rollins to Fred Whiting, 16 March 1943, CPRY. See the notes Paul A. Bennett gathered for a biography of Warde, housed in the uncatalogued Warde Papers at the Grolier Club. For a sympathetic and perceptive eulogy, see Will Ransom's "Warde," 27–37.

11. Johnston, "Fine Books in the Present Market," 952.

12. Garnett, "Printer's Note," in Flanner, *That Endeth Never.*

13. Harlan, *Nash,* 71, 67, and chap. 4, *passim.*

14. R. Grabhorn, "Fine Printing," 46. On one occasion, a prominent San Francisco family hired the Grabhorns to produce a book-length version of the newspaper account of their son's heroic play in the Stanford–University of California football game.

15. Howell, "Two San Francisco Bookmen," 9; Knopf to Adler, 5 May 1955, EAP. Bob Grabhorn admitted that they printed plenty of "terrible" poetry for hire, but they did occasionally turn away such authors. The brothers once intended to discourage a man bearing a manuscript of his own poetry by referring him across town to Nash, whose exorbitant fees were notorious. When the book appeared in print some months later, the Grabhorns snidely speculated that Nash had told the man the job would cost him $10,000 (three times a typical college professor's annual salary at the time), and that he had promptly replied, "Fine. Do you want a deposit?" (R. Grabhorn, "Fine Printing," 24).

16. Nash, "Address before the San Francisco Advertising Club, May 7, 1925," unpublished typescript, JHNC, 21. The following year Nash charged Clark $15,500 for his Christmas book.

17. Hemingway, "American Bohemians in Paris," in *By-Line,* 23.

18. Hart, *Fine Printing,* 23.

19. Nash, prospectus for *Biblia Sacra* (Sancti Francisci: Ioanne Henrico Nash, 1932).

20. Nash to Mrs. Doheny, 27 July 1931, quoted in Harlan, *Chapter Nine,* 60.

21. Rollins, "Not All Lambs Are in Wall Street," *SRL,* 29 May 1929; Rollins, "On Advertisements," *SRL,* 30 June 1928, 1011. Warde to Kittredge, 25 November 1926, FWN.

22. Rollins, *SRL,* 28 December 1929, 611; Rollins, "A Poor Thing," *SRL,* 9 June 1928, 957.

23. See Morrow ad in *SRL,* 21 September 1929, 172; Knopf quoted in John Winterich to Elmer Adler, 13 October 1931, PPNY.

24. Claire Badaracco describes Macy as "a P. T. Barnum in Kelmscott clothing." She characterizes him as a publisher with a "zeal for packaging and marketing skills that did not extend to a concern for literature" (*Trading Words,* 153).

25. Ad, reproduced in "Making New Collectors," 2325.

26. Ibid., 2324. See Badaracco, *Trading Words,* on Macy's marketing innovations and prowess.

27. Rogers to Adler, 19 January 1930, EAP.

28. Rollins, "Limited Editions Club Again," *SRL,* 1 June 1929.

29. Rollins, "A Footnote to Boswell," *SRL,* 30 March 1929, 845.

30. Cerf to Gaige, 10 and 12 July, 27 September 1928, RHC. Aldington's *Poems* was sold at the original fifteen-dollar price — a decision perhaps dictated by the exorbitant thousand-dollar advance Gaige had already paid Aldington.

31. Cerf to Wells, 10 February 1930, 18 December 1929, RHC.

32. Cerf to Wells, 23 April 1930, 17 June 1931, RHC.

33. Currie, *Fishers of Books,* 304; Johnston, *Biblio-Typographica,* 225, 222; B. Warde to Garnett, 27 June 1935, LPC. Garnett abruptly resigned from Carnegie Tech in 1935; apparently he had been asked to recoup the costs of Laboratory Press work by selling rather than giving it to selected recipients.

34. Sargent, "Modern Tendencies," vii, x; Wells, *These Three,* 43. See also Rollins, "The 'Limited' Edition." He disparaged the growing practice of issuing books in both an ordinary and "limited" version, "differing little from each other, with a view toward coddling the snob." This, he warned, would only discredit the more legitimate finely printed books.

35. Troxell, "Collector's Madness," 220.

36. Troxell, "Genial Collector," 328; *PW,* 14 June 1930, 2919.

37. Troxell, "Compleat Collector," *SRL,* 31 August 1929, 96; Troxell, "Fashion of Collecting," 578; Troxell, "Limited Edition," 156. Many book lovers separated the reading function of fine books from an aesthetic, iconic one, however. At least two well-respected collectors not only dismissed literary interests as necessary for book collecting but deemed reading something of a hazard. A. N. L. Munby claimed that "reading one's books is hardly necessary" for the dedicated book lover. "I do read a few," he drolly admitted, "but mostly I just look at or take them down and stroke them from time to time. . . . Book collecting is a full-time occupation, and one wouldn't get very far if one took time off for frivolities like reading" ("Floreat Bibliomania," 41). Gabriel Wells explained that he collected hundreds of editions of Fitzgerald's translation of the *Rubaiyat,* for example, not to read them but to "delight in the variations" among the versions, much as one would prize different performances of the same piece of music. "An overfondness

"Adler-Pynson." *New Yorker*, 12 November 1932, 12–13.

Adorno, Theodor. "Bibliographical Musing." *Grand Street* 39, 3 (1991): 135–48.

"Against Reading." *Saturday Review of Literature*, 21 June 1930, 1137.

Aley, Maxwell. "How Large Is Our Book-Reading Public?" *Publishers' Weekly*, 6 June 1931, 2691.

Allen, Frederick Lewis. *Only Yesterday: An Informal History of the Nineteen-Twenties.* 1931. Rpt. New York: Harper and Row, 1964.

"American Book Production, 1924." *Publishers' Weekly*, 31 January 1925, 385.

"American Book Production, 1926." *Publishers' Weekly*, 22 January 1927, 278–79.

"American Book Production, 1928." *Publishers' Weekly*, 19 January 1929, 274–75.

"American Book Production, 1930." *Publishers' Weekly*, 24 January 1931, 412.

"American Book Production, 1931." *Publishers' Weekly*, 23 January 1932, 368–69.

"America's Expanding Incomes." *Literary Digest*, 4 February 1928, 71–72.

Anderson, Gregg. *Recollections of the Grabhorn Press.* Los Angeles: Primavera Press, 1935.

Anderson, Russell. *The Rowfant Club: A History.* Cleveland: The Rowfant Club, 1955.

The Annual of Bookmaking, 1927–1937. New York: The Colophon, 1938.

Ansbacher, L. J. "On Fine Bookmaking Today." *Publishers' Weekly*, 5 September 1931, 951ff.

"Are the Classics Dying Out?" *Publishers' Weekly*, 1 February 1930, 574.

"Are There Too Many Books? A Debate Before the New York Booksellers' League." *Publishers' Weekly*, 24 December 1927, 2231–35.

Armitage, Merle. *Rockwell Kent.* New York: Knopf, 1932.

Arnold, Edmund C. *Ink on Paper: A Handbook of the Graphic Arts.* New York: Harper and Row, 1963.

Asaf, Allen, and Lynda Wornom. *Members of the Grolier Club, 1884–1984.* New York: Grolier Club, 1986

Babbitt, Irving. *Democracy and Leadership.* Boston: Houghton Mifflin, 1924.

Badaracco, Claire. *American Culture and the Marketplace: R.R. Donnelley's Four American Books Campaign, 1926–1930.* Washington, D.C.: Library of Congress, 1992.

———. *Trading Words: Poetry, Typography, and Illustrated Books in the Modern Literary Economy.* Baltimore: Johns Hopkins University Press, 1995.

Baker, Nicholas. "Books as Furniture." *New Yorker*, 12 June 1995, 84–92.

Baritz, Loren, ed. *The Culture of the Twenties.* Indianapolis: Bobbs-Merrill, 1970.

Barr, Louise. *Presses of Northern California and Their Books, 1900–1933.* Berkeley: The Book Arts Club, University of California, 1934.

Basbanes, Nicholas. *A Gentle Madness: Bibliophiles, Bibliomanes, and the Eternal Passion for Books.* New York: Holt, 1995.

Baughman, Roland. "The Grabhorns." In *Heritage of the Graphic Arts*, 227–39. Ed. Chandler B. Grannis. New York: Bowker, 1972.

Beaujon, Paul. [Beatrice Warde.] "The Machine in Book Composition." *Publishers' Weekly*, 2 February 1929, 570ff.

Beilenson, Peter. *The Story of Frederic W. Goudy.* Mt. Vernon, N.Y.: Peter Pauper Press, 1965.

Belk, Russell W., and Richard W. Pollay. "Images of Ourselves: The Good Life in

Twentieth-Century Advertising." *Journal of Consumer Research* 11 (March 1985): 887–98.

Benjamin, Walter. "The Work of Art in the Age of Mechanical Reproduction." In *Illuminations*, 217–51. Ed. Hannah Arendt. Trans. Harry Zohn. 1955. Rpt. New York: Schocken, 1969.

———. "Unpacking My Library: A Talk about Book Collecting." In *Illuminations*, 59–67. Ed. Hannah Arendt. Trans. Harry Zohn. 1955. Rpt. New York: Schocken, 1969.

Bennett, Jesse Lee. "What We Read and Why We Read It." Part 1: "America Has a Book!" *The Bookman* 42 (October 1925): 119–26.

Bennett, John. "Protest of an Old Timer." *Saturday Review of Literature*, 26 July 1930, 14–15.

Bennett, Paul A. *Elmer Adler in the World of Books*. New York: The Typophiles, 1964.

———, ed. *Books and Printing: A Treasury for Typophiles*. 1951. Rev ed. Cleveland: World, 1963.

———. ed. *Postscripts on Dwiggins*. 2 vols. New York: The Typophiles, 1960.

Bent, Silas. "The Story of the Machine." *World's Work* 58 (June 1929): 40–47.

Bentley, Wilder. *The Printer to the Poet*. Berkeley, Calif.: Archetype Press, 1937.

———. "Wilder Bentley Remembers Porter Garnett." *Fine Print* 1, no. 4 (October 1975): 33–35.

Benton, Megan. "Carl Purington Rollins and the Design of Scholarly Books." *Publishing Research Quarterly* 7 (January 1992): 41–56.

———. "Orchids from Pittsburgh: An Appraisal of the Laboratory Press, 1922–1935." *Library Quarterly* 62 (1992): 28–54.

Bigelow, Charles, Paul Hayden Duensing, and Linnea Gentry, eds. *Fine Print on Type: The Best of Fine Print Magazine on Type and Typography*. San Francisco: Bedford Arts, 1989.

Birkerts, Sven. "The Book as Emblem: The Besieged Stronghold?" *Journal of Scholarly Publishing* 26 (October 1994): 3–7.

———. *The Gutenberg Elegies: The Fate of Reading in an Electronic Age*. Boston: Faber and Faber, 1994.

Bixler, Theodore. "Vigorous and Intelligent Defense of His Alma Mater." *Inland Printer*, January 1924, 649–50.

Blumenthal, Joseph. *Bruce Rogers: A Life in Letters, 1870–1957*. Austin, Tex.: W. Thomas Taylor, 1989.

———. *The Printed Book in America*. Boston: Godine, 1977.

———. *Typographic Years: A Printer's Journey Through a Half Century, 1925–1975*. New York: Beil, 1982.

Blumenthal, Walter Hart. *Bookmen's Trio: Ventures in Literary Philandering*. Worcester, Mass.: Achille J. St. Onge, 1961.

Bolter, Jay David. *Writing Space: The Computer, Hypertext, and the History of Writing*. Hillsdale, N.J.: Lawrence Erlbaum Associates, 1991.

Bonney, Louise. "Books and Interior Decoration." *Publishers' Weekly*, 18 January 1930, 297.

"Book Architects." *Publishers' Weekly*, 12 July 1924, 114–15.

"Book Titles Published by Classes in the United States, 1880–1927." *Publishers' Weekly*, 19 January 1929, 276–77.

"Books and Kitchens." *Atlantic Monthly* 126 (July 1920): 136–37.

"Books and Rooms." *Saturday Review of Literature*, 21 January 1928, 536.

"Books in Ads." *Publishers' Weekly*, 17 November 1928, 2073.

Boris, Eileen. *Art and Labor: Ruskin, Morris, and the Craftsman Ideal in America.* Philadelphia, Temple University Press, 1986.

Borsodi, Ralph. *This Ugly Civilization.* New York: Simon and Schuster, 1929.

The Borzoi 1925: Being a Sort of Record of Ten Years of Publishing. New York: Knopf, 1925.

Bourdieu, Pierre. *Distinction: A Social Critique of the Judgement of Taste.* Trans. Richard Nice. Cambridge, Mass.: Harvard University Press, 1984.

Boyd, Thomas. "The Bibliophile." *Bookman* 64 (January 1927): 614–16.

Bradbury, Malcolm. "The Name and Nature of Modernism." In *Modernism: A Guide to European Literature, 1890–1930,* 19–55. Ed. Malcolm Bradbury and James McFarlane. New York: Viking Penguin, 1976.

Brewer, Reginald. *The Delightful Diversion: The Whys and Wherefores of Book Collecting.* New York: Macmillan, 1935.

Bringhurst, Robert. *The Elements of Typographic Style.* Point Roberts, Wash.: Hartley and Marks, 1992.

Bronner, Simon, ed. *Consuming Visions: Accumulation and Display of Goods in America, 1880–1920.* New York: Norton, 1989.

Brown, R. D. "The Bodley Head Press: Some Bibliographical Extrapolations." *Papers of the Bibliographical Society of America* 61 (1967): 39–50.

Bruccoli, Matthew J. *The Fortunes of Mitchell Kennerley, Bookman.* San Diego: Harcourt, Brace, Jovanovich, 1986.

Bruckner, D. J. R. *Frederic Goudy.* New York: Harry N. Abrams, 1990.

Bullen, Henry L. "An Open Letter [to Carl Rollins]." *Saturday Review of Literature*, 8 February 1927, 724.

Burton, William. "The Decline and Fall of the Limited Editions Club." *American Book Collector* 1, no. 4 (1980): 3–7.

Calkins, Earnest Elmo. "The Market Value of Good Taste." Introduction to *Printing for Commerce: Specimens Exhibited by the Institute, 1926.* New York: John Day, 1927.

Canby, Henry Seidel. "Clear the Shelves: Books in the Home." *Saturday Review of Literature*, 6 December 1930, 411.

Cannon, Carl L. *American Book Collectors and Collecting from Colonial Times to the Present.* New York: H. W. Wilson, 1941.

Carlton, W. N. C. "Henry Edwards Huntington, 1850–1927: An Appreciation." *American Collector* 4 (August 1927): 165–70.

Carpenter, Kenneth. "BR to JHN." *Book Club of California Quarterly Newsletter* 23 (Spring 1958): 29–39.

The Carteret Book Club Register of Officers and Members. Newark, N.J.: Carteret Book Club, 1926.

Cave, Roderick. *The Private Presses.* London: Faber and Faber, 1971.

Cerf, Bennett. *At Random: The Reminiscences of Bennett Cerf.* New York: Random House, 1977.

Chartier, Roger. *The Cultural Uses of Print in Early Modern France.* Trans. Lydia G. Cochrane. Princeton: Princeton University Press, 1987.

——. *Forms and Meanings: Texts, Performances, and Audiences from Codex to Computer.* Philadelphia: University of Pennsylvania Press, 1995.

——. *The Order of Books: Readers, Authors, and Libraries in Europe between the Fourteenth and the Eighteenth Centuries.* Trans. Lydia G. Cochrane. Stanford, Calif.: Stanford University Press, 1994.

Chase, Stuart. *Men and Machines.* New York: Macmillan, 1929.

Cheney, O. H. *Economic Survey of the Book Industry, 1930–1931.* New York: National Association of Book Publishers, 1931.

The Chicago Manual of Style. 14th ed. Chicago: University of Chicago Press, 1993.

Clarke, Jim. "Modernism Has Come to Stay: Dump the Classics in the 'Hell-Box.'" *Direct Advertising* 19 (Fall 1933): 19ff.

Claudy, Carl. "Books as Luxuries." *Publishers' Weekly,* 28 June 1930, 3111.

Cobden-Sanderson, T. J. *The Journals of Thomas James Cobden-Sanderson, 1879–1922.* 2 vols. London: Richard Cobden-Sanderson, 1926.

——. "The Three-fold Purpose of the Doves Press." 1916. In *Cosmic Vision.* Thavies Inn, England: Richard Cobden-Sanderson, 1922.

Cohn, Louis Henry. "Book Madness." *Scribner's,* May 1930, 543–53.

Cole, George Watson. "The Huntington Library." *Library Journal,* 5 September 1922, 745–50.

Cole, W. Arthur. *The Influence of Fine Printing.* Pittsburgh: Carnegie Institute of Technology, 1929.

"Collecting American Literature." *Publishers' Weekly,* 11 April 1931, 1901.

Comparato, Frank E. *Books for the Millions: A History of the Men Whose Methods and Machines Packaged the Printed Word.* Harrisburg, Penn.: Stackpole, 1971.

Connett, Eugene V, III, ed. *A Decade of American Sporting Books and Prints [The Derrydale Press, 1927–1937].* New York: Derrydale, 1937.

Coolidge, Calvin. "Books for Better Homes." *The Delineator* 103 (August 1923): 2.

Cooper-Marshall, Frederick. "The New Generation of Book Makers: Priscilla Crane of Brewer and Warren, Inc." *Publishers' Weekly,* 1 March 1930, 1129–32.

"Covici-Friede, Publishers, in New York." *Publishers' Weekly,* 2 June 1928, 2277.

Cowley, Malcolm, ed. *After the Genteel Tradition: American Writers since 1910.* Gloucester, Mass.: Peter Smith, 1959.

——. *Exile's Return: A Literary Odyssey of the 1920s.* New York: Viking, 1934.

Cram, Norman L. "The Caxton Club of Chicago: Three Generations of Bibliophiles." *Book Club of California Quarterly Newsletter* 21, no. 2 (Spring 1956): 35–44.

Currie, Barton. *Fishers of Books.* Boston: Little, Brown, 1931.

"Damning 'Bibliophilism.'" *Literary Digest,* 10 April 1920, 41.

Dardis, Tom. *Firebrand: The Life of Horace Liveright.* New York: Random House, 1995.

Darnton, Robert. "What Is the History of Books?" In *Reading in America: Literature and Social History,* 27–52. Ed. Cathy Davidson. Baltimore: Johns Hopkins University Press, 1989.

Day, Clarence S. *Story of the Yale University Press Told by a Friend.* New Haven, Conn.: Yale University Press, 1920.

Day, George Parmly. *The Function and Organization of University Presses.* New Haven, Conn.: Yale University Press, 1915.

Day, Kenneth, ed. *Book Typography, 1815–1965, in Europe and the United States of America*. Chicago: University of Chicago Press, 1965.

De la Mare, Walter. *The Printing of Poetry*. London: Double Crown Club, 1931.

De Vinne, Theodore Low. "Masculine Printing." *American Bookmaker* 15 (November 1982): 140–44.

———. "The Printing of Morris." *Book Buyer* 13 (January 1897): 920–23.

"Dedicating a Printing Press: With Solemnity the New Laboratory Press of the Carnegie School of Technology at Pittsburgh Begins Its Activity." *American Printer*, 20 May 1923, 33–35.

Dickinson, Donald C. *Dictionary of American Book Collectors*. New York: Greenwood, 1986.

———. *Henry E. Huntington's Library of Libraries*. San Marino, Calif.: Henry E. Huntington Library and Art Gallery, 1995.

Dickson, S. B. "Patchquilt of Bibliophilia." *Overland Monthly* 84 (August 1926): 248–49.

Dill, Francis P. "The Ideal Book." In *The Ideal Book: Two Essays Jointly Awarded the Prize Offered by the Limited Editions Club*. New York: Limited Editions Club, 1931.

———. "Porter Garnett and the Laboratory Press." *Publishers' Weekly*, 6 February 1932, 671.

Donham, S. Agnes. "Your Income and How to Spend It." *Ladies' Home Journal*, March 1921, 107.

Doud, Margery. "Books for the Home: A Selection for Both Merit and Color." *House Beautiful*, May 1925, 538.

Douglas, Lester. *Notes Along the Typographic Way*. Washington, D.C.: American Institute of Graphic Arts, 1949.

Dreyfus, John. *Bruce Rogers and American Typography*. New York: Cambridge University Press, 1959.

Drucker, Johanna. *The Visible Word: Experimental Typography and Modern Art, 1909–1923*. Chicago: University of Chicago Press, 1994.

Duffus, R. L. *Books: Their Place in a Democracy*. Boston: Houghton Mifflin, 1930.

Dugaid, Paul. "Material Matters." In *The Future of the Book*. Ed. Geoffrey Nunberg. Berkeley and Los Angeles: University of California Press, 1996.

Duke, Maurice. *James Branch Cabell: A Reference Guide*. Boston: G. K. Hall, 1979.

Duncan, Harry. *The Doors of Perception*. Austin, Tex.: W. Thomas Taylor, 1987.

Durant, Will. "In Defense of Outlines." Part 2: "Are the Cultural ABC's Softening Our Brains? A Debate." *Forum* 83 (January 1930): 8–14.

Duryea, Minga Pope. "When Books Become a Decoration." *Arts and Decoration*, February 1926, 45.

"Dutton's Limited Editions." *Publishers' Weekly*, 16 November 1929, 2421.

Dwiggins, W. A. "An Investigation into the Physical Properties of Books." 1919. In *Books and Printing*. Ed. Paul A. Bennett. 129–51. Cleveland: World, 1963.

———. "The Rebirth of Typographical Art." *Saturday Review of Literature*, 18 October 1924, 204–5.

———. "Twenty Years After." 1939. In *Books and Printing*. Ed. Paul A. Bennett. 145–52. Cleveland: World, 1963.

Edman, Irwin. "On American Leisure." *Harper's*, January 1928, 220–25.

"18 Typographic Authorities Discuss Clarke's Modernism . . ." *Direct Advertising*, Winter 1933. 4–16.

Ege, Otto F. "A Decalog for the Making of Fine Books." *Publishers' Weekly*, 21 August 1926, 659–63.

Elsner, John, and Roger Cardinal, eds. *The Cultures of Collecting*. Cambridge, Mass.: Harvard University Press, 1994.

"English View on Limited Editions." *Publishers' Weekly*, 15 June 1929, 2757.

Farquhar, Samuel T. "What's What in the Fine Art of Book Making." San Francisco *Chronicle*, 22, 29 May 1927.

Farrow, Anthony. *George Moore*. Boston: Twayne, 1978.

FauntLeRoy, Joseph. *John Henry Nash, Printer: Legend and Fact in the Development of a Fine Press Intimately Reviewed*. Oakland, Cal.: Westgate Press, 1948.

Fehrenbach, A. J. "The Work of Elmer Adler and the Pynson Printers." *Inland Printer* 80 (February 1928): 769–70.

"Fewer and Better Books." *Atlantic Monthly* 135 (January 1925): 56–64.

Field, Eugene. *The Love Affairs of a Bibliomaniac*. New York: Scribner's, 1896.

Filene, Edward A. "The Ethics of This Machine Age." *Scribner's*, February 1932, 78–80.

"Fine Books in America." *Publishers' Weekly*, 3 September 1927, 684.

Fitzgerald, F. Scott. *The Great Gatsby*. New York: Scribner's, 1925.

Ford, Henry. "Machinery, The New Messiah." *Forum* 79 (March 1928): 359–64.

Fox, Richard W., and T. J. Jackson Lears, eds. *The Culture of Consumption: Critical Essays in American History, 1880–1980*. New York: Pantheon Books, 1983.

Frank, Glenn. "Shall We Scrap Our Machines and Go Back to the Spinning Wheel?" *Magazine of Business*, October 1927, 411ff.

———. "Where Is This Machine Age Taking Us?" *Magazine of Business*, September 1927, 256ff.

Frederick, J. George. "Bookish Snobs." *The Independent*, 11 April 1925, 416.

French, George. "Fifty American Books: A Review of the Exhibition at the Art Center, New York." *American Printer*, 20 June, 1923, 39–42.

Friede, Donald. *The Mechanical Angel: His Adventures and Enterprises in the Glittering 1920s*. New York: Knopf, 1948.

Gaige, Crosby. *Footlights and Highlights*. New York: E. P. Dutton, 1948.

Galbraith, John Kenneth. *The Affluent Society*. 4th ed. Boston: Houghton Mifflin, 1984.

Gallatin, A. F. "Modern Fine Printing in America." *American Magazine of Art*, November 1920, 461–66.

Gans, Herbert J. *Popular Culture and High Culture: An Analysis and Evaluation of Taste*. New York: Basic Books, 1974.

Garnett, Porter. "Again What Is Fine Printing?" *Printing Art* 40 (February 1923): 571–74.

———. *A Documentary Account of the Beginnings of the Laboratory Press*. Pittsburgh: Laboratory Press, 1927.

———. "The Ideal Book." In *Books and Printing*. 1931. Ed. Paul A. Bennett. 115–28. Cleveland: World, 1963.

———, comp. *A Laboratory Press Anthology [Unfinished]: A Collection of Texts Con-*

cerning Art, Belles-Lettres, Philosophy, Craftsmanship, Civilization, Life. . . . Pittsburgh: Laboratory Press, 1935.

———. "The Making and Judging of Books." *Publishers' Weekly*, 22 August 1925, 605–10.

———. "Printer's Note." In Hildegarde Flanner, *That Endeth Never: A Gift*. Pittsburgh: Laboratory Press, 1926.

Garrison, Lydia. "Bookcases as an Integral Part of Interior Architecture." *House Beautiful*, August 1924, 123.

Gaskell, Philip. *A New Introduction to Bibliography*. New York: Oxford University Press, 1972.

Genette, Gerard. *Paratexts: Thresholds of Interpretation*. Trans. Jane E. Lewin. New York: Cambridge University Press, 1997.

Gerould, Katharine Fullerton. "The Plight of the Genteel." *Harper's*, February 1926, 310–19.

Gill, Eric. *An Essay on Typography*. 1936. Boston: Godine, 1993.

Gilman, Dorothy Foster. "The Rich Don't Buy Books." *Publishers' Weekly*, 28 March 1931, 1681–82.

Gilmer, Walker. *Horace Liveright: Publisher of the Twenties*. New York: David Lewis, 1970.

Glick, William J. *William J. Rudge*. New York: The Typophiles, 1984.

Goudy, Frederic W. "What Printing Means to Me." *American Printer*, 20 June 1923, 37–39.

Grabhorn, Edwin. *The Fine Art of Printing*. San Francisco: Grabhorn Press, 1933.

Grannis, Chandler B., ed. *Heritage of the Graphic Arts*. New York: Bowker, 1972.

Grannis, Ruth S. "What Bibliography Owes to Private Book Clubs." *Papers of the Bibliographical Society of America* 23 (1929): 14–33.

Grant, W. V., and Eiden, L. J. *Digest of Educational Statistics*. Washington, D.C.: Government Printing Office, 1982.

A Graphic Survey of Book Production, 1890–1916. Washington, D.C.: Government Printing Office, 1917.

Gray, William S., and Ruth Munroe. *The Reading Interests and Habits of Adults: A Preliminary Report*. New York: Macmillan, 1929.

Greaves, Haslehurst. *The Personal Library: How to Make It and How to Use It*. London: Grafton, 1928.

Greenhood, David. "The Book as an Aesthetic Object." *Fine Print* 2, no. 4 (October 1976): 57–60.

Grolier 75: A Biographical Retrospective. . . . New York: Grolier Club, 1959.

Grosse, Joseph. "An Interview with Elmer Adler." *Central Review* (October 1933): 2–3, 8.

Grover, Edwin O. "Why Not Professors of Books?" *Publishers' Weekly*, 30 November 1929, 2591.

Grover, Sherwood. *Life and Hard Times: or, Sherwood Grover's Twenty-Five Years with the Grabhorn Press*. San Francisco: Roxburghe and Zamarano Clubs, 1968.

"Growth of Limited Editions." *Publishers' Weekly*, 15 June 1929, 2756.

Gunn, Robert. "Crosby Gaige Imprint and Its Value." *Publishers' Weekly*, 6 October 1928, 1471–73.

Guthrie, Jane. "The Decorative Value of Books." *Good Housekeeping*, January 1925, 139.

Haas, Irvin, ed. *Bibliography of Modern American Presses*. Chicago: Black Cat Press, 1935.

———. *Bruce Rogers: A Bibliography. Hitherto Unrecorded Work, 1889–1925, Complete Works 1925–1936. With a Letter of Introduction by Beatrice Warde*. Mt. Vernon, N.Y.: Peter Pauper Press, 1936.

Hackett, Alice Payne. *70 Years of Best Sellers: 1895–1965*. New York: Bowker, 1967.

Hall, David. *On Native Ground: From the History of Printing to the History of Books*. Worcester, Mass.: American Antiquarian Society, 1984.

———. "Readers and Reading in America: Historical and Critical Perspectives." *Proceedings of the American Antiquarian Society* 103 (1993): 337–57.

Halttunen, Karen. "From Parlor to Living Room: Domestic Space, Interior Decoration, and the Culture of Personality." In *Consuming Visions*. Ed. Simon Bronner. New York: Norton, 1989.

"The Harbor Press." *Publishers' Weekly*, 5 January 1929, 81.

Harlan, Robert D. *Chapter Nine: The Vulgate Bible and Other Unfinished Projects of John Henry Nash*. New York: The Typophiles, 1982.

———. *John Henry Nash: The Biography of a Career*. Berkeley and Los Angeles: University of California Press, 1970.

Harper, Henry H. *Booklovers, Bibliomaniacs, and Book Clubs*. Boston: Henry H. Harper, 1904.

Harrington, Frank G. *Praise Past Due: A Memoir of Richard Ellis, Designer and Printer, 1894–1982*. Francestown, N.H.: Typographeum, 1991.

Harris, Neil. "Pictorial Perils: The Rise of American Illustration." In *Cultural Excursions: Marketing Appetites and Cultural Tastes in Modern America*. Chicago: University of Chicago Press, 1990.

Hart, James D. *Fine Printing: The San Francisco Tradition*. Washington, D.C.: Library of Congress, 1985.

———. *A Tribute to Edwin Grabhorn & the Grabhorn Press*. San Francisco: Friends of the San Francisco Library, 1969.

Hazlitt, Henry. "In Dispraise of Fine Books." *The Nation*, 20 May 1931, 559–60.

———. "Who Reads the Classics Now?" *The Nation*, 16 April 1930, 449–51.

Heartman, Charles F. "Erotica." *American Collector* 3 (October 1926): 49–51.

Heininger, Lynn Stevens. *At Home with a Book: Reading in America, 1840–1940*. Rochester, N.Y.: Strong Museum, 1986.

Hemingway, Ernest. "American Bohemians in Paris." In *By-Line: Ernest Hemingway*. Ed. William White. New York: Scribner's, 1967.

Hench, John B. "Toward a History of the Book in America." *Publishing Research Quarterly* 10 (Fall 1994): 9–21.

Hill, John D. "A Business Man Views the Classics." *American Mercury* 61 (August 1945): 167–68.

Hoffman, Frederick J. *The Twenties: American Writing in the Postwar Decade*. Rev ed. New York: Free Press, 1965.

Holden, George Parker. "Shall Tradition Prevent the Adoption of More Legible Type Faces?" *Inland Printer* 82 (January 1929): 4ff.

Holden, John A., and Franklin Spier. "Are There Too Many Books? A Debate Before the New York Booksellers' League." *Publishers' Weekly*, 24 December 1927, 2231ff.

Holden, John Allen, ed. *Private Book Collectors in the United States and Canada*. New York: Bowker, 1925.

Holt, Henry. "The Communication of Literature." *Atlantic Monthly* 96 (August 1905): 577–600.

Hooper, Charles Edwin. *The Country House: A Practical Manual of the Planning and Construction of the Country House and Its Surroundings*. Garden City, N.Y.: Doubleday, Page, 1913.

Horowitz, Daniel. *The Morality of Spending: Attitudes toward the Consumer Society in America, 1875–1940*. Baltimore: Johns Hopkins University Press, 1985.

"How the American Middle Class Lives." *Scribner's*, December 1929, 694–99.

Huxley, Aldous. "The Outlook for American Culture." *Harper's*, August 1927, 265–72.

——. "Typography for the Twentieth-Century Reader." 1928. In *Books and Printing*. Ed. Paul A. Bennett. 344–49. Cleveland: World, 1963.

"Is Modern Civilization Crushing the Soul?" *Current Opinion* 75 (November 1923): 598–99.

Jackson, Holbrook. *The Anatomy of Bibliomania*. New York: Farrar, Straus, 1950.

——. *The Printing of Books*. 1939. Rpt. Freeport, N.Y.: Books for Libraries Press, 1970.

Johnson, Burges. "The Alleged Depravity of Popular Taste." *Harper's*, January 1921, 209–15.

Johnson, James. "The Windsor Press in Retrospect." *Book Club of California Quarterly Newsletter* 26 (Winter 1960): 5–7.

Johnson, James, and Cecil Johnson. "The Regeneration of the Book." *Publishers' Weekly*, 4 August 1928, 406.

Johnston, Paul. "The American 'Fine Book' Bubble." *American Collector* 4 (1927): 119–23.

——. *Biblio-Typographica*. New York: Covici-Friede, 1930.

——. "Books Should Look Like Books." *Publisher's Weekly*, 3 October 1931, 1591ff.

——. "Elmer Adler: The Pynson Printers." *Publishers' Weekly*, 7 March 1931, 1183ff.

——. "Fine Books in America." *American Collector* 5 (October 1927): 77–80.

——. "Fine Books in the Present Market." *Publishers' Weekly*, 6 September 1930, 950ff.

——. "Modernism in Book Design." *Publishers' Weekly*, 1 March 1930, 1121ff.

Jones, Howard Mumford. "The Cult of Short-cut Culture." Part 1: "Are the Cultural ABC's Softening Our Brains? A Debate." *Forum* 83 (January 1930): 5–8.

——, and Richard M. Ludwig. *Guide to American Literature and Its Background since 1890*. 4th ed. Cambridge, Mass.: Harvard University Press, 1972.

Jordan-Smith, Paul. *For the Love of Books: The Adventures of an Impecunious Collector*. New York: Oxford University Press, 1934.

Josephy, Robert. "Trade Bookmaking: Complaint in Three Dimensions." 1935. Books and Printing. Ed. Paul A. Bennett. 167–74. Cleveland: World, 1963.

Kaestle, Carl F., Helen Damon-Moore, Lawrence C. Stedman, Katherine Tinsley, and William Vance Trollinger, Jr. *Literacy in the United States: Readers and Reading since 1880*. New Haven, Conn.: Yale University Press, 1991.

Kemp, Jairus. "In Defense of the Modern Movement—By a True Modernist." *Inland Printer*, March 1929, 69–72.

Kent, Rockwell. *It's Me O Lord: The Autobiography of Rockwell Kent*. New York: Dodd, Mead, 1955.

Keppel, Frederick P., and R. L. Duffus. *The Arts in American Life*. New York: McGraw-Hill, 1933.

Kinross, Robin. *Modern Typography: An Essay in Critical History*. London: Hyphen Press, 1992.

Kittredge, William A. "Of the Better Printing of Books." *Publishers' Weekly*, 12 July 1924, 107ff.

———. "Present Tendencies of the Typography of Books." *Publishers' Weekly*, 22 August 1925, 611–14.

Koopman, Harry Lyman. *The Booklover and His Books*. Boston: Boston Book Co., 1917.

———. "Modern American Printing." *American Mercury* 2 (May 1924): 51–54.

Landow, George. *Hypertext: The Convergence of Contemporary Critical Theory and Technology*. Baltimore: Johns Hopkins University Press, 1992.

———. "Twenty Minutes into the Future, or How Are We Moving beyond the Book?" In *The Future of the Book*. Ed. Geoffrey Nunberg. 210–37. Berkeley and Los Angeles: University of California Press, 1996.

Lanham, Richard A. *The Electronic Word: Democracy, Technology, and the Arts*. Chicago: University of Chicago Press, 1993.

Lawson, Alexander. *Anatomy of a Typeface*. Boston: Godine, 1990.

Le Gallienne, Richard. "The Philosophy of Limited Editions." In *Prose Fancies*. New York: G. P. Putnam's Sons, 1894.

———. "What a Library Should Be Like: Some Suggestions for Those for Whom Books and Their Heritage Are Precious." *House and Garden*, December 1924, 58ff.

Lears, T. J. Jackson. *No Place of Grace: Antimodernism and the Transformation of American Culture, 1880–1920*. New York: Pantheon, 1981.

Lebergott, Stanley. *Pursuing Happiness: American Consumers in the Twentieth Century*. Princeton, N.J.: Princeton University Press, 1993.

Lee, Marshall. *Bookmaking: The Illustrated Guide to Design/Production/Editing*. New York: Bowker, 1979.

Lehman-Haupt, Helmut. *The Book in America: A History of the Making and Selling of Books in the United States*. 2d ed. New York: Bowker, 1952.

Lemperly, Paul. *Among My Books*. Cleveland: The Rowfant Club, 1929.

Leuchtenburg, William E. *The Perils of Prosperity, 1914–32*. Chicago: University of Chicago Press, 1958.

Levine, Lawrence W. *Highbrow/Lowbrow: The Emergence of Cultural Hierarchy in America*. Cambridge, Mass.: Harvard University Press, 1988.

———. "Progress and Nostalgia: The Self Image of the Nineteen Twenties." In *The American Novel and the Nineteen Twenties*. Ed. Malcolm Bradbury and David Palmer. London: Edward Arnold, 1971.

Lewis, Oscar. "The Field of the Book Clubs." *Publishers' Weekly*, 21 August 1926, 663–66.

———. *The First Seventy-Five Years: The Story of the Book Club of California, 1912–1987*. San Francisco: Book Club of California, 1987.

———. "How Not to Be a Publisher." *Book Club of California Quarterly Newsletter* 25 (Summer 1960): 55.

———. "San Francisco Bookstores." *Publishers' Weekly*, 28 August 1926, 731–35.

Lewis, Sinclair. *Babbitt*. 1922. Rpt. New York: New American Library, 1961.

"Limited Editions." *Publishers' Weekly*, 17 November 1928, 2072–73.

"Limited Editions Club." *Publishers' Weekly*, 25 May 1929, 1058–59.

Linden, Eugene. *Affluence and Discontent: The Anatomy of Consumer Societies*. New York: Viking, 1979.

"Literature and the Machine." *Saturday Review of Literature*, 27 April 1929, 945–46.

Loos, Anita. *Gentlemen Prefer Blondes*. New York: Boni and Liveright, 1925.

Lynd, Robert, and Helen Lynd. *Middletown: A Study in American Culture*. New York: Harcourt, Brace, and Company, 1929.

Lynes, Russell. "The Ascending Spiral." *Harper's*, May 1966, 24ff.

———. *The Taste-Makers*. New York: Harper and Brothers, 1949.

MacLeish, Archibald. *The Letters of Archibald MacLeish, 1907 to 1982*. Ed. R. H. Winnick. Boston: Houghton Mifflin, 1983.

Macy, George. *The Limited Editions Club Incorporated*. New York: Limited Editions Club, 1929.

———."The Limited Editions Club Is Organized." *Publishers' Weekly*, 6 April 1929, 1721–22.

Magee, David, and Elinor Raas Heller. *Bibliography of the Grabhorn Press, 1915–1940*. San Francisco: David Magee, 1940.

Magee, David. *Infinite Riches: The Adventures of a Rare Book Dealer*. New York: Paul S. Erikson, 1973.

"Making New Collectors for Limited Editions." *Publishers' Weekly*, 21 November 1931, 2324–26.

"The Making of a Best Seller: The Story of Book Manufacturing at Simon and Schuster." In *The Annual of Bookmaking*. New York: The Colophon, 1938.

Marchand, Roland. *Advertising the American Dream: Making Way for Modernity, 1920–1940*. Berkeley and Los Angeles: University of California Press, 1985.

Marshall, Edward. "Machine-Made Freedom: An Authorized Interview with Thomas Edison." *Forum* 79 (October 1926): 492–97.

Masson, Thomas L. "Domestic Bookaflage." *Independent*, 14 April 1923, 256.

"Master Printer." "Teaching Absurd Typographic Stunts." 72 (October 1923): 83.

Mayes, Will H. "Applied Idealism in the Graphic Arts." *Inland Printer* 72 (December 1923): 481–82.

McCracken, Grant. *Culture and Consumption: New Approaches to the Symbolic Character of Consumer Goods and Activities*. Bloomington: Indiana University Press, 1988.

McCutcheon, George B. *Books Once Were Men: An Essay for Booklovers*. New York: Dodd, Mead, 1925.

McDonald, Thomas W. "Reminiscences of the Grabhorn Press." *Book Club of California Quarterly Newsletter* 14 (Spring 1949): 27–30.

McFarland, J. Horace. "What Is Fine Printing?" *Printing Art* 40 (November 1922): 257–58.

McGann, Jerome J. *Black Riders: The Visible Language of Modernism*. Princeton, N.J.: Princeton University Press, 1993.

——. *The Textual Condition*. Princeton, N.J.: Princeton University Press, 1991.

McGrew, Mac. *American Metal Typefaces of the Twentieth Century*. 2d. ed. New Castle, Del.: Oak Knoll Books, 1993.

McKenzie, D. F. *Bibliography and the Sociology of Texts*. London: The British Library, 1986.

McKitterick, David, ed. *Stanley Morison & D. B. Updike: Selected Correspondence*. New York: Moretus Press, 1979.

McLean, Ruari, ed. *Typographers on Type: An Illustrated Anthology from William Morris to the Present Day*. New York: Norton, 1995.

McMurtrie, Douglas. *The Golden Book: The Story of Fine Books and Bookmaking, Past and Present*. New York: Covici-Friede, 1927.

——. "Modernism in Design." *Publishers' Weekly*, 4 January 1930, 87ff.

——. "Our Medieval Typography." *American Mercury* 12 (September 1927): 94–97.

McPharlin, Paul. "The Marchbanks Press: Fine Book Printers." *Publishers' Weekly*, 5 April 1947, 1947ff.

McWilliams, David Jackson. "On a Piece of Pynson Printers Ephemera." In *Elmer Adler in the World of Books*. Ed. Paul A. Bennett. New York: The Typophiles, 1964.

Melcher, Frederic. "Beatrice L. Warde — Typographer." *Publishers' Weekly*, 2 February 1929, 567–68.

Members of the Grabhorn Press. "The New Art: A Protest Against the Elevation of Printing." *Publishers' Weekly*, 4 August 1928, 405.

Mencken, H. L. *Selected Prejudices*. New York: Modern Library, 1930.

Merz, Charles. "Twentieth-Century Medievalism: The Machine Age on Its Way to a New Order?" *Century* 106 (June 1923): 228–36.

Miers, Earl Schenck. "Richard Ellis, Printer." *Journal of the Rutgers University Library* 5 (December 1941): 39–59.

Moran, James. *Printing Presses: History and Development from the Fifteenth Century to Modern Times*. Berkeley and Los Angeles: University of California Press, 1973.

Morison, Stanley. "First Principles of Typography." 1930. In *Books and Printing*. Ed. Paul A. Bennett. 239–51. Cleveland: World, 1963.

Morris, William. *The Ideal Book: Essays and Lectures on the Arts of the Book*. Ed. William S. Peterson. Berkeley and Los Angeles: University of California Press, 1982.

Moses, Montrose J. "Books for the Guest Room." *House and Garden*, May 1921, 86.

——. "Coming on Books Unexpectedly." *House and Garden*, August 1922, 76.

Mumford, Lewis. *American Taste*. San Francisco: Westgate Press, 1929.

Muensterberger, Werner. *Collecting: An Unruly Passion, Psychological Perspectives*. Princeton, N.J.: Princeton University Press, 1994.

Munby, A. N. L. *Essays and Papers*. Ed. Nicholas Barker. London: Scolar Press, 1978.

Myers, Robin, and Michael Harris, eds. *Bibliophily*. Cambridge, England: Chadwyck-Healey, 1986.

Nash, John Henry. "In Defense of Finely Printed Books." *American Printer*, June 1927, 52–53.

——. Prospectus for *Biblia Sacra*. San Francisco: John Henry Nash, 1932.

Nash, Ray. *C.P.R.: Keeper of the Human Scale.* Montague, Mass.: Dyke Mill, 1954.

"The New Publishing Census." *Publishers' Weekly,* 24 January 1931, 409–10.

Newdigate, B. H. "Preciousness in Printing." *London Mercury* 18 (October 1928): 615–22.

Newton, A. E. *The Amenities of Book Collecting and Kindred Affections.* Boston: Little, Brown, 1929.

——. "What to Collect — and Why." *Saturday Evening Post,* 24 September 1927, 16ff.

Norman, Don Cleveland. *The 500th Anniversary Pictorial Census of the Gutenberg Bible.* Chicago: Cloverdale Press, 1961.

Norris, Beauveau. "Infinite Riches in a Little Room." *Good Housekeeping,* January 1921, 101.

Nunberg, Geoffrey, ed. *The Future of the Book.* Berkeley and Los Angeles: University of California Press, 1996.

Nye, Russel. *The Unembarrassed Muse: The Popular Arts in America.* New York: Dial Press, 1970.

O'Day, Edward F. *John Henry Nash: The Aldus of San Francisco.* San Francisco: San Francisco Bay Cities Club of Printing House Craftsmen, 1928.

——. "Introduction Deprecating Certain Weaknesses of Wives." Introduction to Eugene Field, *Dibdin's Ghost.* San Francisco: John Henry Nash for John S. Drum, 1926.

O'Day, Nell, comp. *A Catalogue of Books Printed by John Henry Nash.* San Francisco: Nash, 1937.

O'Hagan, Anne. "Mary's Got a Book Already." *The Delineator* 87 (October 1920): 69.

O'Hara, Louise M. "John Henry Nash." *Publishers' Weekly,* 2 May 1931, 2217–20.

O'Hara, Palmer. "Book Titles Published by Classes in the United States, 1880–1927." *Publishers' Weekly,* 19 January 1927, 276–77.

Orcutt, William Dana. "In Quest of the Perfect Book." *Atlantic Monthly,* December 1925, 800–809.

——. *The Magic of Books: More Reminiscences and Adventures of a Bookman.* Boston: Little, Brown, 1930.

——. *Master Makers of the Book: Being a Consecutive Story of the Book. . . .* Garden City, N.Y.: Doubleday, Doran, 1928.

Orville, Miles. *The Real Thing: Imitation and Authenticity in American Culutre, 1880–1940.* Chapel Hill: University of North Carolina Press, 1989.

Ortega y Gasset, José. *The Revolt of the Masses.* New York: Norton, 1932.

Otness, Harold M. "A Room Full of Books: The Life and Slow Death of the American Residential Library." *Libraries and Culture* 23 (1988): 111–34.

Parker, Wyman. "The Altschul Book Bequest." *Yale University Library Gazette* 57 (April 1983): 138–44.

Pearson, Edmund Lester. "The Sport of Kings." *Outlook,* 13 February 1924, 272–73.

"Pedigreed Books for Millionaires." *Literary Digest,* 21 February 1925, 59.

Peixotto, Jessica B. *Getting and Spending at the Professional Level: A Study of the Costs of Living an Academic Life.* New York: Macmillan, 1927.

Perrett, Geoffrey. *America in the Twenties.* New York: Simon and Schuster, 1982.

Persons, Stow. *The Decline of American Gentility.* New York: Columbia University Press, 1973.

Peterson, William S. *The Kelmscott Press: A History of William Morris's Typographical Adventure.* Berkeley and Los Angeles: University of California Press, 1991.

Piehl, Frank J. *The Caxton Club, 1895–1995: Celebrating a Century of the Book in Chicago.* Chicago: Caxton Club, 1995.

"Planning for Books." *House and Garden,* November 1924, 110.

Pollard, Alfred W. "The Trained Printer and the Amateur: and the Pleasure of Small Books." 1929. In *Books and Printing.* Ed. Paul A. Bennett. 182–90. Cleveland: World, 1963.

Post, Emily. *The Personality of a House: The Blue Book of Home Design and Decoration.* New York: Funk and Wagnalls, 1930.

Powell, Lawrence Clark. *Books in My Baggage: Adventures in Reading and Collecting.* Cleveland: World, 1960.

"Precious Books for Fuel." *Publishers' Weekly,* 3 January 1931, 90.

Preissig, Vojtèc. "Further Discussion on 'Teaching Absurd Typographic Stunts.'" *Inland Printer* 72 (December 1923): 468.

Private Book Collectors in the United States and Canada with Mention of Their Hobbies. New York: Bowker, 1925, 1928, 1953.

"Prosperity as a Habit." *Saturday Evening Post,* 10 March 1928, 30.

Pupin, Michael. "Romance of the Machine." *Scribner's,* February 1930, 130–37.

Radway, Janice. "The Book of the Month Club and the General Reader." In *Reading in America: Literature and Social History,* 259–84. Ed. Cathy Davidson. Baltimore: Johns Hopkins University Press, 1989.

———. *A Feeling for Books: The Book-of-the-Month Club, Literary Taste, and Middle-Class Desire.* Chapel Hill: University of North Carolina Press, 1997.

Rainey, Lawrence. "The Price of Modernism: Publishing *The Waste Land.*" In *T. S. Eliot: The Modernist in History,* 91–133. Ed. Ronald Bush. Cambridge: Cambridge University Press, 1991.

Ransom, Will. *Private Presses and the Their Books.* New York: Bowker, 1929.

———. "Sanserif: Passing Fancy or Type of Tomorrow?" *American Printer* 90 (June 1930): 33–36.

———. "The Merrymount Press." *Publishers' Weekly,* 14 April 1929, 1617.

———. "Frederic Warde." *Print* 11 (May-June 1941): 27–39.

Recent Social Trends in the United States: Report of the President's Research Committee on Social Trends. New York: McGraw-Hill, 1933.

"The Right to Books." *Bookman,* September 1925, 5.

Rimington, R. C. "Richard W. Ellis: Builder of Books." *Publishers' Weekly,* 2 November 1929, 2207ff.

———. "Valenti Angelo: Master Book-Artist." *Publishers' Weekly,* 21 September 1929, 1373–75.

Ritchie, Ward. *Bookmen and their Brothels: Recollections of Los Angeles in the 1930s.* Los Angeles: Zamarano Club, 1970.

———. "The Forgotten Street of Books." In *A Garland for Jake Zeitlin on the Occasion of the 65th Birthday & the Anniversary of his Fortieth Year in the Book Trade,* 49–58. Ed. J. M. Edelstein. Los Angeles: Grant Dahlstron and Saul Marks, 1967.

———. *Years Touched with Memories.* Clifton, N.J.: AB Bookman Publications, 1992.

Robert, Maurice, and Frederic Warde. *A Code for the Collector of Beautiful Books.* New York: The Limited Editions Club, 1936.

Rogers, Bruce. *Paragraphs on Printing: Elicited from Bruce Rogers in Talks with James Hendrickson on the Functions of the Book Designer.* . . . New York: William Edwin Rudge's Sons, 1943.

——. *PI: A Hodge-Podge of Letters, Papers, Addresses, Written During a Period of Sixty Years by Bruce Rogers.* Cleveland: World, 1953.

Rollins, Carl Purington. *B.R.: America's Typographic Playboy.* New York: Georgian Press, 1927.

——. "About Colophons." *Saturday Review of Literature,* 27 July 1929, 332.

——. "The Artist: His Credo." In *Postscripts on Dwiggin.* Ed. Paul A. Bennett. New York: The Typophiles, 1960.

——. "A Book in Every Home." *Saturday Review of Literature,* 14 June 1930.

——. "Books as Art." *Saturday Review of Literature,* 26 November 1927, 359.

——. "Centaur." *Saturday Review of Literature,* 19 April 1930, 951.

——. "The Colophon." *Saturday Review of Literature,* 12 April 1930, 932.

——. "The Compleat Collector." *Saturday Review of Literature,* 20 April 1929, 940.

——. *Fine Printing and the Small Shop.* Los Angeles: Plantin Press, 1935.

——. "Fifty Books of 1928." *Saturday Review of Literature,* 19 May 1928, 900.

——. "A Footnote to Boswell." *Saturday Review of Literature,* 30 March 1929, 845.

——. "Hand-Press Printing." *Saturday Review of Literature,* 19 January 1929, 612.

——. "Justifying the Beauty of Sound Bookmaking." Rev. of *The Psalms of David in Metre* . . . *Publishers' Weekly,* 2 June 1928, 2299.

——. "The 'Limited' Edition." *Saturday Review of Literature,* 24 January 1931, 559.

——. "Limited Editions Club Again." *Saturday Review of Literature,* 1 June 1929.

——. "Merymount Press." *Saturday Review of Literature,* 28 April 1928, 834.

——. "Modernism in Practice." *Saturday Review of Literature,* 1 February 1930, 702.

——. "Morris's Typographical Adventure." *Printing and Graphic Arts* 6 (June 1958).

——. "Not All Lambs Are in Wall Street." *Saturday Review of Literature,* 29 May 1929.

——. "On Advertisements," *Saturday Review of Literature,* 30 June 1928, 1011.

——. "A Poor Thing." *Saturday Review of Literature,* 9 May 1928, 957.

——. "Printing at Its Best." *Saturday Review of Literature,* 2 November 1929, 356–57.

——. "A Survey of the Making of Books in Recent Years: The United States of America." *The Dolphin* 1 (1933): 288–301.

——. *Theodore Low De Vinne.* New York: The Typophiles, 1968.

——. "Two Small Sets." *Saturday Review of Literature,* 13 September 1930, 131.

——. "Westgate Signed Editions." *Saturday Review of Literature,* 7 September 1929, 120.

Rosenbach, A. S. W. *Books and Bidders: The Adventures of a Bibliophile.* Boston: Little, Brown, 1927.

——. "Why America Buys England's Books." *Atlantic Monthly* 140 (October 1927): 452–59.

Rubin, Joan Shelley. *The Making of Middlebrow Culture.* Chapel Hill: University of North Carolina Press, 1992.

Rummonds, Richard-Gabriel. *Printing on the Handpress*. New Castle, Del.: Oak Knoll Press, 1998.

Russell, Charles Edward. "Take Them or Leave Them: Standardization of Hats and Houses and Minds." *Century* 112 (June 1926): 168–77.

Ruzicka, Rudolph. "W. A. Dwiggins, Artist of the Book." *More Books* 23 (1948): 203–11.

Sadleir, Michael. "Limited Editions." *Publishers' Weekly*, 21 January 1928, 299–302.

Santayana, George. "The Genteel Tradition at Bay." 1931. In *The Genteel Tradition: Nine Essays*. Ed. Douglas L. Wilson. Cambridge, Mass.: Harvard University Press, 1967.

Sargent, George H. *A Busted Bibliophile and His Books*. Boston: Little, Brown, 1928.

——. "Modern Tendencies in Book Collecting." In *Private Book Collectors in the United States and Canada with Mention of Their Hobbies*, vii–xiii. Ed. John Allen Holden. New York: Bowker, 1925.

——. "Should Collectors Read Their Books?" *Bookman* 49 (August 1919): 744–49.

Schad, Robert O. "Henry Edwards Huntington, the Founder and the Library." *Huntington Library Bulletin* 1 (May 1931): 3–32.

Schauffler, Robert Haven. "Mental Good Housekeeping." *Good Housekeeping* 85 (October 1927): 88.

Schreiber, H. R. "The Migration of European Collections to America." *Library Journal* 15 (October 1928): 845–47.

Sedgwick, Ellery, III. "The American Genteel Tradition in the Early Twentieth Century." *American Studies* 25 (Spring 1984): 49–67.

Sedgwick, Henry Dwight. *In Praise of Gentlemen*. Boston: Little, Brown, 1935.

Seitlin, Perry. "Joseph Blumenthal: Printer and Type Designer, of the Spiral Press." *PM* 2 (December 1935): 6–9, 30.

"The Serious Problem of Today." *Publishers' Weekly*, 15 November 1930, 2296–98.

Seymour, Ralph Fletcher. *Some Went This Way: A Forty-Year Pilgrimage Among Artists, Bookmen, and Printers*. Chicago: Ralph Fletcher Seymour, 1945.

Sherman, Stuart P. "Mr. Mencken, the Jeune Fille, and the New Spirit in Letters." In *Americans*. New York: Scribner's 1922.

Siegal, Col. Henry A., Harry C. Marschalk, Jr., and Isaac Oelgart. *The Derrydale Press: A Bibliography*. Goshen, Conn.: The Angler's and Shooter's Press, 1981.

Skinner, Constance Lindsay. "What Well-Dressed Women Are Reading." *North American Review* 227 (April 1929): 430–34.

"Snob Sales." *Saturday Review of Literature*, 7 April 1928, 733.

Soule, Phelps. "Rollins at Montague." *Print* (1941).

Spencer, Herbert. *Pioneers of Modern Typography*. Rev. ed. Cambridge, Mass.: MIT Press, 1982.

Spier, Franklin. "The Return of the Artist." *Publishers' Weekly*, 21 August 1926, 670–74.

Spurgeon, Selena A. *Henry E. Huntington: His Life and His Collections*. San Marino, Calif.: Huntington Library, 1992.

Standard, Paul. "The Limited Editions Club: A New Influence in American Printing." *Penrose's Annual* 37 (1935): 44–49.

——. "Ten Years of Book Making Progress at H. Wolff." In *The Annual of Bookmaking*. New York: The Colophon, 1938.

Stark, Lewis M., comp. "Books Designed by Bruce Rogers: An Exhibition in Honor of

His Eighty-fifth Birthday." *Bulletin of the New York Public Library* 59 (October 1955): 491–504.

Stauffacher, Jack Werner, ed. *Porter Garnett: Philosophical Writings on the Ideal Book.* San Francisco: Book Club of California, 1994.

——. "The Spirit of Porter Garnett at Carnegie." *Carnegie Alumnus* 45 (February 1960): 4–9.

Stearns, Harold E., ed. *Civilization in the United States: An Inquiry by Thirty Americans.* New York: Harcourt, Brace and Co., 1922.

Steinberg, S. H. *Five Hundred Years of Printing.* Rev. John Trevitt. New Castle, Del.: Oak Knoll, 1996.

Stephens, James. *The Letters of James Stephens.* Ed. Richard J. Finneran. London: Macmillan, 1974.

Stetz, Margaret. "Sex, Lies, and Printed Cloth: Bookselling at the Bodley Head in the Eighteen Nineties." *Victorian Studies* 35 (Autumn 1991): 71–86.

Stetz, Margaret, and Mark Samuels Lasner. *England in the 1890s: Literary Publishing at the Bodley Head.* Washington, D.C.: Georgetown University Press, 1990.

Stevens, Frank. "Is the Limited Edition the Solution to the Dollar Book Problem?" *Publishers' Weekly,* 19 July 1930, 250–51.

Stiger, E. T. "William Edwin Rudge: Publisher and Printer of Fine Books." *Creative Art* 7 (1930): 374–77.

Storey, John. "The Politics of the Popular." In *An Introductory Guide to Cultural Theory and Popular Culture,* 181–202. Athens: University of Georgia Press, 1993.

The Story of Yale University Press Told by a Friend. New Haven, Conn.: Yale University Press, 1920.

Strouse, Norman H. *How to Build a Poor Man's Morgan Library.* Detroit: Book Club of Detroit, 1959.

——. "John Henry Nash: A Collector's Appraisal." *Gazette of the Grolier Club,* December 1973, 14–33.

Susman, Warren I. *Culture as History: The Transformation of American Society in the Twentieth Century.* New York: Pantheon, 1984.

Targ, William, ed. *Bouillabaisse for Bibliophiles.* Cleveland: World, 1955.

——. *Carousel for Bibliophiles.* New York: Philip C. Duschnes, 1947.

Teague, W. D. "The Modern Style — If Any." *Publishers' Weekly,* 7 April 1928, 1568–69.

Tebbel, John. *Between Covers: The Rise and Transformation of Book Publishing in America.* New York: Bowker, 1987.

——. *A History of Book Publishing in the United States.* Vol. 3: *The Golden Age between Two Wars, 1920–1940.* New York: Bowker, 1978.

Ten Years and William Shakespeare: A Survey of the Publishing Activities of the Limited Editions Club from October 1929 to October 1940. New York: The Limited Editions Club, 1940.

"Ten Years of Sporting Books." *Publishers' Weekly,* 6 March 1937, 1114–16.

Thaden, J. F. *Standards of Living on Iowa Farms.* Ames: Iowa State College of Agriculture and Mechanic Arts, 1926.

Thompson, Susan Otis. *American Book Design and William Morris.* 2d ed. New Castle, Del.: Oak Knoll, 1996.

Thorpe, James. *Henry Edwards Huntington: A Biography.* Berkeley: University of California Press, 1994.

Tichi, Cecelia. *Shifting Gears: Technology, Literature, Culture in Modernist America.* Chapel Hill: University of North Carolina Press, 1987.

"Too Much Wisdom?" *Publishers' Weekly,* 21 August 1926, 668.

Troxell, George M. "Collector's Madness." *Saturday Review of Literature,* 5 October 1929, 220.

———. "Compleat Collector." *Saturday Review of Literature,* 31 August 1929, 96.

———. "The Fashion of Collecting." *Saturday Review of Literature,* 5 January 1929, 578.

———. "A Genial Collector." *Saturday Review of Literature,* 3 November 1928, 328.

———. "The Limited Edition." *Saturday Review of Literature,* 22 September 1928, 156.

Tschichold, Jan. *The New Typography.* Trans. Ruari McLean. Berkeley: University of California Press, 1995.

"Type Designers and Printers Discuss Sanserif." *American Printer* 90 (July 1930): 39–43.

"The Tyranny of the Classic." *Literary Digest,* 21 June 1924, 29–30.

United States Department of Commerce. *National Income and Product Account Data for 1929–1986.* Washington, D.C.: Bureau of Economic Analysis, 1986.

Updike, D. B. *Notes on the Merrymount Press and Its Work.* Cambridge: Harvard University Press, 1934.

———. *Printing Types: Their History, Forms, and Uses: A Study in Survivals.* 2 vols. Cambridge, Mass.: Harvard University Press, 1922.

———. *Some Aspects of Printing Old and New.* New Haven, Conn.: William Edwin Rudge, 1941.

Van De Water, Frederic. "Books for Babbitt." *World's Work* 58 (June 1929): 68–71.

Van Patten, Nathan. "The Master Typographers of San Francisco." *Publishers' Weekly,* 13 April 1929, 1804–10.

Veblen, Thorstein. *The Theory of the Leisure Class.* 1899. Rpt. New York: Mentor, 1953.

Wagner, Henry. *Bullion to Books: Fifty Years of Business and Pleasure.* Los Angeles: Zamarano Club, 1942.

Walker, Emery. "Printing Fine Editions: Some Governing Principles." *Publishers' Weekly,* 7 December 1929, 2691ff.

Walker, Gay. *The Works of Carl P. Rollins.* New Haven, Conn.: Yale University Library, 1982.

Wallick, Ekin. "Where to Put Books: When There Is No Library: Gaily Bound Volumes in Unexpected Places Add Color and Interest to the Living Room." *House and Garden,* September 1925, 72–73.

Walton, Perry. "Modern Type Best for Punch, Push and Howl." *Direct Advertising* 21, 4 (1934): 6–7.

Warde, Beatrice. *I Am a Communicator: A Selection of Writings and Talks.* Special issue of *Monotype Recorder* 44, no. 1 (Autumn 1970).

———. "On Decorative Printing in America." 1928. In *Fleuron Anthology.* Ed. Francis Meynell and Herbert Simon. Boston: David R. Godine, 1979.

———. "Printing Should Be Invisible." 1932. In *Books and Printing.* Ed. Paul A. Bennett. 109–14. Cleveland: World, 1963.

Warde, Frederic. "On the Work of Bruce Rogers." 1925. In *Fleuron Anthology*. Ed. Francis Meynell and Herbert Simon. Boston: David R. Godine, 1979.

———. "Printers Ornaments on the 'Monotype.'" 1928. In *Typographers on Type*. Ed. Ruari McLean. New York: Norton, 1995.

Warren, Dale. "How to House the Growing Library to Accommodate Both Classes of Books — Those That Are Read and Those That Are Primarily Decorative." *House Beautiful*, June 1926, 778–80.

Weitenkampf, Frank. Review of *The Decorative Work of T.M. Cleland*. *Bookman*, October 1929, 162.

Wells, Gabriel. "The Lure of Collecting." *American Book Collector* 1 (February 1932): 104–7.

———. *These Three*. New York: Rudge, 1932.

Wentz, Roby. *The Grabhorn Press: A Biography*. San Francisco: Book Club of California, 1981.

Wiegand, Willy. "German Presses." *Saturday Review of Literature*, 20 April 1929, 934ff.

Wiggam, Albert Edward. *The Marks of an Educated Man*. Indianapolis, Ind.: Bobbs-Merrill, 1925.

Willis, James F. *Bibliophily; or Booklove*. Boston and New York: Houghton Mifflin Co., 1921.

Willison, Ian, Warwick Gould, and Warren Cherniak, eds. *Modernist Writers and the Marketplace*. New York: St. Martin's, 1996.

Wilson, Christopher P. "The Rhetoric of Consumption: Mass-Market Magazines and the Demise of the Gentle Reader, 1880–1920." In *The Culture of Consumption*. Ed. Richard W. Fox and T. J. Jackson Lears. New York: Pantheon, 1983.

Winship, George Parker. *Daniel Berkeley Updike and the Merrymount Press of Boston, Massachusetts, 1860–1894–1941*. Rochester, N.Y.: Printing House of Leo Hart, 1947.

Winterich, John T. *The Grolier Club, 1884–1950: An Informal History*. New York: Grolier Club, 1950.

———. *Three Lantern Slides: Books, the Book Trade, and Some Related Phenomena in America: 1876, 1901, and 1926*. Urbana: University of Illinois Press, 1949.

———. "While You Wait — ." *Saturday Review of Literature*, 24 October 1931, 239.

Wright, Richardson. "Let's Buy Her a Book." *Bookman* 50 (November 1919): 347–49.

"Your Money's Worth." *Saturday Review of Literature*, 5 May 1928, 837ff.

Zeitlin, Jake. "Developing Interest and Sales in Books of Fine Presses." *Publishers' Weekly*, 10 May 1930, 2421–22.

Zweig, Stefan. *The Old-Book Peddlar and Other Tales for Bibliophiles*. Trans. Theodore W. Koch. Evanston, Ill.: Northwestern University, the Charles Deering Library, 1937.

Index